FIELD BOOK OF
WESTERN
WILD FLOWERS

FIELD BOOK OF WESTERN WILD FLOWERS

THE ULTIMATE GUIDE TO FLOWERS GROWING WEST OF THE ROCKY MOUNTAINS

MARGARET ARMSTRONG
WITH J. J. THORNBER

Skyhorse Publishing

Skyhorse Publishing books may be purchased in bulk at special discounts for sales promotion, corporate gifts, fund-raising, or educational purposes. Special editions can also be created to specifications. For details, contact the Special Sales Department, Skyhorse Publishing, 307 West 36th Street, 11th Floor, New York, NY 10018 or info@skyhorsepublishing.com.

Skyhorse® and Skyhorse Publishing® are registered trademarks of Skyhorse Publishing, Inc.®, a Delaware corporation.

www.skyhorsepublishing.com

10 9 8 7 6 5 4 3 2 1

Library of Congress Cataloging-in-Publication Data is available on file.

ISBN: 978-1-62873-795-0

Printed in China

PREFACE.

In this little book a very large number of the commoner wild flowers growing in the United States, west of the Rocky Mountains, are pictured and described. It is the first attempt to supply a popular field book for the whole West. The field is vast, including within its limits all sorts of climate and soil, producing thousands of flowers, infinite in variety and wonderful in beauty, their environment often as different as that of Heine's *Pine and Palm*. In such strange homes as the Grand Canyon and the Petrified Forest of Arizona, or the deserts of Utah and southern California, we find the oddest desert plants, forced to curious expedients in order to sustain life amidst almost perpetual heat and drought, but often displaying blossoms of such brilliance and delicacy that they might well be envied by their more fortunate sisters, flourishing beside shady waterfalls, in a "happy valley" like Yosemite, or a splendid mountain garden, such as spreads in many-colored parterres of bloom around the feet of Mt. Rainier. On the wind-swept plains hundreds of flowers are to be found; many kinds of hardy plants brighten the salty margins of the sea cliffs, or bloom at the edge of the snow on rocky mountain peaks, while quantities of humble, everyday flowers border our country roadsides or tint the hills and meadows with lavish color.

The field includes the States of Washington, Oregon, California, Idaho, Nevada, Utah, and Arizona and to designate this whole field the term West is used in this book. The term Northwest designates Washington, Oregon, northern Idaho, and northern California, and the term Southwest covers southern California and Arizona. The flowers found only in the Rocky Mountains are not included, and it may be noted here that exceedingly few of the western flowers cross the Rockies and are found in the East.

iii

PREFACE.

This is the only fully illustrated book of western flowers, except Miss Parsons's charming book, which is for California only. The drawings have all been made from life. Allowance must be made for differences in appearance, owing to locality, and the text should be consulted for the size, as, on so small a page, some of the plants must be drawn smaller than others.

Almost all technical botanical terms have been translated into ordinary English, as this book is intended primarily for the general public, but as a large number of the plants given have never before been illustrated, or even described, except in somewhat inaccessible or technical publications, it is hoped that the scientist also may find the contents both interesting and useful.

The nomenclature used, with few exceptions, is that of the American Code. Where these names differ greatly from those in common usage the latter are given as synonyms in brackets, making the book more useful to all readers. The botanical names are marked with an accent. Two accents are used, the grave (`) to indicate the long English sound of the vowel, such as the "i" in "violet," and the acute (´) to show the short sound, such as the "i" in "lily."

Professor J. J. Thornber, of the University of Arizona, is responsible for the botanical accuracy of the text and his knowledge and patient skill have made the book possible.

Thanks are due for most valuable assistance in the determination of a very large number of specimens to Miss Alice Eastwood, of the California Academy of Sciences. Also to Dr. W. L. Jepson, of the University of California; Professor A. O. Garrett, of Salt Lake City; Professor A. R. Sweetser, of the University of Oregon; Mr. S. B. Parish, of San Bernardino, Cal.; Mrs. Henshaw, of Vancouver, B. C.; Dr. A. Davidson, of Los Angeles; and Mr. Marcus E. Jones, of Salt Lake City. Also for advice and assistance to Dr. N. L. Britton, and Dr. H. M. Richards of New York; to Dr. Livingston Farrand, of Colorado; Mr. C. R. Orcutt, of San Diego; Mr. Carl Purdy, of Ukiah, Cal.; Professor Flett, of Mt. Rainier National Park; Miss Winona Bailey, of Seattle; Professor J. H. Paul, of Salt Lake City; and many other kind friends.

The arrangement is that originated by Mr. Schuyler Mathews, in his *Field Book of American Wild Flowers*,

PREFACE.

which has been found very popular in the East, but, in this book, most of the genera, as well as the species, have been very briefly described.

MARGARET ARMSTRONG.

NEW YORK,
   January 1, 1915.

PREFACE.

which has been found very popular in the East, but, in this book, most of the genera, as well as the species, have been very briefly described.

MARGARET ARMSTRONG.

New York,
January 1, 1915.

CONTENTS.

	PAGE
PREFACE	iii
LIST OF COLORED PLATES . . .	xi
TECHNICAL TERMS	xiii
KEY TO FAMILIES	xv

FAMILIES:

Water-plantain (*Alismaceae*) . . .	2
Lily (*Liliaceae*)	4
Iris (*Iridaceae*) . . .	66
Orchid (*Orchidaceae*) . . .	72
Lizard-tail (*Saururaceae*) . . .	80
Sandalwood (*Santalaceae*) . . .	82
Birthwort (*Aristolochiaceae*) . .	84
Buckwheat (*Polygonaceae*) . . .	86
Pigweed (*Chenopodiaceae*) . . .	96
Four-o'clock (*Nyctaginaceae*) . .	100
Carpet-weed (*Aizoaceae*) . . .	108
Pink (*Caryophyllaceae*) . . .	112
Purslane (*Portulacaceae*) . . .	120
Buttercup (*Ranunculaceae*) . .	126
Barberry (*Berberidaceae*) . . .	152
Water Lily (*Nymphaeaceae*) . . .	156
Strawberry Shrub (*Calycanthaceae*) .	158
Poppy (*Papaveraceae*) . . .	160
Bleeding Heart (*Fumariaceae*) . .	168
Mustard (*Cruciferae*) . . .	174
Caper (*Capparidaceae*) . . .	186
Orpine (*Crassulaceae*) . . .	192
Saxifrage (*Saxifragaceae*) . . .	196
Hydrangea (*Hydrangeaceae*) . .	206
Gooseberry (*Grossulariaceae*) . .	210
Apple (*Pomaceae*) . . .	214
Plum (*Drupaceae*) . . .	216
Rose (*Rosaceae*)	218
Pea (*Fabaceae*)	242

CONTENTS.

	PAGE
Senna (*Cassiaceae*)	264
Mimosa (*Mimosaceae*)	266
Krameria (*Krameriaceae*)	268
Caltrop (*Zygophyllaceae*)	268
Flax (*Linaceae*)	270
Wood-sorrel (*Oxalidaceae*)	272
Geranium (*Geraniaceae*)	274
Milkwort (*Polygalaceae*)	278
Meadow Foam (*Limnanthateae*)	278
Buckeye (*Hippocastanaceae*)	280
Buckthorn (*Rhamnaceae*)	282
Mallow (*Malvaceae*)	284
St. John's-wort (*Hypericaceae*)	292
Fouquiera (*Fouquieriaceae*)	294
Violet (*Violaceae*)	296
Loasa (*Loasaceae*)	300
Rock-rose (*Cistaceae*)	304
Cactus (*Cactaceae*)	304
Evening Primrose (*Onagraceae*)	312
Parsley (*Umbelliferae*)	332
Dogwood (*Cornaceae*)	338
Heath (*Ericaceae*)	340
Wintergreen (*Pyrolaceae*)	354
Indian Pipe (*Monotropaceae*)	356
Primrose (*Primulaceae*)	362
Olive (*Oleaceae*)	366
Gentian (*Gentianaceae*)	368
Milkweed (*Asclepiadaceae*)	374
Dogbane (*Apocynaceae*)	378
Buck-bean (*Menyanthaceae*)	380
Morning-glory (*Convolvulaceae*)	380
Phlox (*Polemoniaceae*)	384
Waterleaf (*Hydrophyllaceae*)	402
Borage (*Boraginaceae*)	422
Verbena (*Verbenaceae*)	434
Mint (*Labiatae*)	434
Potato (*Solanaceae*)	458
Figwort (*Scrophulariaceae*)	466
Broom-rape (*Orobanchaceae*)	504
Madder (*Rubiaceae*)	506

CONTENTS.

	PAGE
Valerian (*Valerianaceae*)	508
Honeysuckle (*Caprifoliaceae*)	512
Gourd (*Cucurbitaceae*)	518
Bellflower (*Campanulaceae*)	520
Sunflower (*Compositae*)	522
Chicory (*Chicoriaceae*)	570
INDEX	581

COLORED ILLUSTRATIONS.

FACING PAGE

ORANGE MARIPOSA TULIP	*Frontispiece*
WILD ONION	14
COVENA	16
INDIAN HYACINTH	24
DOGTOOTH VIOLET	28
BRONZE BELLS	38
BUTTERFLY TULIP	62
BUTTER BALLS	92
SAND-VERBENA	104
INDIAN PINK	116
FOOTHILLS LARKSPUR	128
LILAC CLEMATIS	150
CALIFORNIA POPPY	164
BUSH POPPY	166
WESTERN WALLFLOWER	176
CLIFF ROSE	226
BI-COLORED LUPINE	252
WILD SWEET PEA	254
PRIDE OF CALIFORNIA	256
HEDYSARUM PABULARE	260
DESERT SENNA	266
SPOTTED MALLOW	288
SALMON GLOBE MALLOW	290
HEDGEHOG CACTUS	306

COLORED ILLUSTRATIONS

FACING PAGE

Opuntia basilaris	308
Pincushion Cactus	310
White Evening Primrose	326
Western Azalea	342
Snow-Plant	358
Small Shooting Star	366
Canchalagua	370
Scarlet Gilia	392
Large Prickly Gilia	398
Mountain Phacelia	404
Phacelia grandiflora	408
Baby Blue-eyes	412
Ramona incana	438
Thistle Sage	450
Paint Brush	472
Pentstemon cyananthus	480
Pentstemon Parryi	482
Bush Monkey Flower	490
Pink Monkey Flower	492
Wild Valerian	510
Arizona Thistle	524
Easter Daisy	530
Xylorrhiza tortifolia	544
Cut-leaved Balsam-Root . . .	558

TECHNICAL TERMS.

Corolla. The flower-cup composed of one or more divisions called petals.

Petal. One of the divisions of the corolla.

Calyx. A flower-envelope, usually green, formed of several divisions called sepals, protecting the bud.

Sepal. One of the divisions of the calyx.

Anther. The pollen-bearing organ, usually yellow.

Filament. The stalk-like support of the anther.

Stamen. Anther and filament combined.

Ovary. The seed-bearing organ.

Ovary inferior. With the flower-parts growing from above the ovary.

Ovary superior. With the flower-parts growing from below the ovary.

Placenta. That particular portion of the ovary wall to which the ovules are attached.

Ovule. The body in the ovary which becomes a seed.

Style. The stalk-like projection proceeding from the ovary and terminated by the stigma.

Stigma. The generally sticky and sometimes branching termination of the pistil through which pollination takes place.

Pistil. Ovary, style, and stigma combined.

Regular Flower. Generally symmetrical and uniform in the number of its parts.

Perfect Flower. A flower complete in all the common parts.

Staminate. With stamens and without pistils.

Pistillate. With pistils and without stamens.

Polygamous. Pistillate, staminate, and perfect flowers, on the same or on different plants.

Claw. The narrow or stalk-like base of some petals.

Pedicel. The stalk of a flower in a cluster.

TECHNICAL TERMS

Raceme. A flower-cluster in which the flowers are borne along the flower-stalk on pedicels of nearly equal length.

Spike. A flower-cluster in which the flowers have no pedicels and are arranged more or less closely along the flower-stalk.

Bracts. Small scalelike formations.

Involucre. A circle of bracts below a flower-cluster.

Stipule. Small often leaflike formations, confined to the base of the leaf.

Capsule. A dry seed-vessel, composed of more than cne part and splitting open.

Akene. A small dry one-seeded fruit, not splitting open.

A KEY TO THE FAMILIES.

PAGE

A. Parts of the flower nearly always in threes; leaves almost always parallel-veined.

  a. Ovary superior.

    b. Leaves often arrow-shaped; pistils many, in a head.
                              Alismaceae   2

    b. Leaves not arrow-shaped; pistil one.   *Liliaceae*   4

  a. Ovary inferior.

    b. Flowers regular; stamens three.   *Iridaceae*   66

    b. Flowers irregular; stamens one or two. *Orchidaceae*   72

A. Parts of the flower mostly in fours or fives; leaves mostly netted-veined.

  B. Corolla absent; calyx mostly present, sometimes showy.

    a. Ovary superior.

      b. Pistils several to many, distinct. *Ranunculaceae*   126

      b. Pistil one, one to several-celled.

        c. Flowers in long spikes with a white involucre
           at base.   *Saururaceae*   80

        c. Flowers not in long spikes.

          d. Stipules if present sheathing the stem;
             sepals three to six.   *Polygonaceae*   86

          d. Stipules absent; sepals mostly five.
                          Chenopodiaceae   96

    a. Ovary inferior or appearing so by the closely fitting
      calyx.

      b. Ovary six-celled; stamens six to twelve.
                       Aristolochiaceae   84

      b. Ovary one-celled; stamens three to five.

        c. Leaves opposite; flowers often showy.
                      Nyctaginaceae   100

        c. Leaves alternate; flowers not showy.
                        Santalaceae   82

  B. Both corolla and calyx present.

    C. Corolla of separate petals.

      D. Ovary superior.

        a. Stamens more than ten in number.

          b. Pistils several to many, separate or
            united below.

            c. Pistils separate and distinct.

              d. Pistils enclosed in a hollow recep-
                tacle.

                e. Leaves opposite; petals num-
                  erous.   *Calycanthaceae*   158

                e. Leaves alternate; petals most-
                  ly five.   *Rosaceae*   218

             d. Pistils not enclosed in a recep-
                tacle.

                e. Stamens attached to the
                  calyx.   *Rosaceae*   218

                e. Stamens not attached to the
                  calyx.   *Ranunculaceae*   126

A KEY TO THE FAMILIES

PAGE

c. Pistils united below into a lobed or
beaked ovary.
d. Water plants with floating leaves.
Nymphaceae   156
d. Terrestrial or land plants.
e. Pistils forming a ring; filaments united.   *Malvaceae*   284
e. Pistils not forming a ring.
f. Pistils inserted on a convex
receptacle; stamens at-
tached to the calyx.
Rosaceae   218
f. Receptacle not convex; stamens not attached to the
calyx.   *Papaveraceae*   160
b. Pistil one, the styles and stigmas often
several.
c. Ovary one-celled.
d. Style and stigma one.
e. Fruit a drupe (stone-fruit).
Drupaceae   216
e. Fruit an akene tipped with a
tail.   *Rosaceae*   218
d. Styles or stigmas more than one.
e. Sepals falling as the flowers
expand.
f. Sepals two or three; fruit
a capsule.
Papaveraceae   160
f. Sepals four or six; fruit a
berry.   *Ranunculaceae*   126
e. Sepals persistent; low shrubs.
Cistaceae   304
c. Ovary more than one-celled.
d. Water plants with floating leaves.
Nymphaceae   156
d. Plants not growing in water.
e. Leaves with smooth margins
and with transparent dots.
Hypericaceae   292
e. Leaves neither smooth-edged,
nor with transparent dots.
Malvaceae   284
a. Stamens ten or fewer in number.
b. Stamens of the same number as the
petals and opposite them.
c. Ovary more than one-celled; calyx
four- to five-cleft.   *Rhamnaceae*   282
c. Ovary one-celled.
d. Anthers opening by uplifted
valves.   *Berberidaceae*   152
d. Anthers opening by longitudinal
slits.   *Portulacaceae*   120
b. Stamens not of the same number as the
petals, or if of the same number, alternate with them.
c. Ovaries two or more, separate or
partly united.
d. Stamens united with each other
and with the large thick stigma.
Asclepiadaceae   374
d. Stamens free from each other
and from the pistils.
e. Stamens inserted on the
receptacle.
f. Leaves and stems fleshy.
Crassulaceae   192
f. Leaves and stems not
noticeably fleshy.

xvi

PAGE

g. Lobes of ovary two to
five, with a common
style.
h. Ovary two- to three-
lobed.
Limnanthaceae 278
h. Ovary five-lobed.
Geraniaceae 274
g. Ovaries with separate
styles. *Ranunculaceae* 126
e. Stamens inserted on the
calyx.
f. Stamens twice as many as
the pistils. *Crassulaceae* 192
f. Stamens not twice as many
as the pistils.
g. Stipules present.
Rosaceae 218
g. Stipules absent.
Saxifragaceae 196
c. Ovary one, the styles and stigmas
one to several.
d. Ovary with one cell and one
placenta.
e. Corolla forming standard,
wings and keel; filaments
mostly united. *Fabaceae* 242
e. Corolla not of standard, wings
and keel; filaments mostly
not united.
f. Stamens ten or five; fruit
smooth, slender.
Cassiaceae 264
f. Stamens three or four;
fruit spiny, globose.
Krameriaceae 268
d. Ovary with one or more cells
and styles, and two or more
placentae and stigmas.
e. Ovary one-celled.
f. Corolla irregular; petals
and sepals five.
Violaceae 296
f. Corolla regular or nearly so.
g. Ovules attached at the
center or bottom of the
ovary. *Caryophyllaceae* 112
g. Ovules attached on two
placentae.
h. Stamens equal; pod
on a stalk.
Capparidaceae 186
h. Stamens unequal;
pod without a stalk.
Cruciferae 174
e. Ovary more than one-celled.
f. Ovary three-celled; trees
with palmate leaves.
Hippocastanaceae 280
f. Ovary more than three-
celled.
g. Cells of ovary as many
as the sepals.
h. Anthers opening by
terminal pores; dwarf
evergreen shrubby
plants. *Pyrolaceae* 354
h. Anthers opening by
longitudinal slits.

A KEY TO THE FAMILIES

PAGE

      i. Ovules and seeds one or two in each cell.
        j. Herbs with lobed or cut leaves. *Geraniaceae* 274
        j. E v e r g r e e n shrubs with varnished leaves. *Zygophyllaceae* 268
      i. Ovules and seeds several in each cell; leaflets three. *Oxalidaceae* 272
    g. Cells of ovary twice as many as the sepals. *Linaceae* 270

D. **Ovary inferior or more or less so.**
  a. Stamens more than ten in number.
    b. Plant spiny; leaves absent or soon deciduous *Cactaceae* 304
    b. Plant not spiny; leaves persisting for the season.
      c. Leaves three-sided, fleshy. *Aizoaceae* 108
      c. Leaves neither three-sided nor fleshy.
        d. Herbs; leaves rough-hairy. *Loasaceae* 300
        d. Shrubs or trees.
          e. Leaves opposite; stipules none. *Hydrangeaceae* 206
          e. Leaves alternate; stipules present. *Pomaceae* 214
  a. Stamens ten or fewer in number.
    b. Ovules and seeds more than one in each cell.
      c. Ovary one-celled; fruit a berry. *Grossulariaceae* 210
      c. Ovary with two or more cells.
        d. Stamens four or eight.
          e. Shrubs; filaments two-forked at the apex. *Hydrangeaceae* 206
          e. Herbs; filaments not two-forked at the apex. *Onagraceae* 312
        d. Stamens five or ten; styles two or three. *Saxifragaceae* 196
    b. Ovules and seeds only one in each cell.
      c. Stamens mostly ten; ovary partly inferior. *Hydrangeaceae* 206
      c. Stamens less than ten; ovary wholly inferior.
        d. Stamens five; fruit dry. *Umbelliferae* 332
        d. Stamens four; fruit fleshy. *Cornaceae* 338

C. **Corolla with petals more or less united.**
  E. **Ovary superior.**
    a. Stamens more than five in number.
      b. Ovary one-celled.
        c. Placenta one.
          d. Corolla very irregular; stamens not protruding from the corolla. *Fabaceae* 242
          d. Corolla nearly regular; stamens protruding. *Mimosaceae* 266
        c. Placentae two; corolla irregular. *Fumariaceae* 168

PAGE

b. Ovary two to several-celled.
  c. Ovary two-celled; corolla irregular.
          Polygalaceae   278
  c. Ovary three or more-celled; corolla
    regular or nearly so.
    d. Stamens not attached to the
      corolla.
      e. Style one; leaves simple.
              Ericaceae   340
      e. Styles more than one.
        f. Styles three; erect spiny
          shrub.   *Fouquieriaceae*   294
        f. Styles five; low herbs.
              Oxalidaceae   272
    d. Stamens attached to the corolla,
      plants without green foliage
            Monotropaceae   356
a. Stamens five or fewer in number.
  b. Corolla regular.
    c. Stamens free from the corolla.
              Ericaceae   340
    c. Stamens attached to the corolla.
    d. Pistil one.
      e. Stamens of the same number
        as the corolla lobes and op-
        posite them.
              Primulaceae   362
      e. Stamens alternate with the
        corolla lobes or fewer.
        f. Ovary one- or two-celled.
          g. Styles two or occasional-
            ly one.
            h. Capsule usually
              many-seeded; sepals
              united.
              Hydrophyllaceae   402
            h. Capsule few-seeded;
              sepals separate.
              Convolvulaceae   380
          g. Styles one or none.
            h. leaves opposite.
             i. Trees with pinnate
              leaves.   *Oleaceae*   366
             i. Herbs with simple
              s m o o t h-e d g e d
              leaves.
              Gentianaceae   368
            h. Leaves alternate.
             i. Ovary one-celled;
              leaves with three
              leaflets.
              Menyanthaceae   380
             i. Ovary two-celled;
              leaves various.
              Solanaceae   458
        f. Ovary three- or four-celled.
          g. Style one; ovary three-
            celled.
              Polemoniaceae   384
          g. Styles two; ovary four-
            celled.   *Boraginaceae*   422
    d. Pistils two.
      e. Stamens and stigmas united;
        flowers with hood-like ap-
        pendages.   *Asclepidaceae*   374
      e. Stamens and stigmas not
        united; flowers without
        hood-like appendages.
              Apocynaceae   378

A KEY TO THE FAMILIES

PAGE

b. Corolla more or less irregular.
  c. Fruit a many-seeded capsule.
    d. Ovary two-celled.
        Scrophulariaceae   466
    d. Ovary one-celled; plants without
        green foliage.   *Orobanchaceae*   504
  c. Fruit of two or four seed-like nut-
    lets.
    d. Ovary four-lobed; plants mostly
        aromatic.   *Labiatae*   434
    d. Ovary not lobed; plants rarely
        aromatic.   *Verbenaceae*   434

E. Ovary inferior.
  a. Stamens eight or ten; evergreen shrubs.
                 Ericaceae   340
  a. Stamens five or fewer in number.
    b. Plants tendril-bearing. *Cucurbitaceae*   518
    b. Plants not tendril-bearing.
      c. Stamens free, not united.
        d. Leaves alternate; stamens free
          from the corolla. *Campanulaceae*   520
        d. Leaves opposite or whorled; sta-
          mens inserted on the corolla.
          e. Stamens one to three.
             Valerianaceae   508
          e. Stamens four to five.
            f. Leaves opposite, never in
              whorls nor with stipules.
                Caprifoliaceae   512
            f. Leaves opposite and with
              stipules, or in whorls and
              without stipules.
                Rubiaceae   506
      c. Stamens united by their anthers.
        d. Corollas all strap-shaped and per-
          fect; juice milky. *Cichoriaceae*   570
        d. Marginal corollas strap-shaped,
          never perfect; disk corollas per-
          fect; juice not milky.
                Compositae   522

FIELD BOOK
OF
WESTERN WILD FLOWERS

WATER-PLANTAIN FAMILY. *Alismaceae.*

A rather small family, widely distributed, growing in fresh-water swamps and streams. The leaves are all from the root, with long sheathing leaf-stalks, and the flowers are regular and perfect, or with only pistils or only stamens; the sepals three; the petals three; the stamens six or more; the ovaries numerous, superior, developing into dry, one-seeded nutlets.

There are a good many kinds of Sagittaria, with fibrous roots and milky juice; the leaves are usually arrow-shaped; the lower flowers usually pistillate and the upper ones usually staminate; the stamens are numerous and the numerous ovaries are closely crowded and form roundish heads. The name is from the Latin for "arrow," referring to the shape of the leaves.

Arrowhead
Sagittària
latifòlia
White
Summer
North America

An attractive and very decorative plant, with stout, smooth, hollow flower-stems, from eight inches to four feet tall, with very handsome, smooth, olive-green leaves and papery bracts. The flowers are about an inch across, with delicately crumpled, white petals and yellow anthers, forming a bright golden center, and the plants look very pretty standing along the edges of ponds. The leaves are exceedingly variable both in size and shape. This is found throughout North America. The tubers are edible and hence the plant is often called Tule Potato, and they are much eaten by the Chinese in California. The Indian name is Wapato.

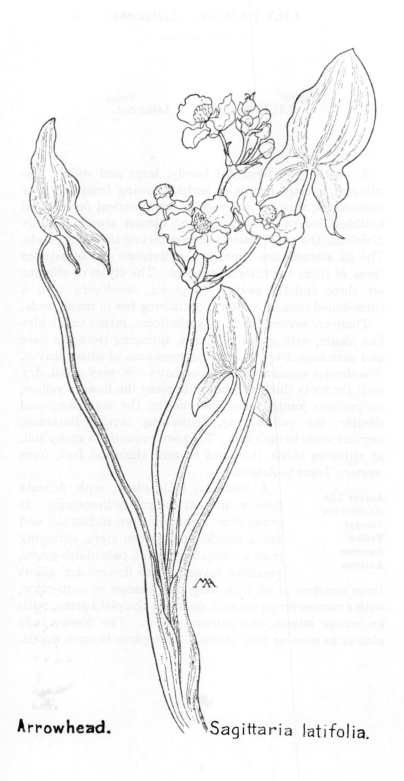

Arrowhead. *Sagittaria latifolia.*

LILY FAMILY. *Liliaceae.*

A wonderfully beautiful family, large and widely distributed, mostly perennial herbs, growing from bulbs or root-stocks, with perfect, regular, symmetrical flowers and toothless leaves. The flower-cup almost always has six divisions, the outer often called sepals and the inner petals. The six stamens are opposite the divisions and sometimes three of them are without anthers. The styles or stigmas are three and the ovary is superior, developing into a three-celled capsule or berry, containing few or many seeds.

There are several kinds of Anthericum, rather small, lily-like plants, with grasslike leaves, springing from the base and surrounded by the fibrous remnants of older leaves. The slender stems are leafless, or have one, very small, dry leaf; the roots thick and fleshy-fibrous; the flowers yellow, on pedicels jointed near the middle; the style long and slender; the pod oblong, containing several flattened, angular seeds in each cell. They are common in rocky soil, at altitudes of six thousand to nine thousand feet, from western Texas to Arizona.

Amber Lily
Anthéricum
Tórreyi
Yellow
Summer
Arizona

A beautiful little plant, with delicate flowers, unusual and pretty in coloring. It grows from eight to fifteen inches tall and has a slender, pale-green stem, springing from a clump of graceful, pale bluish-green, grasslike leaves. The flowers are about three quarters of an inch long, pale orange or corn-color, with a narrow stripe on each division; the pistil green, with an orange stigma; the anthers yellow. The flowers fade almost as soon as they bloom. This grows in open woods.

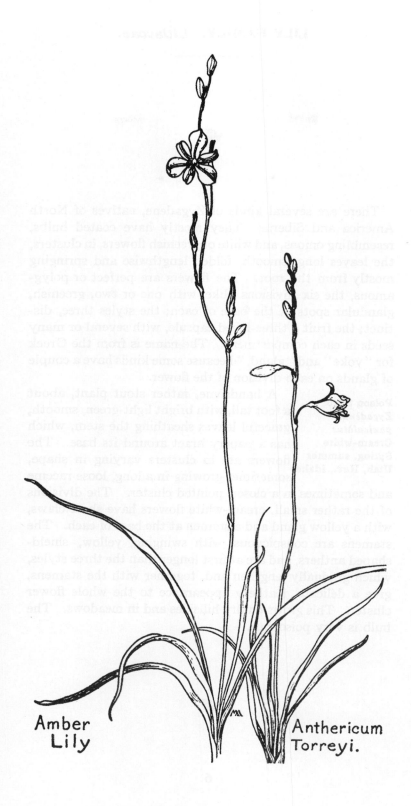

Amber
Lily

Anthericum
Torreyi.

LILY FAMILY. *Liliaceae.*

There are several kinds of Zygadene, natives of North America and Siberia. They mostly have coated bulbs, resembling onions, and white or greenish flowers, in clusters, the leaves long, smooth, folded lengthwise and springing mostly from the root. The flowers are perfect or polygamous, the six divisions alike, with one or two, greenish, glandular spots at the base of each; the styles three, distinct; the fruit a three-lobed capsule, with several or many seeds in each compartment. The name is from the Greek for "yoke" and "gland," because some kinds have a couple of glands on each division of the flower.

Poison Sego
*Zygadènus
paniculàtus*
**Cream-white
Spring, summer
Utah, Nev., Idaho**

A handsome, rather stout plant, about a foot tall, with bright light-green, smooth, graceful leaves sheathing the stem, which has a papery bract around its base. The flowers are in clusters varying in shape, sometimes growing in a long, loose raceme and sometimes in a closer, pointed cluster. The divisions of the rather small, cream-white flowers have short claws, with a yellow gland and a stamen at the base of each. The stamens are conspicuous, with swinging, yellow, shield-shaped anthers, and are at first longer than the three styles, which gradually lengthen and, together with the stamens, give a delicate, feathery appearance to the whole flower cluster. This grows on dry hillsides and in meadows. The bulb is very poisonous.

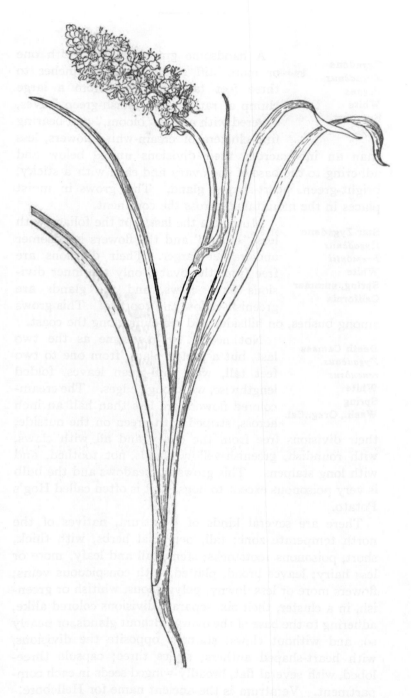

Poison Sego.   **Zygadenus paniculatus.**

LILY FAMILY. *Liliaceae.*

Zygadene
Zygadènus
élegans
White
Summer
U. S.

A handsome graceful plant, with one or more stiff stems, from six inches to three feet tall, springing from a large clump of rather stiff, bluish-green leaves, covered with a pale "bloom," and bearing fine clusters of cream-white flowers, less than an inch across, their divisions united below and adhering to the base of the ovary and each with a sticky, bright-green, heart-shaped gland. This grows in moist places in the mountains, across the continent.

Star Zygadene
Zygadènus
Fremóntii
White
Spring, summer
California

Much like the last, but the foliage with less "bloom" and the flowers handsomer and rather larger. Their divisions are free from the ovary, only the inner divisions have claws, and the glands are greenish-yellow and toothed. This grows among bushes, on hillsides and sea-cliffs along the coast.

Death Camass
Zygadènus
venenòsus
White
Spring
Wash., Oreg.,Cal.

Not nearly so handsome as the two last, but a pretty plant, from one to two feet tall, with dull-green leaves, folded lengthwise, with rough edges. The cream-colored flowers are less than half an inch across, striped with green on the outside, their divisions free from the ovary and all with claws, with roundish, greenish-yellow glands, not toothed, and with long stamens. This grows in meadows and the bulb is very poisonous except to hogs, so it is often called Hog's Potato.

There are several kinds of Veratrum, natives of the north temperate zone; tall, perennial herbs, with thick, short, poisonous rootstocks; stems tall and leafy, more or less hairy; leaves broad, plaited, with conspicuous veins; flowers more or less downy, polygamous, whitish or greenish, in a cluster, their six, separate divisions colored alike, adhering to the base of the ovary, without glands, or nearly so, and without claws; stamens opposite the divisions, with heart-shaped anthers; styles three; capsule three-lobed, with several flat, broadly-winged seeds in each compartment. Veratrum is the ancient name for Hellebore.

Zygadene.

Z. elegans.

Death Camass.

Zygadenus
venenosus.

LILY FAMILY. *Liliaceae.*

False Hellebore
Verátrum
Califórnicum
Greenish-white
Spring
West

The leaves of this plant are its conspicuous feature. A few near the top are long and narrow, but most of them are boat-shaped, with heavy ribs, and from six to twelve inches long. They are bright yellowish-green and, although somewhat coarse, the general effect is distinctly handsome, as we see masses of them growing luxuriantly in rich, moist meadows and marshes in the mountains. When they first come up in the spring, the shoots are packed into green rosettes, in which the leaves are intricately folded, but they soon grow to a height of three to six feet. The flowers are beautiful, in fine contrast to the coarse foliage. They measure about half an inch across and are cream-white, streaked with green, and form a fine cluster about a foot long. The flowers are far prettier and the plants handsomer than their eastern relations and they flourish at an altitude of six to nine thousand feet. The plants are supposed to be poisonous to cattle, but in a recent bulletin of the Agricultural Experiment Station of the State of Washington, it is reported as being a popular food with horses and sheep, particularly the latter, which eat it greedily and without ill effects.

There are several kinds of Hastingsia, perennials, with bulbs or rootstocks; the stamens on the base of the perianth, with swinging anthers; the ovary with a very short stalk and short style.

Reed-lily
Hastíngsia álba
(Schoenolirion)
White
Summer
Oreg., Cal., Nev.

An attractive marsh plant, with a smooth, stiff, bluish stem, over three feet tall, springing from a cluster of long, narrow, sword-like leaves. The slightly sweet-scented flowers are white, about half an inch across, forming a long, graceful, fuzzy wand of bloom, which has a pretty silvery effect and looks interesting at a distance, but is not very striking close by, as the flowers are too colorless. The seeds are black and shiny.

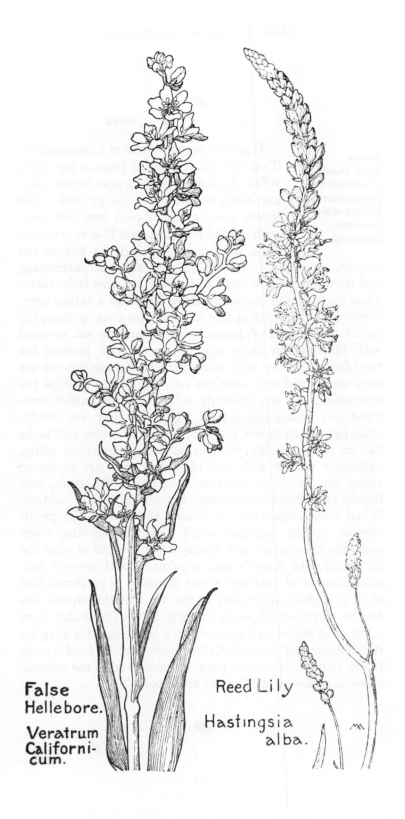

False
Hellebore.

Veratrum
Californi-
cum.

Reed Lily

Hastingsia
alba.

LILY FAMILY. *Liliaceae.*

Amole
Soap Plant
Chlorógalum
pomeridiànum
Silvery-white
Summer
California

There are several kinds of Chlorogalum. This odd plant springs from a big bulb, which is covered with coarse brown fiber and often shows above the ground. The leaves are sometimes over two feet long, with rippled margins, look like very coarse grass, and usually spread out flat on the ground. The plants are conspicuous and look interesting and we wonder what sort of flower is to come from them. Then some day in late summer we find that a rather ugly, branching stalk, four or five feet tall, has shot up from the center of the tuft of leaves. The branches are covered with bluish-green buds, and we watch with interest for the bloom, but we may easily miss it, for the flowers are very short-lived and come out only for a little while in the afternoons. In the lowlands the flowers are rather scattered and straggling, but in Yosemite they are lovely, close by. Each flower is an inch or more across and looks like an airy little lily, with six spreading divisions, white, delicately veined with dull-blue, and they are clustered along the branches, towards the top of the stalk, and bloom in successive bunches, beginning at the bottom. When they commence to bloom, the tips of the petals remain caught together until the last minute, when suddenly they let go and spring apart and all at once the dull stalk, like Aaron's rod, is adorned with several delicate clusters of feathery silver flowers. The thread-like style is slightly three-cleft at the tip and the capsule has one or two blackish seeds in each cell. The bulbs form a lather in water and are used as a substitute for soap by the Indians and Spanish-Californians, and as food by the Pomo Indians, who cook them in great pits in the ground. *Pomeridianum* means "in the afternoon."

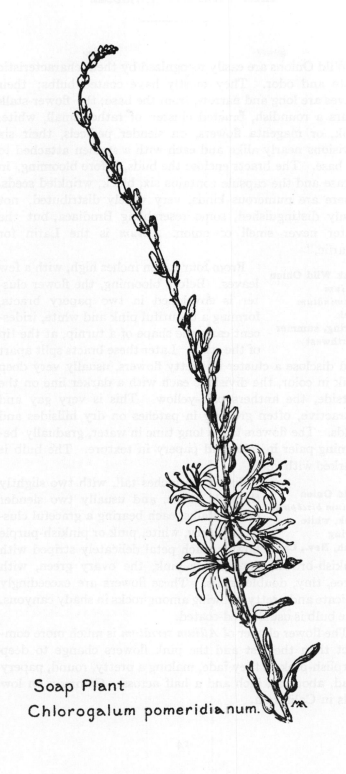

Soap Plant

Chlorogalum pomeridianum.

LILY FAMILY. *Liliaceae*

Wild Onions are easily recognized by their characteristic taste and odor. They mostly have coated bulbs; their leaves are long and narrow, from the base; the flower-stalk bears a roundish, bracted cluster of rather small, white, pink, or magenta flowers, on slender pedicels, their six divisions nearly alike and each with a stamen attached to its base. The bracts enclose the buds, before blooming, in a case and the capsule contains six, black, wrinkled seeds. There are numerous kinds, very widely distributed, not easily distinguished, some resembling Brodiaea, but the latter never smell of onion. *Allium* is the Latin for "garlic."

Pink Wild Onion
Állium
*acuminá
tum*
Pink
Spring, summer
Northwest

From four to ten inches high, with a few leaves. Before blooming, the flower cluster is enveloped in two papery bracts, forming a beautiful pink and white, iridescent case, the shape of a turnip, at the tip of the stalk. Later these bracts split apart and disclose a cluster of pretty flowers, usually very deep pink in color, the divisions each with a darker line on the outside, the anthers pale-yellow. This is very gay and attractive, often growing in patches on dry hillsides and fields. The flowers last a long time in water, gradually becoming paler in color and papery in texture. The bulb is marked with veins.

Wild Onion
Állium biscéptrum
Pink, white
Spring
Utah, Nev., Cal.

Six to ten inches tall, with two slightly thickish leaves, and usually two slender flower stalks, each bearing a graceful cluster of starry, white, pink or pinkish-purple flowers, each petal delicately striped with pinkish-brown, the anthers pink, the ovary green, with three, tiny, double crests. These flowers are exceedingly delicate and pretty, growing among rocks in shady canyons. The bulb is usually red-coated.

The flower cluster of *Allium serrátum* is much more compact than the last and the pink flowers change to deep purplish-pink as they fade, making a pretty, round, papery head, about an inch and a half across. Common on low hills in California.

14

Wild
Onion.

Allium
acuminatum.

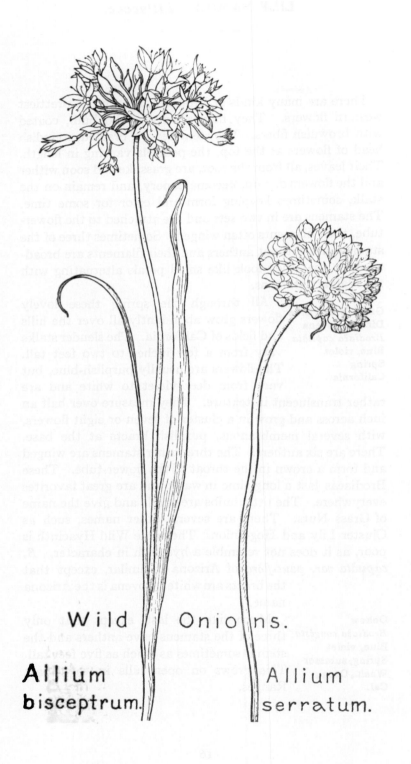

Wild Onions.

Allium
bisceptrum.

Allium
serratum.

LILY FAMILY. *Liliaceae.*

There are many kinds of Brodiaea, among the prettiest western flowers. They have a small, solid bulb, coated with brownish fibers. The stem bears a bracted, roundish head of flowers at the top, the pedicels varying in length. Their leaves, all from the root, are grasslike and soon wither and the flowers dry up, become papery, and remain on the stalk, sometimes keeping form and color for some time. The stamens are in two sets and are attached to the flower-tube, their filaments often winged. Sometimes three of the stamens are without anthers and their filaments are broadened, so that they look like small petals alternating with the ordinary stamens.

Grass Nuts. Blue Dicks. Covena
Brodiaèa capitàta
Blue, violet
Spring
California

All through the spring these lovely flowers grow abundantly all over the hills and fields of California. The slender stalks vary from a few inches to two feet tall. The flowers are usually purplish-blue, but vary from deep-violet to white and are rather translucent in texture. They measure over half an inch across and grow in a cluster of seven or eight flowers, with several membranous, purplish bracts at the base. There are six anthers. The three inner stamens are winged and form a crown in the throat of the flower-tube. These Brodiaeas last a long time in water and are great favorites everywhere. The little bulbs are edible and give the name of Grass Nuts. There are several other names, such as Cluster Lily and Hog-onion. The name Wild Hyacinth is poor, as it does not resemble a hyacinth in character. *B. capitàta var. pauciflòra* of Arizona is similar, except that the bracts are white. Covena is the Arizona name.

Ookow
Brodiaèa congèsta
Blue, violet
Spring, summer
Wash., Oreg., Cal.

Much like the last, except that only three of the stamens have anthers and the stem is sometimes as much as five feet tall. This grows on open hills in the Coast Ranges.

Covena. Brodiaea capitata
var. pauciflora.

Brodiaea capitata
var. pauciflora.

Covena.

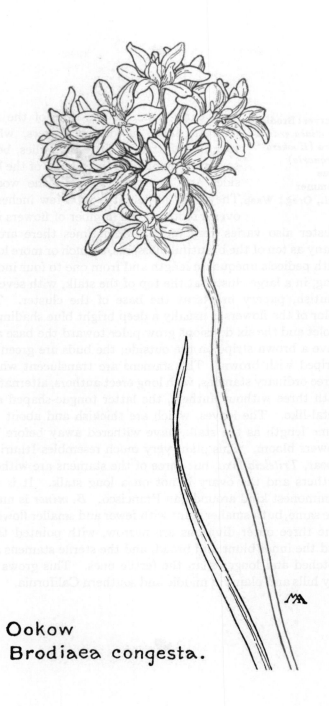

Ookow
Brodiaea congesta.

LILY FAMILY. *Liliaceae.*

Harvest Brodiaea
Brodiaea grandi-flòra (Hookera coronaria)
Blue
Summer
Cal., Oreg., Wash.
In early June, at the time of the hay harvest, these handsome flowers, which look like clusters of little blue lilies, begin to appear among the dried grass of the hill-sides and in open places in the woods. They vary in height from a few inches to over a foot and the number of flowers in a cluster also varies very much. Sometimes there are as many as ten of the beautiful blossoms, an inch or more long, with pedicels unequal in length and from one to four inches long, in a large cluster at the top of the stalk, with several, whitish, papery bracts at the base of the cluster. The color of the flowers is usually a deep bright blue shading to violet and the six divisions grow paler toward the base and have a brown stripe on the outside; the buds are greenish, striped with brown. The stamens are translucent white, three ordinary stamens, with long erect anthers, alternating with three without anthers, the latter tongue-shaped and petal-like. The leaves, which are thickish and about the same length as the stalk, have withered away before the flowers bloom. This plant very much resembles Ithuriel's Spear, *Triteleia laxa*, but three of the stamens are without anthers and the ovary is not on a long stalk. It is the commonest kind around San Francisco. *B. minor* is much the same, but a smaller plant with fewer and smaller flowers. The three outer divisions are narrow, with pointed tips, and the inner blunt and broad, and the sterile stamens are notched and longer than the fertile ones. This grows on dry hills and plains in middle and southern California.

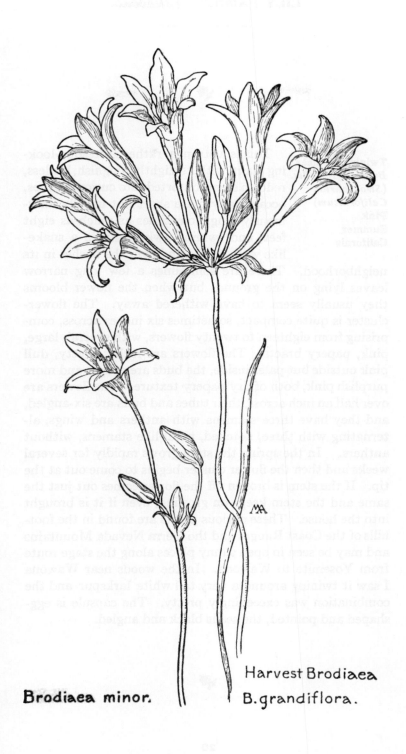

Harvest Brodiaea
B. grandiflora.

Brodiaea minor.

LILY FAMILY. *Liliaceae.*

Twining Brodiaèa
Brodiaèa volùbilis.
*(Stropholirion
Californicum)*
Pink
Summer
California

This is a strange, rather grotesque-look-ing plant, with its slightly roughish, leafless, reddish stem contorted into curious curves, occasionally quite short but usually enor-mously long, sometimes as much as eight feet, and twining awkwardly in a snake-like way around and over the bushes in its neighborhood. There are sometimes a few long narrow leaves lying on the ground, but when the flower blooms they usually seem to have withered away. The flower-cluster is quite compact, sometimes six inches across, com-prising from eighteen to twenty flowers, with several, large, pink, papery bracts. The flowers are rather pretty, dull pink outside but paler inside, the buds are deeper and more purplish pink, both of dry papery texture. The flowers are over half an inch across, their tubes and buds are six-angled, and they have three stamens with anthers and wings, al-ternating with three, notched, petal-like stamens, without anthers. In the spring the stem grows rapidly for several weeks and then the flower cluster begins to come out at the tip. If the stem is broken off the flower comes out just the same and the stem keeps on growing, even if it is brought into the house. These curious plants are found in the foot-hills of the Coast Ranges and the Sierra Nevada Mountains and may be seen in open sunny places along the stage route from Yosemite to Wawona. In the woods near Wawona I saw it twining around a very tall white larkspur and the combination was exceedingly pretty. The capsule is egg-shaped and pointed, the seeds black and angled.

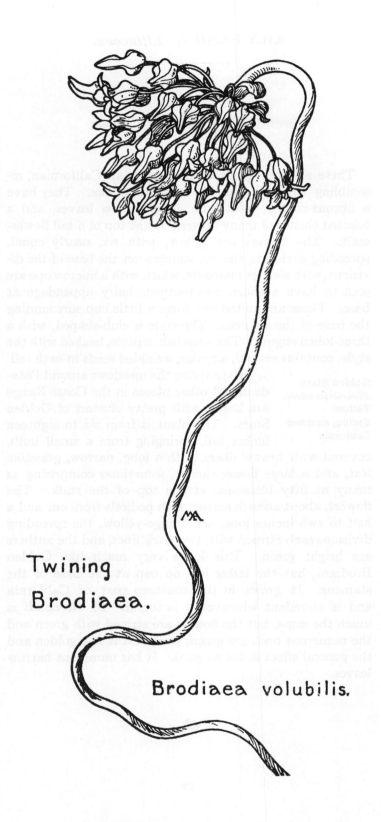

Twining
Brodiaea.

Brodiaea volubilis.

There are four kinds of Bloomeria, all Californian, resembling Brodiaea, but the stamens unlike. They have
a fibrous-coated, solid bulb, long narrow leaves, and a
bracted cluster of many flowers, at the top of a tall flower-
stalk. The flowers are yellow, with six, nearly equal,
spreading divisions, the six stamens on the base of the divisions, with slender filaments, which with a microscope are
seen to have a short, two-toothed, hairy appendage at
base. These are united and form a little cup surrounding
the base of the stamens. The style is club-shaped, with a
three-lobed stigma. The roundish capsule, beaked with the
style, contains several, angular, wrinkled seeds in each cell.

Golden Stars
Bloomèria aùrea
Yellow
Spring, summer
California

In late spring the meadows around Pasadena and other places in the Coast Range
are bright with pretty clusters of Golden
Stars. The plant is from six to eighteen
inches tall, springing from a small bulb,
covered with brown fibers, with a long, narrow, grasslike
leaf, and a large flower-cluster, sometimes comprising as
many as fifty blossoms, at the top of the stalk. The
flowers, about an inch across, with pedicels from one and a
half to two inches long, are orange-yellow, the spreading
divisions each striped with two dark lines, and the anthers
are bright green. This looks very much like Golden
Brodiaea, but the latter has no cup at the base of the
stamens. It grows in the southern part of California
and is abundant wherever it is found. *B. Clevelandi* is
much the same, but the flowers are striped with green and
the numerous buds are green, so that it is less golden and
the general effect is not so good. It has numerous narrow
leaves.

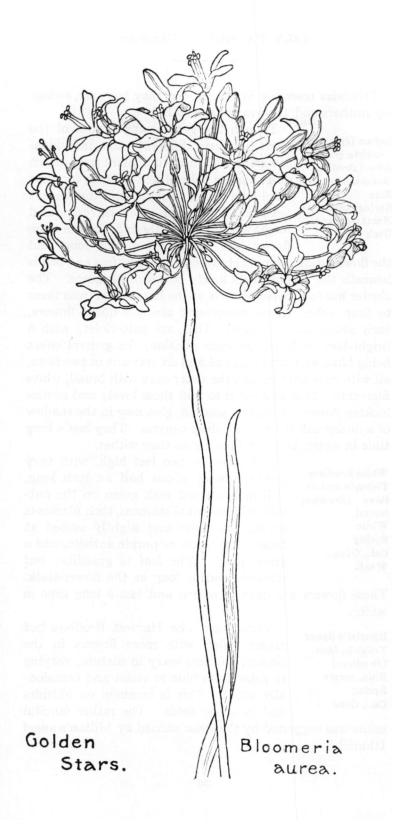

Golden
Stars.

Bloomeria
aurea.

Triteleias resemble Brodiaeas, but they have **six, swing-**ing anthers and the ovary has a stalk.

Indian Hyacinth
Triteleia grandi-
flòra (Brodiaea
Douglasii)
Blue
Spring, summer
Northwest and
Utah

Though the general appearance of the plant is very different, the individual flowers of this beautiful plant very much resemble the bells of a Hyacinth, for they have the same waxy, semi-translucent texture. The bluish-green leaves, folded lengthwise and withering before the flower, are sometimes a foot long and the flower-stalk often reaches a height of two feet and bends beneath the weight of its lovely crown of blossoms. The cluster has four papery bracts at the base and is from three to four inches across, comprising about a dozen flowers, each nearly an inch long. They are pale-violet, with a bright-blue mid-vein on each division, the general effect being blue, with a white pistil and six stamens in two rows, all with blue anthers and the outer ones with broad, white filaments. It is wonderful to find these lovely and exotic-looking flowers, delicately scented, gleaming in the shadow of a dusky oak thicket or a deep canyon. They last a long time in water, becoming papery as they wither.

White Brodiaea
Triteleia hyacin-
thìna (Brodiaea
lactea)
White
Spring
Cal., Oreg.,
Wash.

From one to two feet high, with very pretty flowers, about half an inch long, delicately striped with green on the out-side, with six equal stamens, their filaments broad, triangular and slightly united at base, with yellow or purple anthers, and a green pistil. The leaf is grasslike, but thickish, and as long as the flower-stalk. These flowers are quite common and last a long time in water.

Ithuriel's Spear
Triteleia láxa
(Brodiaea)
Blue, purple
Spring
Cal., Oreg.

Very much like Harvest Brodiaea but rather taller, with more flowers in the cluster, and less waxy in texture, varying in color from blue to violet and occasion-ally white. This is common on hillsides and in adobe fields. The rather fanciful name was suggested by the spear carried by Milton's angel Ithuriel.

Indian Huacint.
Trifeleia grandiflora

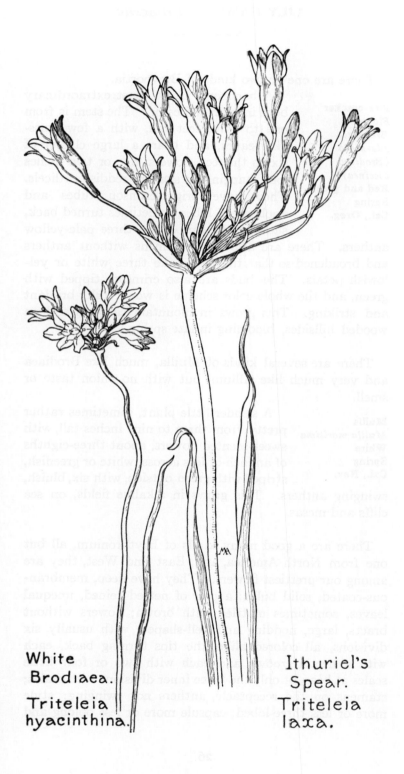

White
Brodiaea.
Triteleia
hyacinthina.

Ithuriel's
Spear.
Triteleia
laxa.

LILY FAMILY. *Liliaceae.*

There are one or two kinds of Brevoortia.

Fire-cracker Flower
Brevoòrtia Ida-Màia
(*Brodiaea coccinea*)
Red and green
Spring
Cal., Oreg.

A handsome plant, most extraordinary both in form and color. The stem is from one to three feet tall, with a few grass-like leaves, and bears a large cluster of six to thirteen flowers, one or two inches long, hanging on slender, reddish pedicels. They have bright-crimson tubes and apple-green lobes, sometimes turned back, showing the tips of the three pale-yellow anthers. There are also three stamens without anthers and broadened so that they look like three white or yellowish petals. The buds are also crimson, tipped with green, and the whole color scheme is wonderfully brilliant and striking. This grows in mountain canyons and on wooded hillsides, blooming in late spring.

There are several kinds of Muilla, much like Brodiaea and very much like Allium, but with no onion taste or smell.

Muilla
Muilla maritima
White
Spring
Cal., Nev.

A slender little plant, sometimes rather pretty, from three to nine inches tall, with sweet-scented flowers, about three-eighths of an inch or less across, white or greenish, striped with green outside, with six, bluish, swinging anthers. This grows in alkaline fields, on sea cliffs and mesas.

There are a good many kinds of Erythronium, all but one from North America, and, East and West, they are among our prettiest flowers. They have deep, membranous-coated, solid bulbs; a pair of netted-veined, unequal leaves, sometimes mottled with brown; flowers without bracts, large, nodding and bell-shaped, with usually six divisions, all colored alike, the tips turning back, each with a nectar-groove, and each with two or four little scales at base, or only the three inner divisions with scales; stamens on the receptacle, anthers not swinging; style more or less three-lobed; capsule more or less oblong and

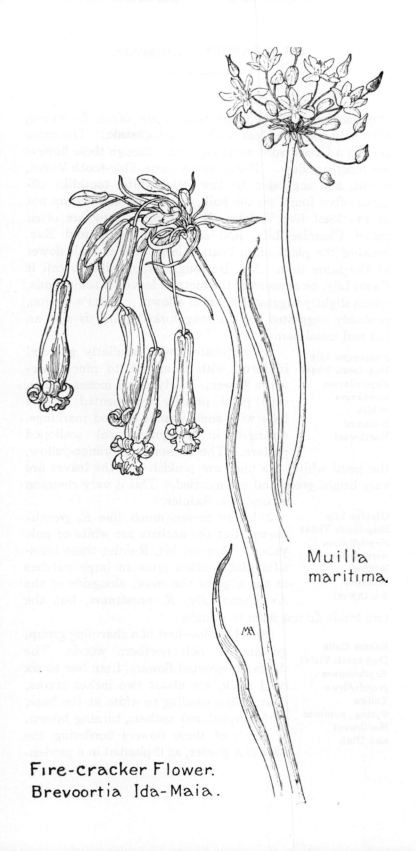

Muilla
maritima.

Fire-cracker Flower.
Brevoortia Ida-Maia.

three-angled. The younger plants are often flowerless, with only one broad leaf, with a long leaf-stalk. The name is from a Greek word meaning "red," though these flowers are mostly yellow. The common name, Dog-tooth Violet, is old, and suggested by the little, white, toothlike off-shoot often found on the bulb, but of course they are not in the least like Violets. In California they are often called Chamise Lily, and sometimes Adam and Eve, because the plant often bears a large and a small flower at the same time. Mr. Burroughs would like to call it Fawn Lily, on account of the mottled leaves of some kinds, which slightly suggest the ears of a fawn. Adder's-tongue, probably suggested by the long forked pistil, is also an old and usual name.

Avalanche Lily
Dog-tooth Violet
Erythrònium
montànum
White
Summer
Northwest

An exquisite kind, peculiarly graceful in form, with from one to nine, pure-white flowers, nearly three inches across, each petal prettily ornamented at the base with some orange-colored markings, arranged in a symmetrical scalloped pattern. The anthers are orange-yellow, the pistil white, the buds are pinkish and the leaves are very bright green and not mottled. This is very common around Mt. Rainier.

Glacier Lily
Dog-tooth Violet
Erythrònium
parviflòrum
Yellow
Summer
Northwest

A lovely flower, much like *E. grandiflorum*, but the anthers are white or pale yellow. Around Mt. Rainier these beautiful plants often grow in large patches at the edge of the snow, alongside of the Avalanche Lily, *E. montanum*, but the two kinds do not seem to mingle.

Easter Bells
Dog-tooth Violet
Erythrònium ,
grandiflòrum
Yellow
Spring, summer
Northwest
and Utah

One of the loveliest of a charming group, growing in rich northern woods. The delicately-scented flowers, from one to six on a stalk, are about two inches across, clear yellow shading to white at the base, with purplish-red anthers, turning brown. A patch of these flowers bordering the edge of a glacier, as if planted in a garden-

Dogtooth
Violet

Erythronium
grandiflorum

Avalanche Lily.
Erythronium montanum.

Glacier Lily.
E parviflorum.

bed, is a sight never to be forgotten. Pushing their bright leaves right through the snow they gayly swing their golden censers in the face of winter and seem the very incarnation of spring. There are several similar kinds. In the Utah canyons these flowers in early spring are a wonderful sight, covering the wooded slopes with sheets of gold, and they seem to me to be the largest and handsomest of their clan, growing at an altitude of six thousand to eleven thousand five hundred feet, and blooming from March to July according to height. Easter Bells is a Utah name.

Desert Lily
*Hesperocállis
undulàta*
**White
Spring
Cal., Ariz.**

This is the only one of its kind, a wonderfully beautiful desert plant, much like an Easter Lily. The stout, pale, bluish stem, from six inches to two feet tall, has a delicate "bloom" and springs from a graceful cluster of narrow leaves, which are a foot and a half long, spreading widely, but not lying quite flat on the ground. They are pale bluish-green, with a narrow, crinkled, white border and folded lengthwise. The buds are bluish and the lovely flowers are about three inches long and pure-white, delicately striped with pale-green and blue on the outside, with yellow anthers and a white stigma, and with a papery bract at the base of each pedicel. The flowers are slightly fragrant and become papery and curiously transparent as they wither. In dry seasons these plants do not bloom at all, but the slightest moisture will cause them to send up a stout stem and crown it with exquisite blossoms, which look extraordinarily out of place on the arid desert sand around Yuma and Ft. Mohave. The bulb is eaten by the Indians.

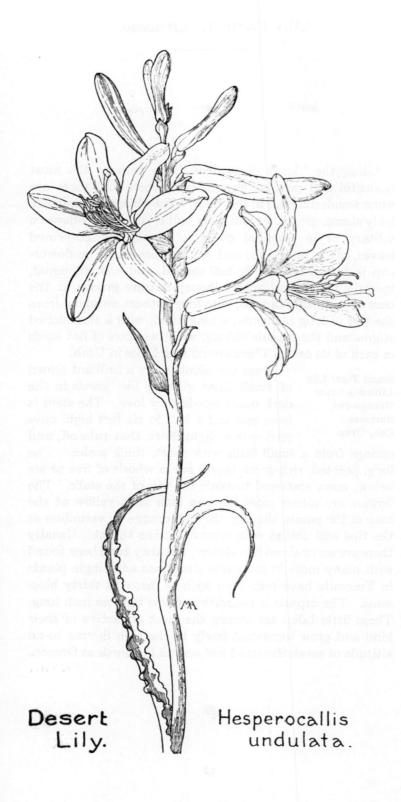

Desert Lily.

Hesperocallis undulata.

LILY FAMILY. *Liliaceae.*

Lilies, the "lords of gardens," are perhaps the most beautiful and popular flowers everywhere and there are some wonderful ones in the West. They have tall, smooth, leafy stems, springing from scaly bulbs; large showy flowers, solitary or in terminal clusters; smooth, netted-veined leaves, often in whorls, and leaflike bracts. The flower-cup is funnel-formed, or bell-shaped, and has six, equal, spreading divisions, with a honey-bearing groove at the base of each; the stamens, with long anthers, swinging from the tips of long filaments; a long pistil, with a three-lobed stigma and the capsule oblong, with two rows of flat seeds in each of its cells. There are no true Lilies in Utah.

Small Tiger Lily
Lílium párvum
Orange-red
Summer
Cal., Oreg.

These tall plants carry a brilliant crown of small lilies, glowing like jewels in the dark moist woods they love. The stem is from one and a half to six feet high, covered with a slight down that rubs off, and springs from a small bulb with short, thick scales. The long, pointed, rich-green leaves are in whorls of five or six below, more scattered towards the top of the stalk. The flowers are rather more than an inch long, yellow at the base of the petals, shading through orange to vermilion at the tips and dotted with crimson in the throat. Usually there are six or seven in a cluster, but they have been found with many more in favorable situations and single plants in Yosemite have been seen with as many as thirty blossoms. The capsule is roundish and less than an inch long. These little Lilies are among the most attractive of their kind and grow somewhat freely in the high Sierras to an altitude of seven thousand feet and as far north as Oregon.

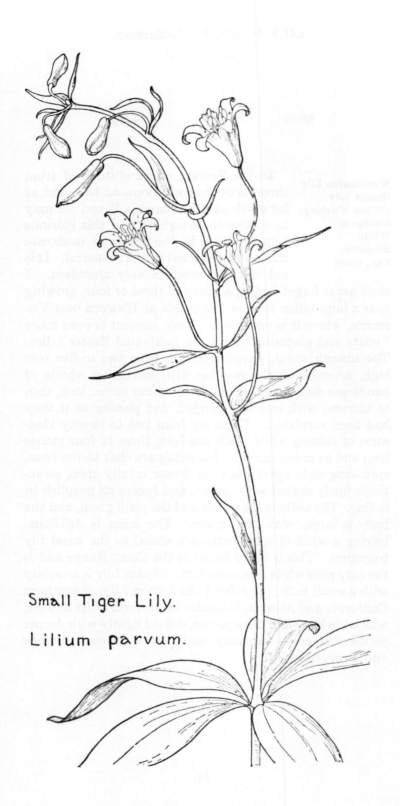

Small Tiger Lily.

Lilium parvum.

LILY FAMILY. *Liliaceae.*

**Washington Lily
Shasta Lily
*Lilium Washing-
tonianum*
White
Summer
Cal., Oreg.**

In the Sierras, at an altitude of from three to over seven thousand feet, and as far north as the Columbia River, we may be fortunate enough to find this glorious Lily, growing in the forest in moderate shade and protected by the chaparral. It is not rare but nowhere very abundant. I shall never forget finding a group of three or four, growing near a huge fallen tree, in the woods at Wawona near Yosemite, where it is very fine. Their raiment is even more "white and glistering" than the cultivated Easter Lilies. The smooth, stout, purplish stem is from two to five feet high, adorned all the way up with successive whorls of handsome dark-green leaves, three or four inches long, thin in texture, with rippling margins, and shining as if they had been varnished. There are from two to twenty blossoms of shining white, each one from three to four inches long and as much across. The petals are cleft to the base, spreading wide apart when the flower is fully open, sometimes finely dotted with purple, and becoming purplish in fading. The anthers are yellow and the pistil green, and the bulb is large, with thin scales. The scent is delicious, having a whiff of spicy carnation added to the usual lily fragrance. This is never found in the Coast Range and is the only pure white American Lily. Shasta Lily is a variety with a small bulb. *L. Pàrryi*, the Lemon Lily, of southern California and Arizona, is similar in the form of its flowers, which are large and clear yellow, dotted lightly with deeper yellow. It grows in shady, moist spots in cool canyons and is very beautiful.

**Washington
Lily.**

**Lilium
Washingtonianum**

LILY FAMILY. *Liliaceae.*

Leopard Lily
*Lilium
pardalinum*
Orange
Summer
Wash., Oreg., Cal.
A magnificent plant, from three to six feet tall, with bright-green leaves, thin in texture, smooth but not shiny, and mostly in whorls. The stem is crowned by a splendid cluster of flowers, usually about half a dozen together, but sometimes as many as thirty on one stalk. They measure three or four inches across and are pale-orange outside and deep-orange inside, spotted with maroon, often blotched with orange-yellow in the throat and tipped with scarlet. The anthers are purplish, changing to reddish-brown, and the pistil is bright-green. These plants often grow in large companies, in moist spots in the mountains, and are un-rivaled in decorative beauty and brilliancy of coloring.

Tiger Lily
*Lilium
Columbianum*
Orange
Summer
Wash., Oreg.
A good deal like the last, but not so large. The petals are more turned back and they are orange-color all over, dotted with dark-red, and the anthers are pale orange-color, ripening to golden-brown. This is common in the Hood River Valley.

**Ruby Lily
Chaparral Lily**
Lilium rubéscens
White, pink
Summer
Cal., Oreg.
A glorious plant, from two to five feet tall, with leaves mostly in whorls, with rippled edges. The stem bears a magnificent cluster of blossoms, most wonderful in coloring, for the buds and young flowers are white, dotted with purple inside, with yellow anthers and a pale-green pistil, but they gradually change to pink, and deepen to ruby-purple as they fade, and the anthers and pistil also darken in color. The effect of the whole cluster is therefore white at the top, shading through pink to almost crimson below. The flowers are even more deliciously fragrant than the Washington Lily, which they resemble, except that they are not quite so large as the latter and stand more erect and the petals are not so spreading. This usually grows among chaparral in the Coast Ranges.

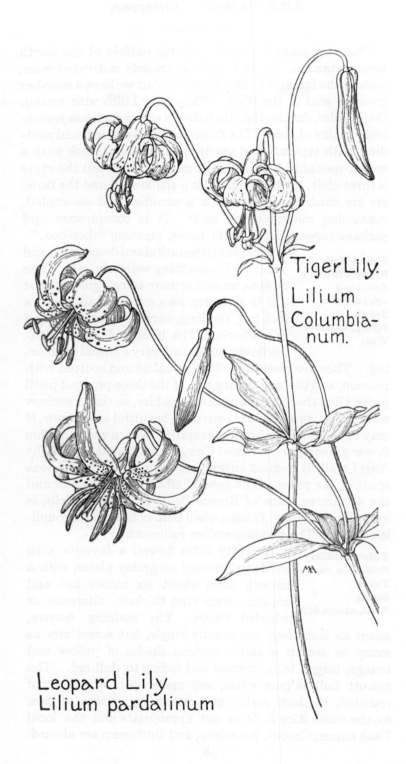

Tiger Lily.
Lilium
Columbia-
num.

Leopard Lily
Lilium pardalinum

LILY FAMILY. *Liliaceae.*

There are many kinds of Fritillaria, natives of the north temperate zone. In the East there are only cultivated ones, such as the familiar Crown Imperial, but we have a number growing wild in the West. They have bulbs with round, thick scales, developing into bulblets and sometimes resembling grains of rice. The flowers are bell-shaped, and nodding, with separate and nearly equal divisions, each with a nectar-spot at its base. They resemble Lilies, but the style is three-cleft, the honey-gland is a shallow pit and the flowers are smaller. The capsule is roundish and six-angled, containing numerous flat seeds. It is conspicuous and perhaps suggested the Latin name, meaning "dice-box."

Bronze Bells
Brown Fritillary
Fritillària
atropurpùrea
Brown
Spring, summer
West

This plant is beautiful and decorative, and yet there is something weird about it. The flowers, an inch or more across, grow four or five in a cluster, on a smooth stalk about a foot tall, the long, narrow leaves scattered or in whorls. The bells, nodding on slender flower-stalks, are very unusual in coloring. They are greenish-yellow, streaked and spotted with maroon, and the long curling tips of the three-pronged pistil project like the forked tongue of an adder, so that somehow we feel that, in a previous existence, beautiful as it is now, it may have been a toad or some reptile. When we found this flower growing in the Grand Canyon, halfway down Bright Angel trail, it seemed entirely suitable to the mysterious spirit of the place. The general effect is bronze-color and the attractive name of Bronze Bells, or Mission Bells, is very appropriate. It has a small bulb of numerous, roundish scales. The pistils are often rudimentary.

Yellow Fritillary
Fritillària pùdica
Yellow
Spring
West, except Ariz.

A pretty little flower, a favorite with children, growing on grassy plains, with a smooth stem about six inches tall, and smooth, somewhat thickish, alternate or whorled leaves. The nodding flowers, about an inch long, are usually single, but sometimes as many as six on a stalk, various shades of yellow and orange, tinged with crimson and fading to dull-red. The smooth bulb is pure white, and made up of a number of rounded, thickish scales not resembling grains of rice, so the name Rice Root is not appropriate and the local Utah names, Crocus, Snowdrop, and Buttercup are absurd.

Bronze
Bells.

Frit illaria
atropurpurea.

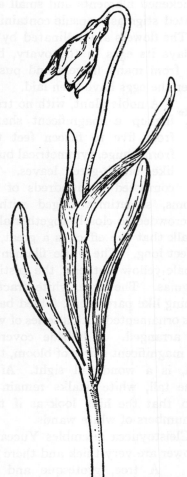

Yellow
Fritillary.

Fritillaria
pudica.

LILY FAMILY. *Liliaceae.*

There are several kinds of Yucca, natives of North and Central America; large plants, with dagger-like leaves, usually with long, thread-like fibers along the margins; flowers with bracts, nodding in a terminal cluster, somewhat bell-shaped, with six, thickish, white divisions; stamens short, with thickened filaments and small anthers; ovary with three united stigmas; capsule containing many, flat, black seeds. The flowers are pollinated by a little white moth, which lays its eggs in the ovary, but previously gathers pollen from many flowers and pushes it against the stigma after the eggs have been laid.

Our Lord's Candle
Spanish Bayonet
Yúcca Whípplei
White
Spring, summer
Cal., Ariz.

A noble plant, with no trunk, but sending up a magnificent shaft of flowers, from five to fifteen feet tall, springing from a huge, symmetrical bunch of dagger-like, bluish-green leaves. The cluster is composed of hundreds of waxy, cream-colored blossoms, sometimes tinged with purple, two inches across, crowded so closely together along the upper part of the stalk that the effect is a great, solid mass of bloom, three feet long. The white filaments are swollen, tipped with pale-yellow anthers; the pistil cream-color, with green stigmas. The large, white bracts are stiff and coarse, something like parchment, folded back so that the pinkish stalk is ornamented with a series of white triangles, symmetrically arranged. A hillside covered with hundreds of these magnificent spires of bloom, towering above the chaparral, is a wonderful sight. After they have blossomed, the tall, white stalks remain standing for some time, so that the hills look as if they had been planted with numbers of white wands.

The genus Cleistoyucca resembles Yucca, but the divisions of the flower are very thick and there is no style.

Joshua Tree
Tree Yucca
Cleistoyúcca
arboréscens
(Yucca)
Greenish-white
Spring, summer
Cal., Ariz., Utah

A tree, grotesque and forbidding in aspect, but with a weird sort of beauty, looming black against the pale desert landscape, with a great, thick, rough trunk, fifteen to thirty feet high, and a few thick, contorted branches, stretching out like a giant's arms and pointing ominously across the sandy waste. The branches

Our Lord's Candle.
Yucca Whipplei.
[very small part of cluster]

LILY FAMILY. *Liliaceae.*

are thatched with the shaggy husks of dead leaves and from their tips they thrust out a great bunch of dagger-like leaves and a big, ponderous cluster of pallid, greenish flowers or heavy, yellowish fruits. The coarse flowers are about two inches across, with a clammy smell like toadstools, and the bracts are dead white. This grows in the Mohave Desert and is at its best around Hesperia, where one may see the most fantastic forest that it is possible to imagine. Elsewhere it is smaller and more like other Yuccas in shape. It was called Joshua Tree by the early settlers, it is said because they fancied that its branches pointed towards the Promised Land. The fruits are relished by the Indians, who utilize the fibers from the leaves for weaving baskets, ropes, hats, horse-blankets, etc., and make a pulp from the stems, used for soap.

There are several kinds of Trillium, of North America and Asia; with tuberous root-stocks; three, netted-veined leaves, in a whorl at the top of the stem; a single flower with three, green sepals, three petals, six, short stamens, and three styles; capsule berry-like and reddish, containing many seeds. The Latin name means "triple."

Wake-robin
Birthroot
Trillium ovàtum
White
Spring, summer
Northwest

A charming plant, about a foot tall, with a single beautiful blossom, set off to perfection by its large, rich green leaves. The flower is two or three inches across, with lovely white petals, which gradually change to deep pink. It is a pleasure to find a company of these attractive plants in the heart of the forest, where their pure blossoms gleam in the cool shade along some mountain brook. They resemble the eastern Large-flowered Trillium and grow in the Coast Ranges.

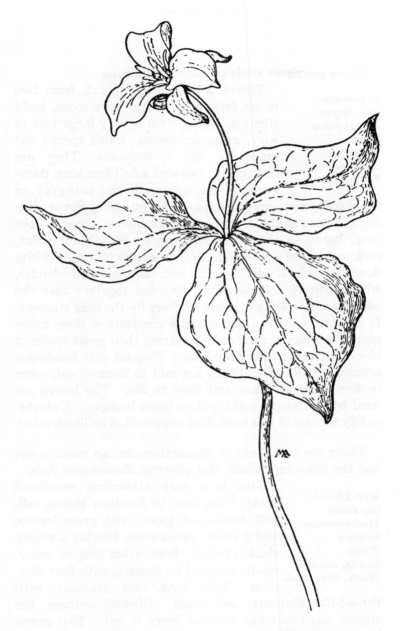

Wake-robin

Trillium ovatum.

LILY FAMILY. *Liliaceae.*

There are three kinds of Xerophyllum.

Squaw-grass
Bear Grass
Xerophýllum
tènax
White
Summer
Northwest

This is a magnificent plant, from two to six feet high, with a very stout, leafy stem, springing from a very large tuft of wiry, grass-like leaves, which spread out gracefully like a fountain. They are from one to two and a half feet long, dark-green on the upper side and pale-gray on the under, with rough edges. The imposing flower cluster is borne at the top of the stalk and is about a foot long, broad at the base and tapering to a blunt point, and composed of hundreds of fragrant, cream-white flowers, each about half an inch across, with slender, white pedicels, and so closely crowded together that the effect is very solid, yet made feathery by the long stamens. It is a fine sight to come across a company of these noble plants in a mountain meadow, rearing their great shafts of bloom far above their neighbors. They are very handsome around Mt. Rainier. They are said to blossom only once in five or seven years and then to die. The leaves are used by Indians in making their finest baskets. Unfortunately the size of this book does not admit of an illustration.

There are two kinds of Maianthemum, an eastern one and the following, which also grows in Europe and Asia.

Wild Lily-of-
the-valley
Maiánthemum
bifòlium
White
Spring, summer
Wash., Oreg., Cal.

This is a very attractive, woodland plant, from four to fourteen inches tall, with handsome, glossy, rich green leaves, and a rather stout stem, bearing a pretty cluster, two or three inches long, of many, small, waxy-white flowers, with four divisions. They have four stamens, with thread-like filaments and small, yellowish anthers, the stigma has two lobes and the berry is red. This grows in rich soil in the mountains and is much handsomer than its eastern relation and strongly sweet-scented. The Latin name means "blooming in May."

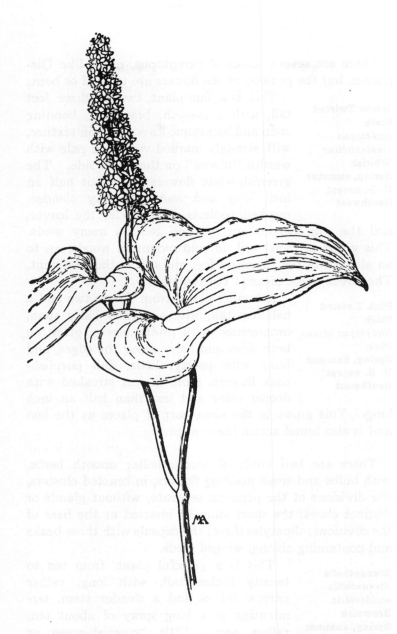

Wild Lily-of-the-valley.

Maianthemum bifolium.

There are several kinds of Streptopus, much like Disporum, but the pedicels of the flowers are twisted or bent.

White Twisted Stalk
Strêptopus amplexifòlius
Whitish
Spring, summer
U. S. except Southwest

This is a fine plant, two or three feet tall, with a smooth, branching, bending stem and handsome leaves, thin in texture, with strongly marked veins and pale with whitish "bloom" on the under side. The greenish-white flowers are about half an inch long and hang on very slender, crooked pedicels, from under the leaves, and the oval berries are red and contain many seeds. This grows in moist soil, in cold mountain woods, up to an altitude of ten thousand feet and across the continent. The Greek name means "twisted stalk."

Pink Twisted Stalk
Strêptopus ròseus
Pink
Spring, summer
U. S. except Southwest

A smaller plant, from one to two and a half feet tall, with a slightly hairy stem, ornamented with pretty leaves, green on both sides and hairy along the edges, and hung with pretty, little, dull purplish-pink flowers, more or less streaked with deeper color and less than half an inch long. This grows in the same sort of places as the last and is also found across the continent.

There are two kinds of Stenanthella; smooth herbs, with bulbs and small nodding flowers, in bracted clusters, the divisions of the perianth separate, without glands or distinct claws; the short stamens inserted at the base of the divisions; the styles three; the capsule with three beaks and containing oblong, winged seeds.

Stenanthella
Stenanthélla occidentàlis
Brownish
Spring, summer
Northwest

This is a graceful plant, from ten to twenty inches tall, with long, rather narrow leaves and a slender stem, terminating in a long spray of about ten, rather pretty, little brownish-green or purplish flowers, each less than half an inch long. This grows in shady places.

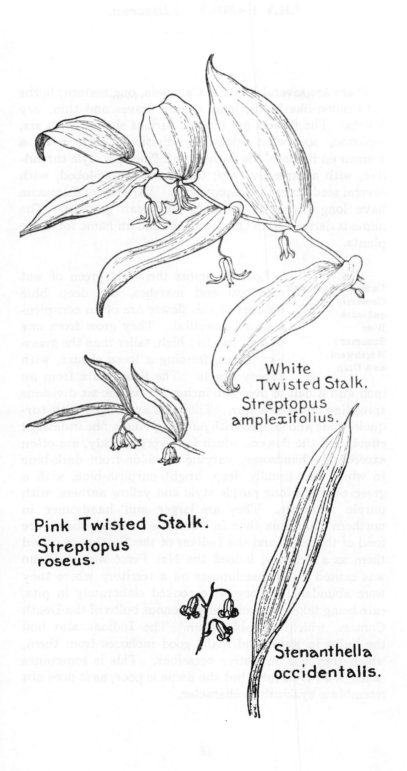

White
Twisted Stalk.
Streptopus
amplexifolius.

Pink Twisted Stalk.
Streptopus
roseus.

Stenanthella
occidentalis.

LILY FAMILY. *Liliaceae.*

There are several kinds of Camassia, one eastern; herbs with onion-like bulbs, long, narrow leaves and thin, dry bracts. The flowers are blue of various shades, with six, separate, somewhat spreading divisions, each with a stamen on its base, the anthers swinging, the style thread-like, with a three-cleft tip; the capsule three-lobed, with several seeds in each compartment. Varieties of Camassia have long been cultivated in European gardens. The name is derived from Quamash, the Indian name for these plants.

Camass, Quamash
Camássia
quámash
Blue
Summer
Northwest
and Utah

Looking across the vivid green of wet meadows and marshes, the deep blue patches of this flower are often conspicuous and beautiful. They grow from one to over two feet high, taller than the grass-like leaves, forming a loose cluster, with papery bracts. The flowers are from an inch and a half to over two inches across, the six divisions spreading out into a star. The buds are tinged with turquoise-blue and striped with purple, giving a fine iridescent effect, and the flowers, which fade very quickly, are often exceedingly handsome, varying in color from dark-blue to white, but usually deep, bright purplish-blue, with a green ovary, a long purple style and yellow anthers, with purple filaments. They are larger and handsomer in northern California than in Yosemite. Grizzly bears are fond of the bulbs and the Indians of the Northwest prized them as a delicacy, indeed the Nez Percé war in Idaho was caused by encroachments on a territory where they were abundant. They were cooked elaborately in pits, care being taken to avoid the poisonous bulbs of the Death Camass, which resemble them. The Indians also boil the bulbs in water and make good molasses from them, which they use on festive occasions. This is sometimes called Wild Hyacinth, but the name is poor, as it does not resemble a hyacinth in character.

48

Camass.   **Camassia quamash.**

LILY FAMILY. *Liliaceae.*

There are six kinds of Clintonia, of North America and Asia; with creeping rootstocks and a few, broad root-leaves; flowers without bracts, their divisions separate, equal or nearly so, each with a stamen at its base; style with two or three, inconspicuous lobes; fruit a berry. These plants were named in honor of De Witt Clinton, Governor of New York, a naturalist, interested in botany, so Thoreau need not have been so annoyed at their having been given this name.

Red Clintonia
Clintònia
Andrewsiàna
Red, pink
Spring, summer
Oreg., Cal.

A magnificent plant, one or two feet high, with five or six, exceedingly hand-some, glossy, rich green leaves, very conspicuous and sometimes a foot long, and a tall, slightly downy flower-stalk, usually with a few flowers scattered along it, and crowned with a large, roundish cluster of beautiful flowers. They are about three-quarters of an inch long, very rich in color, a deep shade of warm reddish-pink, or crimson, not common in flowers. The form of the cluster varies a good deal; sometimes the flowers are not mostly at the top, but clustered quite thickly along all the upper part of the stalk. The large, deep-blue berries are very handsome and, altogether, this is one of our most con-spicuous and attractive woodland plants, especially when growing in the deep shade of redwood forests.

Queen-cup
White Clintonia
Clintònia
uniflòra
White
Spring
Northwest

In rich moist soil, in shady woods, we find this lovely flower, with a white chalice and heart of pale gold, surrounded by two or three, beautiful, large, glossy leaves, resembling those of Lily-of-the-valley, and fairly carpeting the ground in favorable situations. The slender flower-stalk is hairy, six to ten inches tall, and usually bears a single flower, an inch or more across, with pure-white petals that soon drop off. The fruit is a handsome blue berry.

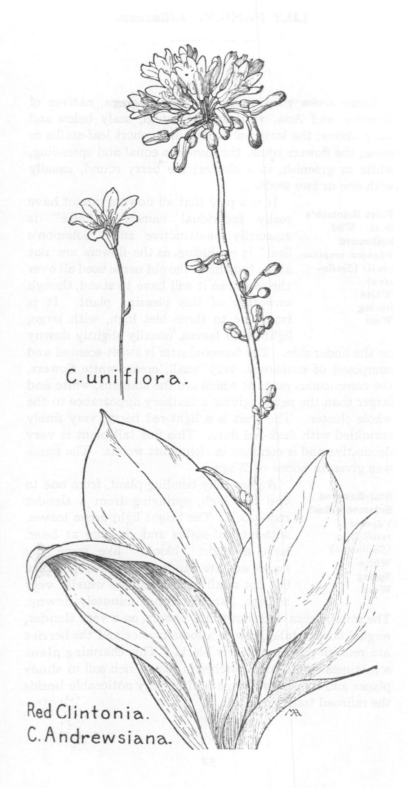

C. uniflora.

Red Clintonia.
C. Andrewsiana.

LILY FAMILY. *Liliaceae.*

There are a good many kinds of **Vagnera**, natives of America and Asia, with a single stem, scaly below and leafy above; the leaves alternate, with short leaf-stalks or none; the flowers small, the divisions equal and spreading, white or greenish, in a cluster; the berry round, usually with one or two seeds.

False Solomon's Seal. Wild Spikenard
Vágnera amplexicáulis (Smilacina)
White
Spring
West

It is a pity that all flowers cannot have really individual names. "False" is especially unattractive and "Solomon's Seal" is confusing, as the flowers are not alike, but this is the old name used all over the world, so it will have to stand, though unworthy of this pleasing plant. It is from one to three feet high, with large, light-green leaves, usually slightly downy on the under side. The flower-cluster is sweet-scented and composed of numerous, very small, cream-white flowers, the conspicuous parts of which are the stamens, white and larger than the petals, giving a feathery appearance to the whole cluster. The fruit is a light-red berry, very finely sprinkled with dark-red dots. This fine tall plant is very decorative and is common in rich moist woods. The name was given in honor of Wagner.

Star-flowered Solomon's Seal
Vágnera sessilifòlia (Smilacina)
White
Spring
West

A gracefully bending plant, from one to two feet high, springing from a slender root-stock. The bright light-green leaves, without leaf-stalks and clasping at base, have a slight "bloom" like some lily leaves and are handsome and conspicuous, but not at all coarse, and are usually very smooth, but sometimes minutely downy. The small, delicate, cream-white flowers, on a very slender, angled flower-stalk, grow in a loose cluster and the berries are reddish-purple or nearly black. This charming plant sometimes forms large patches in moist, rich soil in shady places and its pretty foliage is often very noticeable beside the railroad tracks in Utah.

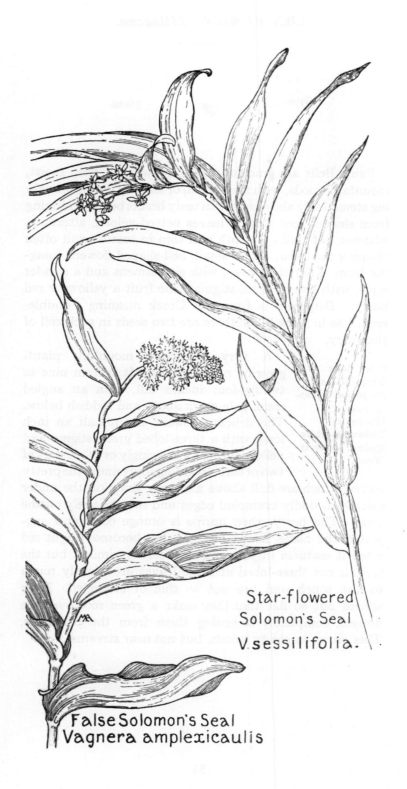

Star-flowered
Solomon's Seal
V. sessilifolia.

False Solomon's Seal
Vagnera amplexicaulis

LILY FAMILY. *Liliaceae.*

Fairy Bells are graceful plants, growing in rich, moist, mountain woods, with smoothish, or slightly hairy, branching stems, leafy above and with scaly bracts below, springing from slender root-stocks; leaves netted-veined, alternate, without leaf-stalks, smooth and thin in texture and often clasping the stem; rather small, bell-shaped flowers, hanging from under the leaves, with six stamens and a slender style, with one or three stigmas; the fruit a yellow or red berry. *Disporum* is from the Greek meaning "double-seed," as in some kinds there are two seeds in each cell of the ovary.

Fairy Bells
Drops of Gold
Disporum trachy-carpum
(Prosartes)
Yellowish-white
Spring, summer
West

A very attractive mountain plant, growing near streams. It is from nine to twenty-four inches tall, with an angled stem, pale green above and reddish below. The delicate flowers, about half an inch long, with a three-lobed green stigma and yellow anthers, grow singly or in clusters of two or three, nodding shyly under the pretty leaves, which are dull above and very shiny on the under side, with oddly crumpled edges and set obliquely on the stem. The berry when unripe is orange color and suggested the name Drops of Gold, but becomes bright red when it matures in June. *D. Hookeri* is similar, but the style is not three-lobed and the leaves are slightly rough to the touch and are not so thin or crumpled. They spread out so flat that they make a green roof over the flowers, completely screening them from the passer-by. This grows in shady woods, but not near streams.

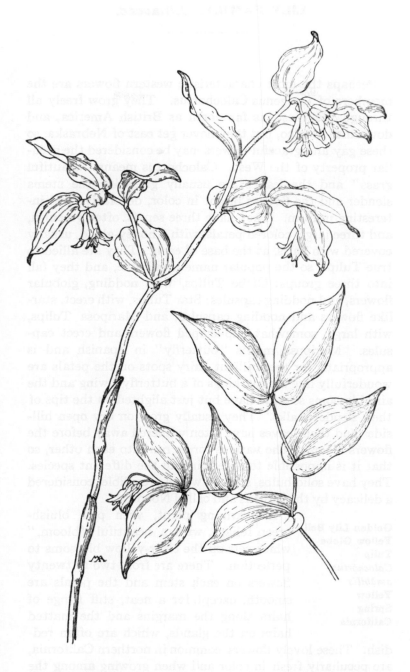

Fairy Bells.

Disporum
trachycarpum.

Drops of Gold.

Disporum
Hookeri.

LILY FAMILY. *Liliaceae.*

Perhaps the most characteristic western flowers are the members of the genus Calochortus. They grow freely all through the West, as far north as British America, and down into Mexico, but they never get east of Nebraska, so these gay and graceful flowers may be considered the peculiar property of the West. Calochortus means "beautiful grass" and the leaves are usually grasslike, the stems slender and the flowers bright in color, decorative and interesting in form. They have three sepals, often greenish, and three large, colored petals, with a honey-gland, usually covered with hairs, at the base of each. They are allied to true Tulips, so the popular name is suitable, and they fall into three groups: Globe Tulips, with nodding, globular flowers, and nodding capsules; Star Tulips, with erect, starlike flowers and nodding capsules; and Mariposa Tulips, with large, somewhat cup-shaped flowers and erect capsules. Mariposa means "butterfly" in Spanish and is appropriate, for the brilliant hairy spots on the petals are wonderfully like the markings of a butterfly's wing and the airy blossoms seem to have but just alighted on the tips of their slender stalks. They usually grow on dry open hillsides and their leaves have often withered away before the flowers bloom. The various forms run into each other, so that it is impossible to determine all the different species. They have solid bulbs, some of which are edible, considered a delicacy by the Indians and called Noonas.

Golden Lily Bell
Yellow Globe
Tulip
Calochórtus amábilis
Yellow
Spring
California

A charming plant, with pale bluish-green foliage, with a beautiful "bloom," which sets off the clear-yellow blossoms to perfection. There are from two to twenty flowers on each stem and the petals are smooth, except for a neat, stiff fringe of hairs along the margins and the matted hairs on the glands, which are often reddish. These lovely flowers, common in northern California, are peculiarly fresh in color and when growing among the grass in the shade of oak trees they have the springlike charm of Daffodils in English woods.

56

Yellow
Globe Tulip.

Calochortus
amabilis.

LILY FAMILY. *Lillaceae.*

Satin-bell. White
Globe Tulip
Calochórtus álbus
White
Spring
California

Beautiful and popular flowers, with a great deal of individuality and quite Japanese in the decorative arrangement of the graceful stems and glossy, rich green foliage. The narrow root-leaf is over a foot long and spreads on the ground and other smaller leaves are disposed along the bending stem, which is from one to two feet tall and hung with pretty light-green buds and beautiful drooping blossoms, over an inch long, pearly white, sometimes tinged with lilac, with a satiny sheen and delicate yet crisp in texture. The papery sepals are greenish-white and the petals are sometimes tinged with purple at the base and are prettily fringed with hairs along the edges and often cross their tips in a very engaging way. They are covered inside with long, silky, white or yellow hairs and the glands are crescent-shaped, with close, short, sticky, white or yellow hairs, and form pale-green humps on the outside of the petals; the anthers are cream-color and the pistil whitish. The capsule is one or two inches long, with a short beak and brown seeds. These plants grow on shady banks in the Coast Ranges and have several pretty common names, such as Lantern of the Fairies and Alabaster Tulip, as well as the misleading name Hairbell, which causes this flower to be confused with the Harebell or Campanula.

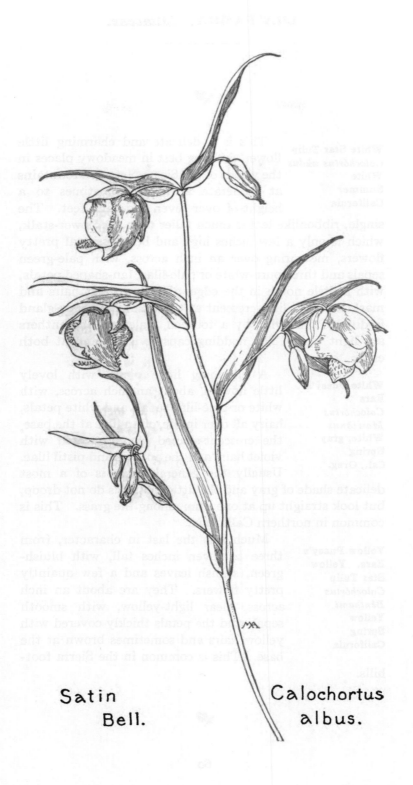

Satin
Bell.

Calochortus
albus.

LILY FAMILY. *Liliaceae.*

White Star Tulip
Calochórtus nùdus
White
Summer
California

This is a delicate and charming little flower, growing best in meadowy places in the woods of the Sierra Nevada Mountains at moderate altitudes, sometimes to a height of over seven thousand feet. The single, ribbonlike leaf is much taller than the flower-stalk, which is only a few inches high and bears several pretty flowers, measuring over an inch across, with pale-green sepals and three pure-white or pale-lilac, fan-shaped petals, with a little notch in the edge, almost without hairs and marked with a lilac crescent at the base; the honey-gland is divided crosswise by a toothed scale and the anthers are light blue. The nodding capsule is pointed at both ends.

White Pussy's
Ears
Calochórtus
Mawednus
White, gray
Spring
Cal., Oreg.

A charming little plant, with lovely little flowers, about an inch across, with white or pale-lilac sepals and white petals, hairy all over inside, often lilac at the base, the crescent-shaped gland covered with violet hairs and the anthers and pistil lilac. Usually the general effect is of a most delicate shade of gray and the little blossoms do not droop, but look straight up at one from among the grass. This is common in northern California.

Yellow Pussy's
Ears. Yellow
Star Tulip
Calochórtus
Bénthami
Yellow
Spring
California

Much like the last in character, from three to seven inches tall, with bluish-green, stiffish leaves and a few quaintly pretty flowers. They are about an inch across, clear light-yellow, with smooth sepals and the petals thickly covered with yellow hairs and sometimes brown at the base. This is common in the Sierra foot-hills.

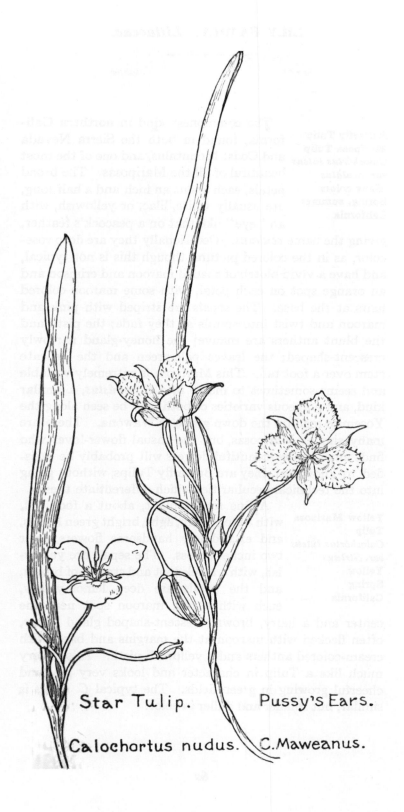

Star Tulip.   Pussy's Ears.

Calochortus nudus. C. Maweanus.

LILY FAMILY. *Liliaceae.*

Butterfly Tulip
Mariposa Tulip
Calochórtus lùteus
var. oculàtus
Many colors
Spring, summer
California

The commonest kind in northern California, found in both the Sierra Nevada and Coast Mountains, and one of the most beautiful of all the Mariposas. The broad petals, each about an inch and a half long, are usually white, lilac, or yellowish, with an "eye" like that on a peacock's feather, giving the name *oculatus*. Occasionally they are deep rose-color, as in the colored picture, though this is not typical, and have a vivid blotch of shaded maroon and crimson and an orange spot on each petal, with some maroon-colored hairs at the base. The sepals are striped with pink and maroon and twist into spirals as they fade; the pistil and the blunt anthers are mauve; the honey-gland narrowly crescent-shaped; the leaves pale-green and the delicate stem over a foot tall. This Mariposa is extremely variable and seems sometimes to merge into *C. venústus*, a similar kind, and gorgeous varieties of both may be seen along the Yosemite road on the down grade to Wawona. There are many similar Mariposas, but the casual flower-lover who finds any of these beautiful flowers will probably be satisfied to know that they are Butterfly Tulips, without going into the technical peculiarities which differentiate them.

Yellow Mariposa
Tulip
Calochórtus lùteus
var. citrìnus
Yellow
Spring
California

A fine robust plant, about a foot tall, with a stout stem, light, bright green leaves, and exceedingly handsome flowers, over two inches across. The sepals are yellowish, with a black spot and streaks of brown, and the petals are deep lemon-yellow, each with a rich maroon spot near the center and a hairy, brown, crescent-shaped gland below, often flecked with maroon at the margins and base, with cream-colored anthers and a yellowish pistil. This is very much like a Tulip in character and looks very gay and cheerful growing in green fields. The typical *C. luteus* is similar, but smaller and duller in color.

Butterfly
Tulip.

Calochortus luteus
var oculatus

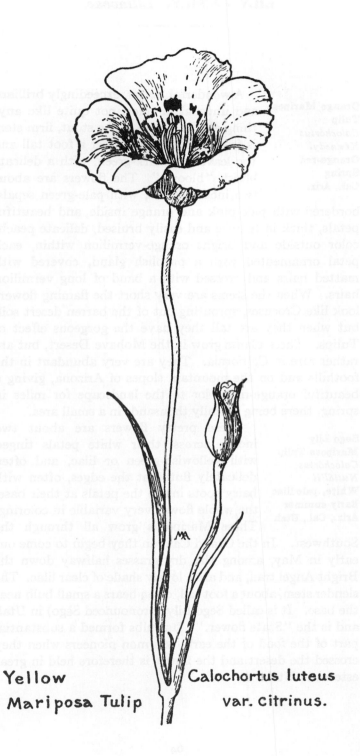

Yellow
Mariposa Tulip

Calochortus luteus
var. citrinus.

LILY FAMILY. *Liliaceae.*

Orange Mariposa Tulip
Calochórtus Kénnedyi
Orange-red
Spring
Cal., Ariz.

A wonderful flower, exceedingly brilliant and unusual in color, not quite like anything else in nature. The stout, firm stem is from two inches to over a foot tall and the leaves are dark-green, with a delicate bluish "bloom." The flowers are about two inches across, with pale-green sepals, bordered with pale-pink and orange inside, and beautiful petals, thick in texture and easily bruised, delicate peach-color outside and bright orange-vermilion within, each petal ornamented with a purplish gland, covered with matted hairs and crossed with a band of long vermilion hairs. When the stems are very short the flaming flowers look like Crocuses, sprouting out of the barren desert soil, but when they are tall they have the gorgeous effect of Tulips. These plants grow in the Mohave Desert, but are rather rare in California. They are very abundant in the foothills and on the mountain slopes of Arizona, giving a beautiful orange-red color to the landscape for miles in spring, there being literally thousands in a small area.

Sego Lily
Mariposa Tulip
Calochórtus Nuttállii
White, pale lilac
Early summer
Ariz., Cal., Utah

These pretty flowers are about two inches across, their white petals tinged with yellowish-green or lilac, and often delicately fluted at the edges, often with hairy spots inside the petals at their base, the whole flower very variable in coloring. These Mariposas grow all through the Southwest. In the Grand Canyon they begin to come out early in May, among the dry grasses halfway down the Bright Angel trail, and are a lovely shade of clear lilac. The slender stem, about a foot tall, often bears a small bulb near the base. It is called Sego Lily (pronounced Sègo) in Utah and is the "State flower." Its bulbs formed a substantial part of the food of the early Mormon pioneers when they crossed the desert and the flower is therefore held in great esteem in Utah.

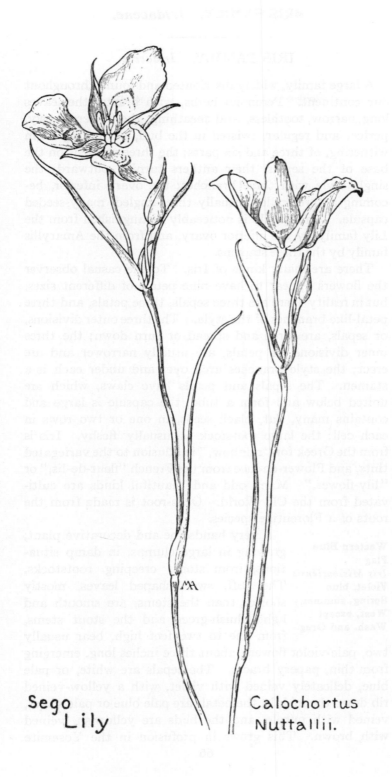

Sego
Lily

Calochortus
Nuttallii.

IRIS FAMILY. *Iridaceae.*

A large family, widely distributed and found throughout our continent. Perennial herbs, with bracts; the leaves long, narrow, toothless, and sheathing; the flowers showy, perfect and regular, twisted in the bud, not falling off in withering, of three and six parts; the three stamens on the base of the sepals, their anthers turning outward; the single style with three branches; the ovary inferior, becoming a three-celled, usually three-angled, many-seeded capsule. This family is noticeably distinguished from the Lily family by the inferior ovary, and from the Amaryllis family by the three stamens.

There are many kinds of Iris. To the casual observer the flowers appear to have nine petals of different sizes, but in reality there are three sepals, three petals, and three petal-like branches of the style. The three outer divisions, or sepals, are large and spread or turn down; the three inner divisions, or petals, are usually narrower and are erect; the style branches arch over and under each is a stamen. The sepals and petals have claws, which are united below and form a tube; the capsule is large and contains many, flat, black seeds, in one or two rows in each cell; the large rootstock is usually fleshy. Iris is from the Greek for "rainbow," in allusion to the variegated tints, and Flower-de-luce from the French "fleur-de-lis," or "lily-flower." Many odd and beautiful kinds are cultivated from the Old World. Orris-root is made from the roots of a Florentine species.

Western Blue Flag
Iris Missouriênsis
Violet, blue
Spring, summer
West, except
Wash. and Oreg.

A very handsome and decorative plant, growing in large clumps, in damp situations, from stout, creeping rootstocks. The stiff, sword-shaped leaves, mostly shorter than the stems, are smooth and light bluish-green and the stout stems, from one to two feet high, bear usually two, pale-violet flowers, about three inches long, emerging from thin, papery bracts. The sepals are white, or pale blue, delicately veined with violet, with a yellow-veined rib down the middle, the petals are pale blue or pale violet, veined with purple, and the buds are yellowish, veined with brown. This grows in profusion in the Yosemite

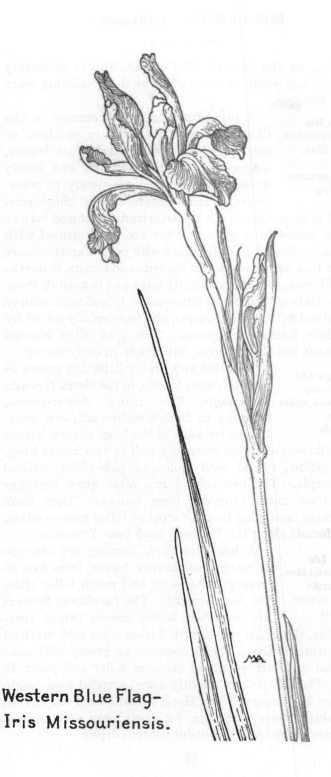

Western Blue Flag-
Iris Missouriensis.

---

meadows, at the foot of El Capitan, and is delicately beautiful, but would be more effective if the coloring were a little stronger.

Douglas Iris
Iris Douglasiàna
Purple, lilac, cream
Spring, summer
Cal., Oreg.

A beautiful kind, very common in the Coast Ranges. It grows in patches, or singly, and has rather dark green leaves, longer than the flower-stalks, and lovely flowers, which vary exceedingly in color. Near the coast they are usually bluish-purple, but in mountain woods they run from violet and mauve to pink, yellow, and white. They are often striped with white and yellow, delicately veined with purple, and measure three or four inches across. In the redwood forests, in northern California, they are peculiarly large and beautiful, their delicate tints of cream and straw-color, tinged with mauve and marked with reddish-purple, and wonderfully set off by their dark forest background. This kind often blooms throughout the rainy season, but chiefly in early spring.

Hartweg's Iris
Iris Hartwégi
Yellow and violet
Summer
California

This odd and pretty little Iris grows in half-dry, open forests, in the Sierra Nevada Mountains. The many flower-stems, from six to twelve inches tall, are over-topped by some of the long, narrow leaves and the flowers are from one and a half to two inches long, either yellow, veined with violet, or pale-violet, veined with purple. The two color forms often grow together and attract much attention from tourists. They look very pretty, springing from a carpet of fallen pine-needles, in the forests along the Wawona road near Yosemite.

Ground Iris
Iris macrosìphon
Blue, purple
Spring, winter
California

A beautiful kind, forming low clumps of many, very narrow leaves, from five to twenty inches long and much taller than the flower-stalks. The handsome flowers are over three inches across, bright purplish-blue, the sepals veined with darker color and marked with a white stripe. This is common on grassy hills near the coast and farther inland becomes taller and paler in color. The flowers are slightly sweet-scented and begin to bloom in January. The Hupa Indians used the leaves for making twine and rope for their nets and snares. There are many other beautiful western Irises.

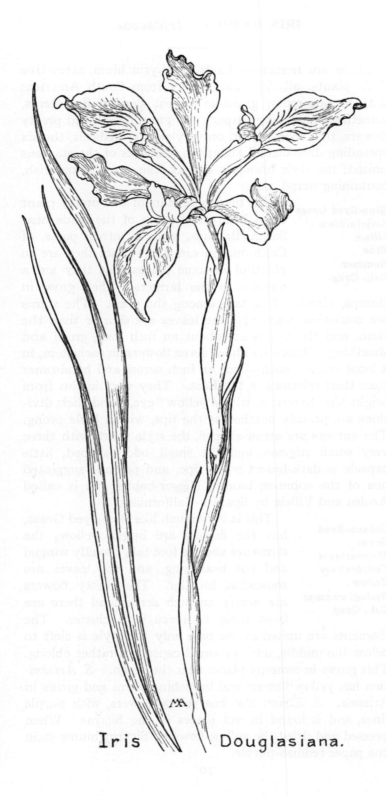

Iris Douglasiana.

IRIS FAMILY. *Iridaceae.*

There are numerous kinds of Sisyrinchium, attractive little plants, all American, many from South America; with fibrous roots; grasslike leaves; slender, flat stems, sometimes branching; papery and green bracts and pretty flowers, that soon wither, on very slender pedicels, the six spreading divisions all alike; the filaments of the stamens united; the style branches slender, the capsule roundish, containing round seeds.

Blue-Eyed Grass
Sisyrinchium béllum
Blue
Summer
Cal., Oreg.

The deep blue stars of this pretty plant are a beautiful feature of the fields near Santa Barbara, and in other parts of California, in summer; in fact they are so plentiful in some places that they are a menace to the farmers. They grow in clumps, about a foot tall, among the grass. The stems are somewhat branching, the leaves are shorter than the stem, and the bracts are about an inch long, green and sheathing. There are about seven flowers on each stem, in a loose cluster, each about an inch across and handsomer than their relations in the East. They vary in tint from bright blue to purple, with a yellow "eye," and their divisions are prettily notched at the tips, with a little prong. The anthers are arrow-shaped, the style short, with three very small stigmas, and the small, oddly-shaped, little capsule is dark-brown when ripe, and perhaps suggested one of the common names, Nigger-babies. It is called Azulea and Villela by Spanish-Californians.

Golden-Eyed Grass
Sisyrinchium Califórnicum
Yellow
Spring, summer
Cal., Oreg.

This is very much like Blue-eyed Grass, but the flowers are bright yellow, the stems are about a foot tall, broadly winged and not branching, and the leaves are somewhat broader. The pretty flowers are nearly an inch across and there are from three to seven in a cluster. The filaments are united at the base only, the style is cleft to below the middle, and the small capsule is rather oblong. This grows in swampy places near the ocean. *S. Arizòni- cum* has yellow flowers and branching stems and grows in Arizona. *S. Élmeri* also has yellow flowers, with purple lines, and is found in wet places in the Sierras. When pressed and dried the yellow-flowered Sisyrinchiums stain the paper reddish-purple.

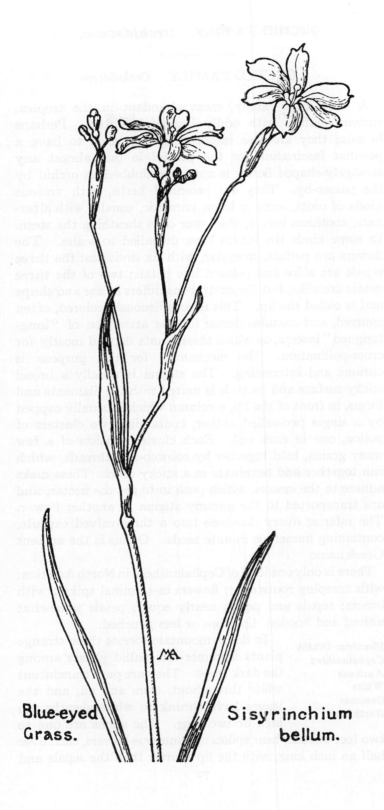

Blue-eyed
Grass.

Sisyrinchium
bellum.

ORCHID FAMILY. *Orchidaceae.*

A very large family, most abundant in the tropics; curious plants, with oddly beautiful flowers. Perhaps because they are also rather rare they seem to have a peculiar fascination for the public; in fact almost any strangely-shaped flower is apt to be dubbed an orchid by the passer-by. They are perennial herbs, with various kinds of roots, some of them parasitic, usually with alternate, toothless leaves, the lower ones sheathing the stem. In some kinds the leaves have dwindled to scales. The flowers are perfect, irregular, with six divisions; the three sepals are alike and colored like petals; two of the three petals are alike, but the central one differs in size and shape and is called the lip. This is conspicuously colored, often spurred, and contains nectar for the attraction of "long-tongued" insects, on which these plants depend mostly for cross-pollination. The mechanism for this purpose is curious and interesting. The stigma is usually a broad sticky surface and its style is united with the filaments and forms, in front of the lip, a column which is usually capped by a single two-celled anther, containing two clusters of pollen, one in each cell. Each cluster consists of a few waxy grains, held together by cobweb-like threads, which run together and terminate in a sticky disk. These disks adhere to the insects, which push in to get the nectar, and are transported to the gummy stigma of another flower. The inferior ovary develops into a three-valved capsule, containing numerous minute seeds. Orchis is the ancient Greek name.

There is only one kind of Cephalanthera in North America; with creeping rootstocks; flowers in terminal spikes, with bracts; sepals and petals nearly equal; petals somewhat united and hooded; lip more or less pouched.

Phantom Orchis
Cephalanthèra
Austinae
White
Summer
Northwest

In dense mountain forests these strange plants shimmer like pallid ghosts among the dark trees. They are pure translucent white throughout, stem and all, and the leaves have shrunk to white sheaths, an inch or two long. The stems are one to two feet tall and bear spikes of numerous flowers, each over half an inch long, with the lip shorter than the sepals and

Phantom Orchis- **Cephalanthera Austinae.**

petals, which are alike. They are beautiful and yet not quite pleasing, for we feel instinctively that there is something unnatural about them and, indeed, the strange absence of any green coloring matter in their make-up indicates that they are incapable of making their own food from the elements and draw their nourishment from decaying vegetation, or are parasitic on other plants. They range northward from Yosemite but are nowhere very abundant. I found several growing near the trail from Little Yosemite Valley to Cloud's Rest and a good many in the woods near the foot of Mt. Shasta, where they seem to be quite common.

There are several kinds of Serapias, widely distributed; tall, stout herbs, with creeping rootstocks and leafy stems; the leaves plaited lengthwise and clasping at base; the flowers with leafy bracts, in terminal racemes. The flowers have no spur; the sepals and petals are separate and nearly equal; the lip broad, free, concave below, constricted near the middle.

Stream Orchis
Chatter-box
Serápias gigantèa
(*Epipactis***)**
Reddish and
greenish-yellow
Summer
West, etc.

A handsome plant, decorative and curious in form and unusual in coloring. It is from one to four feet tall, with a stout, leafy stem bearing three to ten flowers and smoothish leaves, with prominent veins. The sepals are reddish or greenish-yellow and the petals pinkish, veined with maroon. The lip is pouched at the base, with a winged margin and a pendulous tip, which swings freely as if on a hinge, so that it quivers when the plant is shaken. Although the flowers are very handsome this curious tremulous motion, which makes them seem almost alive, gives them a quaint likeness to an old woman in a sunbonnet, with a hooked nose and chattering jaw. They have a slight scent and the plant is quite common along streams and in wet places, in the West and in Colorado and Texas. Some botanists think it is identical with a variety which grows in the Himalaya Mountains. It was named for the Egyptian deity, Serapis.

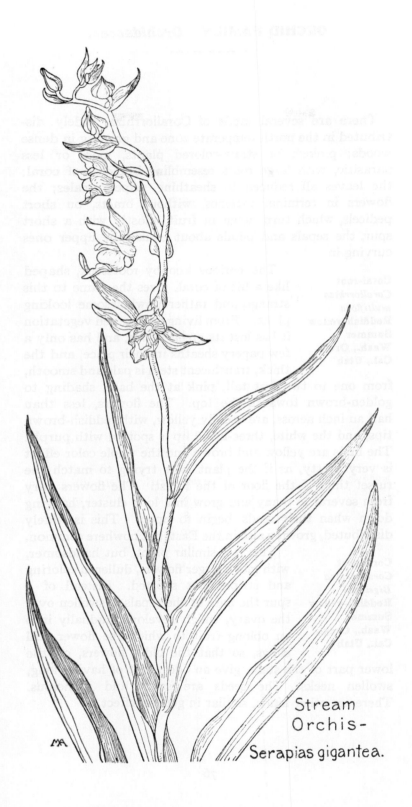

Stream
Orchis-
Serapias gigantea.

MA

ORCHID FAMILY. *Orchidaceae.*

There are several kinds of Corallorrhiza, widely distributed in the north temperate zone and growing in dense woods; pinkish or straw-colored plants, more or less parasitic, with large roots resembling branches of coral; the leaves all reduced to sheathing, papery scales; the flowers in terminal racemes, without bracts, on short pedicels, which turn down in fruit, mostly with a short spur, the sepals and petals about equal, the upper ones curving in.

Coral-root
Corallorrhiza multiflòra
Reddish-yellow
Summer
Wash., Oreg., Cal., Utah

The curious knobby rootstock, shaped like a bit of coral, gives the name to this strange and rather unwholesome looking plant. From living on decayed vegetation it has lost its green leaves, and has only a few papery sheaths in their place, and the thick, translucent stem is pale and smooth, from one to two feet tall, pink at the base, shading to golden-brown towards the top. The flowers, less than half an inch across, are usually yellow, with reddish-brown tips, and the white, three-lobed lip is spotted with purple. The buds are yellow and brown and the whole color effect is very pretty, as if the plant were trying to match the russet tints of the floor of the forest. The flowers vary from several to many and grow in a long cluster, hanging down when their seeds begin to ripen. This is widely distributed, growing also in the East, but nowhere common.

Coral-root
Corallorrhiza Bigelòwii
Reddish-yellow
Summer
Wash., Oreg., Cal., Utah

This is a similar plant, but handsomer, with much larger flowers, duller in coloring and striped not spotted. Instead of a spur the base of the sepals is swollen over the ovary, which develops gradually into an oblong fruit to which the flower still clings, so that the older flowers, on the lower part of the stalk, give an odd effect of having long, swollen necks. The seeds are small and numerous. There are other kinds, similar in general effect.

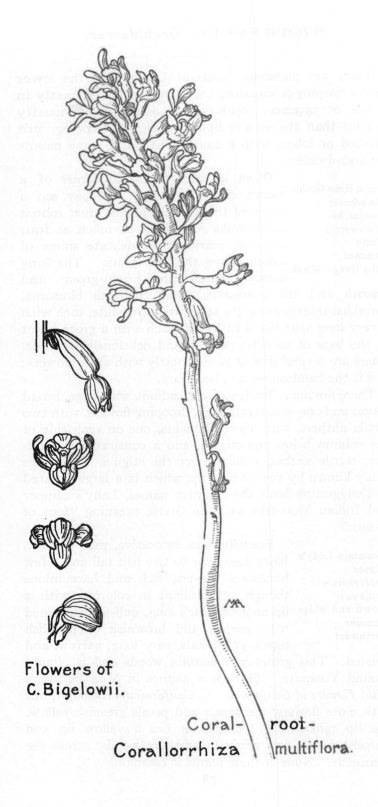

Flowers of
C. Bigelowii.

Coral-   root-
Corallorrhiza   multiflora.

There are numerous kinds of Limnorchis; the lower leaves clasping or sheathing the stem; the flowers mostly in spikes or racemes; sepals nearly equal, petals mostly smaller than the sepals; lip spreading or drooping, not toothed or lobed, with a spur. The Latin name means "marsh-dweller."

Sierra Rein Orchis
Limnórchis leucostáchys
(Habenaria)
White
Summer
Cal., Oreg., Wash.

Often in some favorable corner of a marsh, near the woods, we may see a dozen of these lovely plants, their robust leafy stalks sometimes as much as four feet tall, rearing their delicate spires of bloom above the lush grass. The long narrow leaves are bright-green and smooth and the numerous; small, delicate blossoms, sprinkled thickly along the stem, are pure white, each with a very long spur like a little tail, each with a green bract at the base of its little pedicel, and deliciously fragrant. There are several similar kinds, mostly with green flowers; this is the handsomest and least rare.

There are many kinds of Cypripedium, with large, broad leaves and one or several, large, drooping flowers, with two fertile anthers, with short filaments, one on each side of the column below the stigma, and a conspicuous, petal-like, sterile anther, arching over the stigma. They are easily known by the curious lip, which is a large inflated sac, suggesting both the common names, Lady's Slipper and Indian Moccasin, and the Greek, meaning "foot of Venus."

Mountain Lady's Slipper
Cypripèdium montànum
Brown and white
Summer
Northwest

Beautiful and decorative, with a stout, hairy stem, one to two feet tall and a few handsome flowers, rich and harmonious though not brilliant in coloring, with a lip about an inch long, dull-white, veined with purple, and brownish or purplish sepals and petals, very long, narrow, and twisted. This grows in mountain woods and is found around Yosemite. There is a picture in Miss Parsons's *Wild Flowers of California.* *C. Califórnicum* is similar, but with more flowers, the sepals and petals greenish-yellow, the lip pinkish. *C. parviflòrum* has a yellow lip and purplish sepals and grows in northern woods, across the continent. None of these plants is common.

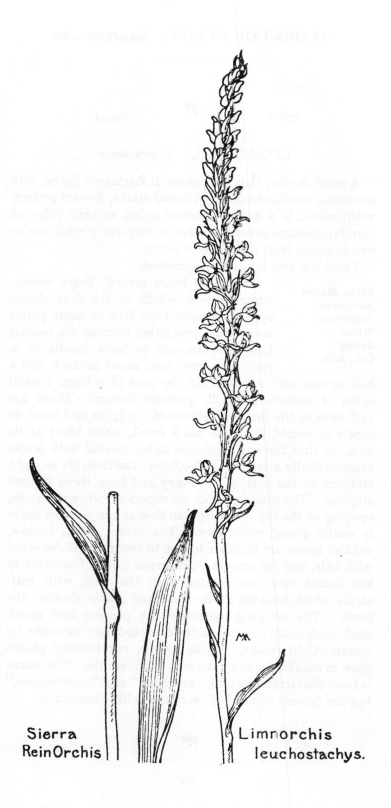

Sierra
ReinOrchis

Limnorchis
leuchostachys.

LIZARD-TAIL FAMILY. *Saururaceae.*

LIZARD-TAIL. *Saururaceae.*

A small family; ours are perennial astringent herbs, with alternate, toothless leaves, with leaf-stalks; flowers perfect, with bracts, in a dense, terminal spike, without calyx or corolla; stamens generally three or six; ovary with one to five stigmas; fruit a capsule or berry.

There are two kinds of Anemopsis.

Yerba Mansa
Anemópsis
Califórnica
White
Spring
Cal., Ariz.

This plant bears several, large, cream-white flowers, which at the first glance appear to have from five to eight petals and a long, projecting knob in the center, but what appears to be a corolla is in reality an involucre, about an inch and a half across, and surrounding the base of a long, conical spike of numerous, small, greenish flowers. These are half-sunk in the fleshy substance of the spike and have no sepals or petals, but each has a small, white bract at its base, so that the spike appears to be covered with scales symmetrically arranged. The flower has from six to eight stamens on the base of the ovary and from three to four stigmas. The ovaries, which are superior, form small pods, opening at the top when ripe, so that in the end the spike is neatly pitted with holes. The rather thick, hollow, reddish stems are from six inches to two feet tall, covered with hair, and the smooth, light-green leaves, from two to ten inches long, are mostly from the root, with leaf-stalks which broaden at the base and partly sheathe the stem. The creeping rootstocks are peppery and acrid, used medicinally, and considered exceedingly valuable by Spanish-Californians. These pretty, odd-looking plants grow in alkaline or salty swamps in the south. The name is from the Greek meaning "anemone" and "appearance," but the flowers do not look very much like Anemones.

Yerba mansa.

Anemopsis Californica.

SANDALWOOD FAMILY. *Santalaceae.*

SANDALWOOD FAMILY. *Santalaceae.*

This is a very small family in this country, for they prefer the tropics, and in those regions some are trees. Ours are usually parasitic on the roots of their neighbors. They have toothless, mostly alternate leaves, mostly without leaf-stalks or stipules, and small flowers, with a four- or five-lobed calyx and no corolla. The four or five stamens are opposite the calyx lobes, at the edge of a fleshy disk, and the ovary is one-celled and inferior, with one style, developing into a one-seeded fruit.

There are four kinds of Comandra, one of them European; smooth, perennial herbs, with alternate leaves, and flowers in clusters, without bracts. The calyx is more or less bell-shaped, usually with five lobes, its tube lined with a disk, the stamens inserted at base of the lobes and the anthers attached to the lobes by tufts of hairs.

Pale Comandra
Comándra pállida
Flesh-color,
greenish, purplish
Spring, summer
Northwest, Nev.,
Utah, Ariz.

This is a rather pretty plant, growing from a few inches to about a foot tall, branching and rather woody below, with pale-green, smooth, slightly thickish, rather stiff leaves, which are reduced to pinkish scales on the lower stem. The flowers are small, usually flesh-color, thickish in texture, with slender pedicels, and form terminal, rather flat-topped clusters. The fruit, which is about the size of a small pea, is crowned by the remains of the calyx, like a rose-hip. This is common on dry plains and hillsides and is noticeable because of its pale and somewhat peculiar coloring.

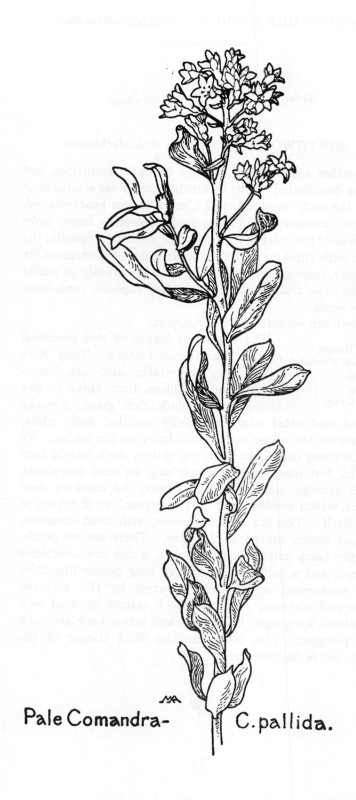

Pale Comandra— C. pallida.

BIRTHWORT FAMILY. *Aristolochiaceae.*

BIRTHWORT FAMILY. *Aristolochiaceae*

A rather small family, chiefly of warm countries, but widely distributed; herbs or shrubs; the leaves alternate or from the root, with leaf-stalks, more or less heart-shaped, without stipules; the flowers perfect, mostly large, symmetrical or irregular in form, with or without a corolla; the calyx with three or six lobes, or irregular; the stamens six to many, inserted on the pistil; the ovary wholly or partly inferior; the fruit a mostly six-celled capsule, containing many seeds.

There are several kinds of Asarum.

Wild Ginger
Ásarum Hartwégi
Brown
Spring
Cal., Oreg.

The handsome leaves of this perennial are its conspicuous feature. They have long, hairy leaf-stalks and are heart-shaped and toothless, from three to five inches broad, dark rich green, prettily veined and often also beautifully mottled with white, smooth on the upper surface and hairy on the under. We notice them immediately in the damp, dark woods they live in, but unless we look carefully we miss the single, large, strange, purplish-brown flower, the color of dead leaves, which nestles close to the ground as if trying to hide itself. This has twelve stamens, with stout filaments, and six styles, united at the base. There are no petals, but the hairy calyx has three lobes, which are sometimes an inch and a half long, and have long points like tails. The seed-vessel is roundish, crowned by the withered calyx and stamens. The rootstock cannot be used as a substitute for ginger, but smells and tastes very aromatic and pungent. This resembles the Wild Ginger of the East, but is handsomer.

84

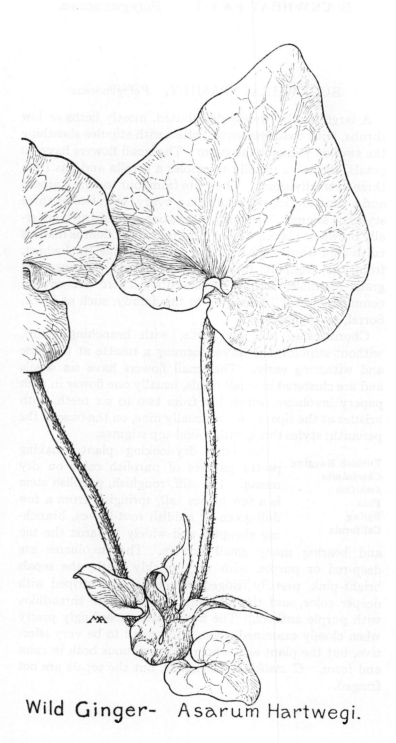

Wild Ginger- Asarum Hartwegi.

BUCKWHEAT FAMILY. *Polygonaceae.*

BUCKWHEAT FAMILY. *Polygonaceae.*

A large family, widely distributed, mostly herbs or low shrubs, with toothless leaves, often with stipules sheathing the swollen joints of the stem. The small flowers have no petals, the calyx usually resembles a corolla and has from three to six divisions. There are from four to nine stamens and a superior, mostly triangular, ovary, with two or three styles or stigmas, becoming a dry, one-seeded fruit, generally brown or black. The kind from which flour is made is cultivated from northern Asia, and the name Buckwheat, from the German, means "beech-wheat," because the grain resembles minute beech-nuts. There are several common "weeds" belonging to this family, such as Dock, Sorrel, and Smartweed.

Chorizanthes are low herbs, with branching stems, without stipules, the leaves forming a rosette at the base and withering early. The small flowers have six sepals and are clustered in small heads, usually one flower in each papery involucre, which has from two to six teeth, with bristles at the tips; stamens usually nine, on the base of the perianth; styles three, with round-top stigmas.

Turkish Rugging
Chorizánthe fimbriáta
Pink
Spring
California

An odd, dry-looking plant, making pretty patches of purplish color on dry mesas. The stiff, roughish, purplish stem is a few inches tall, springing from a few dull-green or reddish root-leaves, branching abruptly and widely towards the top and bearing many small flowers. The involucres are deep-red or purple, with very prickly teeth, the sepals bright-pink, prettily fringed with white and striped with deeper color, and the filaments are long and threadlike, with purple anthers. The flowers are exceedingly pretty when closely examined, though too small to be very effective, but the plant as a whole is conspicuous both in color and form. *C. staticoïdes* is similar, but the sepals are not fringed.

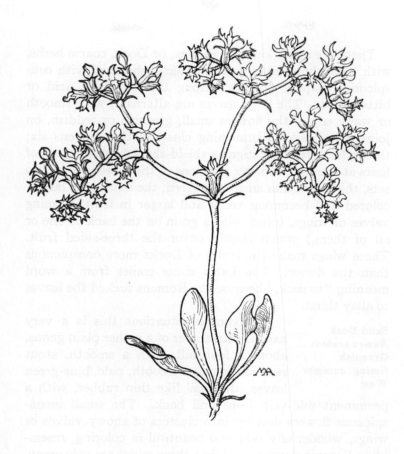

Turkish
Rugging-

Chorizanthe
fimbriata

BUCKWHEAT FAMILY. *Polygonaceae.*

There are many kinds of Rumex, or Dock, coarse herbs, with leafy, branching, grooved stems, sheathed with conspicuous, papery stipules, strong tap-roots and acid or bitter juice. The large leaves are alternate, with smooth or wavy edges; the flowers small, greenish or reddish, on jointed pedicels, in branching clusters; the stamens six; the styles three, the stigmas shield-shaped, with a tuft of hairs at the tip. The six divisions of the flower are in two sets, the three outer small and green, the inner ones larger, colored and becoming veiny and larger in fruit, forming valves or wings, (often with a grain on the back of one or all of them,) which closely cover the three-sided fruit. These wings make the fruits of Docks more conspicuous than the flower. The Latin name comes from a word meaning "to suck," because the Romans sucked the leaves to allay thirst.

Sand Dock
Rùmex venòsus
Greenish
Spring, summer
West

In favorable situations this is a very handsome member of a rather plain genus, about a foot tall, with a smooth, stout reddish stem and smooth, pale, blue-green leaves, that feel like thin rubber, with a prominent mid-vein front and back. The small inconspicuous flowers develop into clusters of showy valves or wings, wonderfully odd and beautiful in coloring, resembling Begonia flowers. At first these wings are pale green, but they gradually brighten until they are all shades of salmon, rose-color, and red, fading to brown, and forming lovely combinations of vivid color, particularly against the arid background of the sand hills they frequent, and they last a long time in water and are exceedingly decorative. If these wings, which are nearly an inch across, are pulled apart, a three-sided akene, like a little nut, will be found inside them.

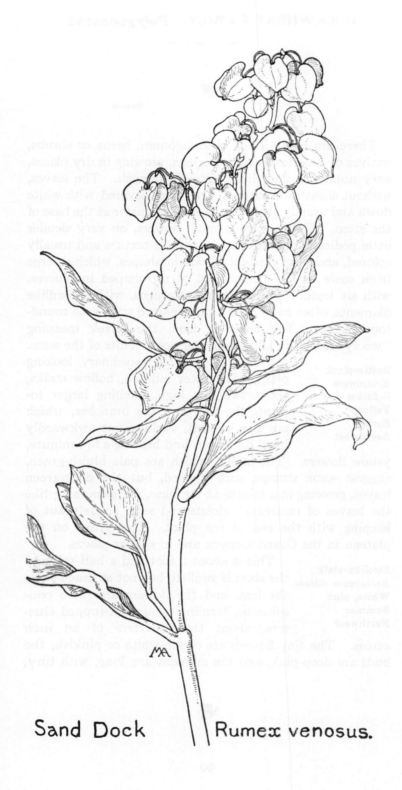

Sand Dock   Rumex venosus.

BUCKWHEAT FAMILY. *Polygonaceae.*

There are many kinds of Eriogonum, herbs or shrubs, natives of America, mostly western, growing in dry places, very numerous and difficult to distinguish. The leaves, without sheaths or stipules, are often covered with white down and usually grow in a spreading cluster at the base of the stem. The numerous small flowers, on very slender little pedicels, have six sepals, thin in texture and usually colored, and form clusters of various shapes, which emerge from more or less bell-shaped or top-shaped involucres, with six teeth. There are nine stamens, with threadlike filaments, often hairy, and a three-parted style with round-top stigmas. The name is from the Greek meaning "wooly knees," in allusion to the wooly joints of the stem.

Bottle-plant
Eriógonum
inflátum
Yellow
Spring
Southwest

This is a most extraordinary looking plant, with queer inflated, hollow stalks, about two feet high, swelling larger towards the top, and the branches, which are also swollen, sticking out awkwardly in all directions and bearing a few minute, yellow flowers. The stalks, which are pale bluish-green, suggest some strange sort of reed, but the dark-green leaves, growing in a rosette at the base, are something like the leaves of cultivated violets and seem entirely out of keeping with the rest of the plant. This grows on the plateau in the Grand Canyon and in similar places.

Swollen-stalk
Eriógonum elátum
White, pink
Summer
Northwest

This is about a foot and a half tall and the stem is swollen, but not so much so as the last, and the flowers are more conspicuous, forming rather flat-topped clusters, about three-quarters of an inch across. The tiny flowers are cream-white or pinkish, the buds are deep-pink, and the stamens are long, with tiny,

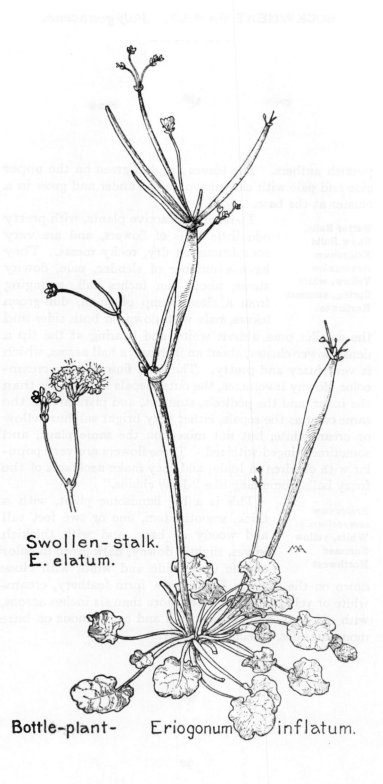

Swollen-stalk.
E. elatum.

Bottle-plant- Eriogonum inflatum.

pinkish anthers. The leaves are dull-green on the upper side and pale with close down on the under and grow in a cluster at the base.

**Butter Balls,
Snow Balls**
*Eriógonum
orthocàulon*
**Yellow, white
Spring, summer
Northwest**

These are attractive plants, with pretty odd little balls of flowers, and are very conspicuous on dry, rocky mesas. They have a number of slender, pale, downy stems, about ten inches tall, springing from a close clump of small, dull-green leaves, pale with down on both sides and the smaller ones almost white, and bearing at the tip a dense flower-cluster, about an inch and a half across, which is very fuzzy and pretty. The little flowers have cream-color, downy involucres, the outer sepals are broader than the inner, and the pedicels, stamens, and pistil are all the same color as the sepals, either very bright sulphur-yellow or cream-white, but not mixed on the same plant, and sometimes tinged with red. These flowers are very popular with children in Idaho and they make necklaces of the fuzzy balls, something like "daisy chains."

*Eriógonum
compósitum*
**White, yellow
Summer
Northwest**

This is a big handsome plant, with a thick, smooth stem, one or two feet tall and woody at base, and with thickish leaves, slightly downy, dark green in color on the upper side and white with close down on the under. The flowers form feathery, cream-white or yellow clusters, often more than six inches across, with red buds, and are beautiful and conspicuous on bare mountainsides, smelling of honey.

Butter Balls.

Eriogonum
orthocaulon.

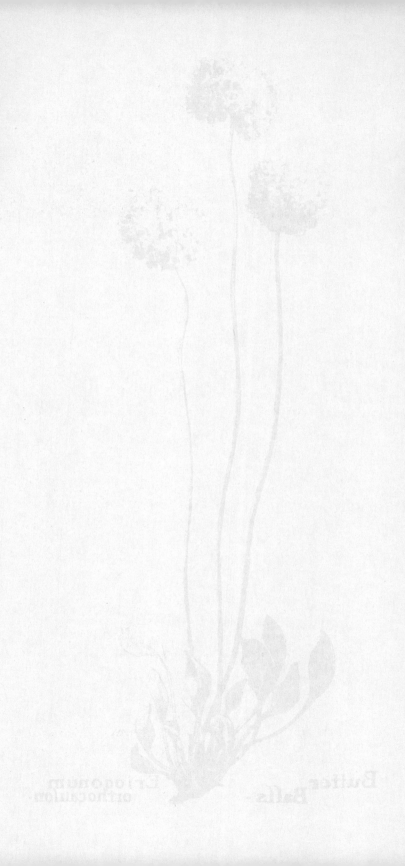

Butter
Balls

Eriogonum
orthocaulon

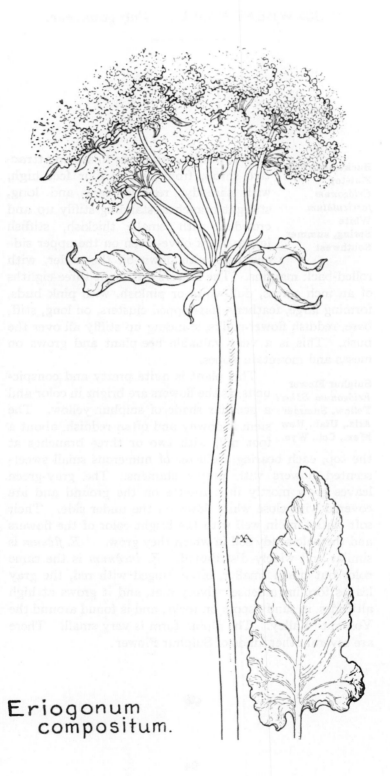

Eriogonum
compositum.

BUCKWHEAT FAMILY. *Polygonaceae.*

**Buckwheat Bush,
Flat-top
*Eriógonum
fasciculàtum*
White
Spring, summer
Southwest**
In favorable situations this is an attractive shrub, from two to four feet high, with shreddy, reddish bark and long, straight branches, standing stiffly up and crowded with small, thickish, stiffish leaves, dark olive-green on the upper side and pale with down on the under, with rolled-back margins. The flowers are about three-eighths of an inch across, dull-white or pinkish, with pink buds, forming large, feathery, flat-topped clusters, on long, stiff, bare, reddish flower-stalks, standing up stiffly all over the bush. This is a very valuable bee-plant and grows on mesas and mountain slopes.

**Sulphur Flower
Eriógonum Bàkeri
Yellow, Summer
Ariz., Utah, New
Mex., Col., Wyo.**
This plant is quite pretty and conspicuous, as the flowers are bright in color and a peculiar shade of sulphur yellow. The stem is downy and often reddish, about a foot tall, with two or three branches at the top, each bearing a cluster of numerous small sweet-scented flowers with pretty stamens. The gray-green leaves grow mostly in a rosette on the ground and are covered with close white down on the under side. Their soft tints tone in well with the bright color of the flowers and the pale sandy soil in which they grow. *E. flàvum* is similar and widely distributed. *E. incànum* is the same color but much smaller, often tinged with red, the gray leaves forming a dense velvety mat, and it grows at high altitudes, in sandy spots on rocks, and is found around the Yosemite Valley. The alpine form is very small. There are several other kinds of Sulphur Flower.

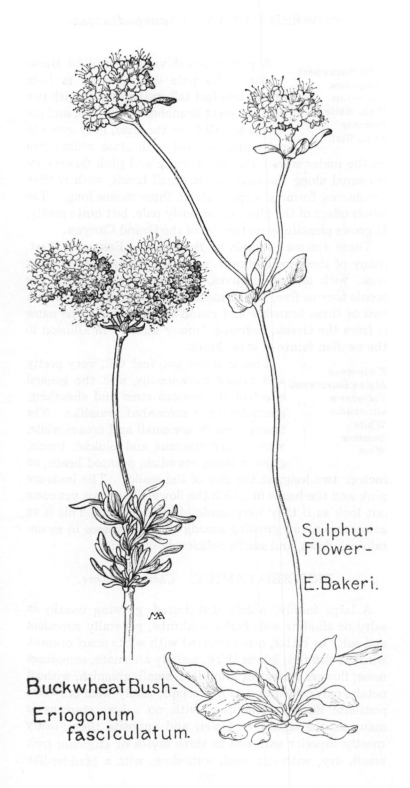

Sulphur
Flower-
E.Bakeri.

Buckwheat Bush-
Eriogonum
fasciculatum.

PIGWEED FAMILY. *Chenopodiaceae.*

Wild Buckwheat
Eriógonum racemòsum
Pink, white
Summer
Ariz., Utah

A pretty desert variety of Wild Buckwheat. The pale downy stem is from one to two feet tall, rather stout, with two or three erect branches at the top, and the leaves are all from the base, gray-green in color and covered with close white down on the under side. The small white and pink flowers are clustered along the branches in small heads, with reddish involucres, forming a spike about three inches long. The whole effect of the plant is curiously pale, but quite pretty. It grows plentifully on the rim of the Grand Canyon.

There are many kinds of Polygonum, East and West, many of them insignificant, some aquatic, some woody at base, with alternate leaves, and sheathing stipules; the sepals four or five; the stamens five to nine; the style with two or three branches and round-top stigmas. The name is from the Greek, meaning "many knees," in allusion to the swollen joints of some kinds.

Knot-weed
Alpine Smartweed
Polýgonum bistortòides
White
Summer
West

This is about two feet tall, very pretty and rather conspicuous, and the general effect of the smooth stem and sheathing, green leaves is somewhat grasslike. The flowers, which are small and cream-white, with pretty stamens and pinkish bracts, grow in close, roundish, pointed heads, an inch or two long, at the tips of the stalks. The buds are pink and the heads in which the flowers have not yet come out look as if they were made of pink beads. This is an attractive plant, growing among the tall grasses in mountain meadows, and smells deliciously of honey.

PIGWEED FAMILY. *Chenopodiaceae.*

A large family, widely distributed, growing usually in salty or alkaline soil; herbs or shrubs, generally succulent and salty or bitter, often covered with white scurf or meal, without stipules; leaves thick, usually alternate, sometimes none; flowers perfect or imperfect, small, greenish, without petals; calyx with two to five sepals, rarely with only one, pistillate flowers sometimes with no calyx; stamens as many as the sepals, or fewer, and opposite them; ovary mostly superior with one to three styles or stigmas; fruit small, dry, with one seed, sometimes with a bladder-like

96

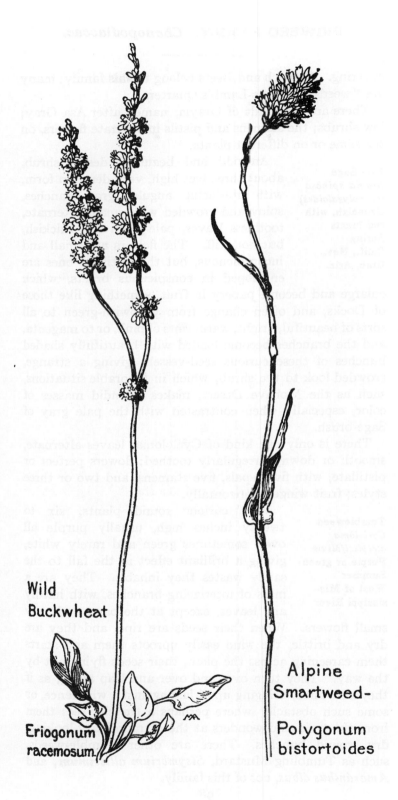

Wild
Buckwheat

Eriogonum
racemosum.

Alpine
Smartweed-

Polygonum
bistortoides

PIGWEED FAMILY. *Chenopodiaceae.*

covering. Spinach and Beets belong to this family; many are "weeds," such as Lamb's Quarters.

There are two kinds of Grayia, named after Asa Gray; low shrubs; the stamens and pistils in separate flowers, on the same or on different plants.

Hop Sage
Gràyia spinòsa
(*G. polygaloides*)
Greenish, with
red bracts
Spring
Calif., Nev..
Utah, Ariz.

An odd and beautiful desert shrub, about three feet high, very dense in form, with interlacing, angular, gray branches, spiny and crowded with small, alternate, toothless leaves, pale-green and thickish, but not stiff. The flowers are small and inconspicuous, but the pistillate ones are enveloped in conspicuous bracts, which enlarge and become papery in fruit, something like those of Docks, and often change from yellowish-green to all sorts of beautiful, bright, warm tints of pink, or to magenta, and the branches become loaded with beautifully shaded bunches of these curious seed-vessels, giving a strange, crowded look to the shrub, which in favorable situations, such as the Mohave Desert, makes splendid masses of color, especially when contrasted with the pale gray of Sage-brush.

There is only one kind of Cycloloma; leaves alternate, smooth or downy, irregularly toothed; flowers perfect or pistillate, with five sepals, five stamens, and two or three styles; fruit winged horizontally.

Tumbleweed
Cyclolòma
atriplicifòlium
Purple or green
Summer
West of Mis-
sissippi River

Very curious round plants, six to twenty inches high, usually purple all over, sometimes green and rarely white, giving a brilliant effect in the fall to the sandy wastes they inhabit. They are a mass of interlacing branches, with hardly any leaves, except at the base, and very small flowers. When their seeds are ripe, and they are dry and brittle, the wind easily uproots them and starts them careening across the plain, their seeds flying out by the way. They turn over and over and leap along, as if they were alive, bringing up at last against a wire fence, or some such obstacle, where perhaps a traveler sees them from the train and wonders at the extraordinary-looking, dry, round bunches. There are other Tumble-weeds, such as Tumbling Mustard, *Sisymbrium allissimum*, and *Amaránthus álbus*, not of this family.

98

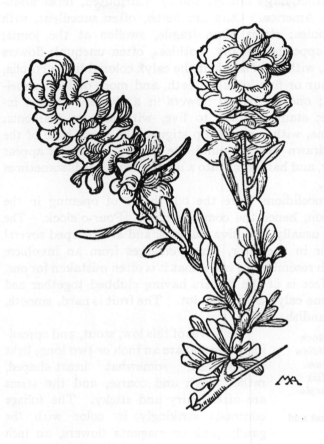

Hop
Sage-

Grayia
polygaloides.

FOUR-O'CLOCK FAMILY. *Nyctaginaceae.*

A rather large family, widely distributed, most abundant in America. Ours are herbs, often succulent, with no stipules; stems often fragile, swollen at the joints; leaves opposite, usually toothless, often unequal; flowers perfect, with no petals, but the calyx colored like a corolla, with four or five lobes or teeth, and more or less funnel-shaped; one or several flowers in a cluster with an involucre; stamens three to five, with slender filaments; style one, with a round-top stigma; the green base of the calyx drawn down around the ovary, making it appear inferior, and hardening into a nutlike fruit; seeds sometimes winged.

Quamoclidions have the odd habit of opening in the afternoon, hence the common name, Four-o'clock. The flowers usually have five stamens, and are grouped several together in a cluster, which emerges from an involucre so much resembling a calyx that it is often mistaken for one. The effect is of the flowers having clubbed together and made one calyx do for the lot. The fruit is hard, smooth, and roundish.

Four-o'clock
Quamoclidion multiflòrum.
(Mirabilis)
Pink, purple
Spring
Southwest and Col.

The leaves of this low, stout, and spreading perennial are an inch or two long, light bluish-green, somewhat heart-shaped, rather rough and coarse, and the stems are often hairy and sticky. The foliage contrasts strikingly in color with the gaudy pink or magenta flowers, an inch across and slightly sweet-scented, the shape of Morning-glories and resembling them, as they have the same stripes of deeper color. The long stamens droop to one side, the pistil is long and purple and the bell-shaped involucre contains about six flowers. These plants are conspicuous and quite handsome. They grow on the plateau in the Grand Canyon.

There are several kinds of Hesperonia, much like Quamoclidion, but the bell-shaped involucre contains only one flower, which is also bell-shaped, usually with five separate stamens. The fruit is roundish, not angled or ribbed, usually smooth.

Four o'clock- **Quamoclidion multiflorum.**

FOUR-O'CLOCK FAMILY. *Nyctaginaceae.*

California Four-o'clock
Hesperònia
Califórnica.
(*Mirabilis*)
Magenta, pink
Spring, summer
California

This is very common in southern California and forms quite large, low clumps cf rather yellowish green, sticky and hairy foliage, sprinkled with numbers of bright little flowers, opening in the afternoon. The base is woody and the weak, hairy stems are supported on bushes, as if climbing over them. The leaves are rather thick, about an inch long, and the flowers are open bell-shaped, about three-quarters of an inch across, usually magenta, but often pink of various shades, sometimes quite pale in tint with long stamens drooping to one side, and the involucre is often purplish and very hairy and sticky. The effect at a distance is gay and attractive, though the plant is not quite so pretty close by.

Hesperònia
glutinòsa var.
grácilis
White, pinkish
Spring
Arizona

This has a straggling, hairy, sticky stem, over a foot long, and thickish, dull-green leaves, hairy and sticky. The flowers are about half an inch long, white or tinged with pink, and are rather delicate and pretty, though the plant is not especially attractive. It blooms at night, the flowers gradually closing with the morning sun. This variety is common in the southern part of the state, in mountain canyons, and *Hesperonia glutinosa* is common in the north.

There are several kinds of Abronia, all American, with branching, usually sticky-hairy stems, thick, toothless leaves, with leaf-stalks, in pairs and one of each pair somewhat larger than the other. The flowers are more or less salver-form, with five lobes, a threadlike style, and from three to five, unequal stamens, on the tube of the perianth and not protruding from it. They are numerous and in clusters, with involucres, on long flower-stalks, from the angles of the leaves. The fruit is winged. The name is from the Greek meaning graceful, but most of these plants are rather awkward in their manner of growth.

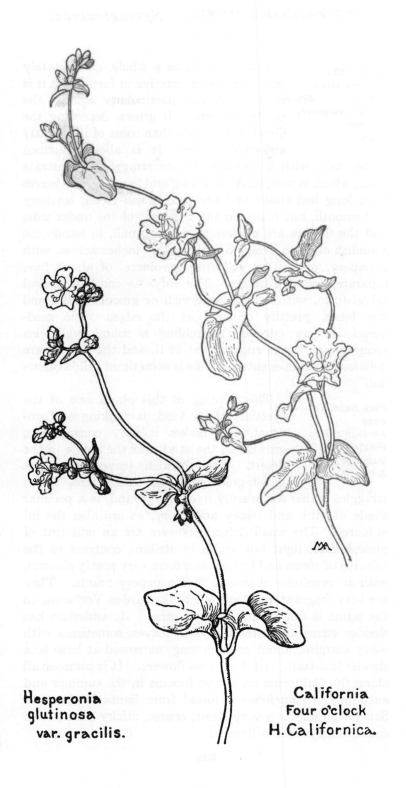

**Hesperonia
glutinosa
var. gracilis.**

**California
Four o'clock
H. Californica.**

FOUR-O'CLOCK FAMILY. *Nyctaginaceae.*

Sand Puffs
Abrònia sàlsa
White
Spring, summer, autumn
Utah

This plant is, as a whole, so delicately tinted and so decorative in form, that it is most attractive, particularly against the sandy soil where it grows, deserving the Greek name more than some of its slightly awkward sisters. It is about fourteen inches tall, with a stoutish, rather straggling, prostrate stem, which is pale, pinkish, sticky and fuzzy. The leaves have long leaf-stalks and are pale bluish-green, leathery and smooth, but fuzzy on the mid-vein of the under side, and the flowers are numerous, rather small, in handsome roundish clusters, which are about two inches across, with a papery, pinkish or yellowish involucre, of about five, separate, rounded bracts. The calyx is corolla-like and salver-form, with a long, yellowish or greenish tube and five lobes, prettily crinkled at the edges. The seed-vessel is very curious, resembling a round, yellowish sponge, with hooks sticking out of it, and the flowers are deliciously sweet-scented. This is sometimes called Snowball.

Pink Sand-Verbena
Abrònia villòsa
Pinkish-lilac
Summer
Ariz., Cal., Utah

The coloring of this plant, one of the prettiest of its kind, is striking and unusual, and makes it very conspicuous, growing in the sand near the sea or in the desert. The thickish leaves are light bluish-green and the thick stem, which straggles rather awkwardly over the ground, is a peculiar shade of pink and sticky and hairy, as are also the involucres. The small delicate flowers are an odd tint of pinkish-lilac, light but vivid, in striking contrast to the coloring of stems and foliage, and form very pretty clusters, with an involucre of five to fifteen papery bracts. They are very fragrant and look much like garden Verbenas, so the name is not so unhappy as some. *A. umbellàta* has slender stems and almost smooth leaves, sometimes with wavy margins, about an inch long, narrowed at base to a slender leaf-stalk, and deep-pink flowers. It is common all along the California coast and blooms in the summer and autumn. *A. marítima* is found from Santa Barbara to San Diego and is a very stout, coarse, sticky plant, with small, deep-magenta flowers.

Sand
Verbena

Abronia
villosa

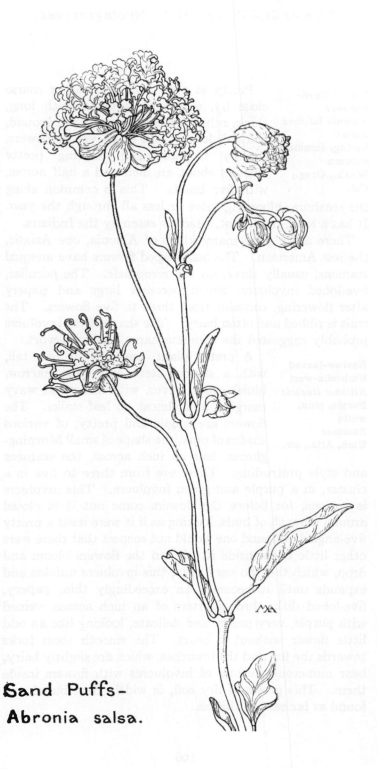

Sand Puffs—
Abronia salsa.

Yellow Sand-Verbena
Abrònia latifòlia
Yellow
Spring, summer, autumn
Wash., Oreg., Cal.

Pretty at a distance, but rather coarse close by, a straggling plant, with long, thick, rubbery stems, lying on the ground, thickish leaves, and small yellow flowers, slightly fragrant and forming pretty clusters about an inch and a half across, with five bracts. This is common along the seashore, blooming more or less all through the year. It has a long, thick root, which is eaten by the Indians.

There are a good many kinds of Allionia, one Asiatic, the rest American. The bell-shaped flowers have unequal stamens, usually three, on the receptacle. The peculiar, five-lobed involucre, which becomes large and papery after flowering, contains from three to five flowers. The fruit is ribbed and often hairy. The shape of the involucre probably suggested the common name Umbrella-wort.

Narrow-leaved
Umbrella-wort
Alliònia lineàris
Purple, pink, white
Summer
Utah, Ariz., etc.

A pretty plant, one to four feet tall, with a slender stem and long, narrow, bluish-green leaves, with somewhat wavy margins, and almost no leaf-stalks. The flowers are fragile and pretty, of various shades of pink, the shape of small Morning-glories, half an inch across, the stamens and style protruding. There are from three to five in a cluster, in a purple and green involucre. This involucre is curious, for before the flowers come out it is closed around a bunch of buds, looking as if it were itself a pretty five-angled bud, and one would not suspect that there were other little buds inside it. When the flowers bloom and drop, which they do very soon, this involucre unfolds and expands until it becomes an exceedingly thin, papery, five-lobed disk, three-quarters of an inch across, veined with purple, very pretty and delicate, looking like an odd little flower without a heart. The smooth stem forks towards the top and the branches, which are slightly hairy, bear numerous clusters of involucres with flowers inside them. This grows in dry soil, is widely distributed and found as far east as Illinois.

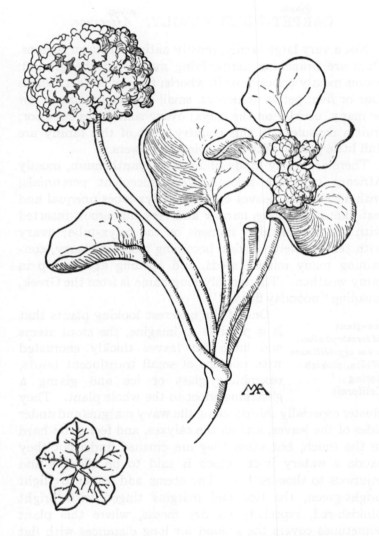

Involucre of
Allionia linearis.

Yellow Sand Verbena
Abronia latifolia.

CARPET-WEED FAMILY. *Aizoaceae.*

Not a very large family, mostly natives of warm regions. Ours are branching herbs, lying mostly on the ground; leaves mostly opposite or in whorls; flowers perfect; sepals four or five; petals numerous, small or none; stamens few or many, usually on the calyx; ovary sometimes superior; fruit a capsule. In this country most of this family are dull little plants, with inconspicuous flowers.

There are many kinds of Mesembryanthemum, mostly African; ours are smooth, very succulent perennials; without stipules; leaves opposite; calyx-lobes unequal and leaf-like; petals long, narrow and very numerous, inserted with the innumerable stamens on the calyx-tube; ovary with ten or twelve styles, becoming a sort of berry, containing many minute seeds, and opening at the top in rainy weather. The terribly long name is from the Greek, meaning "noonday flower."

Ice-plant
Mesembryánthe-mum crystállinum
White, pinkish
Spring
California

One of the queerest looking plants that it is possible to imagine, the stout stems and large flat leaves thickly encrusted with millions of small translucent beads, resembling glass or ice and giving a glistening effect to the whole plant. They cluster especially thickly along the wavy margins and under sides of the leaves, and on the calyxes, and feel quite hard to the touch, but when they are crushed underfoot they exude a watery juice, which is said to be alkaline and injurious to shoe-leather. The stems and leaves are light bright-green, the tips and margins tinged with bright pinkish-red, especially on dry mesas, where this plant sometimes covers the ground for long distances with flat rosettes, forming a thick, red carpet, beautiful in color. In shadier, damper places, such as the crevices in the sea-cliffs at La Jolla, it becomes quite a large, tall plant,

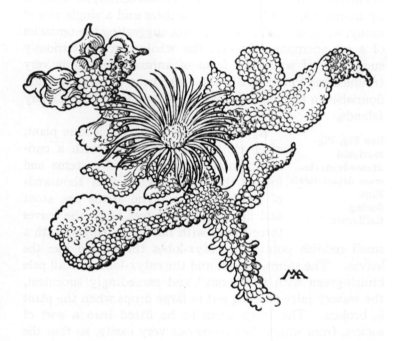

Ice-plant
Mesembryanthemum crystallinum.

scarcely tinged with red and very glistening. The flowers are about an inch across, with a greenish center, surrounded by numerous, small, yellowish anthers and a single row of many, white or flesh-colored petals, suggesting the tentacles of a sea-anemone. In fact the whole plant is curiously suggestive of some low form of animal life. It is very troublesome to farmers in the south near the sea, and also flourishes in the Mohave Desert, in France and the Canary Islands.

Sea Fig, Fig-marigold
Mesembryánthe-mum aequilaterále
Pink
Spring
California

A very strange and conspicuous plant, often clothing sandy slopes with a curious mantel of trailing, fleshy stems and foliage thickly sprinkled with thousands of gaudy flowers. The stems are stout and flattish, several feet long; the leaves three-sided, with flat faces, tipped with a small reddish point; the calyx-lobes three-sided like the leaves. The stems, leaves, and the calyx-lobes are all pale bluish-green with a "bloom" and exceedingly succulent, the watery juice running out in large drops when the plant is broken. The twigs seem to be fitted into a sort of socket, from which they come out very easily, so that the plant comes apart almost at a touch. The fragrant flowers are two or three inches across, bright but crude in color, the numerous, purplish-pink petals resembling the rays of a composite and encircling a fuzzy ring of innumerable stamens, with white, threadlike filaments and small, straw-colored anthers, around a dark-green center, composed of the top of the calyx and the six to ten styles of the ovary. This accommodating plant is very useful and ornamental in hot, sandy places, where not much else will grow, and may be seen hanging its long stems over the sea-cliffs all along the coast, from Patagonia to Marin County in California. It also grows in Africa and is extensively cultivated. The fruit is edible, with pulp and tiny seeds something like a fig.

Sea Fig-
Mesembryanthemum aequilaterale.

PINK FAMILY. *Caryophyllaceae.*

A large family, widely distributed, most abundant in the northern hemisphere, including both the handsome Pinks and the insignificant Chickweeds. They are herbs, with regular, mostly perfect flowers, with four or five sepals; usually with four or five petals, sometimes with none; stamens as many, or twice as many, as the petals; ovary superior, one-celled; styles two to five in number; fruit a capsule, containing several or many, kidney-shaped seeds, opening by valves, or by teeth, at the top; leaves opposite, toothless; stems usually swollen at the joints. The name Pink comes from the petals of some kinds being cut into points, or "pinked."

There are numerous kinds of Arenaria, widely distributed, difficult to distinguish, with small, white flowers with five petals, usually not notched, ten stamens and usually three styles; leaves usually long and narrow, often stiff and growing in tufts; capsule roundish, splitting into usually three valves, each with two parts. These plants often grow in dry, sandy places, some at very high altitudes, some by the sea, hence the Latin name meaning "sandy," and the common one, Sandwort.

Fendler's Sand-wort
Arenària Féndleri
White
Summer
Utah, Ariz., etc.

This has pretty little white flowers, about half an inch across, and is variable. Sometimes the stem is roughish, only three or four inches tall, springing from a tuft of small leaves, stiff and almost prickly. Sometimes the stem is smooth, six or eight inches tall, and the leaves resemble rather fine, stiff grass. This grows on dry hills and mountains, up to thirteen thousand feet, from Nebraska and Wyoming to Utah, Arizona, and New Mexico.

There are many kinds of Silene, widely distributed, more or less sticky plants, hence the common name, Catchfly; flowers mostly rather large; calyx inflated or tubular, with five teeth; petals five, with long claws, which often have scales at the top, forming a "crown"; stamens ten; styles usually three; capsule opening by three or six teeth at the tip; seeds numerous.

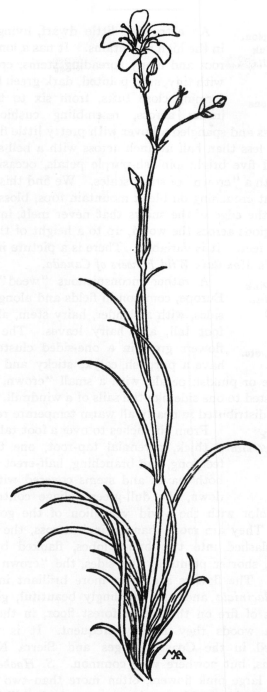

Sandwort-   Arenaria Fendleri.

PINK FAMILY. *Caryophyllaceae.*

Moss Campion.
Cushion Pink
Silène acaulis
Purple
Summer
Alpine regions

An attractive little dwarf, living only in the high mountains. It has a long tap-root and many spreading stems, crowded with tiny, stiff, pointed, dark-green leaves, forming close tufts, from six to twenty inches across, resembling cushions of harsh moss and spangled all over with pretty little flowers. They are less than half an inch across with a bell-shaped calyx and five bright pinkish-purple petals, occasionally white, with a "crown" of small scales. We find this brave little plant crouching on bleak mountain tops, blossoming gayly at the edge of the snows that never melt, in arctic alpine regions across the world, up to a height of thirteen thousand feet. It is variable. There is a picture in Mrs. Henshaw's *Mountain Wild Flowers of Canada.*

Windmill Pink
Silène Ánglica
(*S. Gallica*)
White
Spring
Northwest, etc.

A rather inconspicuous "weed" from Europe, common in fields and along road-sides, with a slender, hairy stem, about a foot tall, and hairy leaves. The small flowers grow in a one-sided cluster and have a purplish calyx, sticky and hairy, and white or pinkish petals, with a small "crown," each petal twisted to one side like the sails of a windmill. This is widely distributed in nearly all warm temperate regions.

Indian Pink
Silène Califórnica
Red
Summer
Northwest

From six inches to over a foot tall, with a thick, perennial tap-root, one to two feet long, and branching, half-erect stems, both leaves and stems covered with fine down, the dull-green foliage contrasting well in color with the vivid vermilion of the gorgeous flowers. They are more than an inch across, the petals usually slashed into two broad lobes, flanked by two narrower, shorter points at the sides, the "crown" conspicuous. The flowers are even more brilliant in color than *S. laciniata* and are startlingly beautiful, glowing like coals of fire on the brown forest floor, in the open mountain woods they usually frequent. It is widely distributed in the Coast Ranges and Sierra Nevada Mountains, but nowhere very common. *S. Hookeri* has beautiful large pink flowers, often more than two inches across, sometimes white, and grows on shady hillsides in the Northwest, except in Idaho.

Windmill Pink-
Silene Anglica

Indian Pink-
Silene Californica.

PINK FAMILY. *Caryophyllaceae.*

Indian Pink
Silène laciniàta
Red
Summer
California

This has handsome conspicuous flowers, clear vermilion or pinkish-scarlet in color, about an inch and a half across, with the five petals prettily slashed at the ends into four long divisions. Each petal has two little crests, which form a pretty "crown" in the throat of the corolla. The roughish, slender stems, from one to over two feet high, have several branches, the flowers growing two or three at the ends. The leaves are long, narrow, and rather rough and the whole plant is hairy and sticky. This is common around Pasadena and other places in southern California and is beautiful on Point Loma, where the brilliant flowers gleam among the underbrush like bits of flame. *S. laciniàta var. Gréggii* is common in Arizonia and New Mexico.

Silène Lyalli
White
Summer
Northwest

Rather pretty, with a slender stem about a foot tall, smooth, bluish-green leaves, and flowers about three-quarters of an inch across; the calyx much inflated, yellowish-white and papery, with brownish veins, and the petals cream-color, with two lobes and a "crown."

There are a few kinds of Vaccaria, of Europe and Asia, smooth annuals, with clasping leaves and red or pink flowers in terminal clusters; calyx five-angled and inflated in fruit, five-toothed, without bracts; petals longer than the calyx, without appendages; stamens ten; styles two. Both the Latin and common names allude to the value of some kinds for fodder.

Cow-herb
Vaccària vaccària
(Saponaria)
Pink
Summer
Across the continent

Quite pretty, with a leafy, branching stem, from one to three feet tall, bluish-green leaves, and flowers less than an inch long, with a ribbed, yellowish-green calyx, with reddish teeth, and the petals a very pretty and unusual shade of deep, warm reddish-pink, veined with deeper color. This is a European "weed," common in waste places and cultivated fields.

Indian Pink.
Silene laciniata.

Indian Pink
Silene laciniata

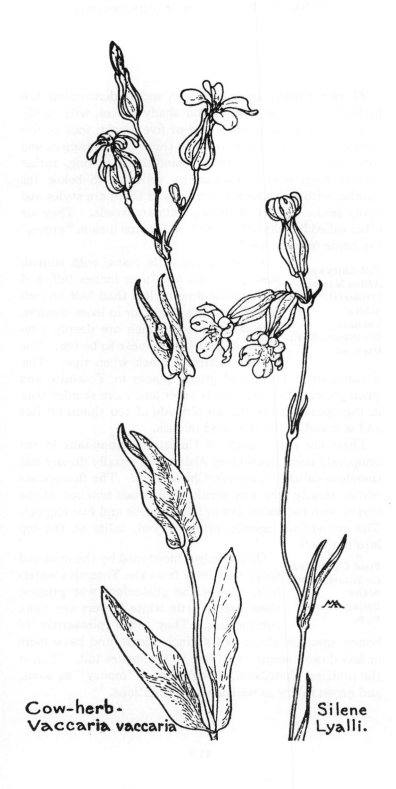

Cow-herb.
Vaccaria vaccaria

Silene
Lyalli.

PINK FAMILY. *Caryophyllaceae.*

There are many kinds of Alsine, widely distributed, low herbs, liking moist ground and shady places, with small, starry white flowers; with four or five sepals; four or five petals, deeply two-lobed or none; three to ten stamens and three to five styles; capsule roundish or oblong, rather shorter than that of Cerastium, splitting to below the middle, with twice as many valves as there are styles and many seeds. Many of these plants are weeds. They are often called Stitchwort. The Greek name means "grove," the home of some kinds.

Tall Chickweed
Alsine lóngipes.
(*Stellaria*)
White
Summer
Northwest, Nev., Utah, etc.

An attractive little plant, with smooth stems, from six to fifteen inches tall, and pretty little flowers, less than half an inch across, growing singly, or in loose clusters, with white petals which are deeply two-lobed, so that they appear to be ten. The capsule is almost black when ripe. This is common in moist and grassy places in Yosemite and when growing in the shade is taller and more slender than in the open. It reaches an altitude of ten thousand feet and is found in the East and in Asia.

There are many kinds of Cerastium, abundant in the temperate zone, resembling Alsine, but usually downy and therefore called Mouse-ear Chickweeds. The flowers are white, usually with five sepals, five petals notched at the tips or with two lobes, ten or five stamens and five stigmas. The cylindrical capsule, often curved, splits at the top into ten teeth.

Field Chickweed
Cerástium arvénse
White
Spring, summer
U. S.

On the ledges moistened by the mist and spray that blow from the Yosemite waterfalls, among the glistening, wet grasses, these pretty little white flowers are quite conspicuous. They smell pleasantly of honey, measure about half an inch across, and have more or less downy stems, from five to ten inches tall. This is the prettiest Cerastium, though not so "mousy" as some, and grows in dry as well as moist situations.

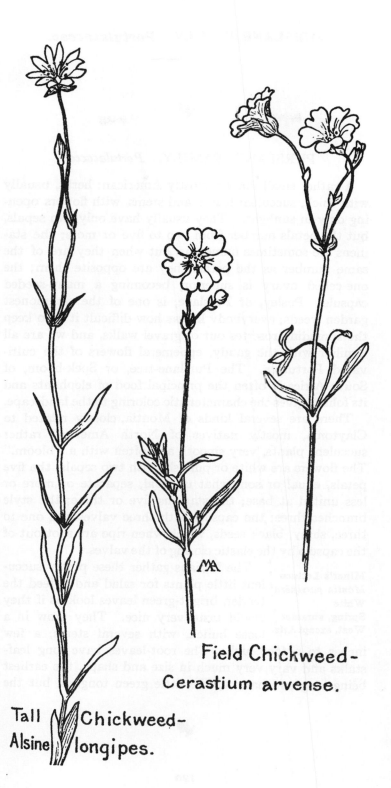

Field Chickweed-
Cerastium arvense.

Tall Chickweed-
Alsine longipes.

PURSLANE FAMILY. *Portulacaceae.*

PURSLANE FAMILY. *Portulacaceae.*

A rather small family, mostly American; herbs, usually with thick, succulent leaves and stems, with flowers opening only in sunlight. They usually have only two sepals, but the petals number from two to five or more; the stamens are sometimes numerous, but when they are of the same number as the petals they are opposite them; the one-celled ovary is superior, becoming a many-seeded capsule. Pusley, or Purslane, is one of the commonest garden weeds; everybody knows how difficult it is to keep the spreading rosettes out of gravel walks, and we are all familiar with the gaudy, ephemeral flowers of the cultivated Portulaca. The Purslane-tree, or Spek-boom, of South Africa is often the principal food of elephants and its foliage gives the characteristic coloring to the landscape.

There are several kinds of Montia, closely related to Claytonia, mostly natives of North America, rather succulent plants, very smooth and often with a "bloom." The flowers are white or pinkish, with two sepals; the five petals, equal or somewhat unequal, separate or more or less united at base; the stamens five or three; the style branches three; the capsule with three valves and one to three, shiny, black seeds, which when ripe are shot out of the capsule by the elastic closing of the valves.

Miner's Lettuce
Móntia parviflòra
White
Spring, summer
West, except Ariz.

The Indians gather these pretty succulent little plants for salad and indeed the tender, bright-green leaves look as if they would taste very nice. They grow in a loose bunch, with several stems, a few inches to a foot high. The root-leaves have long leafstalks and vary very much in size and shape, the earliest being long and narrow, like little green tongues, but the

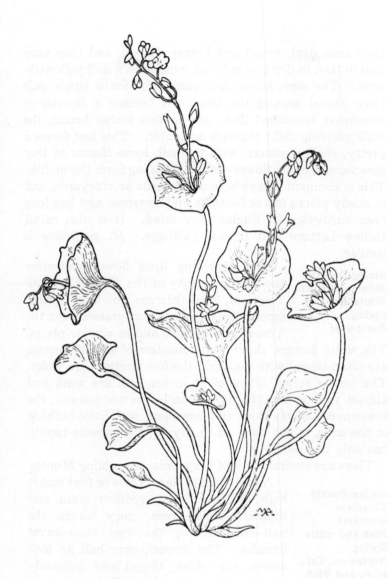

Miner's
Lettuce-

Montia
parviflora.

later ones oval, round and kidney-shaped, and they vary
also in tint, in dry places being sometimes a dull yellowish-
pink. The stem-leaves are quite odd, for a single pair
have united around the stem and become a circular or
somewhat two-lobed disk, one or two inches broad, the
stalk piercing right through its center. This leaf forms a
pretty, shallow saucer, with a small, loose cluster of tiny
flowers, on slender flower-stalks, springing from the middle.
This is common everywhere in orchards or vineyards, and
in shady places in the foothills and canyons, and has long
been cultivated in England for salad. It is also called
Indian Lettuce and Squaw Cabbage. *M. perfoliàta* is
similar.

Spring Beauty
Móntia parvijòlia
White and pink
Spring
Northwest

This charming little flower resembles
the Spring Beauty of the East, *Claytonia
Virginica*, and blooms in late spring,
among the ferns and wet grasses near the
Yosemite waterfalls and in similar places.
The white flowers, about three-quarters of an inch across,
are often tinged with pink and the five stamens are violet.
The tender stems, about eight inches tall, are weak and
almost trailing and the pale-green leaves are smooth, the
lower ones slightly thick and succulent, with little bulblets
in the axils, which drop off in drying; the capsule mostly
has only one seed.

There are several kinds of Claytonia, resembling Montia.

Spring Beauty
Claytònia
lanceolàta
Pink and white
Spring
Northwest, Cal.,
Nev., and Utah

A pretty little plant, three or four inches
high, with a juicy, reddish stem and
thickish, bluish-green, juicy leaves, the
root-leaf narrow, the two stem-leaves
broader. The flowers, over half an inch
across, are white, tinged and delicately
veined with pink, with a little yellow at
the base of the petals; the pistil and stamens pink; the two
sepals yellowish-green. This grows on moist mountain
slopes, up to an altitude of nine thousand feet, sometimes at the edge of the snow, is pretty and delicate and
also resembles the eastern Spring Beauty.

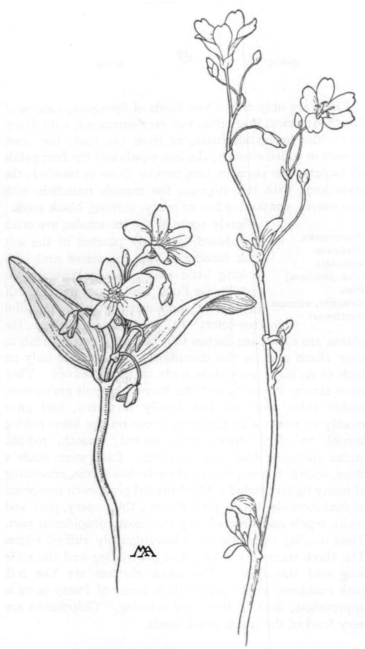

Spring Beauties
Claytonia lanceolata. Montia parvifolia.

PURSLANE FAMILY. *Portulacaceae.*

There are only one or two kinds of Spraguea, natives of North America; low herbs, not very succulent, with fleshy roots; the leaves alternate, or from the root; the small flowers in coiled clusters; the two sepals and the four petals all papery; the stamens one, two, or three in number; the style long, with two stigmas; the capsule roundish, with two valves, containing few or many, shining, black seeds.

Pussy-paws
Spràguea umbellàta
(*Calyptridium*)
Pink
Summer, autumn
Northwest

Sandy spots in the mountains are often brightened by lovely patches of the soft pink blooms of this attractive and odd-looking little plant. Near Wawona, on the Glacier Point trail, I saw at least half an acre of sand carpeted with beautiful rose-color. In moderate altitudes the plants are about ten inches tall, but they get dwarfish as they climb and on the mountain-tops they are only an inch or so high, with close mats of small leaves. They have strong tap-roots and the leaves are dull gray-green, rather thick and stiff but hardly succulent, and grow mostly in rosettes at the base, those on the stem having shrunk to mere bracts, with several, smooth, reddish stalks springing from among them. Each stem bears a close, roundish head, two or three inches across, consisting of many tightly-coiled tufts of shaded pink, each composed of innumerable, small, pink flowers, the papery, pink and white sepals and bracts being the most conspicuous part. They overlap each other and have daintily ruffled edges. The three stamens are long and protruding and the style long and threadlike. The flower-clusters are like soft pink cushions, so the pretty little name of Pussy-paws is appropriate, both to form and coloring. Chipmunks are very fond of the small, black seeds.

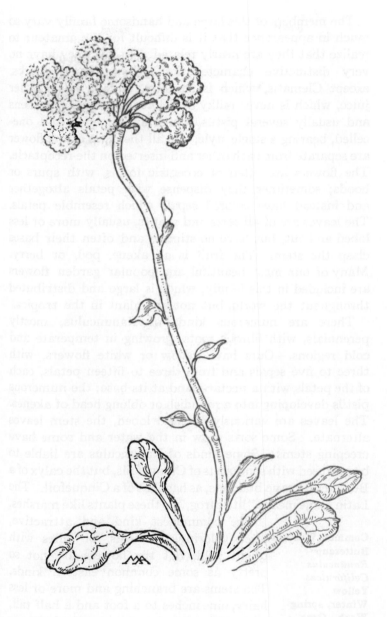

Pussy-paws- **Spraguea umbellata.**

BUTTERCUP FAMILY. *Ranunculaceae.*

The members of this large and handsome family vary so much in appearance that it is difficult for the amateur to realize that they are nearly related. In fact they have no very distinctive characteristics. They are all herbs, except Clematis, which is shrubby, and all have bitter juice, which is never milky or colored, numerous stamens and usually several pistils, which are superior and one-celled, bearing a single style, and all the parts of the flower are separate from each other and inserted on the receptacle. The flowers are often of eccentric forms, with spurs or hoods; sometimes they dispense with petals altogether and instead have colored sepals which resemble petals. The leaves are of all sorts and shapes, usually more or less lobed and cut, but have no stipules and often their bases clasp the stem. The fruit is an akene, pod, or berry. Many of our most beautiful and popular garden flowers are included in this family, which is large and distributed throughout the world, but not abundant in the tropics.

There are numerous kinds of Ranunculus, mostly perennials, with fibrous roots, growing in temperate and cold regions. Ours have yellow or white flowers, with three to five sepals and from three to fifteen petals, each of the petals with a nectar-gland at its base; the numerous pistils developing into a roundish or oblong head of akenes. The leaves are variously cut and lobed, the stem leaves alternate. Some sorts grow in the water and some have creeping stems. Some kinds of Ranunculus are liable to be confused with some sorts of Cinquefoils, but the calyx of a Buttercup has no bractlets, as has that of a Cinquefoil. The Latin name means "little frog," as these plants like marshes.

Common Western Buttercup
Ranúnculus Califórnicus
Yellow
Winter, spring
Wash., Oreg., Cal.

The commonest kind and attractive, often coloring the fields for miles with bright gold, but the flowers are not so pretty as some common eastern kinds. The stems are branching and more or less hairy, nine inches to a foot and a half tall, with dark-green leaves, smooth, hairy or velvety, and velvety, hairy buds. The flowers are about an inch across, with from nine to sixteen, bright-yellow, shiny petals and pale-green sepals, turned

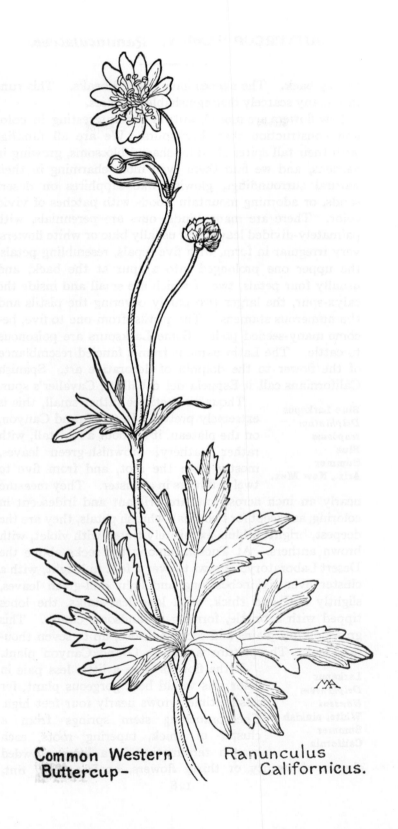

Common Western Buttercup-   Ranunculus Californicus.

BUTTERCUP FAMILY. *Ranunculaceae.*

closely back. The akenes have hooked beaks. This runs into many scarcely distinguishable varieties.

Few flowers are more beautiful and interesting in color and construction than Larkspurs. We are all familiar with their tall spires of oddly-shaped blossoms, growing in gardens, and we find them even more charming in their natural surroundings, glowing like sapphires on desert sands, or adorning mountain woods with patches of vivid color. There are many kinds; ours are perennials, with palmately-divided leaves and usually blue or white flowers, very irregular in form, with five sepals, resembling petals, the upper one prolonged into a spur at the back, and usually four petals, two of which are small and inside the calyx-spur, the larger two partly covering the pistils and the numerous stamens. The pistils, from one to five, become many-seeded pods. Some Larkspurs are poisonous to cattle. The Latin name is from a fancied resemblance of the flower to the dolphin of decorative art. Spanish Californians call it Espuela del caballero, Cavalier's spur.

Blue Larkspur
Delphinium scapòsum
Blue
Summer
Ariz., New Mex.

Though sometimes rather small, this is extremely pretty. In the Grand Canyon, on the plateau, it is about a foot tall, with rather leathery, brownish-green leaves, mostly from the root, and from five to twelve flowers in a cluster. They measure nearly an inch across and are brilliant and iridescent in coloring, as except for two small whitish petals, they are the deepest, brightest blue, exquisitely tinted with violet, with brown anthers. At Tucson, among the rocks above the Desert Laboratory, it grows to over a foot in height, with a cluster over six inches long and light dull-green leaves, slightly stiff and thick, with long leaf-stalks, the lobes tipped with a bristle, forming a handsome clump. This grows on dry plains and rocky hillsides, up to seven thousand feet. The picture is from a Grand Canyon plant.

Larkspur
Delphinium Hánseni
White, pinkish
Summer
California

If the flowers were a little less pale in color this would be a gorgeous plant, for it sometimes grows nearly four feet high. The branching stem springs from a cluster of thick, tapering roots, each branch terminating in a long, crowded cluster of twenty or thirty flowers, opalescent in tint,

Foothills
Larkspur.

Delphinium
scaposum

Foothills   Delphinium
Larkspur   scaposum

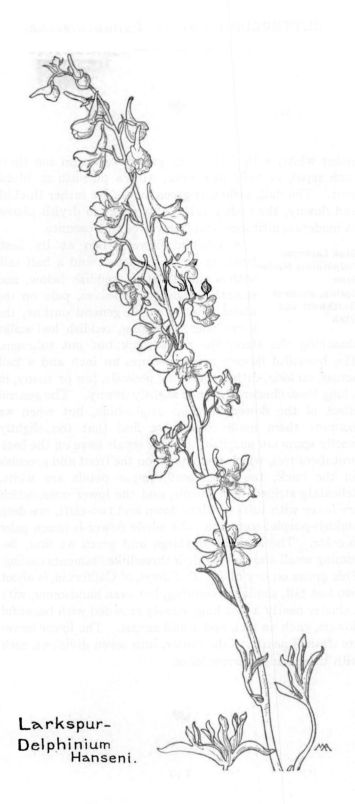

Larkspur—
Delphinium
Hanseni.

either white, with a bluish or greenish spot on the tip of each sepal, or very pale pink, with a purplish or bluish spot. The dull, yellowish-green leaves are rather thickish and downy, the pods erect. This grows in dryish places, at moderate altitudes, and freely around Yosemite.

Blue Larkspur
Delphinium bicolor
Blue
Spring, summer
Northwest and Utah

A splendid flower when at its best, from six inches to a foot and a half tall, with a smooth stem, reddish below, and smooth, bright-green leaves, pale on the under side, round in general outline, the lower ones with long, reddish leaf-stalks sheathing the stem, the roots thick but not tuberous. The beautiful flowers are sometimes an inch and a half across, on long, rather spreading pedicels, few or many, in a long loose cluster, the buds slightly downy. The general effect of the flowers is deep bright-blue, but when we examine them more closely we find that the slightly woolly spurs are purplish, the blue sepals have on the back protuberances, which are pinkish on the front and greenish on the back, the two, small, upper petals are white, delicately striped with purple, and the lower ones, which are fuzzy with tufts of white down and two-cleft, are deep pinkish-purple; sometimes the whole flower is much paler in color. The anthers are large and green at first, becoming small and yellow, their threadlike filaments curling. This grows on dry hills. *D. Párryi*, of California, is about two feet tall, similar in coloring, but even handsomer, with a cluster nearly a foot long, closely crowded with beautiful flowers, each an inch and a half across. The lower leaves are slashed nearly to the center, into seven divisions, each with three, long, narrow lobes.

Blue Larkspur—
Delphinium bicolor.

BUTTERCUP FAMILY. *Ranunculaceae.*

Very handsome, over a foot tall, the upper stem downy, the lower more or less hairy and the leaves more or less velvety. The flowers are an inch or more long and rather few, with long pedicels, forming a loose cluster. They are downy on the outside, all bright-purple, except the two upper petals, which are white tipped with purple, the lower petals edged and tipped with hairs, the spur stoutish and wrinkled. These flowers, though described as blue, seem to me to have more true purple than most Larkspurs. They probably vary a good deal in color. This grows in the Coast Ranges and the Sacramento Valley. There are many similar blue Larkspurs.

Sacramento Larkspur
Delphinium variegàtum
Purple
Spring, summer
California

Scarlet seems an odd color for a Larkspur, but there are two red ones in the West. This is an exceedingly airy, graceful plant and suggests a Columbine more than a Larkspur. The stem is slender and branching, from one to over two feet tall, with a "bloom"; the leaves thickish, smooth, dark rich green on the upper side and pale on the under. The flowers are far apart, from two to twelve, on long pedicels, forming a very loose, open cluster. Each flower is about an inch long; the sepals scarlet shading to yellow, the spur tipped with deeper red, the petals yellow tipped with crimson, not woolly, the two upper notched and much larger than the two lower ones, which are small and slashed into two points, the edges of both sepals and petals more or less hairy; the buds pale yellowish-green, tinged with pink and red. These charming flowers have an elfin look all their own, as they swing their little pointed red caps in the light shade of cool canyons along the mountain streams they love. In southern California we find *D. cardinàle*, a handsomer plant, sometimes six feet tall, its flowers larger and deeper red and forming a larger, closer cluster.

Scarlet Larkspur, Christmas-horns
Delphinium nudicaùle
Red
Spring
Wash., Oreg., Cal.

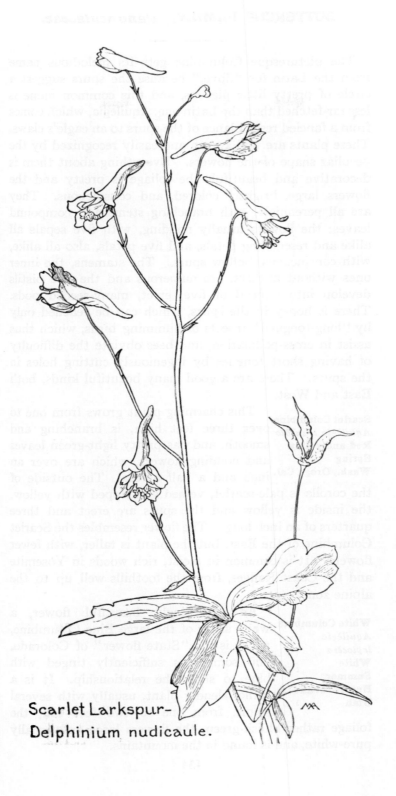

Scarlet Larkspur—
Delphinium nudicaule.

BUTTERCUP FAMILY. *Ranunculaceae.*

The picturesque Columbine gets its melodious name from the Latin for "dove," because the spurs suggest a circle of pretty little pigeons, and this common name is less far-fetched than the Latin one, Aquilegia, which comes from a fancied resemblance of the spurs to an eagle's claws. These plants are well known and easily recognized by the peculiar shape of the flowers. Everything about them is decorative and beautiful, the foliage is pretty and the flowers large, brightly colored, and conspicuous. They are all perennials, with branching stems and compound leaves; the flowers usually nodding, with five sepals all alike and resembling petals, and five petals, also all alike, with conspicuous, hollow spurs. The stamens, the inner ones without anthers, are numerous and the five pistils develop into a head of five, erect, many-seeded pods. There is honey in the spurs, which can be reached only by "long-tongued" insects or humming birds, which thus assist in cross-pollination, and bees obviate the difficulty of having short tongues by ingeniously cutting holes in the spurs. There are a good many beautiful kinds, both East and West.

Scarlet Columbine
Aquilègia truncàta
Red and yellow
Spring
Wash., Oreg., Cal.

This charming plant grows from one to over three feet high, is branching and smooth, and has pretty light-green leaves and nodding flowers, which are over an inch and a half across. The outside of the corolla is pale-scarlet, veined and tipped with yellow, the inside is yellow and the spurs are erect and three quarters of an inch long. The flower resembles the Scarlet Columbine of the East, but the plant is taller, with fewer flowers. It is common in moist, rich woods in Yosemite and the Coast Ranges, from the foothills well up to the alpine zone.

White Columbine
Aquilègia
leptocèra
White
Summer
Northwest and
Utah

An exceedingly beautiful flower, a white sister of the large Blue Columbine, which is the "State flower" of Colorado, and sometimes sufficiently tinged with blue to show the relationship. It is a rather slender plant, usually with several stems, from one to two feet tall, the foliage rather bluish-green, the flowers large and usually pure-white, and is found in the mountains.

134

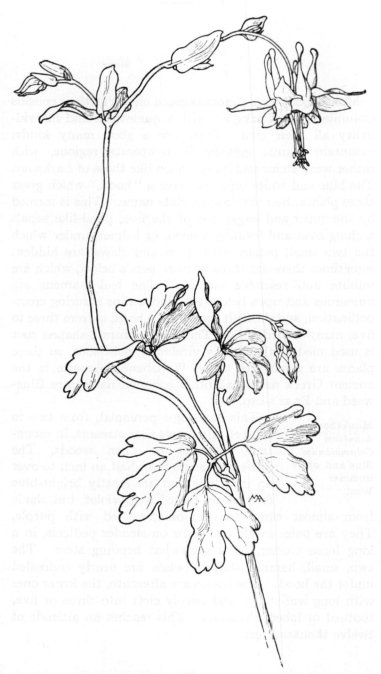

Scarlet Columbine-   Aquilegia truncata.

BUTTERCUP FAMILY. *Ranunculaceae.*

Monkshoods have almost as much charm as their cousins Columbine and Larkspur, with a quaintness and individuality all their own. There are a good many kinds; mountain plants, growing in temperate regions, with rather weak stems and leaves much like those of Larkspur. The blue and white blossoms have a "hood," which gives these plants their very appropriate name. This is formed by the upper and larger one of the five, petal-like sepals arching over and forming a hood, or helmet, under which the two small petals, with spurs and claws, are hidden; sometimes there are three or more petals below, which are minute and resemble stamens. The real stamens are numerous and ripen before the pistils, thus ensuring cross-pollination, and the fruit consists of a head, of from three to five, many-seeded pods. The thick or turnip-shaped root is used medicinally and is virulently poisonous, so these plants are sometimes called Wolfsbane. Aconite is the ancient Greek name and other common names are Blue-weed and Friar's-cap.

Monkshood
Aconìtum
Columbiànum
Blue and white
Summer
West

This handsome perennial, from two to six feet tall, grows near streams, in mountain meadows or open woods. The flowers measure from half an inch to over an inch long and are mostly bright-blue and white, tinged with violet, but shade from almost white to deep-blue, veined with purple. They are paler inside and grow on slender pedicels, in a long loose cluster, on a somewhat bending stem. The two, small, hammer-shaped petals are nearly concealed under the hood. The leaves are alternate, the lower ones with long leaf-stalks, and deeply cleft into three or five, toothed or lobed, divisions. This reaches an altitude of twelve thousand feet.

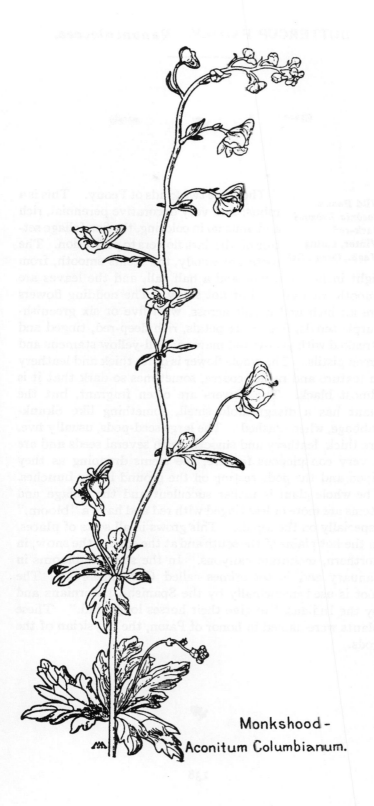

Monkshood-
Aconitum Columbianum.

BUTTERCUP FAMILY. *Ranunculaceae.*

Wild Peony
Paeònia Bròwnii
Dark-red
Winter, spring
Wash., Oreg., Cal.
There are two kinds of Peony. This is a robust and very decorative perennial, rich and unusual in coloring, the fine foliage setting off the dark flowers to perfection. The roots are woody, the stems smooth, from eight inches to a foot and a half tall, and the leaves are smooth, rich green, but not shiny. The nodding flowers are an inch and a half across, with five or six greenish-purple sepals, five or six petals, rich deep-red, tinged and streaked with yellow and maroon; dull-yellow stamens and green pistils. The whole flower is quite thick and leathery in texture and rather coarse, sometimes so dark that it is almost black. The flowers are often fragrant, but the plant has a disagreeable smell, something like Skunk-cabbage, when crushed. The large seed-pods, usually five, are thick, leathery and smooth, with several seeds and are a very conspicuous feature, the stems drooping as they ripen and the pods resting on the ground in big bunches. The whole plant is rather succulent and the foliage and stems are more or less tinged with red and have a "bloom," especially on the sepals. This grows in all sorts of places, in the hot plains of the south and at the edge of the snow, in northern, mountain canyons. In the south it blooms in January and is sometimes called Christmas-rose. The root is used medicinally by the Spanish-Californians and by the Indians, "to give their horses long wind." These plants were named in honor of Paion, the physician of the gods.

Wild Peony-   Paeonia Brownii.

There are only a few kinds of Actaea, tall perennials, with large, alternate, thrice-compound leaves and small, white flowers, in short, terminal clusters. The sepals number about four and resemble petals; the petals are from four to ten, or sometimes none, with claws; the stamens are numerous, with conspicuous white filaments; the one pistil has a broad, somewhat two-lobed, stigma, and the fruit is a large, showy, red or white, somewhat poisonous berry, containing many, smooth, flat seeds.

Baneberry
Actaea argùta
White
Spring, summer
West, except Ariz.

This is a fine plant, from one to two feet tall, with a stoutish, smooth, branching stem and handsome leaves, prettily cut, with pointed teeth, thin and soft in texture, with conspicuous veins. The sepals and petals of the small cream-white flowers are less conspicuous than the numerous white stamens, which give a very feathery appearance to the flower-cluster, which is one or two inches long and speckled with the dark tips of the pistils. The sepals and petals drop off early and the stamens lengthen, so that the cluster becomes very airy and delicate. The general effect of the plant, which grows near shady mountain streams, is striking and graceful. It grows also in the East and is sometimes slightly sweet-scented, but often has an unpleasant smell. The handsome, poisonous berries are oval or round, red or white, with a polished surface, and contain many seeds. This reaches an altitude of ten thousand feet. A very similar kind, *A. viridiflòra*, grows in the mountains of Arizona.

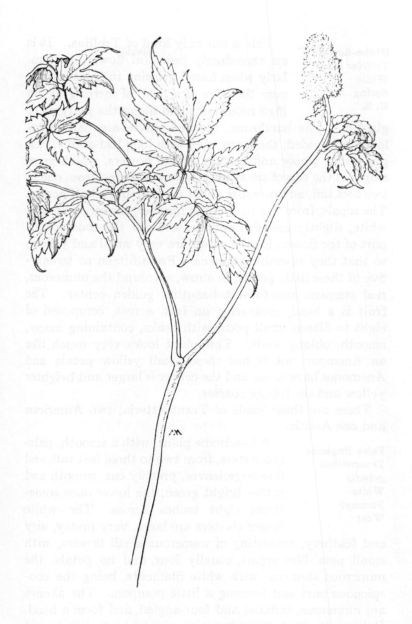

Baneberry—   Actaea arguta.

BUTTERCUP FAMILY. *Ranunculaceae.*

Globe-flower
Tróllius láxus
White
Spring
U. S.

This is our only kind of Trollius. It is an exceedingly beautiful flower, particularly when found growing in the snow, or near the edge of a field of melting ice, in high mountains and along the margins of glaciers. The handsome, toothed leaves are palmately-lobed or divided, the lower ones with long leaf-stalks, rich green and glossy and setting off the flowers, which grow singly at the tips of smooth, rather weak stems, from one to two feet tall, and measure about an inch and a half across. The sepals, from five to seven in number, are large, cream-white, slightly greenish outside, and are the conspicuous part of the flower, for the petals are very small and yellow, so that they resemble stamens. From fifteen to twenty-five of these little petals, in a row, surround the numerous, real stamens and form a beautiful golden center. The fruit is a head, measuring an inch across, composed of eight to fifteen small pods, with beaks, containing many, smooth, oblong seeds. This plant looks very much like an Anemone but it has these small yellow petals and Anemones have none, and the center is larger and brighter yellow and the foliage coarser.

There are three kinds of Trautvetteria, two American and one Asiatic.

False Bugbane
Trautvettèria
grándis
White
Summer
West

A handsome plant, with a smooth, pale-green stem, from two to three feet tall, and fine large leaves, prettily cut, smooth and rather bright green, the lower ones sometimes eight inches across. The white flower clusters are large, very pretty, airy and feathery, consisting of numerous small flowers, with small petal-like sepals, usually four, and no petals, the numerous stamens, with white filaments, being the conspicuous part and forming a little pompon. The akenes are numerous, inflated and four-angled, and form a head. It is a pity that this attractive plant has such a horrid name. It grows in moist woods at Mt. Rainier and in similar places.

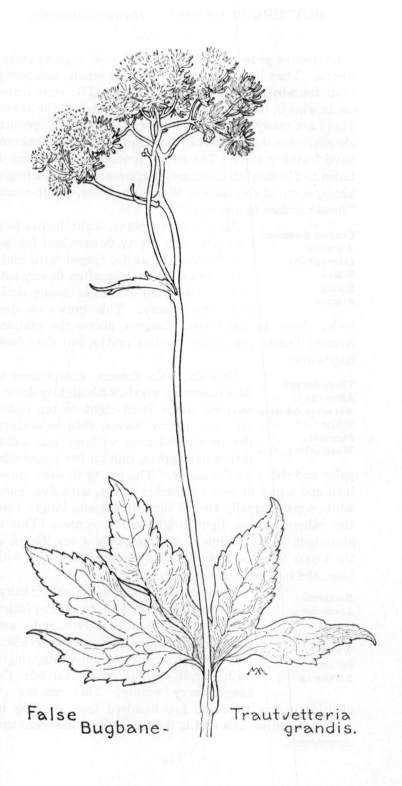

False
Bugbane-
Trautvetteria
grandis.

BUTTERCUP FAMILY. *Ranunculaceae.*

Anemones grow in temperate and cold regions everywhere. They have no petals, but their sepals, numbering from four to twenty, resemble petals. The stem-leaves are in whorls, forming a kind of involucre below the flower. There are many kinds; some have nearly smooth, pointed akenes, some densely woolly ones, and in some the akenes have feathery tails. The name, pronounced anemòne in Latin and in English anémone, is appropriate to the fragile kinds, such as the eastern Wood Anemone, for it means "flower shaken by the wind."

Canyon Anemone
Anemòne
sphenophýlla
White
Spring
Arizona

An attractive plant, eight inches to a foot tall, with pretty flowers and foliage. The flowers are white, tinged with pink, less than an inch across, often downy outside, and the head of fruit is oblong, sleek, and silky downy. This grows on dry, rocky slopes in the Grand Canyon, above the plateau. Around Tucson the flowers are less pretty, but the foliage handsomer.

Three-leaved
Anemone
Anemòne deltoìdea
White
Summer
Wash., Oreg., Col.

Delicate, pale flowers, conspicuous in dark mountain woods, with slightly downy, purplish stems, from eight to ten inches tall, and pretty leaves, thin in texture, the involucre-leaves without leaf-stalks, rather light-green, dull on the upper side, paler and shiny on the under. The pretty flowers are an inch and a half to over two inches across, with five, pure-white sepals, usually two of them larger and longer than the others, and a light bright-yellow center. This is abundant at Mt. Rainier. *A. quinquefòlia var. Gràyi*, of the Coast Ranges, is similar, the flower often tinged with blue, the involucre-leaves with leaf-stalks.

Northern
Anemone
Anemòne
parviflòra
White
Summer
Northwest

A pretty little plant, with a rather hairy, reddish stem, from four to twelve inches tall, glossy, dark-green leaves, paler and downy on the under side, and flowers about half an inch across, cream-white, tinged with purple or blue on the outside; the akenes very woolly. This reaches an altitude of ten thousand five hundred feet, growing in the East and in Asia and is the smallest of the mountain Anemones.

144

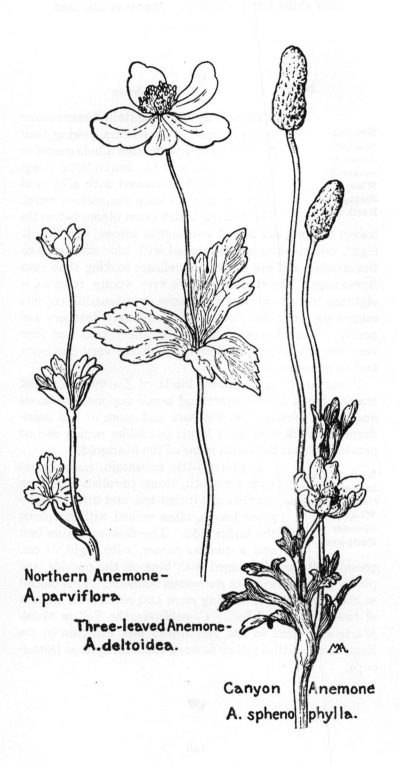

**Northern Anemone—
A. parviflora**

**Three-leaved Anemone—
A. deltoidea.**

**Canyon Anemone
A. sphenophylla.**

Western Anemone
Anemòne occidentàlis
White
Spring
Northwest

These beautiful mountain flowers bloom in early spring, sometimes poking their pretty faces right through a hole melted in a snow-bank, and the brave little things are quite thickly covered with silky wool all over, as if to keep themselves warm. The flowers, which often bloom before the leaves expand, are about two inches across, with five to eight, cream-white sepals, tinged with blue and hairy on the outside, and are much less delicate looking than most Anemones. The stout stems are very woolly, from six to eighteen inches tall, and the leaves are beautiful, cut into numerous, very fine divisions, exceedingly feathery and pretty. The akenes have long, feathery tails and form very large, silky, fluffy heads, which are very handsome and conspicuous.

There are a good many kinds of Caltha, succulent marsh plants, of temperate and arctic regions; the leaves undivided, mostly from the base and more or less heart-shaped; the flowers with large, petal-like sepals and no petals. This is the Latin name of the Marigold.

White Marsh Marigold
Càltha leptosèpala
White
Summer
Northwest

A pretty little mountain, marsh plant with a smooth, stout, purplish stem from four to eight inches tall, and smooth, light-green leaves, often veined with purple on the under side. The flowers are an inch and a quarter across, with eight or ten, cream-white sepals, tinged with blue on the outside, and pretty golden centers of numerous stamens. This blooms at the edge of the retreating snow and reaches an altitude of twelve thousand feet. *C. palústris*, the Yellow Marsh Marigold, found in the Northwest and common in the East, has beautiful yellow flowers, resembling large Buttercups.

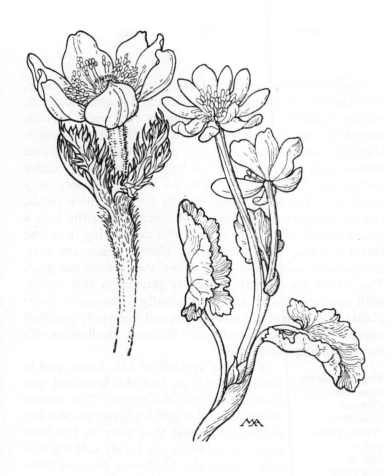

Western
Anemone-

Anemone occidentalis

White Marsh
Marigold-

Caltha leptosepala.

BUTTERCUP FAMILY. *Ranunculaceae.*

There are many varieties of Clematis, or Virgin's Bower, familiar to us all, both East and West, and general favorites, widely distributed and flourishing in temperate regions; perennials, woody below, which is unusual in this family. Usually they are beautiful trailing vines, which climb over bushes and rocks, holding on by their twisting, curling leaf-stalks. The flowers have no petals, or only very small ones, but their sepals, usually four, resemble petals; the stamens are numerous. The numerous pistils form a round bunch of akenes, their styles developing into long feathery tails, and these gray, plumy heads are very conspicuous and ornamental, when the flowers are gone. The leaves are opposite, which is unusual in this family, with slender leaf-stalks, and are usually compound. Some plants have only staminate flowers and some only pistillate ones, and the appearance is quite different, the flowers with stamens being handsomer.

Virgin's Bower, Pipe-stem
Clématis lasiántha
White, pale-yellow
Spring
California

Near the summit of Mt. Lowe, and in similar places, we find this beautiful vine clambering over the rocks. The flowers measure an inch and a quarter to over two inches across and they vary in tint from almost pure white to a lovely soft shade of pale-yellow, the handsome clusters forming a beautiful contrast to the dark-green foliage. The stamens and pistils are on different plants. The flowers, leaves, and stems are all more or less velvety and the akenes have tails an inch long, forming a head, about two inches across. The flowers are often so numerous as to make conspicuous masses of pale color on canyon sides, in the Coast Range and Sierra Nevada Mountains.

Virgin's Bower— Clematis lasiantha.

BUTTERCUP FAMILY. *Ranunculaceae.*

There are a few kinds of Atragene, resembling Clematis.

Purple Clematis
Atrágene occidentàlis (Clematis)
Violet, blue
Summer
West

This is péculiarly attractive, as the flowers are large and beautiful and the foliage very pretty. The leaves are divided into three, pointed leaflets, which are thin in texture, light bright-green and prettily cut or lobed, and the trailing or climbing stems are almost smooth, slender and purplish above and woody below. The flowers, which are not in clusters, measure from two to three inches across, with four, sometimes five, violet or blue sepals, spreading widely as the flower grows older, and the outer stamens are broad and resemble small petals. The flowers are followed by handsome feathery heads, which are large and silky. This pretty vine is found in the Grand Canyon, not far below the Rim, and in many mountain places. The foliage varies somewhat in different climates.

There are many kinds of Thalictrum, not easily distinguished, widely distributed, a few in the Andes, India, and Africa; perennials, with tall stems, from a short rootstock, and handsome, compound leaves; the flowers perfect or imperfect, many, small, in clusters, with four to seven sepals and no petals; the akenes tipped with the long styles and forming a head. Some of these plants have a disagreeable smell. They grow in moist places, both East and West.

Meadow Rue
Thalíctrum
Féndleri
Greenish-white
Summer
West

Though its flowers are small and colorless, this plant is conspicuous for delicacy and grace. The leaves of tender green suggest the fronds of Maidenhair Fern and are almost as beautiful, while the flowers are odd and pretty. A shower of numerous, pale-yellow stamens, with purplish, threadlike filaments, falls from the center of four, greenish-white sepals and forms a charming little tassel. These tassels hang on the ends of very slender pedicels, in loose clusters. The smooth stems are from one to three feet tall and the smooth leaves are thin in texture, thrice-compound, with many, rounded leaflets, the lower leaves with long leafstalks. This Meadow Rue has its pistils and stamens on different plants, the flowers with tassels of stamens being prettier and more conspicuous than the small, green, pistillate ones. The variety *Wrìghtii* is common in Arizona.

Lilac Clematis.
Atragene occidentalis.

Lilac Clematis
Atragene occidentalis

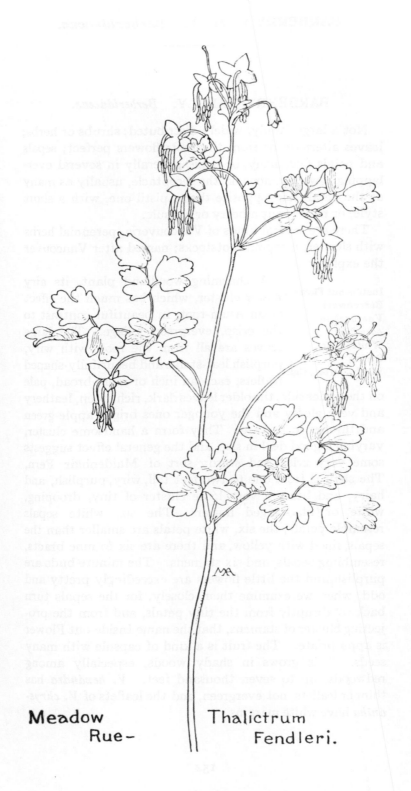

**Meadow
Rue—**

**Thalictrum
Fendleri.**

BARBERRY FAMILY. *Berberidaceae.*

BARBERRY FAMILY. *Berberidaceae.*

Not a large family, widely distributed; shrubs or herbs; leaves alternate or from the root; flowers perfect; sepals and petals few, many, or none, generally in several overlapping rows; stamens on the receptacle, usually as many as the petals and opposite them; pistil one, with a short style, or none; fruit a berry or capsule.

There are several kinds of Vancouveria, perennial herbs with slender, creeping rootstocks; named after Vancouver the explorer.

Inside-out Flower,
Barrenwort
Vancouvèria
parviflòra
White, lilac
Spring
Wash., Oreg., Cal.

A charming woodland plant, its airy flower cluster, which has much the effect of an Alum-root, in beautiful contrast to the crisp, evergreen foliage. The large leaves are all from the root, with wiry, purplish leaf-stalks and beautifully-shaped leaflets, each an inch or more broad, pale on the under side, the older leaves dark, rich green, leathery and very glossy and the younger ones bright apple-green and thinner in texture. They form a handsome cluster, varying a good deal in size, and the general effect suggests some very crisp and sturdy sort of Maidenhair Fern. The stem is from one to two feet tall, wiry, purplish, and hairy, and bears a very loose cluster of tiny, drooping, white or lilac-tinged flowers. The six, white sepals resemble petals; the six, white petals are smaller than the sepals, lined with yellow, and there are six to nine bracts, resembling sepals, and six stamens. The minute buds are purplish and the little flowers are exceedingly pretty and odd, when we examine them closely, for the sepals turn back so abruptly from the tiny petals, and from the projecting cluster of stamens, that the name Inside-out Flower is appropriate. The fruit is a kind of capsule with many seeds. This grows in shady woods, especially among redwoods, up to seven thousand feet. *V. hexándra* has thinner leaflets, not evergreen, and the leaflets of *V. chrysántha* have white margins.

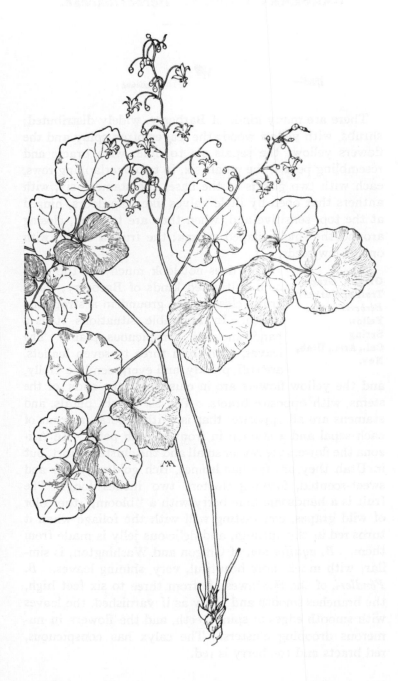

Inside-out
Flower-

Vancouveria
parviflora.

BARBERRY FAMILY. *Berberidaceae.*

There are many kinds of Barberry, widely distributed; shrubs, with yellow wood; the leaves often spiny and the flowers yellow; the sepals six to nine, with bracts and resembling petals; the petals six, in two overlapping rows, each with two glands at the base; the stamens six, with anthers that open by little valves like trap-doors, hinged at the top, sensitive and, when they are touched, closing around the shield-shaped stigma; the fruit a berry, with one or few seeds.

Oregon Grape, Trailing Barberry
Bérberis rèpens
Yellow
Spring
Cal., Ariz., Utah, Nev.

This does not look much like the common cultivated kinds of Barberry, for it grows close to the ground in a straggling bunch. In favorable situations it is a handsome and conspicuous plant. The leaves, with from three to seven leaflets, are stiff, prickly, and evergreen like Holly, and the yellow flowers are in clusters at the ends of the stems, with opposite bracts. The six sepals, petals, and stamens are all opposite, that is, with a petal in front of each sepal and a stamen in front of each petal. In Arizona the flowers are rather small and the clusters short, but in Utah they are far handsomer, rich golden-yellow and sweet-scented, forming clusters two inches long. The fruit is a handsome blue berry with a "bloom," the color of wild grapes, contrasting well with the foliage when it turns red in the autumn, and delicious jelly is made from them. *B. aquifòlium*, of Oregon and Washington, is similar, with much more beautiful, very shining leaves. *B. Féndleri*, of the Southwest, is from three to six feet high, the branches smooth and shiny as if varnished, the leaves with smooth edges or spiny teeth, and the flowers in numerous drooping clusters. The calyx has conspicuous, red bracts and the berry is red.

Oregon Grape-

Berberis repens.

WATER LILY FAMILY. *Nymphaeaceae.*

Sweet-after-Death
Áchlys triphýlla
White
Summer
Wash., Oreg., Cal.

The only kind, an attractive perennial, popular on account of its sweet-smelling foliage, which, however, is not fragrant until the leaves are dried. It has a very slender rootstock and only one large leaf, with a very long, slender leaf-stalk and three, oddly-shaped leaflets, from two to six inches across, bright-green, smooth and thin in texture, but not glossy. The single, very slender flower-stalk, from one to two feet tall, bears a crowded spike of many, tiny, scentless, white flowers, without either calyx or corolla, but consisting of a cluster of stamens, with long, threadlike filaments, the outer ones broader, and a pistil with a broad stigma and no style. The effect of the cluster is feathery and pretty and the broad leaf is very conspicuous, on account of its size and shape. The crescent-shaped fruit contains one seed, is at first fleshy, but becomes dry and leathery. This grows in the woods in the Coast Ranges, from near sea-level up to seven thousand feet. It is also called Vanilla Leaf and Deer-foot.

WATER LILY FAMILY. *Nymphaeaceae.*

A small family, widely distributed in fresh-water lakes and streams; aquatic, perennial herbs, with thick, horizontal rootstocks, or with tubers, large, floating, or erect leaves, and large, solitary flowers, with long flower-stalks; sepals three to twelve; petals three to many; stamens six to numerous; ovary superior, stigmas distinct or united into a disk. We have no white Water Lilies in the West.

Indian Pond Lily,
Spatter-dock
Nympháea poly-sépala (Nuphar)
Yellow
Summer
Cal., Oreg., Wash., Col., Wyo.

Like the eastern Spatter-dock, this is a coarse, but rather handsome and decorative plant. The leathery leaves are shaped like a rounded heart and sometimes a foot long. The cup-shaped calyx, two to four inches across, is the conspicuous part of the flower, consisting of seven to twelve, thickish sepals, yellow and petal-like, the outer greenish. There are twelve to eighteen

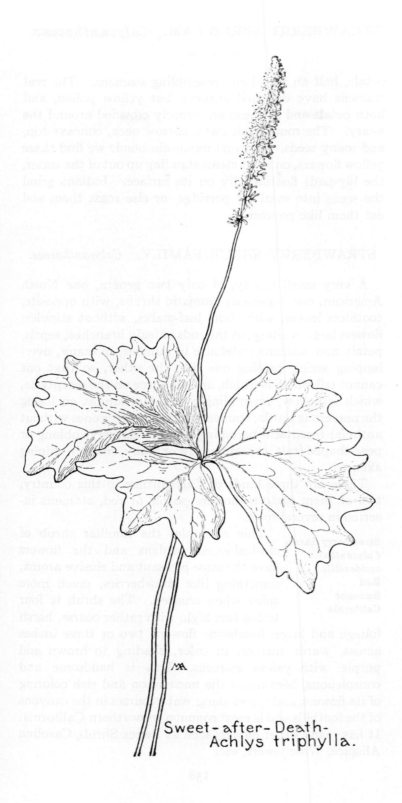

Sweet-after-Death-
Achlys triphylla.

petals, half an inch long, resembling stamens. The real stamens have dark-red anthers, but yellow pollen, and both petals and stamens are densely crowded around the ovary. The round fruit has a narrow neck, concave top, and many seeds. In quiet mountain ponds we find these yellow flowers, on stout stems standing up out of the water, the lily-pads floating idly on its surface. Indians grind the seeds into meal for porridge, or else roast them and eat them like popcorn.

STRAWBERRY SHRUB FAMILY. *Calycanthaceae.*

A very small family, of only two genera, one North American, one Japanese; aromatic shrubs, with opposite, toothless leaves, with short leaf-stalks, without stipules; flowers large, solitary, at the ends of leafy branches; sepals, petals, and stamens, indefinite in number, in many, overlapping series, passing one into the other, so that one cannot tell which is which, and all borne on the receptacle, which is hollow, resembling a rose-hip, almost enclosing the numerous pistils; stamens short, the inner ones without anthers; receptacle becoming a large, leathery, oblong or pear-shaped fruit, containing few or many, smooth, shining akenes.

There are three kinds of Calycanthus in this country, two of them eastern; flowers purple or red, stamens inserted in several rows.

Strawberry Shrub
Calycánthus
occidentàlis
Red
Summer
California

This resembles the familiar shrub of old-fashioned gardens and the flowers have the same pleasant and elusive aroma, something like strawberries, much more spicy when crushed. The shrub is four to ten feet high, with rather coarse, harsh foliage and large, handsome flowers, two or three inches across, warm maroon in color, shading to brown and purple, with yellow stamens. This is handsome and conspicuous, because of the uncommon and rich coloring of its flowers, and grows along watercourses in the canyons of the foothills and is most common in northern California. It has many other names, such as Sweet Shrub, Carolina Allspice, Wineflowers, etc.

Strawberry Shrub—

Calycanthus occidentalis.

POPPY FAMILY. *Papaveraceae.*

POPPY FAMILY. *Papaveraceae.*

A rather large family, widely distributed, most abundant in the north temperate zone; herbs, rarely shrubs, with milky, mostly yellow juice and narcotic or acrid properties; the leaves mostly alternate, without stipules; the parts of the flower usually all separate and distinct, borne on a top-shaped receptacle. There are usually two sepals, which fall off when the blossom opens, and usually four petals, overlapping and crumpled in the bud; the stamens are usually numerous and conspicuous, with thread-like filaments; the superior ovary becomes a many-seeded capsule.

There are only two kinds of Romneya, much alike, smooth, stout, perennial herbs, several feet high, with colorless sap, the leaves alternate and more or less divided; three sepals, each with a broad wing on the back; six, large, white petals; many stamens; the ovary covered with bristles. These plants are nowhere common, but are found from Santa Barbara south, and in lower California sometimes grow in great profusion. They are extensively cultivated and much admired abroad.

Matilija Poppy,
Giant Poppy
Romnèya
trichocàlyx
White
Summer
California

This is often considered the handsomest flower in the West and it would be hard to find anything more beautiful and striking than its magnificent blossoms. The plant has somewhat the effect of a Peony-bush, sometimes, in cultivation, as much as five feet high, with many smooth stems and handsome, smooth, light-green foliage, the leaves cut and lobed, those near the top with a few prickles. The splendid flowers are enormous, from five to nine inches across, with diaphanous, white petals, crinkled like crêpe tissue-paper, and bright golden centers, composed of hundreds of yellow stamens surrounding a greenish-white pistil. The blossoms remain open for several days. The hard, round buds are covered with short, brown hairs. This is the true Matilija Poppy, (pronounced Matfliha,) as it is the kind that grows in the canyon of that name, but the tremendous floods of 1914 drowned most of these beautiful plants in that locality. *R. Còulteri* is similar, but the buds are smooth and the stems more robust.

Matilija Poppy—   Romneya trichocalyx.

POPPY FAMILY. *Papaveraceae.*

There are several kinds of Argemone, natives of the warmer parts of America, with bitter, yellow juice, spiny-toothed leaves and large, conspicuous flowers, the buds erect; sepals two or three, with odd little horns; petals twice as many as the sepals; stamens numerous; style very short, with a radiate stigma; capsule prickly, oblong, opening at the top, containing numerous seeds.

Thistle Poppy,
Milk Thistle
Argemòne hispida
White
Summer
Southwest

The prickly, bluish-green foliage of this decorative and handsome plant is thistle-like both in form and color. The leafy, branching stems, two or three feet high, are covered with dense, white or yellowish prickles and bear several lovely flowers, over three inches across, with delicately crumpled, white petals and beautiful golden centers, composed of numerous yellow stamens, both stem and leaves having a bluish "bloom." The three prickly green sepals each have a spine-like beak and form a queer-looking, three-horned bud; the pistil has a purplish, cap-shaped stigma, with six lobes, and the prickly ovary becomes a very prickly capsule. This grows in dry places and looks very beautiful and striking when we find its fragile flowers waving in the wind against a background of hot desert sand. It varies a good deal in prickliness and in the form both of plant and flower. When there is only one large flower in bloom, surrounded by a circle of prickly buds, it suggests a fairy princess, guarded by a retinue of fierce warriors. The flowers are often quite broad and flat, and then are sometimes given the prosaic name of Fried-eggs.

There are many kinds of Papaver; with milky juice, leaves lobed or cut, nodding flower buds, showy regular flowers, with two or three sepals and four to six petals. The stigmas are united to form a disk with rays and the fruit is a round or oblong capsule, opening near the top. Both the Latin and common name, Poppy, are ancient. Opium is made from *P. somniferum* of the Mediterranean.

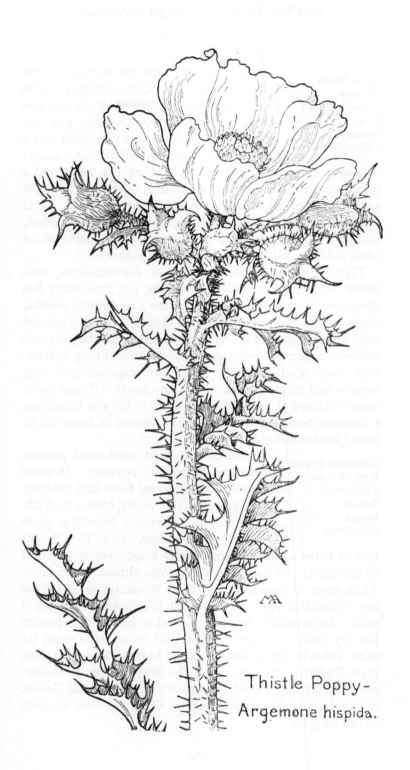

Thistle Poppy—
Argemone hispida.

POPPY FAMILY. *Papaveraceae.*

Wind Poppy
Papáver
heterophýllum
Red
Spring
California

A slender, graceful plant, one or two feet tall, with smooth, branching, purplish stems, smooth leaves, variously cut and lobed, and charming flowers, gay yet delicate. They are about an inch and a half across, usually with four, scarlet petals, each with a spot of maroon at the base, and a bright-green pistil and maroon filaments with pale-yellow anthers. The buds and seed-pods are smooth. This varies a good deal, smells strong of opium when picked, and its flowers glow like jewels among the underbrush on open hillsides, but fall to pieces when gathered.

There are a good many kinds of Eschscholtzia, with bitter, watery juice; leaves alternate, cut into many fine divisions; buds erect; flowers yellow; receptacle cuplike, often with a rim; the two sepals united to form a pointed cap, which is pushed off by the four petals as they expand; stamens numerous, with short filaments and long anthers; style very short, usually with four stigmas; pod long, narrow and ribbed, containing many seeds. These plants were collected at San Francisco in 1816 by von Chamisso, a German poet and naturalist, and named in honor of his friend Eschscholtz, a botanist.

California Poppy
Eschschóltzia
Califórnica
Yellow
Spring
Cal., Oreg.

Probably the most celebrated western flower and deservedly popular. It varies a great deal in general form and coloring, but is usually a fine plant, over a foot tall, with stems and leaves a beautiful shade of light bluish-green, and the flowers two or three inches across, usually bright-yellow, shading to orange at the base, but sometimes almost cream-color. They open in sunlight and when blooming in quantities are a beautiful sight, covering the hillsides with a cloth of gold. In southern Arizona a similar kind often borders the dry beds of streams with bright color, with much the same value in the landscape as the Marsh Marigolds along New England streams. It is the State flower of California and has many poetic Spanish names, such as Torosa, Amapola, and Domidera, besides Copa de Oro, meaning "Cup of gold."

California
Poppy.

Eschscholtzia
Californica.

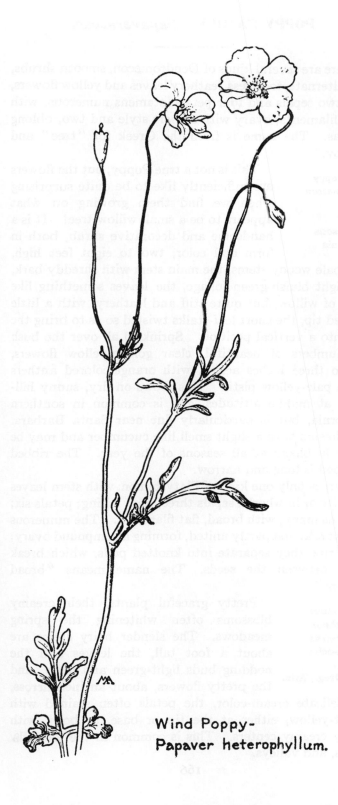

Wind Poppy-
Papaver heterophyllum.

POPPY FAMILY. *Papaveraceae.*

There are several kinds of Dendromecon, smooth shrubs, with alternate, toothless, leathery leaves and yellow flowers, with two sepals and four petals; stamens numerous, with short filaments; ovary with a short style and two, oblong stigmas. The name is from the Greek for "tree" and "poppy."

Tree Poppy
Dendromécon rígida
Yellow
All seasons
California

This is not a true Poppy, but the flowers are sufficiently like to be quite surprising when we find them growing on what appears to be a small willow tree! It is a handsome and decorative shrub, both in form and color, two to eight feet high, with pale woody stems, the main stem with shreddy bark, and light bluish-green foliage, the leaves something like those of willow, but quite stiff and leathery, with a little pointed tip, the short leaf-stalks twisted so as to bring the leaf into a vertical position. Sprinkled all over the bush are numbers of beautiful, clear golden-yellow flowers, one to three inches across, with orange-colored anthers and a pale-yellow pistil. This grows on dry, sunny hillsides, at middle altitudes, and is common in southern California, but is particularly fine near Santa Barbara. The flowers have a slight smell like cucumber and may be found in bloom at all seasons of the year. The ribbed seed-pod is long and narrow.

There is only one kind of Platystemon, with stem leaves opposite or in whorls; sepals three, soon falling; petals six; stamens many, with broad, flat filaments. The numerous pistils are at first partly united, forming a compound ovary; when ripe they separate into knotted pods, which break apart between the seeds. The name means "broad stamens."

Cream-cups
Platystèmon Califórnicus
Cream-color
Spring
Cal., Oreg., Ariz.

Pretty graceful plants, their creamy blossoms often whitening the spring meadows. The slender hairy stems are about a foot tall, the leaves and the nodding buds light-green and hairy, and the pretty flowers, about an inch across, are delicate cream-color, the petals often stained with bright-yellow, either at the tip or base, or both, with pretty creamy centers. This is common in the foothills, plains, and valleys.

Bush Poppy.

Dendromecon rigida.

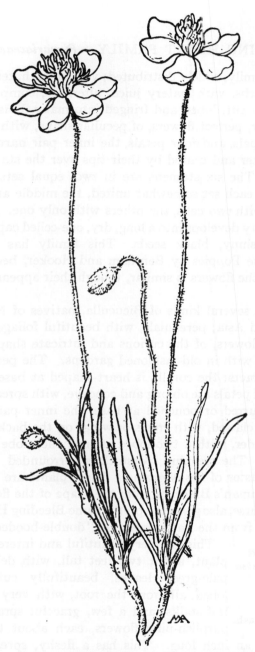

Cream-cups- Platystemon Californicus.

BLEEDING HEART FAMILY. *Fumariaceae.*

BLEEDING HEART FAMILY. *Fumariaceae.*

A small family, widely distributed; very smooth, tender, perennial herbs, with watery juice; alternate, compound leaves, finely cut, lobed and fringed into many divisions, and irregular, perfect flowers, of peculiar shape, with two, scale-like sepals, and four petals, the inner pair narrower than the outer and united by their tips over the stamens and style. The six stamens are in two, equal sets, the filaments of each set somewhat united, the middle anther of each set with two cells, tne others with only one. The superior ovary develops into a long, dry, one-celled capsule, containing shiny, black seeds. This family has been united to the Poppies by Bentham and Hooker, because the plan of the flowers is similar, though their appearance is unlike.

There are several kinds of Bicuculla, natives of North America and Asia; perennials, with beautiful foliage and decorative flowers, of the curious and intricate shape we are familiar with in old-fashioned gardens. The pedicels have two bracts; the corolla is heart-shaped at base; the outer pair of petals are oblong and concave, with spreading tips and spurred or pouched at base, the inner pair are narrow and clawed, with crests or wings on the back; the style is slender, with a two-lobed stigma, each lobe with two crests. The creeping rootstock is surrounded by a bulb-like cluster of fleshy grains. These plants are often called Dutchman's Breeches, from the shape of the flower, which, of course, also gives the pretty name Bleeding Heart. Bicuculla is from the Latin, meaning "double-hooded."

Bleeding Heart
Bicucúlla formòsa
(*Dicentra*)
Pink
Summer
Cal., Oreg., Wash.

This is a very beautiful and interesting plant, about two feet tall, with delicate pale-green leaves, beautifully cut and lobed, all from the root, with very long leaf-stalks, and a few, graceful sprays of purplish-pink flowers, each about three-quarters of an inch long. This has a fleshy, spreading

168

Bleeding
Heart.

Bicuculla
formosa.

rootstock and grows in shady spots, in rich, moist woods, at moderate altitudes, but is not very common. It is found in the Yosemite Valley. *B. uniflòra* is a diminutive alpine plant, from one to three inches high, usually with only one white or flesh-colored flower, about half an inch long, which is often hidden among dead leaves. This grows in rich soil on mountain sides in the Wasatch and Teton Mountains and in the Sierra Nevada, and is found in the Yosemite Valley and on Mt. Lyall, at a height of ten thousand five hundred feet. This is called Squirrel Corn and Steer's Head.

Golden Eardrops
*Bicucúlla
chrysántha*
(Dicentra)
Yellow
Summer
California

The general appearance of this handsome plant is striking and Japanese in effect, and the coloring of the feathery, pale-green foliage and the golden-yellow flowers is exceedingly odd and beautiful. The large, finely-cut leaves are sometimes a foot long, and resemble delicate ferns, and the smooth, stout, rather coarse flower-stems bear a few pretty flowers, which are a soft shade of yellow, about three-quarters of an inch long, the usual Bleeding Heart shape, but not drooping, and with a strong narcotic odor, much like that of poppies. This is sometimes as much as four feet high and grows in sunny places on dry ridges in the Coast Ranges, but is nowhere common.

There are many kinds of Capnoides, natives of the north temperate zone and Africa. They have oddly-shaped flowers, something like Bleeding Heart, but with only one spur, at the back on the upper side, instead of two. The name is from the Greek, meaning "smokelike," in allusion to the odor of some kinds.

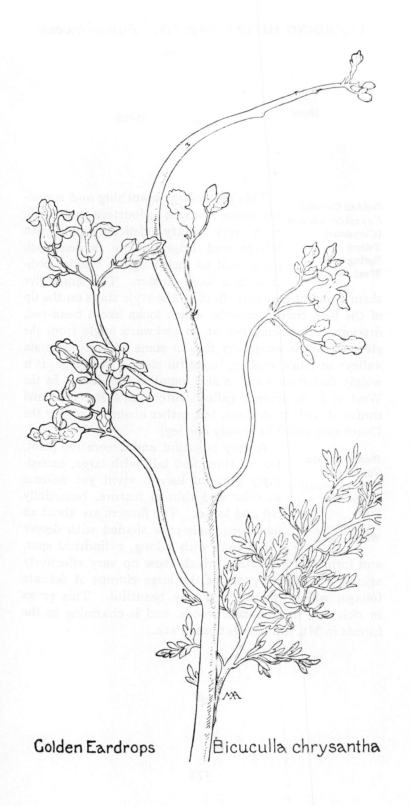

Golden Eardrops   Bicuculla chrysantha

BLEEDING HEART FAMILY. *Fumariaceae.*

Golden Corydal
Capnoìdes aùreum
(Corydalis)
Yellow
Spring
West

This has hollow, branching and spreading stems, from six to fourteen inches tall, with very pretty, delicate, pale-green foliage and bright-yellow flowers, each about half an inch long, on slender pedicels, in a loose cluster. The spurs give them a quaint and pert effect. The style stays on the tip of the long curved capsule, which looks like a bean-pod, drooping or sticking out at an awkward angle from the stem. This is especially fine in some of the mountain valleys in Utah, making beautiful clumps of foliage; it is widely distributed and is also found in the East. In the West it is sometimes called Dutchman's Breeches and confused with that plant, but rather absurdly so, for the Dutchman could have only one leg!

Pink Corydalis
Capnoìdes
Scoùleri
(Corydalis)
Pink
Summer
Wash., Oreg.

A very beautiful and decorative plant, two or three feet tall, with large, exceedingly graceful leaves, vivid yet delicate in color and thin in texture, beautifully cut and lobed. The flowers are about an inch long, pale-pink shaded with deeper color, each with a long, cylindrical spur, and form pretty clusters, which show up very effectively against the tender green of the large clumps of delicate foliage, which are conspicuously beautiful. This grows in rich soil, in mountain woods, and is charming in the forests in Mt. Rainier National Park.

Golden
Corydal-
C. aureum.

Pink.Corydalis-
Capnoides Scouleri.

MUSTARD FAMILY. *Cruciferae.*

A large family, widely distributed. Both the English and Latin names are appropriate, for the watery juice of these plants is pungent, like mustard, and the flowers spread out their four petals in the form of a cross. They are herbs, the leaves alternate or from the root, usually with no leaf-stalks. The flowers have four petals, with claws; four sepals, the two outer ones narrow, apt to drop off; six stamens, two of them short. The ovary is superior, usually with a single style and stigma, and usually develops into a pod, divided in two by a transparent partition, which remains after the pod has opened from below; in some kinds the pod remains closed. The flowers generally grow in clusters and though they are often small they produce honey and so are frequented by bees and flies. The family is easily recognized by the four petals and in most species by two stamens being shorter than the others, but the flowers are so much alike that the various kinds have to be determined by examining the fruit. Radish and Horse-radish, Mustard and Water-cress all belong to this family, as well as many familiar garden flowers, such as Sweet Alyssum, Candytuft, Rockets, and Stocks, and many are common weeds, such as Peppergrass and Shepherd's Purse.

There are several kinds of Dentaria, smooth perennials, with rather large white or pink flowers and tuberous root-stocks.

**Milk Maids,
Pepper-root
*Dentària
Califórnica*
White, pink
Spring
Cal., Oreg.**
A charming plant, with a purplish stem, from six inches to two feet tall, and pretty leaves, varying in shape, those from the root being roundish in outline, or with three leaflets, but the stem-leaves with three or five leaflets. The flowers are about three-quarters of an inch across, with pure-white or pale-pink petals. This is one of the loveliest of the early spring flowers in the Coast Ranges and usually found in damp spots, both in woods and open places, often whitening the meadows with its blossoms.

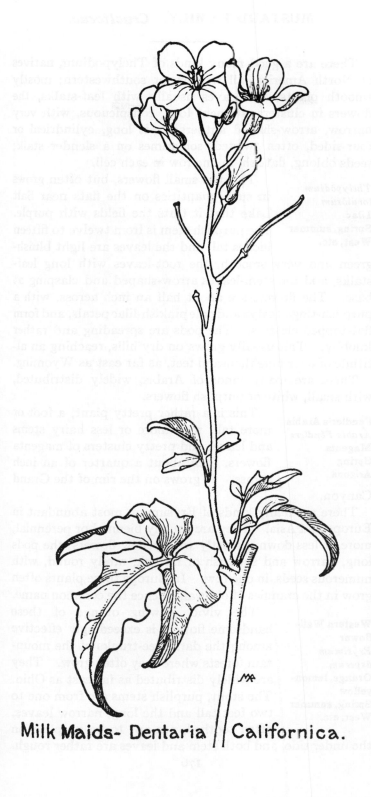

Milk Maids- Dentaria Californica.

MUSTARD FAMILY. *Cruciferae.*

There are a good many kinds of Thelypodium, natives of North America, all western or southwestern; mostly smooth plants, the leaves usually with leaf-stalks, the flowers in clusters; stamens long, conspicuous, with very narrow, arrow-shaped anthers; pods long, cylindrical or four-sided, often twisted, sometimes on a slender stalk; seeds oblong, flattish, in one row in each cell.

Thelypòdium torulòsum
Lilac
Spring, summer
West, etc.

This has small flowers, but often grows in such quantities on the flats near Salt Lake that it tints the fields with purple. The purplish stem is from twelve to fifteen inches tall and the leaves are light bluish-green and very smooth; the root-leaves with long leaf-stalks, and the stem-leaves arrow-shaped and clasping at base. The flowers are about half an inch across, with a purplish-tinged calyx and pale pinkish-lilac petals, and form flat-topped clusters. The pods are spreading and rather knobby. This usually grows on dry hills, reaching an altitude of over nine thousand feet, as far east as Wyoming.

There are many kinds of Arabis, widely distributed, with small, white or purplish flowers.

Fendler's Arabis
Árabis Féndlers
Magenta
Spring
Arizona

This is a rather pretty plant, a foot or more tall, with more or less hairy stems and leaves and pretty clusters of magenta flowers, each about a quarter of an inch across. It grows on the rim of the Grand Canyon.

There are many kinds of Erysimum, most abundant in Europe and Asia. They are usually biennial or perennial, more or less downy; mostly with yellow flowers; the pods long, narrow and squarish or flattish, rarely round, with numerous seeds, in one row. In Europe these plants often grow in the crannies of old walls, hence the common name.

Western Wall-flower
Erýsimum ásperum
Orange, lemon-yellow
Spring, summer
West, etc.

The vivid glowing orange of these handsome flowers is exceedingly effective among the dark tree-trunks of the mountain forests where they often grow. They are widely distributed as far east as Ohio. The stout, purplish stems are from one to two feet tall and the long, narrow leaves, often toothed, are apt to be purplish on the under side, and both stem and leaves are rather rough.

176

Western
Wall-flower

Erysimum
asperum

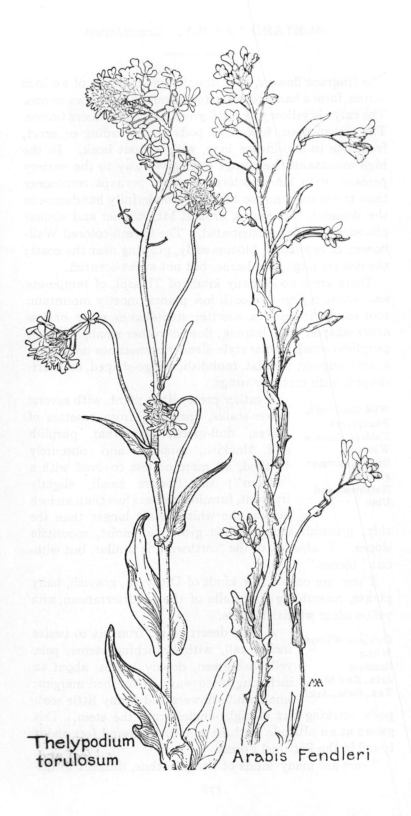

Thelypodium
torulosum

Arabis Fendleri

The fragrant flowers, each about three-quarters of an inch across, form a handsome cluster, about three inches across. The calyx is yellow, the pistil green, and the anthers brown. The conspicuous, four-sided pods are spreading or erect, from one to five inches long, with a stout beak. In the high mountains the orange-color gives way to the variety *perénne*, with lemon-colored flowers, perhaps commoner than the orange, not so tall, and wonderfully handsome in the Wasatch Mountains, around Mt. Rainier and similar places, and widely distributed. The Cream-colored Wall-flower, *E. capitátum*, blooms early, growing near the coast; the flowers large, handsome, but not sweet-scented.

There are a good many kinds of Thlaspi, of temperate and arctic regions: smooth low plants, mostly mountain; root-leaves forming a rosette; stem-leaves more or less arrow-shaped and clasping; flowers rather small, white or purplish; sepals blunt; style slender, sometimes none, with a small stigma; pod flat, roundish, wedge-shaped, or heart-shaped, with crests or wings.

Wild Candytuft, Pennycress
Thláspi glaùcum
White
Spring, summer, autumn
Northwest and Utah

A rather pretty little plant, with several flower-stalks, springing from rosettes of leaves, dull-green, somewhat purplish and thickish, smooth and obscurely toothed, all more or less covered with a "bloom"; the flowers small, slightly fragrant, forming clusters less than an inch across, the white petals longer than the thin, greenish sepals. This grows on moist, mountain slopes. *T. alpéstre*, of the Northwest, is similar, but without "bloom."

There are only a few kinds of Díthyrea, grayish, hairy plants, resembling Biscutella of the Mediterranean, with yellowish or whitish flowers.

Dithýrea Wislizéni
White
Summer
Ariz., New Mex., Tex., Okla., Ark.

A little desert plant, from six to twelve inches tall, with branching stems; pale, yellowish-green, downy leaves, about an inch long, with wavy or toothed margins; small white flowers and funny little seed-pods, sticking out at right-angles from the stem. This grows at an altitude of three to four thousand feet and is found in the Petrified Forest.

There are many kinds of Streptanthus, difficult to dis-

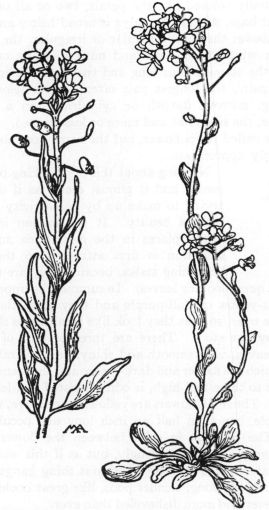

**Dithyrea
Wislizeni.**

**Wild Candytuft -
Thlaspi glaucum.**

tinguish, smooth plants, often with a "bloom"; stems branching; leaves often clasping at base, the lower ones usually more toothed or lobed than the upper. The flowers are very peculiar in shape, not like most Mustards, but suggesting the shape of a Bleeding Heart flower; the sepals usually colored like the petals, two or all of them bulging at base, so that the calyx is broad below and contracted above; the corolla regular or irregular, the petals purple or white, with claws and narrow, wavy or crisp borders; the stamens four long and two short, or in three unequal pairs, the longest pair often united below; the pods long, narrow, flattish or cylindrical, on a broad receptacle; the seeds flat and more or less winged. These plants are called Jewel-flower, but the name does not seem particularly appropriate.

Shield-leaf
Streptánthus tortuòsus
Yellowish, purplish
Summer
California

Nothing about this odd-looking plant is pretty and it almost seems as if it were trying to make up by eccentricity for its lack of beauty. It is common in dry, sandy places in the mountains and our attention is first attracted to the tall, branching stalks, because they are strung with such queer-looking leaves. In summer the upper ones are bright-yellow or dull-purple and they clasp the stem and curve over, so that they look like small brass shields, pierced by the stem. There are three or four of these curving leaves, very smooth and shiny, and several more below, which are flatter and dark-green, and the stem, from six inches to three feet high, is oddly twisted and leans to one side. The small flowers are yellowish or mauve, veined with purple, less than half an inch long and peculiar in shape. The contrast in color between the flowers and leaves is very odd and very ugly, but as if this were not enough, later in the season the curious thing hangs itself with ridiculously long, slender pods, like great hooks, and looks queerer and more disheveled than ever.

Arizona Streptanthus
Streptánthus Arizònicus
White
Spring
Arizona

Prettier and not so queer-looking as the last. The leaves are arrow-shaped, clasping at base, rather leathery, bluish-green, with a "bloom" and tinged with purple on the backs, the lower ones toothed, and the pods are about two inches long, flat and tinged with purple. The flowers are

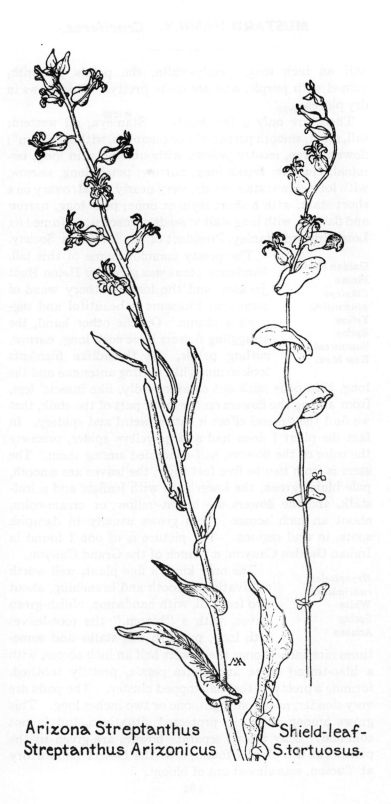

Arizona Streptanthus
Streptanthus Arizonicus

Shield-leaf-
S. tortuosus.

half an inch long, pearly-white, the petals yellowish, veined with purple, and are quite pretty. This grows in dry places.

There are only a few kinds of Stanleya, all western; tall, stout, smooth perennials, or biennials, with a "bloom"; flowers large, mostly yellow, without bracts, in long, terminal, clusters; sepals long, narrow; petals long, narrow, with long claws; stamens six, very nearly equal; ovary on a short stalk, with a short style or none; pods long, narrow and flattish, with long stalks; seeds numerous. Named for Lord Edward Stanley, President of the Linnaean Society.

Golden Prince's Plume
Stánleya pinnatífida
Yellow
Spring
Southwest and New Mex.

The pretty common name of this tall, handsome plant was given by Helen Hunt Jackson and the long, feathery wand of numerous blossoms is beautiful and suggests a plume. On the other hand, the straggling flowers have such long, narrow, curling petals, the threadlike filaments look so much like curling antennae and the long, thin pods stick out so awkwardly, like insects' legs, from among the flowers on the lower part of the stalk, that we find the general effect is rather weird and spidery. In fact the plant I drew had a large yellow spider, precisely the color of the flowers, half-concealed among them. The stem is from two to five feet high; the leaves are smooth, pale bluish-green, the lower ones with leaflets and a leaf-stalk, and the flowers are bright-yellow, or cream-color, about an inch across. This grows usually in dampish spots, in arid regions. The picture is of one I found in Indian Garden Canyon, a branch of the Grand Canyon.

Dryopétalon runcinátum
White
Spring
Arizona

The only kind, a fine plant, well worth cultivation; smooth and branching, about two feet tall, with handsome, bluish-green leaves, with a "bloom," the root-leaves with long, purplish leaf-stalks and sometimes nine inches long; the flowers half an inch across, with a lilac-tinged calyx and white petals, prettily toothed, forming a pretty, rather flat-topped cluster. The pods are very slender, nearly straight, one or two inches long. This grows among rocks, in protected situations, and is not common. Only a few, separate flowers are given in the picture, as the plant I found, near the Desert Laboratory at Tucson, was almost out of bloom.

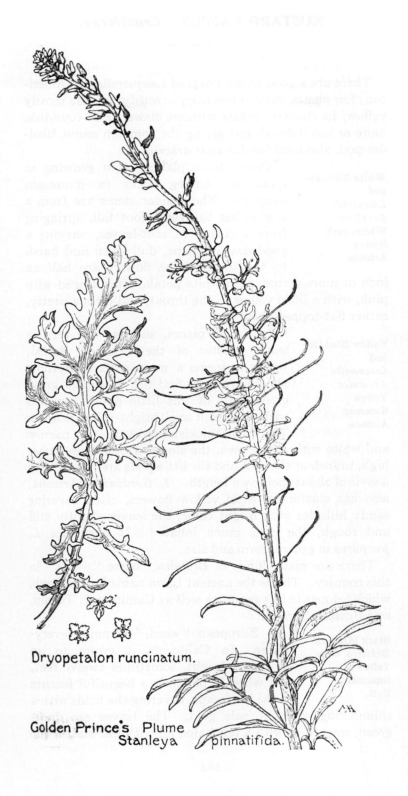

Dryopetalon runcinatum.

Golden Prince's Plume
Stanleya pinnatifida.

There are a good many kinds of Lesquerella, all American; low plants, more or less hairy or scurfy; flowers mostly
yellow, in clusters; petals without claws; pods roundish,
more or less inflated, and giving the common name, Bladder-pod, also used for *Isomeris arborea.*

**White Bladder-
pod**
*Lesquerélla
purpùrea*
White, pink
Spring
Arizona

Pretty little plants, often growing in
quantities among rocks in mountain
canyons. The slender stems are from a
few inches to over a foot tall, springing
from a cluster of root-leaves, varying a
good deal in shape, dull-green and harsh
to the touch. The flowers are half an
inch or more across, with white petals, often tinged with
pink, with a little yellow in the throat, and form a pretty,
rather flat-topped cluster.

**Yellow Bladder-
pod**
*Lesquerélla
Arizónica*
Yellow
Summer
Arizona

In desert places, such as the terrible
sandy wastes of the Petrified Forest,
where it seems a miracle that anything
should grow, we find the close, pale, gray-
green tufts of this little plant, crowned
with racemes of small bright-yellow flowers.
The small, thickish leaves are long, narrow
and white with close down, the stems, about three inches
high, branch at the root and the little pods are tipped with
a style of about their own length. *L. Gordóni,* of Arizona,
also has clusters of little yellow flowers, often covering
sandy hillsides with bright color; the leaves slightly stiff
and rough, the pods much inflated. It resembles *L.
purpurea* in general form and size.

There are many kinds of Brassica, coarse "weeds" in
this country. This is the ancient Latin name for Cabbage,
which belongs to this genus, as well as Cauliflower, Turnip,
and Brussels Sprouts.

Black Mustard
Brássica nìgra
Yellow
Summer
U. S.

A European "weed," common everywhere. In California it grows to an
enormous height, sometimes twelve feet,
and when in bloom is a beautiful feature
of the landscape, covering the fields with a
shimmering sheet of pale gold. The leaves are dark-
green, smooth or with a few hairs, all with leaf-stalks, the

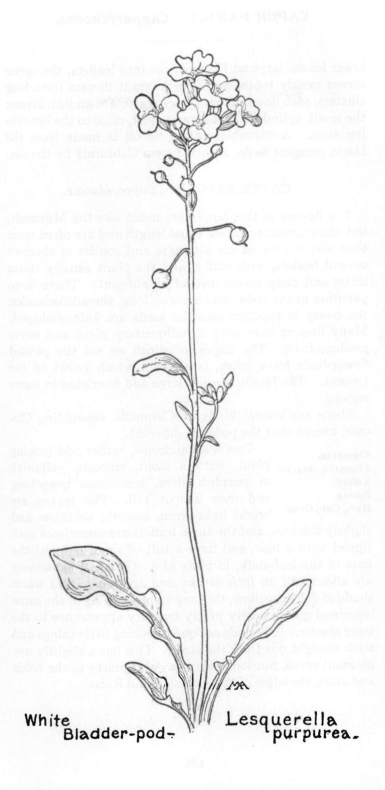

White
Bladder-pod—

Lesquerella
purpurea.

---

lower leaves large and jagged, cut into leaflets, the upper leaves mostly toothless. The fragrant flowers form long clusters, each flower about three-quarters of an inch across; the small, cylindrical pods stand erect, close to the branching stem. A valuable, antiseptic oil is made from the black, pungent seeds, exported from California by the ton.

CAPER FAMILY. *Capparidaceae.*

The flowers of this family are much like the Mustards, but the stamens are all of equal length and are often more than six; the leaves are alternate and consist of three or several leaflets, with stalks, and the plant usually tastes bitter and disagreeable instead of pungent. There is no partition in the pods, which are on long, threadlike stalks; the ovary is superior and the seeds are kidney-shaped. Many flowers have only a rudimentary pistil and never produce fruit. The Caper, of which we eat the pickled flower-buds for a relish, is a shrub which grows in the Levant. The family is quite large and flourishes in warm regions.

There are several kinds of Cleomella, resembling Cleome, except that the pods are different.

Cleomella
Cleomélla lóngipes
Yellow
Spring
Nev., Cal., Oreg.

This is a handsome, rather odd-looking plant, with a stout, smooth, yellowish or purplish stem, sometimes branching and over a foot tall. The leaves are bright light-green, smooth, toothless and slightly thickish, and the three leaflets are sometimes each tipped with a hair, and have a tuft of small hairs at the base of the leaf-stalk, in place of a stipule. The flowers are about half an inch across, and are a beautiful warm shade of golden-yellow, the long stamens being of the same color and giving a very pretty feathery appearance to the large cluster. The pods are queer-looking little things and stick straight out from the stem. This has a slightly unpleasant smell, but looks very gay and pretty in the fields and along the edges of the mesas around Reno.

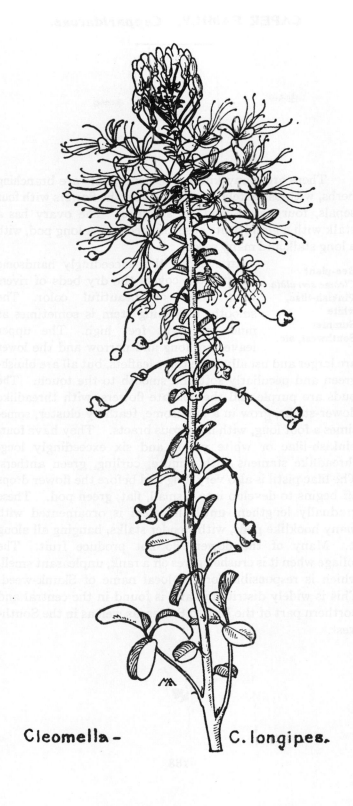

Cleomella - **C. longipes.**

CAPER FAMILY. *Capparidaceae.*

There are many kinds of Cleome; ours are branching herbs, with palmately-divided leaves; the flowers with four sepals, four petals, and six stamens. The ovary has a stalk with a gland at its base and becomes a long pod, with a long stalk and many seeds.

Bee-plant
Cleòme serrulàta
Pinkish-lilac,
white
Summer
Southwest, etc.

In Arizona this exceedingly handsome plant often covers the dry beds of rivers with acres of beautiful color. The smooth, branching stem is sometimes as much as eight feet high. The upper leaves are long and narrow and the lower are larger and usually have three leaflets, but all are bluish-green and peculiarly soft and smooth to the touch. The buds are purple and the delicate flowers, with threadlike flower-stalks, grow in a handsome, feathery cluster, sometimes a foot long, with numerous bracts. They have four, pinkish-lilac or white petals and six exceedingly long, threadlike stamens with minute, curling, green anthers. The lilac pistil is also very long and before the flower drops off begins to develop into a small, flat, green pod. These gradually lengthen, until the stem is ornamented with many hooklike pods, with slender stalks, hanging all along it. Many of the flowers do not produce fruit. The foliage when it is crushed gives off a rank, unpleasant smell, which is responsible for the local name of Skunk-weed. This is widely distributed and is found in the central and northern part of the United States, as well as in the Southwest.

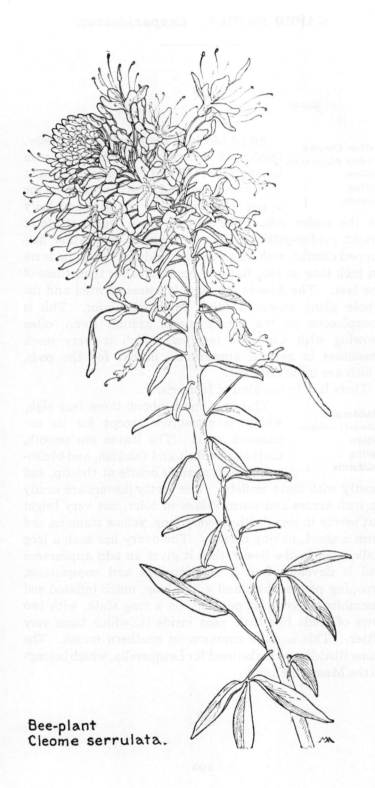

Bee-plant
Cleome serrulata.

CAPER FAMILY. *Capparidaceae.*

Yellow Cleome
Cleòme platycàrpa
Yellow
Spring
Nevada
An odd-looking plant, with very pretty, feathery flower-clusters. The hairy stem is over a foot tall and the leaves are bright yellowish-green and mostly smooth on the upper side, with hairy margins and hairy on the under side. The flowers are a warm shade of bright golden-yellow and form a handsome, rather flat-topped cluster, with long stamens, and the oblong pods are an inch long or less, flat and much broader than those of the last. The flowers are slightly sweet-scented and the whole plant exudes a faint unpleasant odor. This is conspicuous on the dreary mesas around Reno, often growing with *Cleomella longipes*, which it very much resembles in general appearance, except for the pods, which are quite different.

There is only one kind of Isomeris.

Bladderpod
Isómeris arbòrea
Yellow
Spring
California
This is a shrub about three feet high, which is attractive except for its unpleasant smell. The leaves are smooth, toothless, stiffish and thickish, and bluish-green, with a small bristle at the tip, and mostly with three leaflets. The pretty flowers are nearly an inch across and warm yellow in color, not very bright but pretty in tone, with six very long, yellow stamens, and form a short, oblong cluster. The ovary has such a long stalk, even in the flower, that it gives an odd appearance and it develops into a very curious and conspicuous, drooping pod, an inch and a half long, much inflated and resembling a very fat pea-pod, on a long stalk, with two rows of seeds like little peas inside it, which taste very bitter. This is quite common on southern mesas. The name Bladderpod is also used for Lesquerella, which belongs to the Mustard Family.

Bladderpod— Isomeris arborea.

ORPINE FAMILY. *Crassulaceae.*

A rather large family, widely distributed; odd-looking, mostly very succulent herbs, with smooth, fleshy leaves and stems, without stipules; flowers in clusters; sepals, petals, pistils, and stamens, all of the same number, usually four or five, sometimes the stamens twice as many; ovary superior; receptacle with honey-bearing scales, one behind each pistil; pistils separate, developing into small dry pods, containing few or many, minute seeds. Some of these plants look like tiny cabbages and we are all familiar with their tight little rosettes in the formal garden-beds of hotels and railway stations, where they are so stiff and unattractive that we hardly recognize them when we find them looking exceedingly pretty in their natural homes. The Latin name means "thick."

There are many kinds of Sedum, no one kind very widely distributed; fleshy herbs; leaves usually alternate; flowers star-like, often in one-sided clusters; stamens and pistils sometimes in different flowers on different plants; sepals and petals four or five; stamens eight or ten, on the calyx, the alternate ones usually attached to the petals; styles usually short. The Latin name means "to sit," because these plants squat on the ground, and Stonecrop is from their fondness for rocks.

Douglas Stonecrop
Sèdum Douglásii
Yellow
Spring, summer
Northwest

This makes beautiful golden patches, on dry slopes or more or less open hilltops, usually among limestone rocks. The reddish stems are from six to ten inches tall, the leaves are rather long and narrow, thick but flat, forming pretty pale-green rosettes, more or less tinged with pink and yellow, and the pretty starry flowers are three-quarters of an inch across, bright-yellow, with greenish centers, the stamens giving a feathery appearance.

Yosemite Stonecrop
Sèdum
Yosemitènse
Yellow
Summer
California

On moss-covered rocks, moistened by the glistening spray blowing from the Yosemite waterfalls, we find these beautiful plants, covering the stones with a brilliant, many-colored carpet. The flowers are stars of brightest gold, about half an inch across and delicately scented, and form flat-topped clusters, three or four inches across.

Douglas Stone-crop
S. Douglasii

Yosemite Stonecrop-
Sedum Yosemitense.

The upper part of the stalk, which is about six inches tall, and the upper leaves are delicate bluish-green, but both stem and leaves shade to vivid scarlet at the base. Spreading out on the ground from the base of the stem in all directions are numerous little runners, each bearing at the end a small rosette of thick, blue-green leaves, forming a beautiful contrast to the vivid color of flowers and stems. The leaves and runners are very brittle and break off at a touch.

There are several kinds of Dudleya; perennials, very thick and fleshy; root-leaves in a conspicuous rosette, stem-leaves mostly bract-like, usually with a broad, clasping base; flowers mostly yellow or reddish; calyx conspicuous, with five lobes; petals united at base; stamens ten. Most of these plants grow in the South, often on rocks, in such shallow soil, that they would die in dry weather, except that the juicy leaves retain their moisture for a long time and nourish the plant. They resemble Sedum in appearance, but as the petals are more or less united the flowers are not starlike. The Indians make poultices out of the leaves.

Hen-and-Chickens
Dúdleya Nevadénsis (Cotyledon)
Orange-red
Summer
California

The succulent, reddish flower-stalks of this handsome plant bear large, loose, rather flat-topped clusters of orange-red flowers, on coiling branches, and are about a foot tall, with scaly bracts, springing from a large handsome rosette on the ground of very thick, pale-green leaves, often tinged with pink. Other smaller rosettes form a circle around it, hence its nice little common name. *D. pulverulénta (Echeveria)* is beautiful but weird-looking. It has red flowers, and the rosette, resembling a small Century-plant, is covered all over with a white powder which, among ordinary herbage, gives an exceedingly striking and ghostlike effect. This plant is sometimes a foot and a half across, with as many as eight, tall stalks, and is found from San Diego to Santa Barbara.

Hen-and-Chickens- Dudleya Nevadensis.

SAXIFRAGE FAMILY. *Saxifragaceae.*

A large family, almost all herbs, living usually in temperate regions. They have no very peculiar characteristics and resemble the Rose Family, but sometimes their leaves are opposite, usually they have no stipules and have fewer stamens than Roses, not more than twice as many as the sepals, and usually the pistils, from two to five in number, with distinct styles, are united to form a compound ovary, which is superior or partly inferior; sepals usually five; petals four, five, or rarely none, alternate with the sepals; petals and stamens borne on the calyx; fruit a dry pod or berry, containing numerous seeds. The Latin name means "rock breaker," as many grow among rocks.

There are several kinds of Parnassia, of north temperate and arctic regions; smooth perennials; leaves toothless, almost all from the root; flowers single; sepals five; petals five, each with a cluster of sterile filaments, tipped with glands, at the base; fertile stamens five, alternate with the petals; ovary superior, or partly inferior, with a very short style, or none, usually with four stigmas; fruit a capsule, containing numerous winged seeds. These plants were called Grass of Parnassus by Dioscorides, but are not grass-like. They resemble the other members of this family so little that they have been made into a separate family by some botanists.

Grass of Parnassus
Parnássia fimbriàta
White
Summer
Northwest

A charming plant, with several slender stems, about a foot tall, springing from a large cluster of handsome, very smooth, glossy leaves. The flowers are about an inch across and have cream-white petals, delicately veined with green and prettily fringed towards the base, and pale yellow anthers. At the base of each petal there is a queer little stiff cluster of sterile filaments, like a tiny green hand. This grows on banks of streams and in moist places, reaching an altitude of eleven thousand feet. *P. Californica* is similar, but the petals not fringed.

There are several kinds of Leptasea, perennials, with alternate, thick or stiffish leaves; flowers white or yellow, single or in terminal clusters; sepals five; petals five, with claws or claw-like bases; stamens ten; ovary mostly superior.

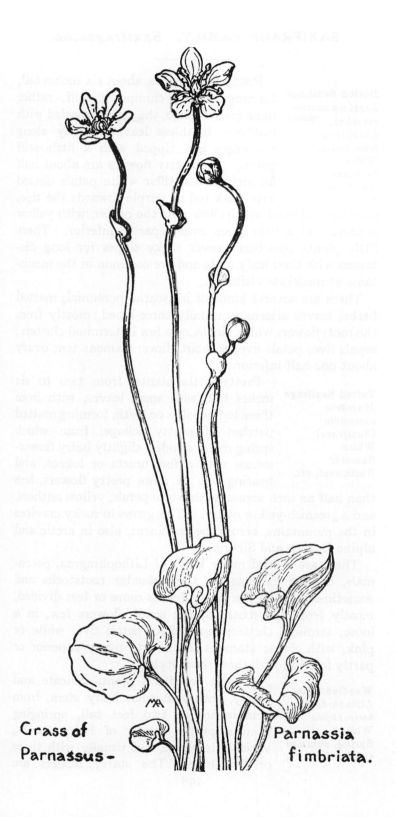

Grass of
Parnassus-

Parnassia
fimbriata.

SAXIFRAGE FAMILY. *Saxifragaceae.*

Dotted Saxifrage
Leptàsea austro-montàna.
(*Saxifraga bronchialis*)
White
Summer
Northwest

Pretty little plants, about six inches tall, forming matted clumps of stiff, rather dark green foliage, the twigs crowded with leathery, toothless leaves, bristly along the edges and tipped with a little stiff point. The pretty flowers are about half an inch across, their white petals dotted with dark red or purple towards the tips, sometimes dotted with yellow near the center, with yellow anthers and a pale green ovary, partly inferior. These little plants sometimes cover rocky slopes for long distances with their leafy mats and are common in the mountains at moderate altitudes.

There are several kinds of Muscaria, perennial, matted herbs; leaves alternate, usually three-lobed, mostly from the root; flowers white, single, or a few in terminal clusters; sepals five; petals five, without claws; stamens ten; ovary about one-half inferior.

Tufted Saxifrage
Muscària caespitòsa
(*Saxifraga*)
White
Summer
Northwest, etc.

Pretty little plants, from two to six inches tall, with small leaves, with from three to five lobes or teeth, forming matted patches of pretty foliage, from which spring many slender, slightly hairy flower-stems, with a few bracts or leaves, and bearing one or more pretty flowers, less than half an inch across, with white petals, yellow anthers, and a greenish-yellow ovary. This grows in rocky crevices in the mountains, across the continent, also in arctic and alpine Europe and Siberia.

There are a good many kinds of Lithophragma, perennials, bearing bulblets on their slender rootstocks and sometimes also on the stems; leaves more or less divided, mostly from the root; stipules small; flowers few, in a loose, terminal cluster; sepals five; petals five, white or pink, with claws; stamens ten, short; ovary superior or partly inferior, with three short styles.

Woodland Star
Lithophrágma heterophýlla
White
Spring, summer
California

A little woodland plant, delicate and pretty, with a slender, hairy stem, from nine inches to two feet tall, springing from a pretty cluster of hairy leaves, variable in shape, but usually with three or five lobes. The starry flowers are

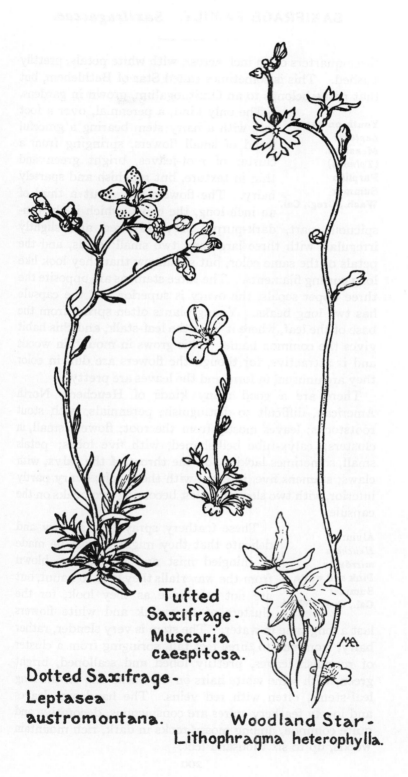

Tufted
Saxifrage-
Muscaria
caespitosa.

Dotted Saxifrage-
Leptasea
austromontana.

Woodland Star-
Lithophragma heterophylla.

three-quarters of an inch across, with white petals, prettily slashed. This is sometimes called Star of Bethlehem, but that name belongs to an Ornithogalum, grown in gardens.

Youth-on-age
Leptáxis
Menziěsii.
(Tolmiea)
Purplish
Summer
Wash., Oreg., Cal.

The only kind, a perennial, over a foot tall, with a hairy stem bearing a graceful wand of small flowers, springing from a cluster of root-leaves, bright green and thin in texture, but roughish and sparsely hairy. The flowers are about a third of an inch long, the calyx, which is the conspicuous part, dark-purple or pinkish-red and slightly irregular, with three large and two small sepals, and the petals of the same color, but so narrow that they look like long curling filaments. The three stamens are opposite the three upper sepals, the ovary is superior and the capsule has two long beaks. Young plants often spring from the base of the leaf, where it joins the leaf-stalk, and this habit gives the common name. This grows in mountain woods and is attractive, for though the flowers are dull in color they are unusual in form and the leaves are pretty.

There are a good many kinds of Heuchera, North American, difficult to distinguish; perennials, with stout rootstocks; leaves mostly from the root; flowers small, in clusters; calyx-tube bell-shaped, with five lobes; petals small, sometimes lacking, on the throat of the calyx, with claws; stamens five, inserted with the petals; ovary partly inferior, with two slender styles, becoming two beaks on the capsule.

Alumroot
Heuchèra
micrántha
Pink and white
Summer
Cal., Oreg., Wash.

These feathery sprays are so airy and delicate that they might almost be made of mingled mist and moonshine, blown from the waterfalls they love to haunt, but are not so fragile as they look, for the clusters of tiny pink and white flowers last a long time in water. The stem is very slender, rather hairy, from one to three feet tall, springing from a cluster of roundish leaves, prettily lobed and scalloped, bright green, with some white hairs on the backs and on the long leaf-stems, often with red veins. The handsome leaves and lovely feathery spires are conspicuous, decorative and quite common, among mossy rocks in dark, rich mountain woods, up to six thousand feet.

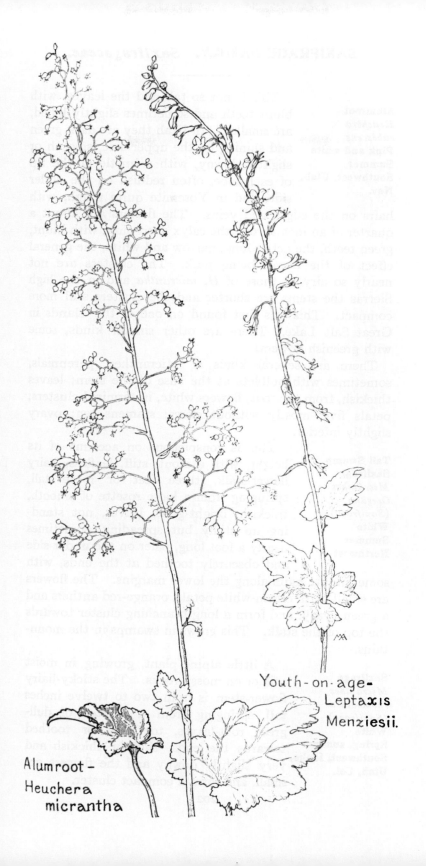

Youth-on-age-
Leptaxis
Menziesii.

Alumroot-
Heuchera
micrantha

SAXIFRAGE FAMILY. *Saxifragaceae.*

Alumroot
Heuchèra
rubéscens
Pink and white
Summer
Southwest, Utah,
Nev.

This is not so tall and the leaves, with blunt teeth and sometimes slightly lobed, are smaller. In Utah they are dark green and shining on the upper side, smooth or slightly downy, with a bristle at the tip of each lobe, often reddish on the under side, and in Yosemite quite rough, with hairs on the edges and veins. The flowers are about a quarter of an inch across, the calyx deep-pink, with blunt, green teeth, the petals long, narrow and white, the general effect of the flower being pink. The clusters are not nearly so airy as those of *H. micrantha* and in the high Sierras the stems are shorter and the clusters still more compact. This was first found on one of the islands in Great Salt Lake. There are other similar kinds, some with greenish flowers.

There are several kinds of Micranthes, perennials, sometimes with bulblets at the base of the stem; leaves thickish, from the root; flowers white, in terminal clusters; petals five, mostly without claws; stamens ten; ovary slightly inferior.

Tall Swamp
Saxifrage
Micránthes
Oregàna
(Saxifraga)
White
Summer
Northwest

This is conspicuous on account of its height, with a stout, stiff, leafless, hairy flower-stalk, three feet or more tall, springing from a loose rosette of smooth, thickish, bright-green leaves, not standing up stiffly but spreading, sometimes nearly a foot long, paler on the under side and obscurely toothed at the ends, with some minute hairs along the lower margins. The flowers are small, with cream-white petals, orange-red anthers and a green ovary, and form a long branching cluster towards the top of the stalk. This grows in swamps in the mountains.

Saxifrage
Micránthes
rhomboídea
(Saxifraga)
White
Spring, summer
Southwest, Idaho,
Utah, Col.

A little alpine plant, growing in moist soil, or on mossy rocks. The sticky-hairy flower-stem is from two to twelve inches tall, springing from a cluster of dull-green root-leaves, toothless, or toothed towards the ends, slightly thickish and very slightly downy and the flowers are small, and form a compact cluster.

202

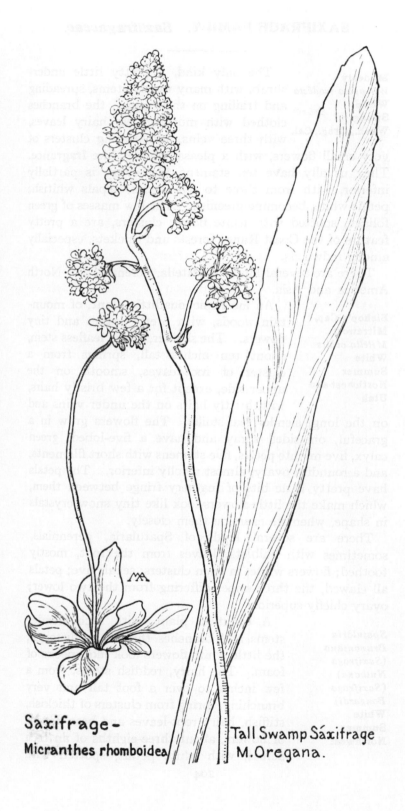

Saxifrage-
Micranthes rhomboidea

Tall Swamp Sáxifrage
M.Oregana.

SAXIFRAGE FAMILY. *Saxifragaceae.*

Modesty
Whipplea modésta
White
Spring
Wash., Oreg., Cal.

The only kind, a pretty little under-shrub, with many woody stems, spreading and trailing on the ground, the branches clothed with more or less hairy leaves, with three veins, and bearing clusters of very small flowers, with a pleasant honey-like fragrance. They usually have ten stamens, the ovary is partially inferior, with from three to five styles; sepals whitish; petals white, becoming greenish. The low masses of green foliage, spotted with white flower clusters, are a pretty feature of the Coast Range forests and thickets, especially among redwoods.

There are several kinds of Mitella, perennials, of North America and Asia.

Bishop's Cap,
Mitrewort
Mitélla ovális
White
Summer
Northwest and Utah

An inconspicuous little plant, of mountain woods, with pretty leaves and tiny flowers. The slender, hairy, leafless stem, about ten inches tall, springs from a cluster of root-leaves, smooth on the upper side, except for a few bristly hairs, with bristly hairs on the under veins and on the long, slender leaf-stalks. The flowers grow in a graceful, one-sided spray and have a five-lobed, green calyx, five minute petals, five stamens with short filaments, and a roundish ovary, almost wholly inferior. The petals have pretty little bits of feathery fringe between them, which make the little flowers look like tiny snow crystals in shape, when we examine them closely.

There are several kinds of Spatularia, perennials, sometimes with bulblets; leaves from the root, mostly toothed; flowers white, in open clusters; sepals five; petals all clawed, the three upper differing from the two lower; ovary chiefly superior.

Spatulària
Brunoniàna
(Saxifraga
Nutkana)
(Saxifraga
Bongardi)
White
Summer
Northwest

A beautiful plant, with such slender stems and branches that, at a distance, the little white flowers look like specks of foam. The hairy, reddish stems, from a few inches to over a foot tall and very branching, spring from clusters of thickish, stiffish, hairy root-leaves and bear dozens of flowers, about three-eighths of an inch across, with white petals, spotted with

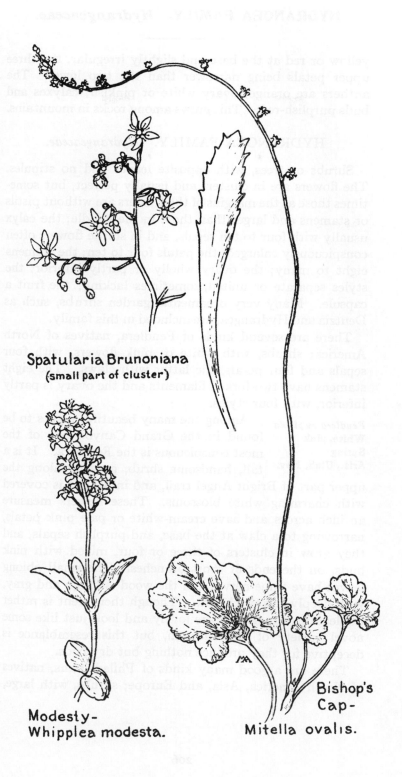

Spatularia Brunoniana
(small part of cluster)

Modesty-
Whipplea modesta.

Bishop's
Cap-
Mitella ovalis.

yellow or red at the base and slightly irregular, the three upper petals being narrower than the two lower. The anthers are orange; ovary white or pinkish; calyxes and buds purplish-red. This grows among rocks in mountains.

HYDRANGEA FAMILY. *Hydrangeaceae.*

Shrubs or trees, with opposite leaves and no stipules. The flowers are in clusters and usually perfect, but sometimes those at the margins of the clusters are without pistils or stamens and larger than those in the middle; the calyx usually with four to ten sepals, and in sterile flowers often conspicuously enlarged; the petals four to ten; the stamens eight to many; the ovary wholly or partly inferior; the styles separate or united, sometimes lacking; the fruit a capsule. Many very ornamental garden shrubs, such as Deutzia and Hydrangea, are included in this family.

There are several kinds of Fendlera, natives of North America; shrubs, with white or pink flowers, with four sepals and four petals, the latter with claws. The eight stamens have two-forked filaments and the ovary is partly inferior, with four styles.

Féndlera rupícola
White, pink
Spring
Ariz., Utah, Nev.

Among the many beautiful plants to be found in the Grand Canyon one of the most conspicuous is the Fendlera. It is a tall, handsome shrub, growing along the upper part of Bright Angel trail, and in May it is covered with charming white blossoms. These flowers measure an inch across, and have cream-white or pale pink petals, narrowing to a claw at the base, and purplish sepals, and they grow in clusters of three or four, mixed with pink buds, on the ends of short branches. The small oblong leaves have three nerves and the wood is tough and gray, with deeply furrowed bark. Though their scent is rather unpleasant, the flowers are lovely and look just like some novel variety of fruit-blossom, but this resemblance is deceptive for they produce nothing but dry pods.

There are a good many kinds of Philadelphus, natives of North America, Asia, and Europe; shrubs, with large,

Fendlera rupicola.

HYDRANGEA FAMILY. *Hydrangeaceae.*

white or cream-colored flowers; the calyx top-shaped, with four or five lobes; the petals four or five; the stamens twenty to forty, inserted on a disk; the ovary inferior, with three to five styles; the capsule top-shaped, containing many oblong seeds. These plants were named in honor of King Ptolemy Philadelphus. They are often called Mock-Orange, because the flowers often resemble orange-blossoms. The commonest name, Syringa, is confusing, because that is the generic name of the Lilac.

Syringa
Philadélphus
Calijórnicus
White
Summer
Cal., Oreg., Wash.

In June and July, in the high Sierras, up to an altitude of four thousand feet, this lovely shrub forms fragrant thickets of bloom. It looks very much like the familiar garden Syringa and the smell is just as delicious. The bush is from four to twelve feet high, with smooth, pale, woody stems, dark-green leaves, sometimes slightly toothed, very smooth and shiny, and pretty flowers, in clusters at the ends of the branches. They are each about an inch across, with four or five, cream-white petals, rolled in the bud, and a golden center, composed of numerous, bright-yellow stamens.

Small Syringa
Philadélphus
microphýllus
White
Summer
Ariz., Cal.,
New Mex.

A small shrub, not nearly so handsome as the last, from two to three feet high, with slender, pale-gray, woody stems, branching very abruptly. The small leaves are smooth and very bright green on the upper side, but the under side is very pale and covered with close white down. The flowers are much smaller than the garden Syringa, with white petals and numerous yellow stamens, the calyx reddish outside and downy within, and have a delicious smell, like lemon-blossoms. This pretty little shrub may be found growing in small shady canyons, in northern Arizona and elsewhere in the Southwest.

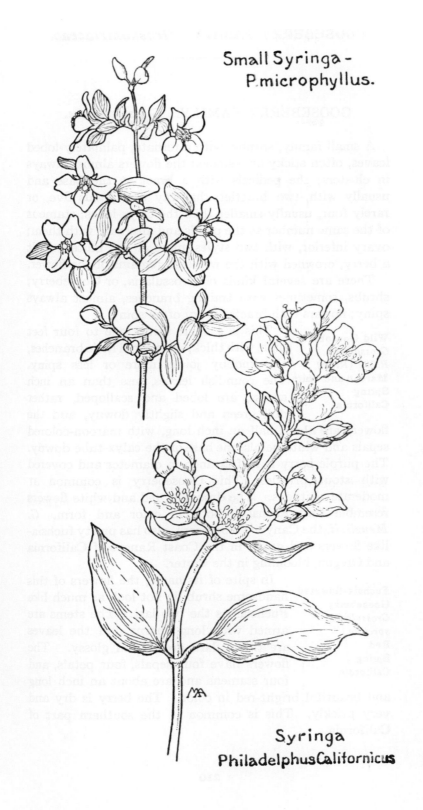

Small Syringa -
P.microphyllus.

Syringa
Philadelphus Californicus

GOOSEBERRY FAMILY. *Grossulariaceae.*

A small family, shrubs, with alternate, palmately-lobed leaves, often sticky or resinous; the flowers almost always in clusters; the pedicels with a bract at the base and usually with two bractlets halfway up; petals five, or rarely four, usually smaller than the calyx-lobes; stamens of the same number as the petals and alternate with them; ovary inferior, with two styles, more or less united; fruit a berry, crowned with the withered remains of the flower.

There are several kinds of Grossularia, or Gooseberry; shrubs, sometimes with trailing branches, almost always spiny; flowers with bracts; ovary often spiny.

Wild Gooseberry
Grossulària
Roèzli (Ribes)
Maroon and white
Spring
California

This is a stout shrub, one to four feet high, with thick, short, rigid little branches, the knobby joints more or less spiny. The roundish leaves, less than an inch across, are lobed and scalloped, rather dull green and slightly downy, and the flowers are about half an inch long, with maroon-colored sepals and white petals, the base of the calyx-tube downy. The purple berry is half an inch in diameter and covered with stout prickles. This Gooseberry is common at moderate altitudes. The drooping, red and white flowers resemble tiny Fuchsias, both in color and form. *G. Menzièsii,* the Canyon Gooseberry, also has pretty fuchsia-like flowers and grows in the Coast Ranges of California and Oregon, blooming in the winter.

Fuchsia-flowered
Gooseberry
Grossulària
speciòsa
Red
Spring
California

In spite of its name, the flowers of this handsome shrub do not look as much like Fuchsias as the two last. The stems are armed with long thorns and the leaves are thick, dark green, and glossy. The flowers have four sepals, four petals, and four stamens and are about an inch long and beautiful bright-red in color. The berry is dry and very prickly. This is common in the southern part of California.

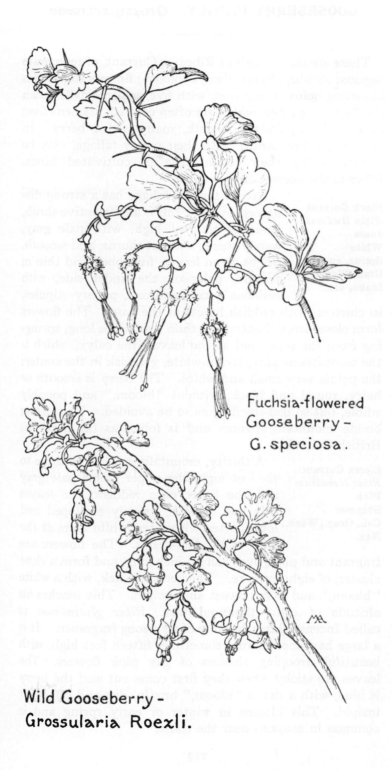

Fuchsia-flowered
Gooseberry—
G. speciosa.

Wild Gooseberry—
Grossularia Roexli.

GOOSEBERRY FAMILY. *Grossulariaceae.*

There are many kinds of Ribes, or Currant, of temperate regions; shrubs, almost always smooth; flowers sometimes blooming before the leaves, with five petals, smaller than the five calyx-lobes, which are often colored; stamens five; ovary inferior, fruit a smooth, many-seeded berry. In general the low shrubs, with their pretty foliage, may be recognized by their resemblance to cultivated kinds. Ribes is the ancient Arabic name.

Black Currant
Rìbes Hudsoni-
ànum
White
Spring, summer
Utah, Wash.,
Idaho, etc.

Except that its foliage has a strong disagreeable smell, this is an attractive shrub, three to six feet high, with pale gray, woody stems, without thorns, and smooth, bright green leaves, five-lobed and thin in texture, paler on the under side, with resinous dots and broad, papery stipules, in clusters, with reddish bracts at the base. The flowers form close, erect clusters, less than two inches long, springing from the same bud as the leaves; the calyx, which is the conspicuous part, cream-white, greenish in the center; the petals very small and white. The berry is smooth or hairy, round and black, without "bloom," and possibly edible, but so bad-smelling as to be avoided. This grows beside mountain streams and is found as far north as British Columbia.

Sierra Currant
Rìbes Nevadénse
Pink
Summer
Cal., Oreg., Wash.,
Nev.

A thrifty, mountain bush, from three to six feet high, the upper stems pale gray and the lower ones reddish; the leaves thin and smooth, prettily scalloped and lobed, often with a few white hairs at the base of the leaf-stalks. The flowers are fragrant and pink, over half an inch long, and form a close cluster, of eight or more. The berry is black, with a white "bloom," and tastes sweet and insipid. This reaches an altitude of eight thousand feet. *Rìbes glutinòsum* is called Incense-shrub, because of its strong fragrance. It is a large handsome shrub, sometimes fifteen feet high, with beautiful drooping clusters of gay pink flowers. The leaves are sticky when they first come out and the berry is blue, with a dense "bloom," bristly, dry and bitter, or insipid. This blooms in winter or early spring and is common in canyons near the coast.

Sierra Currant-
Ribes
Nevadense

Black
Currant-
R.Hudsonianum.

APPLE FAMILY. *Pomaceae.*

Golden, Missouri or Buffalo Currant
Ribes aureum
Yellow
Spring, summer
West, etc.

A very handsome bush, from five to twelve feet high, with pretty foliage and smooth, pinkish-gray, woody stems. The bright green leaves, with three or five lobes, are thin in texture, with a few hairs on the leaf-stalks, fresh and glossy-looking, and setting off the bright clusters of clear yellow flowers, of which the calyx, half an inch across, with a long greenish-yellow tube, is the conspicuous part. The small petals are sometimes yellow, but often bright red and the fruit is smooth, yellow, red, or black, and edible. This is deliciously fragrant and spicy, very handsome and attractive, growing beside brooks and in moist canyons, where sometimes, in masses, it has at a distance the effect of Forsythia, but purer in color. It grows as far east as Missouri and is often cultivated.

APPLE FAMILY. *Pomaceae.*

A rather large family, widely distributed, including many attractive trees and shrubs, such as Mountain Ash and Hawthorn, as well as Pears and Apples, with pretty blossoms and conspicuous, often edible fruits; leaves alternate; stipules small; flowers regular, perfect, single or in clusters; calyx usually five-toothed or five-lobed; petals mostly five, usually with claws; stamens numerous, or rarely few, separate, with small anthers; ovary inferior and compound; styles one to five. The calyx-tube gradually thickens and becomes a "pome," or apple-like fruit, in which the core is the ovary.

There are several kinds of Amelanchier, of the north temperate zone; shrubs or trees, with thornless branches and white flowers, usually in clusters; calyx-tube bell-shaped, with five narrow sepals; petals five; stamens numerous, on the throat of the calyx; styles two to five in number, united and hairy at base; ovary wholly or partly inferior; fruit small and berry-like. The name is from the French for the Medlar. These shrubs are called Shad-bush in the East, because they bloom just when the shad are beginning to run in the rivers.

Golden Currant — Ribes aureum.

PLUM FAMILY. *Drupaceae.*

Service-berry, June-berry
Amelánchier alnifólia
White
Spring, summer
West, etc.

A pretty shrub with woody, branching stems, reddish twigs and smooth, bright green leaves, sometimes downy on the under side, toothed only at the ends. The flowers, less than an inch across, have long, narrow, straggling petals, and are so mixed with leaves, and crowded so irregularly on the branches, that the effect is rather ragged. The roundish, pulpy, black fruit is liked by the Indians, but though sweet is insipid. When thickets of this shrub are in bloom on mountainsides the effect is very pretty, especially in Utah, where the shrubs are more compact and the flowers less straggling than in Yosemite, giving at a distance much the effect of Hawthorn. It grows as far east as Nebraska and in British Columbia.

PLUM FAMILY. *Drupaceae.*

A rather small family, widely distributed, trees or shrubs, the bark exuding gum, the foliage, bark, and seeds bitter, containing prussic acid; leaves alternate, toothed, with leaf-stalks; stipules small; flowers mostly perfect, regular, single or in clusters; calyx five-lobed, dropping off after flowering; petals five, inserted on the calyx; stamens numerous, inserted with the petals; pistil one in our genera; ovary superior, developing into a stone-fruit.

There are many kinds of Prunus, including Cherry as well as Plum, with white or pink flowers and usually edible fruits. Prunus is the ancient Latin name for plum.

Holly-leaved Cherry, Islay
Prùnus ilicifòlia
White
Summer
California

Mountain slopes near Santa Barbara are beautiful in June with the creamy flowers of this very ornamental evergreen shrub, from five to twenty-five feet high, with shiny, leathery, dark green leaves, with prickly edges, looking much like Holly. The small flowers form close but feathery clusters, from one to three inches long, and smell pleasantly of honey. The sweetish fruit, not particularly good to eat, is a dark red cherry, about half an inch in diameter. In dry places these shrubs are small, but in favorable situations, such as the old mission gardens, where they have been growing for perhaps a hundred years, they develop into small trees.

Islay -
Prunus ilicifolia.

Service-berry -
Amelanchier alnifolia.

ROSE FAMILY. *Rosaceae.*

A large and important family, widely distributed and including some of our loveliest flowers and most delicious fruits; herbs, shrubs, or trees; generally with stipules and usually with alternate leaves; the flowers rich in pollen and honey and usually perfect. The calyx usually five-lobed, often with bracts, with a disk adhering to its base; the petals of the same number as the calyx-lobes, separate or none; the stamens usually numerous, separate, with small anthers; the ovary superior, or partly inferior; the pistils few or many, separate or adhering to the calyx, sometimes, as in the true Rose, enclosed and concealed in a hollow receptacle; the fruit of various kinds and shapes.

There are several kinds of Opulaster, branching shrubs, with clusters of white flowers and grayish or reddish, shreddy bark.

Ninebark
Opuláster
malváceus
(Physocarpus)
White
Summer
Northwest, Utah,
Ariz.

This is a handsome bush, from three to six feet high, with pretty, almost smooth, bright green leaves, with large stipules. The flowers are sweet-smelling, about half an inch across, with cream-white petals, and form very beautiful and conspicuous rounded clusters, about three inches across, the long stamens giving a very feathery appearance. At a distance this shrub has the effect of Hawthorn in the landscape. It grows on mountainsides in rich soil.

Apache Plume
Fallùgia paradóxa
White
Spring
Ariz., New Mex.

There are two kinds of Fallugia. This is usually a low undershrub, but in the Grand Canyon, on the plateau, it is a fine bush, four or five feet high, with pale woody, branching stems; the small, some-what downy, evergreen leaves, resembling those of the Cliff Rose, but the flowers larger. They are white, two inches across, like a Wild Rose in shape, with beautiful golden centers, and grow on long, slender, downy flower-stalks, at the ends of the branches. Individually, they are handsomer than the flowers of the Cliff Rose, but not nearly so effective, as the bloom is much more scattered. The calyx-tube is downy inside and the five sepals alternate with five, small, long, narrow bractlets. The hairy pistils are on a small

Ninebark—   Opulaster malvaceus.

conical receptacle, surrounded by a triple row of very numerous stamens on the margin of the calyx-tube.

Wild Roses are widely distributed in the northern hemisphere and are too familiar to need much description. There are numerous kinds; some are climbing, all are prickly and thorny, with handsome, often fragrant, flowers and compound leaves, with toothed edges. The numerous yellow stamens are on the thick margin of a silky disk, which nearly closes the mouth of the calyx. The numerous pistils develop into akenes, or small, dry, one-seeded fruits. These look like seeds and we find them inside the calyx-tube, which in ripening enlarges and becomes round or urn-shaped. These swollen calyx-tubes are the "hips," which turn scarlet and add so much to the beauty of the rose-bush when the flowers are gone. Rosa is the ancient Latin name.

Fendler's Rose
Ròsa Féndleri
Pink
Spring, summer
Idaho, Utah, Ariz.

This is a very handsome thrifty bush, about four feet high, with smooth, or slightly downy, bright green leaves, and thorny stems, with slightly curved thorns. The flowers are more or less fragrant and about two inches across, with bright pink petals, which gradually become paler as they fade, and pretty crimson-tipped buds. This has smooth "hips" and is a beautiful and conspicuous kind, growing in valleys and along streams, up to an altitude of nine thousand feet. It is widely distributed and variable, probably including several forms.

California Wild Rose
Ròsa Califórnica
Pink
Spring, summer, autumn
Cal., Oreg.

A large bush, three to six feet high, with erect, branching stems, armed with a few, stout thorns, which turn back. The leaves are more or less downy, especially on the under side, with from three to seven leaflets, and the flowers usually form a cluster of few or many and are each from one to nearly two inches across, with pale pink petals. They are lovely flowers, with a delicious fragrance, and are common at low and moderate altitudes in California, usually growing near streams.

Rosa Fendleri.

California Wild Rose- R.Californica.

ROSE FAMILY. *Rosaceae.*

Redwood Rose
Ròsa gymnocàrpa
Pink
Spring, summer
Northwest

A charming kind, delicate both in foliage and flower, usually growing in shady, mountain woods. The slender bush is from one to three feet high, with dark brown stems, armed with some straight, slender thorns, and light green leaves, usually with quite a number of neat little leaflets, smooth and thin in texture. The flowers are an inch or less across, usually single, with light yellow centers and bright pink petals, very clean and fresh in tone, usually deeper towards the margins. The sepals are not leafy at the tips, the flower-stalks, and sometimes the leaf-stalks also, are covered with small, dark, sticky hairs and the buds are tipped with carmine. Neither leaves nor flowers are fragrant.

Mountain Misery
Chamaebàtia
foliolòsa
White
Summer
California

This is the only kind. In open places, in the Sierra forests, the ground is often carpeted for acres with the feathery foliage of this charming shrub, sprinkled all over with pretty white flowers. Mountain Misery does not at first seem an appropriate name for so attractive a plant, but when we walk through the low, green thickets we find not only that the tangled branches catch our feet but that the whole plant is covered with a strong-smelling, resinous substance, which comes off on our clothes in a most disagreeable manner. On a warm day the forest is filled with the peculiar, medicinal fragrance and when, later in the season, we unpack our camping outfit we are apt to be puzzled by the smell of "Pond's Extract" which our clothes exhale. The shrub is usually less than two feet high, with downy, evergreen foliage, the numerous small leaflets so minutely subdivided and scalloped that they have the appearance of soft ferns. The flowers resemble large strawberry-blossoms, and have a top-shaped, five-lobed calyx, many yellow stamens and one pistil, becoming a large, leathery akene. The smell and foliage attract attention and the shrub has many names, such as Bear-mat and Kittikit, or Kit-kit-dizze, so-called by the Indians. Bears do not eat it, so the name Bear-clover is poor, and Tarweed belongs to another plant. It is used medicinally.

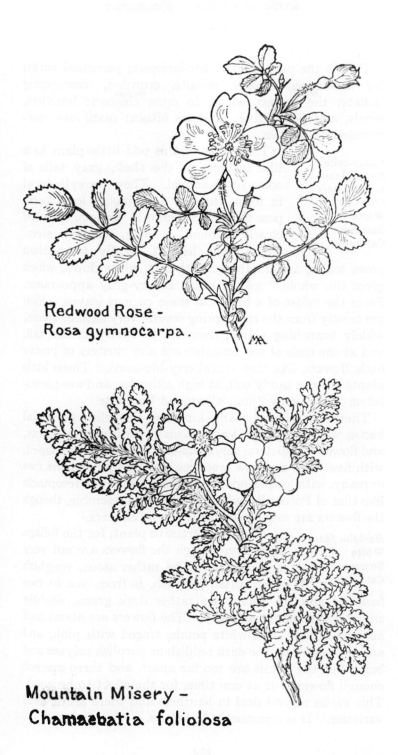

Redwood Rose -
Rosa gymnocarpa.

Mountain Misery -
Chamaebatia foliolosa

ROSE FAMILY. *Rosaceae.*

This is the only kind of Stellariopsis; perennial herbs; the leaves with many, minute, crowded, overlapping leaflets; the flowers white, in open clusters; bractlets, sepals, and petals five; stamens fifteen; pistil one, surrounded by bristles.

Pussy-tails
Stellariópsis
santolinoìdes
(*Ivesia*)
White
Summer
California

The leaves of this odd little plant look like catkins, or the sleek, gray tails of some little animal. They are cylindrical in form, three or four inches long, composed of many minute leaflets, crowded closely around a long, central stem. These little leaflets, hardly more than green scales, are smothered with soft, white down, which gives the whole "tail" a silky, silvery-gray appearance. From the midst of a bunch of these curious leaves, which are mostly from the root, spring several very slender stems, widely branching above, from six to twelve inches tall, and at the ends of the branches are airy clusters of pretty little flowers, like tiny strawberry-blossoms. These little plants grow in sandy soil, at high altitudes, and are plentiful on the gravelly "domes" around Yosemite.

There are a good many kinds of Horkelia; perennial herbs, with compound leaves, usually with many leaflets, and flowers in clusters; calyx cup-shaped, or saucer-shaped, with five teeth and five bractlets; stamens ten; pistils two or many, with long slender styles, and borne on a receptacle like that of Potentilla, which these plants resemble, though the flowers are usually smaller, in closer clusters.

Horkèlia fúsca
White
Summer
Cal., Oreg., Nev.

A rather attractive plant, for the foliage is pretty, though the flowers are not very conspicuous. The rather stout, roughish stem, often purplish, is from one to two feet tall and the leaves are rather dark green, slightly sticky and sometimes downy. The flowers are about half an inch across, with white petals, tinged with pink, and are well set off by the dark reddish or purplish calyxes and buds, but the petals are too far apart, and there are not enough flowers out at one time, for the effect to be good. This varies a good deal in hairiness and there are several varieties. It is common in Yosemite.

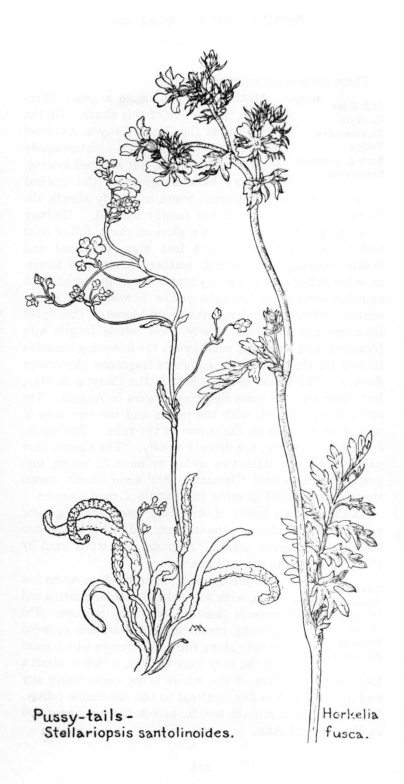

Pussy-tails -
Stellariopsis santolinoides.

Horkelia
fusca.

ROSE FAMILY. *Rosaceae.*

There are several kinds of Cowania.

Cliff Rose
Cowània
Stansburiàna
Yellow
Spring, summer
Southwest

Altitude and soil make a great difference in the beauty of this shrub. On the rocky rim of the Grand Canyon it is from four to eight feet high, picturesquely gnarled and twisted, but stunted looking, the gray bark hanging off the crooked branches and thick, distorted trunk in untidy shreds, the flowers pale, scanty, and but faintly scented. Halfway down Bright Angel trail it is a glorious thing, full of color and fragrance, about twelve feet high, luxuriant and healthy-looking. The small, leathery, evergreen leaves, crowded in bunches along the branches, are glossy and rich in color, setting off the light yellow flowers, with golden centers, which form long wands of bloom. The upper branches are clustered closely their whole length with blossoms, and when the wind sways the flowering branches to and fro they exhale an exquisite fragrance like orange flowers. The bloom is at its best in the Canyon in May, but there are still some lingering flowers in August. The calyx is top-shaped, with the petals and the two rows of numerous stamens on the throat of the tube. The pistils, from five to twelve, are densely woolly. The akenes have pale, silky-hairy tails, two inches or more in length, suggesting gone-to-seed Clematis. For some occult reason this shrub is called Quinine Bush at the Grand Canyon.

There are two kinds of Aruncus, resembling Spiraea; with small white flowers, the stamens and pistils in separate flowers on different plants. Aruncus is a word used by Pliny to designate a goat's beard.

Goat's Beard
Arúncus sylvéster
(*Spiraea aruncus*)
White
Summer
Northwest, etc.

A pretty plant, from three to seven feet high, with somewhat branching stems and smooth leaves, thin in texture. The minute, cream-white flowers are crowded closely along the many sprays which make up the very loose cluster, which is about a foot long, the effect of the whole being exceedingly airy and graceful and in fine contrast to the handsome foliage. This grows in mountain woods, across the continent and in Europe and Asia.

Cliff
Rose.

Cowania
Stansburiana.

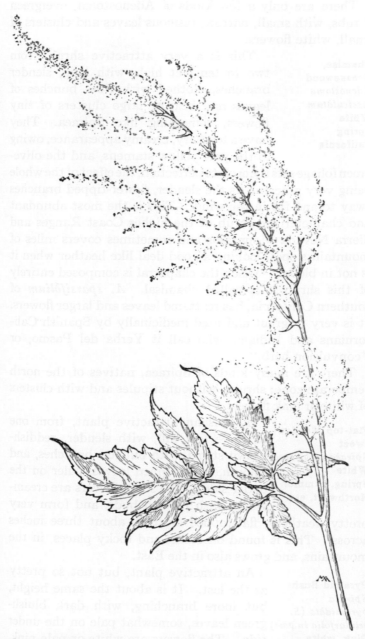

Goat's Beard-   Aruncus sylvester.

ROSE FAMILY. *Rosaceae.*

There are only a few kinds of Adenostoma, evergreen shrubs, with small, narrow, resinous leaves and clusters of small, white flowers.

**Chamise,
Greasewood**
*Adenóstoma
fasciculàtum*
**White
Spring
California**

This is a very attractive shrub, from two to ten feet high, with long, slender branches, clothed with close bunches of leaves and bearing large clusters of tiny flowers, something like Spiraea. They have a feathery, creamy appearance, owing to the pale yellow stamens, and the olive-green foliage sets them off to perfection, the effect of the whole being very graceful, as the slender, flower-tipped branches sway to and fro in the wind. This is the most abundant and characteristic shrub of the higher Coast Ranges and Sierra Nevada Mountains and sometimes covers miles of mountain slopes, looking a good deal like heather when it is not in bloom. When the chaparral is composed entirely of this shrub it is called chamisal. *A. sparsifólium* of southern California, has scattered leaves and larger flowers. It is very fragrant and used medicinally by Spanish Californians and Indians, who call it Yerba del Pasmo, or "convulsion herb."

There are many kinds of Spiraea, natives of the north temperate zone; shrubs, without stipules and with clusters of white or pink flowers.

Flat-top Meadow-sweet
Spiraèa corymbòsa
**White
Spring, summer
Northwest, etc.**

This is an attractive plant, from one to three feet tall, with slender, reddish-brown stems, with but few branches, and smooth, bright green leaves, paler on the under side. The small flowers are cream-white, with pinkish buds, and form very pretty, feathery, flat-topped clusters, about three inches across. This is found on banks and rocky places, in the mountains, and grows also in the East.

Pyramid Bush
*Spiraèa
pyramidàta (S.
betulaefolia in part)*
**Pink, white
Spring, summer
Northwest**

An attractive plant, but not so pretty as the last. It is about the same height, but more branching, with dark bluish-green leaves, somewhat pale on the under side. The flowers are white or pale pink, with deep pink buds, and form long clusters, not so feathery as the last, because the stamens are not so long. This grows in the mountains.

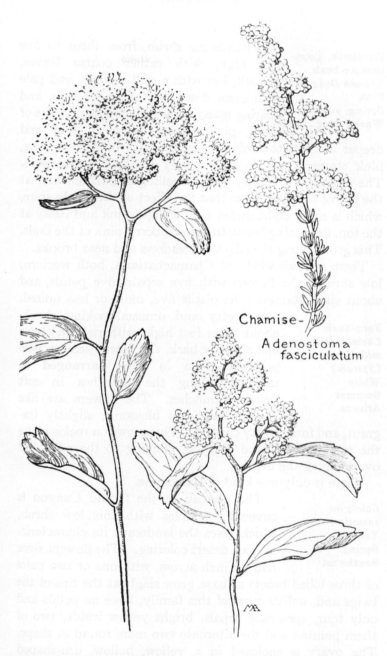

Chamise-
Adenostoma
fasciculatum

Flat-top Meadow-sweet -
Spiraea corymbosa.

Pyramid Bush -
S. pyramidata.

ROSE FAMILY. *Rosaceae.*

**Hardhack,
Steeple-bush
Spiræa Doúglasii
Pink
Spring, summer
Wash., Oreg., Cal.**
A handsome shrub, from three to five feet high, with rather coarse leaves, smooth, but with a dull surface, and pale with close down on the under side, and bearing many beautiful, compact spires of small, pink flowers, warm in tone and deeper in color towards the center, with numerous, long, pink stamens, which give a very feathery appearance. The flowers are slightly sweet-smelling and bloom first at the top of the cluster, so that the effect of the whole spire, which is six or eight inches long, is light pink and fuzzy at the top, deepening below to the raspberry-pink of the buds. This grows along the edges of meadows and near brooks.

There are two kinds of Chamaebatiaria, both western; low shrubs; the flowers with five sepals, five petals, and about sixty stamens; the pistils five, more or less united.

**Fern-bush
*Chamaebatiària
millefòlium*
(*Spiraea*)
White
Summer
Arizona**
A pretty and unusual-looking shrub, about three feet high, with reddish stems and shreddy bark, the downy leaves, pale yellowish-green in color, arranged at intervals along the branches in soft feathery bunches. The flowers are like small strawberry blossoms, slightly fragrant, and form pretty clusters. This grows on rocks, along the rim of the Grand Canyon, clinging to the edge and overhanging the depths.

There is only one kind of Coleogyne.

**Coleógyne
ramosíssima
Yellow
Spring
Southwest**
The plateau in the Grand Canyon is covered for miles with this low shrub, which gives the landscape its characteristic pale desert coloring. The flowers, over half an inch across, with one or two pairs of three-lobed bracts at base, grow singly at the tips of the twigs and, unlike most of this family, have no petals and only four, spreading sepals, bright yellow inside, two of them pointed and the alternate two more round in shape. The ovary is enclosed in a yellow, hollow, urn-shaped receptacle, surrounded by numerous stamens inserted on its base; the yellow anthers with threadlike filaments.

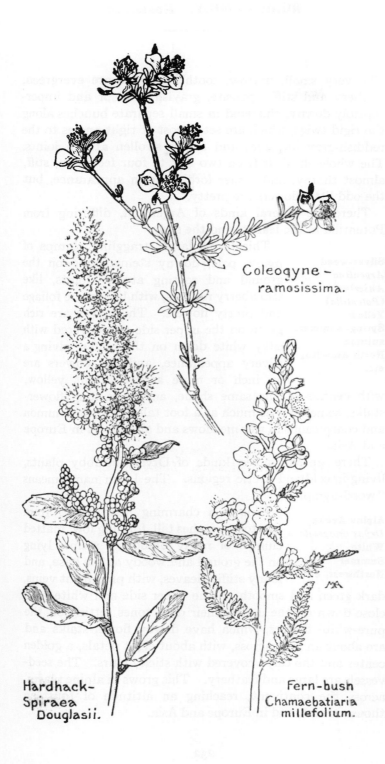

Coleogyne –
ramosissima.

Hardhack-
Spiraea
Douglasii.

Fern-bush
Chamaebatiaria
millefolium.

The very small, narrow, toothless leaves are evergreen, leathery and stiff, opposite, grayish in color and imperceptibly downy, clustered in small separate bunches along the rigid twigs, which are set almost at right angles to the reddish-gray branches and rather swollen at the joints. The whole shrub is from two feet to four feet high, stiff, almost thorny, and rather forbidding in appearance, but the odd little flowers are pretty.

There are several kinds of Argentina, differing from Potentilla in the leaflets and the style.

Silver-weed
Argentìna
Anserìna
(Potentilla)
Yellow
Spring, summer, autumn
North America, etc.

This forms large straggling clumps of many, pale, downy stems, lying on the ground and rooting at the joints, like strawberry runners, with handsome foliage and pretty flowers. The leaves are rich green on the upper side and covered with silky white down on the under, giving a silvery appearance, and the flowers are an inch or more across, bright yellow, with centers of the same shade, and have long flower-stalks, sometimes as much as a foot tall. This is common and conspicuous in wet meadows and also grows in Europe and Asia.

There are only a few kinds of Dryas, shrubby plants, living in cold and arctic regions. The Latin name means "wood-nymph."

Alpine Avens
Drỳas octopétala
White
Summer
Northwest, etc.

This is a charming little plant, from two to five inches tall, forming low, matted clumps of many branching stems, lying on the ground and woody at the base, and many stiffish leaves, with prominent veins, dark green and smooth on the upper side and white with close down on the under, their dark tones setting off the pure-white flowers, which have downy flower-stalks and are about an inch across, with about eight petals, a golden center and the calyx covered with sticky hairs. The seed-vessels are large and feathery. This grows in alpine places, across the continent, reaching an altitude of fourteen thousand feet, and in Europe and Asia.

Silver-weed -
Argentina Anserina.

Alpine Avens- Dryas octopetala.

ROSE FAMILY. *Rosaceae.*

There are many kinds of Cinquefoils, mostly natives of the north temperate zone, usually herbs, with compound leaves and yellow, white or purple flowers, always with pedicels; the flat or cup-shaped calyx, with five, main teeth, alternating with five, tooth-like bractlets; petals five, broad, often notched; stamens numerous, with thread-like filaments and small anthers, near the base of the calyx-cup; pistils numerous, on the conical, hairy receptacle, which does not become fleshy or juicy, each pistil maturing into a dry, seed-like akene. Potentilla means "powerful," as some sorts are medicinal. They often resemble Butter-cups, but never have shiny petals, and Buttercups do not have bractlets between the calyx-lobes.

Arctic Cinquefoil
Potentilla
emarginàta
Yellow
Summer
Northwest

A dear little plant, forming low tufts, two or three inches high, with thin, brown-ish stipules, bright green leaves, more or less hairy, and bright yellow flowers, deeper in color towards the center and about half an inch across. This grows in high northern mountains across the continent and in Siberia.

Silky Cinquefoil
Potentilla
pectinisécta
Yellow
Spring, summer
Utah, Ariz., Wyo.

The foliage of this plant is a lovely shade of silvery gray, which suits the yellow flowers. It has several stoutish, reddish, stems, a foot to a foot and a half tall, springing from clumps of leaves, with long leaf-stalks and five to seven leaflets. The bright-yellow flowers are each three-quarters of an inch across and the whole plant is conspicuously covered with long, thick, white, silky down, particularly on the under side of the leaves.

Shrubby Cinque-foil
Dasiphora
fruticòsa
(*Potentilla*)
Yellow
Spring, summer
West, etc.

This is the only kind of Dasiphora, a pretty shrub, very branching and leafy, one to four feet high, dotted all over with charming flowers. The bark is shreddy and the gray-green leaves are covered with silky down, with rolled back margins, and paler on the under side. The flowers, single or in clusters, are over an inch across, with clear yellow petals and deeper yellow anthers. This is common in the mountains, across the continent, up to an altitude of ten thousand feet, and is a troublesome weed in northern New England. It is also found in Europe and Asia.

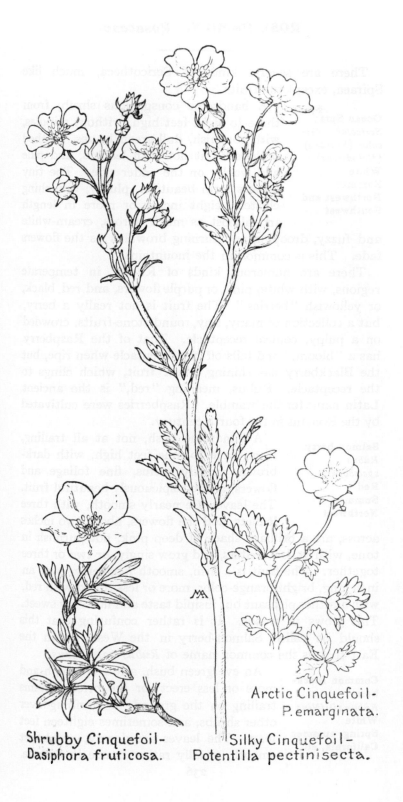

Shrubby Cinquefoil-
Dasiphora fruticosa.

Arctic Cinquefoil-
P. emarginata.

Silky Cinquefoil-
Potentilla pectinisecta.

ROSE FAMILY. *Rosaceae.*

There are several kinds of Sericotheca, much like Spiraea, except the fruits.

Ocean Spray
Sericothèca discolor (Spiraea)
(Holodiscus)
White
Summer
Northwest and Southwest

A handsome conspicuous shrub, from three to eight feet high, without stipules, with roughish, dull-green leaves, toothed or lobed, but not with leaflets, and pale and woolly on the under side. The tiny flowers form beautiful, plumy, branching clusters, eight inches or more in length and almost as much across, cream-white and fuzzy, drooping and turning brownish as the flowers fade. This is common in the mountains.

There are numerous kinds of Rubus, in temperate regions, with white, pink, or purple flowers, and red, black, or yellowish "berries." The fruit is not really a berry, but a collection of many, tiny, round stone-fruits, crowded on a pulpy, conical receptacle. That of the Raspberry has a "bloom," and falls off the receptacle when ripe, but the Blackberry has shining, black fruit, which clings to the receptacle. Rubus, meaning "red," is the ancient Latin name for the bramble. Raspberries were cultivated by the Romans in the fourth century.

Salmon-berry
Rùbus
spectàbilis
Red
Summer
Northwest

A handsome bush, not at all trailing, from three to nine feet high, with dark-brown, prickly stems, fine foliage and flowers, and conspicuously beautiful fruit. The leaves are nearly smooth, with three leaflets, and the flowers, about two inches across, are a brilliant shade of deep pink, not purplish in tone, with yellow centers, and grow singly, or two or three together. The fruit is a firm, smooth raspberry, over an inch long, bright orange-color, more or less tinted with red, with a rather pleasant but insipid taste and not very sweet. This grows in woods. It is rather confusing that this should be called Salmon-berry in the West, for in the East that is the common name of *Rubus parviflorus*.

Common Blackberry
Rùbus vitifòlius
White
Spring, summer
California, etc.

An evergreen bush, a few feet high and more or less erect; or the prickly stems trailing on the ground, or climbing over other shrubs, and sometimes eighteen feet long. The leaves are downy, or almost smooth, usually rather coarse in texture.

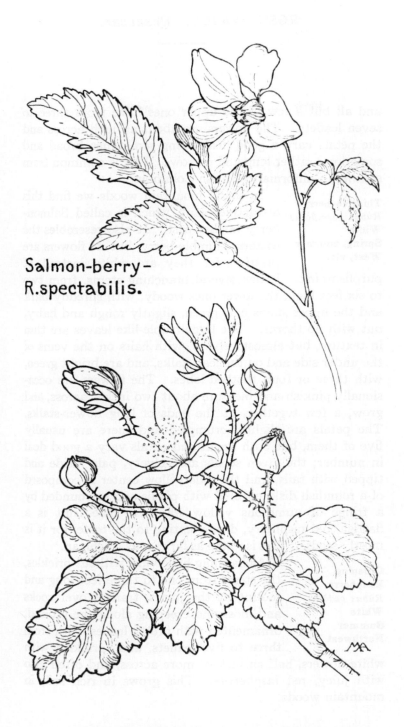

Salmon-berry –
R.spectabilis.

Common Blackberry – Rubus vitifolius.

and all but a few of the upper ones have from three to seven leaflets. The flowers are about an inch across and the petals vary a good deal, being sometimes broad and sometimes rather long and narrow. This is common from southern California to British Columbia.

Thimble-berry
Rùbus parviflòrus
White
Spring, summer
West, etc.

In shady mountain woods we find this attractive plant, which is called Salmon-berry farther east. It also resembles the eastern Thimble-berry, but its flowers are prettier, for they are white instead of purplish-pink. It has several branching stems, from two to six feet high, the lower ones woody, with shreddy bark and the upper stems pale green, slightly rough and hairy, but with no thorns. The large maple-like leaves are thin in texture, but almost velvety, with hairs on the veins of the under side and on the leaf-stalks, and are bright green, with three or four, toothed lobes. The flowers are occasionally pinkish and measure about two inches across, and grow, a few together, at the ends of long flower-stalks. The petals are slightly crumpled and there are usually five of them, but both sepals and petals vary a good deal in number; the green sepals are velvety, pale inside and tipped with tails, and the pale yellow center is composed of a roundish disk, covered with pistils and surrounded by a fringe of numerous yellow stamens. The fruit is a flattish, red raspberry, disappointing to the taste, for it is mostly seeds. This is found as far east as Michigan.

Creeping
Raspberry
Rùbus pedàtus
White
Summer
Northwest

A charming little vine, without prickles, the stems from one to three feet long and rooting at the joints, trailing over rocks and moss and creeping along the ground, ornamented with pretty leaves, with from three to five leaflets, and sprinkled with white flowers, half an inch or more across, and often also with juicy, red raspberries. This grows in rich soil, in mountain woods.

Thimble-berry-
Rubus parviflorus.

Creeping Raspberry-
R. pedatus.

ROSE FAMILY. *Rosaceae.*

There are a good many kinds of Strawberry, natives of the north temperate zone and the Andes. They are perennials, with running stems, rooting at the joints; the flowers white, or rarely pink, with slender, often drooping pedicels, forming loose clusters; the flower-stalks springing from tufts of root-leaves, which have three, toothed leaflets and a pair of sheathing stipules at the base of the long leaf-stalk; the sepals five, alternating with sepal-like bractlets; the petals five, with short claws and not notched; the stamens numerous, with slender filaments; the receptacle roundish or cone-shaped, becoming enlarged, red and juicy, in fruit, bearing minute, dry akenes, scattered over its surface, or set in pits. Fragum is the Latin name for strawberry, meaning "fragrant."

Wood Strawberry
Fragària bracteàta
White
Spring, summer
West

A slender little plant, growing in light shade, in rich soil, along streams, in rocky woods and producing runners very freely. The stipules are papery and reddish, the thin, dull-green leaves are slightly silky on the upper side, when young, and the leaflets are sharply and coarsely toothed, somewhat wedge-shaped, broad at the tips, the two side ones uneven at base. There is usually a little bract, halfway up, on both the flower-stalk and the leaf-stalk. The flowers are nearly an inch across, with fuzzy, bright yellow centers, and the fruit is light red, with a good flavor, somewhat cone-shaped, the akenes scattered over its smooth, shining, even surface and but slightly attached to it.

Sand Strawberry
Fragària
Chiloénsis
White
Spring, summer
Wash., Oreg., Cal.

A charming plant, a few inches tall, with thick, glossy, dark green leaves, paler and hairy on the under side, and pure-white flowers, with bright yellow centers. They are about an inch across and are well set off by the masses of dark foliage. This has large, delicious berries and grows abundantly on beaches and sand dunes near the sea, from San Francisco to Alaska. It is often cultivated.

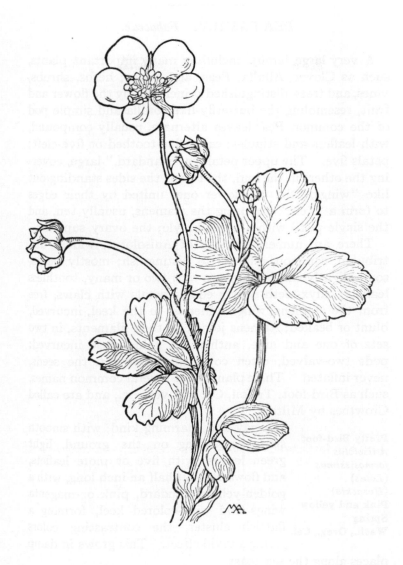

**Sand Strawberry—
Fragaria Chiloensis.**

PEA FAMILY. *Fabaceae.*

A very large family, including many important plants, such as Clover, Alfalfa, Peas, and Beans; herbs, shrubs, vines, and trees, distinguished principally by the flower and fruit, resembling the butterfly-like corolla and simple pod of the common Pea; leaves alternate, usually compound, with leaflets and stipules; calyx five-toothed or five-cleft; petals five. The upper petal, or "standard," large, covering the others in the bud, the two at the sides standing out like "wings," the two lower ones united by their edges to form a "keel," enclosing the stamens, usually ten, and the single pistil with a curved style; the ovary superior.

There are numerous kinds of Anisolotus, widely distributed, common, difficult to distinguish; mostly herbs, some slightly shrubby; leaves with two or many, toothless leaflets; calyx-teeth nearly equal; petals with claws, free from the stamens, wings adhering to the keel, incurved, blunt or beaked; stamens joined by their filaments, in two sets of one and nine, anthers all alike; style incurved; pods two-valved, often compressed between the seeds, never inflated. These plants have several common names, such as Bird-foot, Trefoil, Cat's-clover, etc., and are called Crowtoes by Milton.

Pretty Bird-foot
Anisolótus
formosissimus
(Lotus)
(Hosackia)
Pink and yellow
Spring
Wash., Oreg., Cal.

A gay and charming kind, with smooth stems, spreading on the ground, light green leaves, with five or more leaflets, and flowers about half an inch long, with a golden-yellow standard, pink or magenta wings and wine-colored keel, forming a flattish cluster, the contrasting colors giving a vivid effect. This grows in damp places along the sea-coast.

Bird-foot
Anisolótus
argyraèus (Lotus)
(Hosackia)
Yellow
Spring
California

A shrubby, branching plant, a foot and a half high, forming a pretty clump, two or three feet across, with downy, gray-green stems and foliage, sprinkled with clover-like heads of yellow flowers. The leaflets are slightly thickish, covered with silky down, the twigs and young leaves silvery-white. The small flowers are a soft shade of warm-yellow, and the buds form neat, fuzzy, silvery balls. This grows on dry hillsides in the Catalina Islands.

242

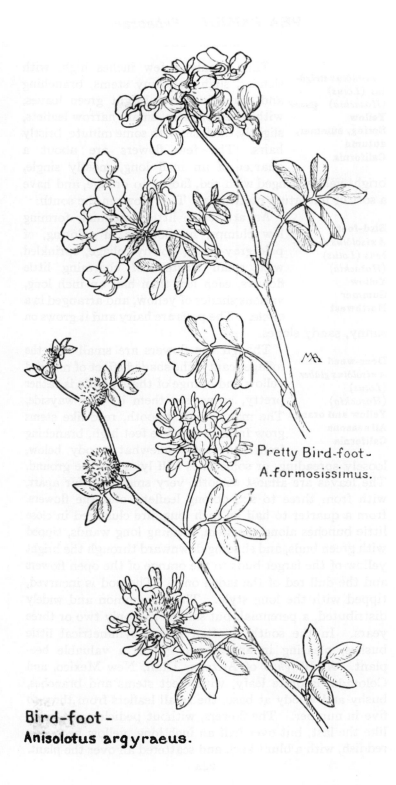

Pretty Bird-foot -
A. formosissimus.

Bird-foot -
Anisolotus argyraeus.

A nisolòtus strigò-sus (Lotus) (Hosackia)
Yellow
Spring, summer, autumn
California

This is only a few inches high, with slender, slightly downy stems, branching and spreading, and bright green leaves, with seven or more, small, narrow leaflets, slightly thickish, with some minute, bristly hairs. The few flowers are about a quarter of an inch long, mostly single, bright yellow, tinged with red, fading to orange, and have a sort of miniature prettiness. This grows in the south.

Bird-foot
A nisolòtus decúm-bens (Lotus) (Hosackia)
Yellow
Summer
Northwest

An attractive little perennial, forming low clumps, harmonious in coloring, of pale gray-green, downy foliage, sprinkled with small clusters of charming little flowers, each less than half an inch long, various shades of yellow, and arranged in a circle. The pods are hairy and it grows on sunny, sandy slopes.

Deer-weed
A nisolòtus glàber (Lotus) (Hosackia)
Yellow and orange
All seasons
California

Though the flowers are small and the foliage scanty, the shaded effect of mingled yellow and orange of these plants is rather pretty, as we see them by the wayside, The many, long, smooth, reed-like stems grow from two to five feet high, branching from the root, somewhat woody below, loosely spreading, or sometimes half lying on the ground. The leaves are almost smooth, very small and far apart, with from three to six, oblong leaflets, and the flowers, from a quarter to half an inch long, are clustered in close little bunches along the stem, forming long wands, tipped with green buds, and shading downward through the bright yellow of the larger buds to the orange of the open flowers and the dull red of the faded ones. The pod is incurved, tipped with the long style. This is common and widely distributed, a perennial, but said to live only two or three years. In the south it often makes symmetrical little bushes, pleasing in appearance. It is a valuable bee-plant. *A. Wrìghtii* of Arizona, Utah, New Mexico, and Colorado, is quite leafy, with erect stems and branches, bushy and woody at base, the small leaflets from three to five in number. The flowers, without pedicles, are much like the last, but over half an inch long, yellow becoming reddish, with a blunt keel, and scattered all over the plant.

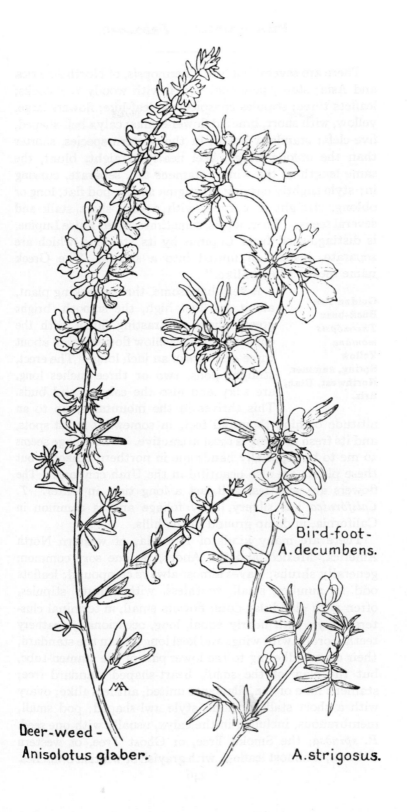

Bird-foot-
A.decumbens.

Deer-weed-
Anisolotus glaber.

A.strigosus.

PEA FAMILY. *Fabaceae.*

There are several kinds of Thermopsis, of North America and Asia; stout, perennial herbs, with woody rootstocks; leaflets three; stipules conspicuous, leaf-like; flowers large, yellow, with short, bracted flower-stalks; calyx bell-shaped, five-cleft; standard broad, in the western species, shorter than the oblong wings, keel nearly straight, blunt, the same length as the wings; stamens ten, separate, curving in; style slightly curving in, stigma small; pod flat, long or oblong, straight or curved, with a very short stalk and several seeds. Thermopsis, sometimes called False Lupine, is distinguished from Lupinus by its stamens, which are separate, instead of united into a sheath. The Greek name means "lupine-like."

Golden Pea
Buck-bean
Thermópsis
montàna
Yellow
Spring, summer
Northwest, Utah,
Ariz.

A very handsome, thrifty-looking plant, about two feet high, the smooth, bright green foliage contrasting finely with the clusters of clear yellow flowers, each about three-quarters of an inch long. The erect, straight pods, two or three inches long, are silky and also the calyxes and buds. This thrives in the mountains, up to an altitude of nine thousand feet, in somewhat moist spots, and its fresh coloring is most attractive. The foliage seems to me to be especially handsome in northern Arizona, but these plants are also beautiful in the Utah canyons. The flowers are scentless and last a long time in water. *T. Califórnica* has silvery, silky foliage and is common in California, in damp ground in the hills.

There are many kinds of Parosela, of western North America, Mexico, and the Andes, no one sort common; generally shrubs; leaves almost always compound; leaflets odd in number, small, toothless, with minute stipules, often with glandular dots; flowers small, in terminal clusters; calyx with nearly equal, long, occasionally feathery teeth; corolla with wings and keel longer than the standard, their claws adhering to the lower part of the stamen-tube, but the claw of the small, heart-shaped standard free; stamens nine or ten, filaments united, anthers alike; ovary with a short stalk, or none, style awl-shaped; pod small, membranous, included in the calyx, usually with one seed. *P. spinósa*, the Smoke Tree, or Ghost Tree, of western Arizona, is almost leafless, with grayish or whitish branches.

Golden Pea — Thermopsis montana.

PEA FAMILY. *Fabaceae.*

Parosèla Cali-
fórnica (Dalea)
Blue
Spring
California

This little spiny desert shrub grows two or three feet high and is conspicuous on account of the odd contrast in color between its foliage and flowers. The woody stems and branches are very pale in color and the very small leaflets, so narrow and stiff that they look like evergreen needles, are covered with pale down and have glandular dots. All over this colorless foliage are sprinkled small spikes of indigo-blue flowers, so dark in color that the effect, against a background of desert sand, is of pale gray, speckled with black. It has a pleasant smell like balsam.

Parosèla Émoryi
(Dalea)
Magenta
Spring, summer
Southwest

A low, desert shrub, with slender, abruptly branching stems and small, soft, thickish leaves, usually with three leaflets, obscurely toothed, the stems and leaves all thickly covered with white down. The flower-clusters are about three-quarters of an inch across, like a small clover-head, the woolly calyxes giving a yellowish-gray effect to the whole cluster, which is ornamented with a circle of tiny purple flowers. The effect of these specks of dark color on the pale bush is odd; the plant smells like balsam and grows in sandy soil.

Chaparral Pea
Xylothērmia
monlàna
(Pickeringia)
Crimson
Spring, summer
California

This is the only kind, an evergreen shrub, flourishing on dry hills in the Coast Ranges, with tough, crooked branches and stout spines, forming chaparral so dense that it is impossible to penetrate. It grows from three to eight feet high, the gnarled, knotty, black branches terminating in long spines, which are often clothed with small leaves nearly to the end, the leaves with one to three, small leaflets and without stipules. The bush is often covered with quantities of pretty, bright, deep purplish-pink flowers, three-quarters of an inch long, forming a fine mass of color. The calyx has four, short, broad teeth; the petals are equal, the standard roundish, with the sides turned back and a paler spot at base, the wings oblong, the keel straight; the filaments of the ten stamens not united; the pod is two inches long, flat, straight, sickle-shaped when young. This very rarely produces fruit. Stevenson was probably describing this shrub when he wrote, "Even the low thorny chaparral was thick with pea-like blossoms."

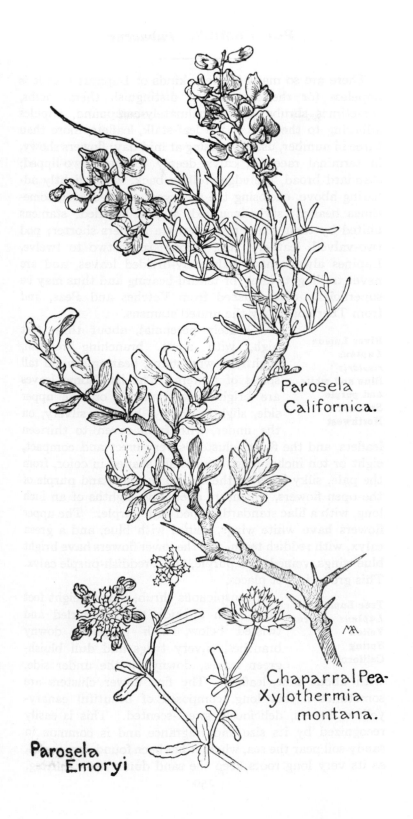

Parosela
Californica.

Chaparral Pea-
Xylothermia
montana.

Parosela
Emoryi

PEA FAMILY. *Fabaceae.*

There are so many western kinds of Lupinus that it is hopeless for the amateur to distinguish them; herbs, sometimes shrubs; leaves palmately-compound, stipules adhering to the base of the leaf-stalk, leaflets, more than three in number, usually closing at mid-day; flowers showy, in terminal racemes; calyx deeply toothed, two-lipped; standard broad, the edges rolling back, wings lightly adhering above, enclosing the incurved, pointed keel, sometimes beaked; style incurved, stigma bearded; stamens united by their filaments, alternate anthers shorter; pod two-valved, leathery, flat, oblong; seeds two to twelve. Lupines always have palmately-divided leaves, and are never trailing, twining, or tendril-bearing and thus may be superficially distinguished from Vetches and Peas, and from Thermopsis, by the united stamens.

River Lupine
Lupìnus rivulàris
Blue and white and purple
Summer
Northwest

A stately perennial, about three feet high, with stout, branching reddish, slightly downy stems, bearing several tall spires of flowers. The handsome leaves are bright green, smooth on the upper side, slightly downy, but not silvery, on the under, with from seven to thirteen leaflets, and the flower-cluster is very erect and compact, eight or ten inches long, beautifully shaded in color, from the pale, silky buds at the tip, to the blue and purple of the open flowers, which are about five-eighths of an inch long, with a lilac standard, tipped with purple. The upper flowers have white wings, veined with blue, and a green calyx, with reddish teeth, and the lower flowers have bright blue wings, veined with purple, and a reddish-purple calyx. This grows in wet places.

Tree Lupine
Lupìnus arbòreus
Yellow
Spring
California

A conspicuous shrub, four to eight feet high, with a thick trunk, gnarled and twisted below, with purplish, downy branches, silvery twigs and dull bluish-green leaves, downy on the under side, with about nine leaflets. The fine flower clusters are sometimes a foot long, composed of beautiful canary-yellow flowers, deliciously sweet-scented. This is easily recognized by its size and fragrance and is common in sandy soil near the sea, where it has been found very useful, as its very long roots keep the sand dunes from shifting.

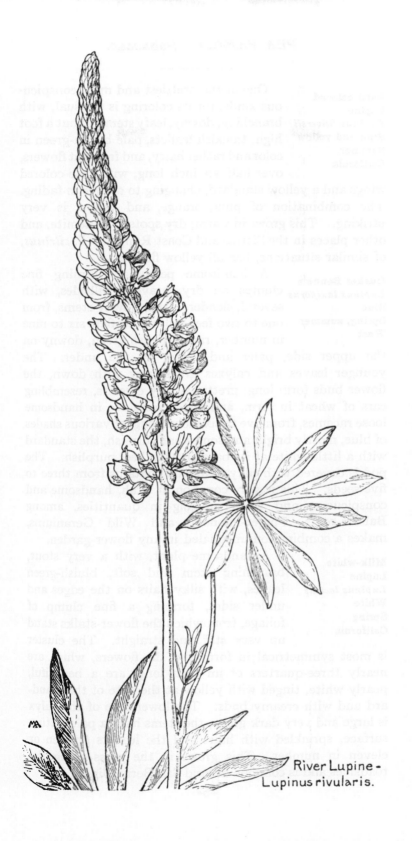

River Lupine -
Lupinus rivularis.

PEA FAMILY. *Fabaceae.*

Parti-colored Lupine
Lupìnus Stìversii
Pink and yellow
Summer
California

One of the prettiest and most conspicuous kinds, for its coloring is unusual, with branching, downy, leafy stems, about a foot high, thickish leaflets, pale bluish-green in color and rather hairy, and fragrant flowers, over half an inch long, with rose-colored wings and a yellow standard, changing to orange in fading. The combination of pink, orange, and yellow is very striking. This grows in warm, dry spots in Yosemite, and other places in the Sierras and Coast Ranges. *L. citrìnus,* of similar situations, has all yellow flowers.

Quaker Bonnets
Lupìnus laxiflòrus
Blue
Spring, summer
West

A handsome perennial, forming fine clumps on dry, gravelly hillsides, with several, slender, rather downy stems, from one to two feet tall, the leaflets six to nine in number, rather bluish-green, downy on the upper side, paler and silkier on the under. The younger leaves and calyxes are silvery with down, the flower buds form long, pretty, silvery clusters, resembling ears of wheat in form, and the flowers are in handsome loose racemes, from five to six inches long, of various shades of blue, mostly bright and somewhat purplish, the standard with a little white at its base and the keel purplish. The pod is covered with silky hairs and contains from three to five seeds. This is very common in Utah, handsome and conspicuous, and when growing in quantities, among Balsam-roots, Forget-me-nots, and Wild Geraniums, makes a combination unequaled in any flower-garden.

Milk-white Lupine
Lupìnus lactèus
White
Spring
California

A handsome plant, with a very stout, branching stem and soft, bluish-green leaves, with silky hairs on the edges and under sides, forming a fine clump of foliage, from which the flower-stalks stand up very stiff and straight. The cluster is most symmetrical in form and the flowers, which are nearly three-quarters of an inch long, are a beautiful, pearly white, tinged with yellow at the base of the standard and with creamy buds. The lower lobe of the calyx is large and very dark green, the stems have a pale, satiny surface, sprinkled with hairs and the leaflets are ten or eleven in number. This grows in the grass along the roadsides and is common around San Bernardino.

Bi-colored
Lupine.

Lupinus
Stiversii.

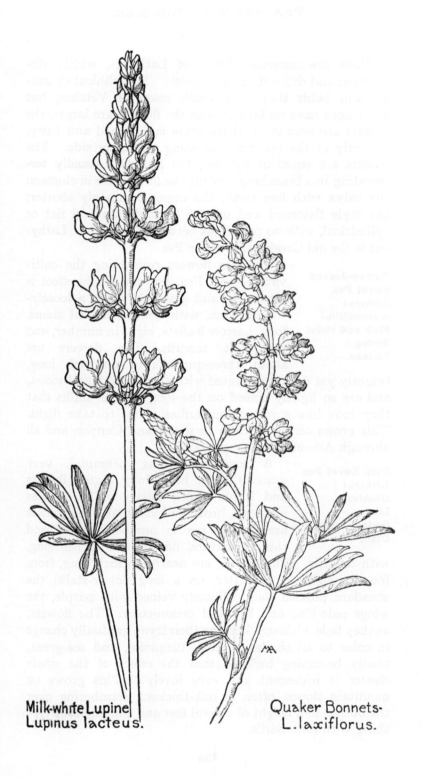

Milk-white Lupine
Lupinus lacteus.

Quaker Bonnets-
L. laxiflorus.

PEA FAMILY. *Fabaceae.*

There are numerous kinds of Lathyrus, widely distributed and difficult to distinguish. In technical character and habit they very much resemble Vetches, but sometimes have no tendrils and the flowers are larger, the leaflets are broader, and the style is flattened and hairy, not only at the tip, but also along the upper side. The leaflets are equal in number, the leaf-stalk usually terminating in a branching tendril; the flowers are in clusters; the calyx with five teeth, the upper commonly shorter; the style flattened and usually twisted; the pod flat or cylindrical, with no partitions between the seeds. Lathyrus is the old Greek name of the Pea.

Narrow-leaved Sweet Pea
Láthyrus graminifólius
Pink and violet
Spring
Arizona

This has flowers resembling the cultivated Sweet Pea, but the whole effect is more airy and graceful. It is a loosely-trailing vine, with slender, angled stems, long, narrow leaflets, eight in number, and three-cleft tendrils. The flowers are about three-quarters of an inch long, brightly yet delicately tinted with shaded pink and violet, and are so lightly poised on the long slender stalks that they look like a row of butterflies about to take flight. This grows on the plateau in the Grand Canyon and all through Arizona in the mountains.

Utah Sweet Pea
Láthyrus Utahénsis
Lilac
Spring, summer
Utah, Col.

A smooth, trailing perennial, very graceful, with beautifully tinted flowers and bright green foliage. The stipules are large, broad and leafy, and the leaflets are usually ten in number, veined and thin in texture, one or two inches long, with tendrils. The flowers are nearly an inch long, from four to eight in a cluster, on a long flower-stalk; the standard pinkish-lilac, delicately veined with purple, the wings pale lilac and the keel cream-color. The flowers, as they fade, although keeping their form, gradually change in color to all shades of blue, turquoise, and sea-green, finally becoming buff, so that the effect of the whole cluster is iridescent and very lovely. This grows on mountain slopes, often in oak-thickets, clambering over the bushes to a height of several feet and clinging to everything with its tendrils.

Wild
Sweet Pea.

Lathyrus
graminifolius.

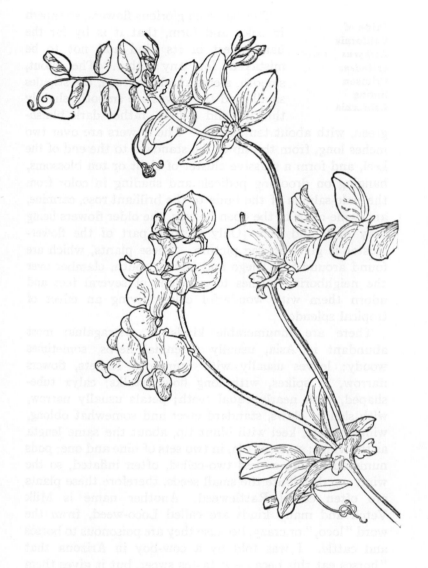

Utah Sweet Pea-   **Lathyrus Utahensis**

PEA FAMILY. *Fabaceae.*

**Pride of
California
*Láthyrus
spléndens*
Crimson
Spring
California**
This has such glorious flowers, so superb in color and form, that it is by far the handsomest of its kind and not to be mistaken for any other. The stout, smooth, stems are dark green, the stipules small, and the leaves are smooth, slightly thickish and stiffish, rather dark bluish-green, with about ten leaflets. The flowers are over two inches long, from the tip of the standard to the end of the keel, and form a massive cluster of eight or ten blossoms, hanging on drooping pedicels and shading in color from the pale-salmon of the buds to the brilliant rose, carmine, and wine-color of the open flowers, the older flowers being very dark and rich. Only a small part of the flower-cluster is given in the picture. These plants, which are found around San Diego and farther south, clamber over the neighboring bushes to a height of several feet and adorn them with wonderful color, giving an effect of tropical splendor.

There are innumerable kinds of Astragalus; most abundant in Asia, usually perennial herbs, sometimes woody; leaves usually·with numerous leaflets, flowers narrow, in spikes, with long flower-stalks; calyx tube-shaped, with nearly equal teeth; petals usually narrow, with slender claws, standard erect and somewhat oblong, wings oblong, keel with blunt tip, about the same length as the wings; stamens ten, in two sets of nine and one; pods numerous, more or less two-celled, often inflated, so the wind can distribute the small seeds, therefore these plants are often called Rattleweed. Another name is Milk Vetch and many kinds are called Loco-weed, from the word "loco," or crazy, because they are poisonous to horses and cattle. I was told by a cow-boy in Arizona that "horses eat this because it tastes sweet, but it gives them water on the brain and they die, unless the skull is split with an axe and the water is let out!"

*Astrágalus
Menzièsii*
**White
Spring, summer
California**
A decorative plant, its pale flowers contrasting well with the dark foliage, with stout, branching stems, from two to three feet tall, hairy above, and many leaflets, dark-green on the upper side, hairy and paler on the under. The flowers are half an

256

Pride of
California.

Lathyrus
splendens.

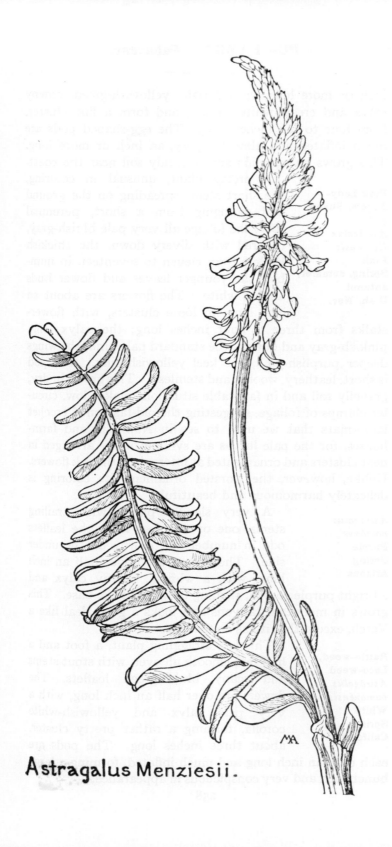

Astragalus Menziesii.

inch or more long, with a pale, yellowish-green, downy calyx and cream-white corolla, and form a fine cluster, from four to ten inches long. The egg-shaped pods are much inflated and almost papery, an inch or more long. This grows on sea-cliffs and in sandy soil near the coast.

Pink Lady-
fingers, Sheep-
pod
Astrágalus
Utahénsis
Pink
Spring, summer,
autumn
Utah, Nev.

A pretty plant, unusual in coloring, the short stems spreading on the ground and springing from a short, perennial root; the foliage all very pale bluish-gray, covered with silvery down, the thickish leaflets from eleven to seventeen in number, the younger leaves and flower buds almost white. The flowers are about an inch long, in loose clusters, with flower-stalks from three to four inches long; the calyx long, pinkish-gray and downy, the standard pale pink, the wings deeper purplish-pink, the keel yellowish-pink. The pod is short, leathery, woolly, and stemless. This grows in dry, gravelly soil and in favorable situations makes low, circular clumps of foliage, suggesting the old-fashioned crochet lamp-mats that we used to see in New England farm-houses, for the pale leaves are symmetrically arranged in neat clusters and ornamented at intervals with pink flowers. Unlike, however, the worsted ornament, its coloring is delicately harmonious and beautiful.

Astrágalus
nothóxys
Purple
Spring
Arizona

A very slender plant, with trailing stems, one or two feet long, the leaflets odd in number and downy on the under side. The flowers are about half an inch long, with a whitish, downy calyx and a bright purple corolla, shading to white at the base. This grows in mountain canyons and looks a good deal like a Vetch, except that it has no tendrils.

Rattle-weed,
Loco-weed
Astrágalus
pomonénsis
White
Spring
California

This is a straggling plant, a foot and a half tall, smooth all over, with stout stems and many bluish-green leaflets. The flowers are over half an inch long, with a very pale calyx and yellowish-white corolla, forming a rather pretty cluster, about three inches long. The pods are each over an inch long and much inflated, forming a large bunch, odd and very conspicuous in appearance.

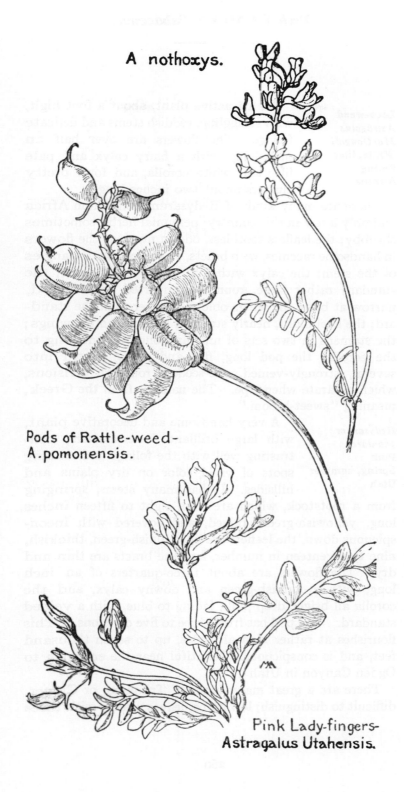

A nothoxys.

Pods of Rattle-weed-
A. pomonensis.

Pink Lady-fingers-
Astragalus Utahensis.

PEA FAMILY. *Fabaceae.*

Loco-weed
A strágalus
MacDoùgali
White, lilac
Spring
Arizona

An attractive plant, about a foot high, with straggling, reddish stems and delicate foliage. The flowers are over half an inch long, with a hairy calyx and pale lilac and white corolla, and form pretty clusters about two inches long.

There are many kinds of Hedysarum, some from Africa and only a few in this country; perennial herbs, sometimes shrubby; the leaflets toothless, odd in number; the flowers in handsome racemes, with bracts, on stalks from the angles of the stem; the calyx with five, nearly equal teeth; the standard rather large, round, or inverted heart-shaped, narrow at base, the wings oblong, shorter than the standard; the keel blunt, nearly straight, longer than the wings; the stamens in two sets of nine and one, not adhering to the corolla; the pod long, flat, and oddly jointed into several, strongly-veined, one-seeded, roundish divisions, which separate when ripe. The name is from the Greek, meaning "sweet-broom."

Hedýsarum
pab·ldre
Pink
Spring, summer
Utah

A very handsome and decorative plant, with large brilliant flower-clusters, contrasting well with the foliage and making spots of vivid color on dry plains and hillsides. It has many stems, springing from a rootstock, which are from eight to fifteen inches long, yellowish-green, ridged, and covered with inconspicuous down, the leaflets are light bluish-green, thickish, nine to seventeen in number, and the bracts are thin and dry. The flowers are about three-quarters of an inch long, with a pinkish-green and downy calyx, and the corolla all bright deep pink, fading to blue, with a veined standard. The pod has from three to five divisions. This flourishes at rather high altitudes, up to seven thousand feet, and is conspicuously beautiful near the entrance to Ogden Canyon in Utah.

There are a great many kinds of Trifolium, or Clover, difficult to distinguish; low herbs; leaves usually with three

Hedysarum pabulare.

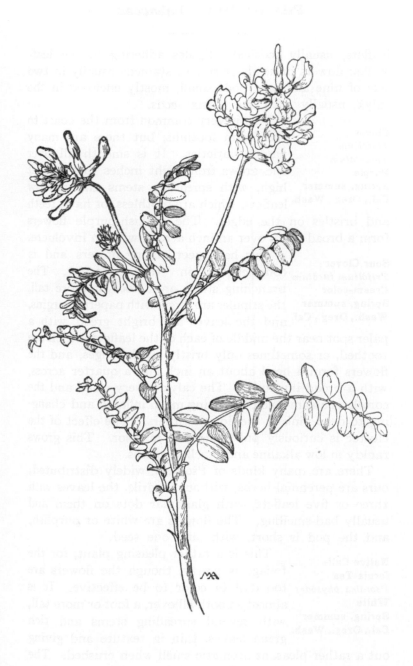

Loco-weed-   Astragalus MacDougali.

PEA FAMILY. *Fabaceae.*

leaflets, usually toothed; stipules adhering to the leaf-stalks; flowers in heads or spikes; stamens usually in two sets of nine and one; pods small, mostly enclosed in the calyx, usually with one to six seeds.

Clover
Trifòlium tridentàtum
Purple
Spring, summer
Cal., Oreg., Wash.
This is very common from the coast to the Sierra foothills, but there are many named varieties. It is smooth all over and grows from eight inches to two feet high, with spreading stems and narrow leaflets, which are toothless, or have teeth and bristles on the edges. The pinkish-purple flowers form a broad head, over an inch across, with an involucre.

Sour Clover
Trifòlium fucàtum
Cream-color
Spring, summer
Wash., Oreg., Cal.
This has queer-looking flowers and is conspicuous on that account. The branching stems are a foot or more tall, the stipules are large, with papery margins, and the leaves are bright green, with a paler spot near the middle of each of the leaflets, which are toothed, or sometimes only bristly on the edges, and the flowers form a head about an inch and a quarter across, with a broad involucre. The calyx is very small and the corolla is cream-color, becoming much inflated and changing to deep pink as the flower withers. The effect of the cluster is curiously puffy and odd in color. This grows rankly in low alkaline and brackish places.

There are many kinds of Psoralea, widely distributed; ours are perennial herbs, without tendrils, the leaves with three or five leaflets, with glandular dots on them and usually bad-smelling. The flowers are white or purplish, and the pod is short, with only one seed.

Native Cali-
fornia Tea
Psoràlea physòdes
White
Spring, summer
Cal., Oreg., Wash.
This is a rather pleasing plant, for the foliage is pretty, though the flowers are too dull in color to be effective. It is almost smooth all over, a foot or more tall, with several spreading stems and rich green leaves, thin in texture and giving out a rather pleasant aromatic smell when crushed. The flowers are less than half an inch long, with a somewhat hairy calyx, covered with dots and becoming inflated in fruit, and a yellowish-white corolla, more or less tinged with purple. This is common in the woods of the Coast Ranges. The foliage was used as tea by the early settlers.

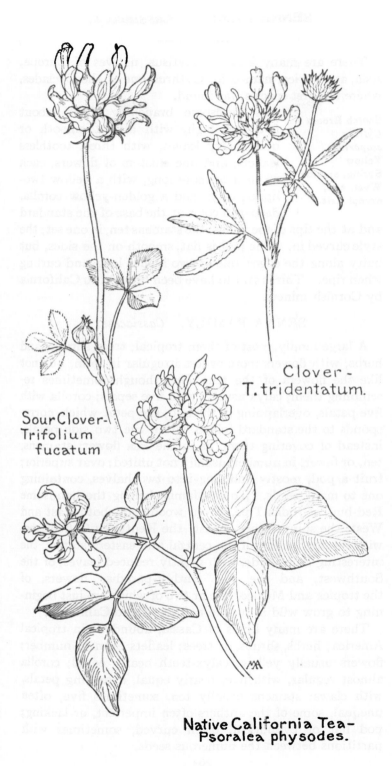

Clover—
T. tridentatum.

Sour Clover—
Trifolium
fucatum

Native California Tea—
Psoralea physodes.

SENNA FAMILY. *Cassiaceae.*

There are many kinds of Cytisus, natives of Europe, Asia, and Africa, named for Cythrus, one of the Cyclades, where the first species was found.

Scotch Broom
Cytisus
scopàrius
Yellow
Spring, summer
West, etc.,
except Ariz.

A handsome branching shrub, about five feet high, with almost smooth or quite hairy leaves, with three, toothless leaflets, and fine clusters of flowers, each an inch or more long, with a yellow two-lipped calyx and a golden-yellow corolla, deeper in color at the base of the standard and at the tips of the wings; the stamens ten, in one set; the style curved in. The pod is flat, smooth on the sides, but hairy along the edges, one or two inches long and curling when ripe. This is said to have been brought to California by Cornish miners.

SENNA FAMILY. *Cassiaceae.*

A large family, most of them tropical; trees, shrubs, and herbs, with flowers more or less irregular in form, but not like the flowers of the true Pea, though sometimes resembling them; calyx usually with five sepals; corolla with five petals, overlapping in the bud, the petal which corresponds to the standard folded within the two side petals, instead of covering them, as in the Pea flower; stamens, ten, or fewer, in number, usually not united; ovar superior; fruit a pod, mostly splitting into two halves, containing one to many seeds. To this family belong the handsome Red-bud, or Judas Tree, of our woodlands, both East and West; the spiny Honey-locust; the Kentucky Coffee-tree, with its fine foliage, of the central and eastern states; the interesting Palo Verde, with greatly reduced leaves, of the Southwest, and the fine Bird-of-paradise flowers, of the tropics and Mexico, one or two of which are just beginning to grow wild in southern Arizona and California.

There are many kinds of Cassia, abundant in tropical America; herbs, shrubs, or trees; leaflets even in number; flowers usually yellow; calyx-teeth nearly equal; corolla almost regular, with five, nearly equal, spreading petals, with claws; stamens usually ten, sometimes five, often unequal, some of the anthers often imperfect, or lacking; pod flat or cylindrical, often curved, sometimes with partitions between the numerous seeds.

Scotch Broom—
Cytisus scoparius

MIMOSA FAMILY. *Mimosaceae.*

**Desert Senna,
Golden Cassia
Cássia armàta
Yellow
Spring
Southwest**
The peculiar orange-yellow of these handsome flowers at once attracts our attention, for their tint is quite different from the greenish-yellow, which is so much more common. They grow in the desert, forming big clumps, two feet high and two or three feet across, but have almost no foliage. The numerous, smooth stems are very pale in color, often bluish or gray, with a few dark-green leaves, with six, very small, stiff leaflets, and bearing clusters of numerous, sweet-smelling flowers, almost regular and about three-quarters of an inch across, with a downy calyx and the small, flat pod also downy.

MIMOSA FAMILY. *Mimosaceae.*

A large family, most of them tropical; herbs, shrubs, or trees; leaves alternate, generally compound, usually with two or three leaflets; flowers small, regular and perfect, in clusters; calyx with three to six lobes or teeth; petals of the same number, separate, or more or less united, neither sepals nor petals overlapping in the bud; stamens as many as the petals, or twice as many, or numerous, separate or united; ovary superior; fruit a pod.

There are several kinds of Calliandra, low shrubs or herbs.

**Fairy Dusters
*Calliàndra
eriophýlla*
Pink
Spring
Arizona**
An odd little shrub, pretty and very Japanese in character, about a foot tall, with a few, pale-gray, spreading branches and very scanty foliage. The small leaves are cut into many tiny leaflets and look like those of a Mimosa, the buds are deep pink and the flowers are in clusters towards the ends of the branches and slightly sweet-scented. They are very queer-looking, but exceedingly pretty, for the purplish calyx and corolla are so small that the flower appears to be merely a tuft of many stamens, about an inch long, with threadlike filaments, white at base and shading to bright pink at the tips. The pistil is also long and pink, so the whole effect is a bunch of pink fuzz, airy in form and delicately shaded in color. These little shrubs sometimes bloom when they are only a few inches high, looking very quaint, like dwarf plants in a toy garden, and are among the earliest spring flowers.

Desert Senna
Cassia armata.

Fairy Dusters - Calliandra eriophylla.

KRAMERIA FAMILY. *Krameriaceae.*

A small family, distributed from the southern United States to Chili; hairy herbs or low shrubs, without stipules; leaves alternate; two bracts on the flower-stalk; flowers purplish, irregular, perfect; sepals four or five, usually large, the outer one commonly wider than the others; petals usually five, smaller than the sepals, the three upper ones with long claws, often united by their claws, sometimes the middle one of the three lacking, the two lower ones reduced to mere fleshy glands and not resembling petals; stamens three or four, united at least at base; ovary superior, with a slender style; fruit spiny, seed one.

Crimson-beak
Kramèria Gràyi
Purplish-pink
Spring
Arizona

A desert shrub, with a pleasant smell like balsam, two to four feet high, with gray, woody stems, abruptly branching, armed with long, brown and gray thorns, and clothed with very small, silvery-gray leaves, downy and thickish. The flowers are curious in shape and color, with five, large, purplish-pink sepals and five, small petals, the two lower ones minute and reduced to glands. The pistil is dark red, the three stamens have green filaments and red anthers, the ovary is downy and prickly, and the downy buds are pale pink.

CALTROP FAMILY. *Zygophyllaceae.*

Not a large family, widely distributed in warm and tropical regions; ours are herbs or shrubs, with opposite or alternate, compound leaves, with stipules and toothless leaflets; flowers complete, usually with five sepals and five petals, and usually twice the number of stamens, with swinging anthers, alternate stamens sometimes longer, filaments often with a small scale near the middle; ovary superior, usually surrounded at the base by a disk; style one, with a five- to ten-lobed stigma; fruit dry.

There are several kinds of Covillea.

Creosote-bush,
Hediondilla
Covíllea glutinòsa
(Larrea Mexicana)
Yellow
All seasons
Southwest

A graceful, evergreen shrub, common in arid regions and a characteristic feature of the desert landscape, filling the air with its very strong, peculiar odor. It is from three to ten feet high, with many little branches, with blackish knots at the joints, clothed with sticky, dull yellowish-

268

Creosote-bush –
Covillea glutinosa.

Crimson-beak –
Krameria Grayi.

green foliage, the thickish, resinous leaflets very small, in pairs, with almost no leaf-stalk, and uneven at base. The pretty flowers are nearly an inch across, with bright yellow petals, with claws, and silky, greenish-yellow sepals which soon drop off. The filaments are broadened below into wings and have a scale on the inner side. The ovary is covered with pale, silky hairs, so that the older flowers have a silky tuft in the center, and becomes a round, densely hairy fruit, with a short stalk, tipped with the slender style. These little white, silky balls of down are very conspicuous and, as they are mingled with yellow flowers, the bush has an odd and pretty effect of being spotted all over with yellow and white.

FLAX FAMILY. *Linaceae.*

A small family, widely distributed in temperate and tropical regions. Ours are smooth herbs, with loosely clustered, complete flowers, having five sepals; five petals, alternating with the sepals; five stamens, alternating with the petals, with swinging anthers and filaments united at the base; ovary superior; fruit a capsule, containing eight or ten, oily seeds.

There are many kinds of Flax, sometimes shrubby at base; with tough fibers in the bark; leaves without stipules, sometimes with glands at base in place of real stipules; flowers mostly blue or yellow. There are numerous, small-flowered, annual kinds, difficult to distinguish and usually somewhat local. *L. usitatissimum*, an annual, with deep blue flowers, is the variety which, from time immemorial, has furnished the world with linen from its fiber and oil from its seeds. Linum is the ancient Latin name.

Blue Flax
Lìnum Lewisii
Blue
Spring, summer
West, etc.
An attractive plant, from one to two feet tall, with several, erect stems, springing from a woody, perennial root, with numerous, small, narrow, bluish-green leaves and loose clusters of pretty flowers, each about an inch across. The petals, delicately veined with blue, vary in tint from sky-blue to almost white, with a little yellow at the base. This is common and widely distributed, from Manitoba to Texas and westward, but the fiber is not strong enough to be used commercially.

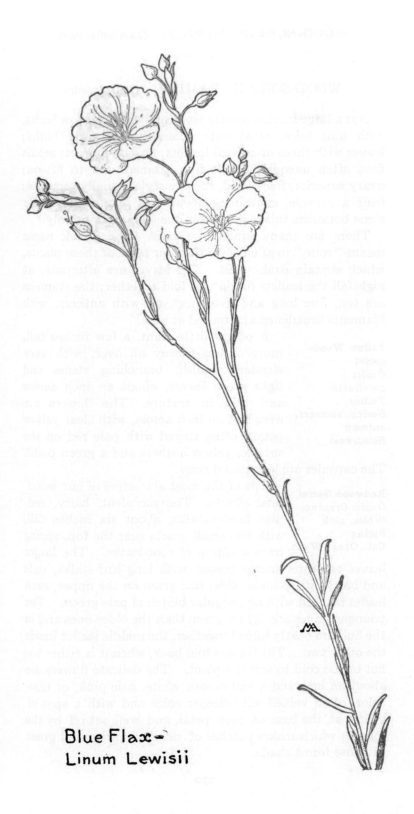

Blue Flax -
Linum Lewisii

WOOD-SORREL FAMILY. *Oxalidaceae.*

Not a large family, mostly tropical. Ours are low herbs, with sour juice, often with rootstocks or scaly bulbs; leaves with three or several leaflets; flowers perfect; sepals five, often unequal; petals five, stamens ten to fifteen; ovary superior, five-celled, the five styles usually separate; fruit a capsule, containing several or many seeds. By some botanists this is merged in the Geranium Family.

There are many kinds of Oxalis. The Greek name means "sour," in allusion to the sour taste of these plants, which contain oxalic acid. The leaves are alternate, at nightfall the leaflets droop and fold together; the stamens are ten, five long and five short, all with anthers, with filaments broadened and united at base.

Yellow Wood-sorrel
Óxalis corniculàta
Yellow
Spring, summer, autumn
Southwest

A pretty little plant, a few inches tall, more or less downy all over, with very slender, reddish, branching stems and light green leaves, about an inch across and thin in texture. The flowers are over half an inch across, with clear yellow petals, often tinged with pale red on the outside, yellow anthers and a green pistil. The capsules are long and downy.

Redwood Sorrel
Óxalis Oregàna
White, pink
Spring
Cal., Oreg., Wash.

One of the most attractive of our woodland plants. The succulent, hairy, reddish flower-stalks, about six inches tall, with two small bracts near the top, spring from a clump of root-leaves. The larger leaves are three inches across, with long leaf-stalks, pale and hairy on the under side, rich green on the upper, each leaflet marked with an irregular blotch of pale green. The younger leaves are lighter green than the older ones and in the bud are neatly folded together, the middle leaflet inside the other two. The leaflets fold back, when it is either too hot or too cold to suit the plant. The delicate flowers are about an inch and a half across, white, pale pink, or rose-color, often veined with deeper color and with a spot of yellow at the base of each petal, and well set off by the foliage, which makes patches of rich and variegated green in dense forest shade.

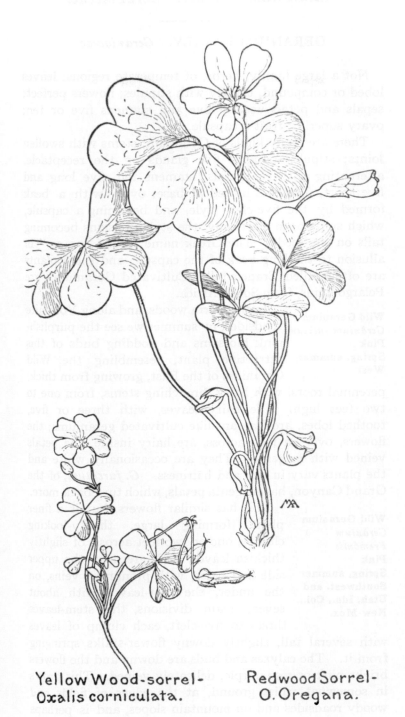

Yellow Wood-sorrel-
Oxalis corniculata.

Redwood Sorrel-
O. Oregana.

GERANIUM FAMILY. *Geraniaceae.*

GERANIUM FAMILY. *Geraniaceae.*

Not a large family, herbs, of temperate regions; leaves lobed or compound, usually with stipules; flowers perfect; sepals and petals usually five and stamens five or ten; ovary superior; fruit a capsule.

There are many kinds of Geranium; stems with swollen joints; stipules papery; five glands on the receptacle, alternating with the petals; stamens ten, five long and five short, filaments united at base; ovary with a beak formed by the five-cleft style, and becoming a capsule, which splits open elastically, the style-divisions becoming tails on the seeds. The Greek name means "crane," in allusion to the long beak of the capsule, and these plants are often called Crane's-bill. Cultivated Geraniums are Pelargoniums, from South Africa.

Wild Geranium
Gerànium incìsum
Pink
Spring, summer
West

In the Sierra woods, and along Yosemite roadsides, in summer we see the purplish-pink blossoms and nodding buds of this attractive plant, resembling the Wild Geranium of the East, growing from thick, perennial roots, with hairy, branching stems, from one to two feet high. The hairy leaves, with three or five, toothed lobes, are fragrant like cultivated geraniums; the flowers, over an inch across, are hairy inside, the petals veined with magenta. They are occasionally white and the plants vary in size and hairiness. *G. furcàtum*, of the Grand Canyon, has magenta petals, which turn back more.

Wild Geranium
Gerànium
Fremóntii
Pink
Spring, summer
Southwest. and Utah, Ida., Col., New Mex.

This has similar flowers, but is a finer plant, forming large, thrifty-looking clumps, one or two feet across, of slightly thickish leaves, dark green on the upper side and paler, with prominent veins, on the under, the root-leaves with about seven, main divisions, the stem-leaves three- to five-cleft, each clump of leaves with several tall, slightly downy flower-stalks springing from it. The calyxes and buds are downy and the flowers bright pink or rose-purple, delicately veined. This grows in somewhat moist ground, at the edges of fields and woody roadsides and on mountain slopes, and is perhaps the handsomest of its clan.

Geranium
incisum.

Wild Geranium–
G Fremontii.

GERANIUM FAMILY. *Geraniaceae.*

Long-stalked Crane's-bill
Gerànium columbìnum
Purple
Spring, summer
California, etc.

A slender plant, about a foot tall, with pinkish, hairy stems and pretty leaves, thin in texture, with a dull surface; the seed-vessels erect, with bristly beaks. The flowers grow in pairs and are less than half an inch across, with hairy calyxes and notched, purple or magenta petals. This is naturalized from Europe, and common in the East and grows along roadsides, at the edges of fields and woods.

There are many kinds of Erodium, three native in the Southwest and several more introduced, weeds in the Old World and important forage plants in the West; leaves often unequal, with one stipule on one side and two on the other. They resemble Geranium, flower and fruit being nearly the same, but only five of the stamens have anthers, the alternate ones being scale-like, without anthers; styles hairy inside. The Greek name means "heron," in allusion to the long beak of the capsule.

Red-stem Filaree
Eròdium cicutàrium
Pink
All seasons
West, etc.

Though not native, this is the commonest kind, in the interior and semi-arid regions, and most valued for forage. When young it forms rosettes close to the ground, but grows taller and more straggling. The stems are often reddish; the leaves somewhat hairy; the flowers small, in clusters of four to eight, with four bracts at the base; the petals purplish-pink, with darker veins, and hairy at the base, the two upper petals slightly smaller; the sepals tipped with one or two bristles. The ovary is beaked by the united styles, the beak, when the seeds ripen, separating into five, long tails, which twist spirally when dry and untwist when moistened. This is common west of the Rockies, blooming more or less all the year round, varying in size in different soils. Filaree is a corruption of the Spanish Alfilerilla, from "alfiler," a "pin." Other names are Pinkets, Pinclover, Storksbill, and Clocks, so-called by children because they amuse themselves by watching the tails twist about like the hands of a clock. White-stem Filaree, *E. moschàtum,* common in rich soil, has larger, coarser leaves and a faint scent.

276

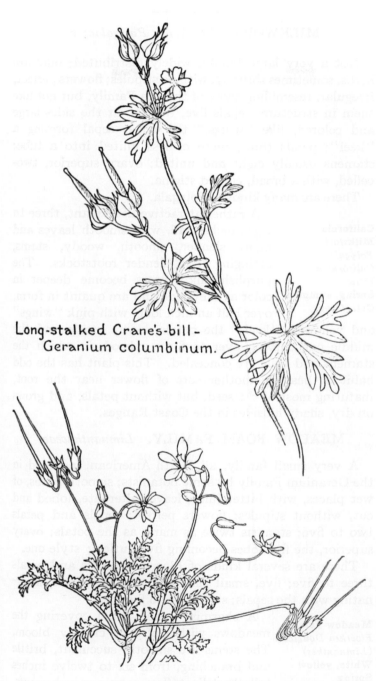

Long-stalked Crane's-bill -
Geranium columbinum.

Red-stem Filaree -
Erodium cicutarium.

MILKWORT FAMILY. *Polygalaceae.*

Not a very large family, widely distributed; ours are herbs, sometimes shrubby, with no stipules; flowers perfect, irregular, resembling those of the Pea Family, but not like them in structure; sepals five, the two at the sides large and colored, like "wings," the upper sepal forming a "keel"; petals three, more or less united into a tube; stamens usually eight and united; ovary superior, two-celled, with a broad, curved stigma.

There are many kinds of Polygala.

California Milkwort *Polýgala Califórnica* **Pink** **Spring, summer** **Cal., Oreg.**
A rather attractive little plant, three to eight inches tall, with smooth leaves and many slender, smooth, woody, stems, springing from slender rootstocks. The purplish-pink flowers become deeper in color as they fade and are quaint in form, over half an inch long, with pink "wings" and yellowish "keel," the petals downy inside and the middle one curving over to form a hood, in which the stamens and style are concealed. This plant has the odd habit of bearing another sort of flower near the root, maturing most of the seed, but without petals, and grows on dry, shady hillsides in the Coast Ranges.

MEADOW FOAM FAMILY. *Limnanthaceae.*

A very small family, all North American, included in the Geranium Family by some botanists; smooth herbs, of wet places, with bitter juice; leaves alternate, lobed and cut, without stipules; flowers perfect; sepals and petals two to five; stamens twice as many as the petals; ovary superior, the five lobes becoming five nutlets; style one.

There are several kinds of Floerkea; sepals and petals three to five; five, small glands on the receptacle, alternating with the sepals; style two- to five-cleft.

Meadow Foam *Floérkea Douglásii* (*Limnanthes*) **White, yellow** **Spring** **Cal., Oreg.**
A charming plant, often covering the meadows with drifts of creamy bloom. The stems are smooth, succulent, brittle and branching, from six to twelve inches tall; the delicate flowers over an inch across, the petals hairy at base, sometimes pinkish, but usually white and yellow.

Meadow Foam-
Floerkea Douglasii

California Milk-wort
Polygala Californica.

BUCKEYE FAMILY. *Hippocastanaceae.*

BUCKEYE FAMILY. *Hippocastanaceae.*

A small family, widely distributed; trees or shrubs, with opposite, compound leaves, no stipules and terminal clusters of irregular flowers, some perfect and some with only pistils or only stamens; the calyx tubular or bell-shaped, with five, unequal lobes or teeth; the petals four or five, unequal, with claws; the stamens five to eight, with long filaments; the ovary superior, with no stalk, three-celled, with a slender style; the capsule leathery, roundish or slightly three-lobed, smooth or spiny, with one to three, large, polished seeds.

There are a good many kinds of Aesculus, or Horse Chestnut, natives of America and Asia; the leaves palmately compound, with toothed leaflets; the flowers of two sorts, the fertile ones few in number, near the top of the cluster, with long, thick styles, and the sterile flowers with short styles.

California Buckeye
Aésculus Califórnica
White
Spring, summer
California

One of our handsomest western shrubs, usually from ten to fifteen feet tall, with gray bark, and dark bluish-green foliage, the leaflets from five to seven in number, glossy on the upper side, pale and dull on the under, and firm in texture. The flowers have a rather heavy scent and are about an inch across, with four or five, slightly irregular, white petals, which become pink in fading, a pinkish ovary and long stamens with curling, white filaments, unequal in length, with buff anthers. They are crowded in a magnificent, pyramidal cluster, about a foot long, which has a pinkish-red, downy stem, and the buds are also downy and pinkish, so that the color effect is warm-pink above, merging into cream-white below, the whole made feathery by the long stamens. The shrub has a rounded top of rich green foliage, symmetrically ornamented with spires of bloom, standing up quite stiffly all over it. The large, leathery pod contains a big, golden-brown nut, supposed to be poisonous to cattle. The leaves fall off very early in the season, leaving the pods hanging on the bare branches. This is at its best in the mountain valleys of middle California, sometimes becoming a good-sized tree.

California Buckeye-   Aesculus Californica

BUCKTHORN FAMILY. *Rhamnaceae.*

BUCKTHORN FAMILY. *Rhamnaceae.*

A large family; shrubs, or small trees, of temperate and warm regions, some with bitter, astringent properties, often thorny; leaves mostly alternate; stipules minute; flowers often in showy clusters, small, regular; calyx-lobes and stamens four or five; petals usually four or five, sometimes lacking, with claws. The short calyx-tube is lined with a fleshy disk and on this are borne the petals and the stamens, alternate with the sepals and opposite the petals, with swinging anthers. In some cases, some of the flowers have only pistils or only stamens. The ovary superior or partly inferior; the fruit a berry or capsule.

There are many kinds of Ceanothus, largely western; flowers small, blue or white, in clusters; calyx bell-shaped, five-lobed, with a colored, petal-like border; petals five, the tips arching to form a tiny hood, with long claws; stamens five, long, protruding, with threadlike filaments; ovary partly inferior; style three-cleft; capsule splitting open elastically so as to scatter the three, hard nutlets, The flowers make a soapy lather when rubbed in water, hence the name Soap-bush, and the kinds with rigid branches are called Buckbrush. Red-root is another name. Mountain Lilac is the commonest name, but misleading. Lilacs belong to another family.

Squaw Carpets, Mahala Mats
Ceanòthus prostràtus
Blue
Spring, summer
Cal., Oreg.

This decorative shrub is common in the Sierras and carpets the forest floor with a rich green, leafy mat, sprinkled with small, feathery clusters of blue flowers. The trailing stems are clothed with leathery leaves, opposite and very glossy, and the little flowers are deep purplish-blue, with yellow stamens, and slightly scented. These plants are equally attractive late in the season when the flowers are replaced by scarlet seed-vessels, with three horns.

Snow Brush, Mountain Lilac
Ceanòthus velùtinus
White
West, except Ariz.

A fine shrub, two to twelve feet high, with stout trunk and branches, easily recognized by its leaves, which are rich green, thick and resinous, shiny as if varnished on the upper side and sometimes rich chocolate-brown in color, but pale on the under side, with three, con-

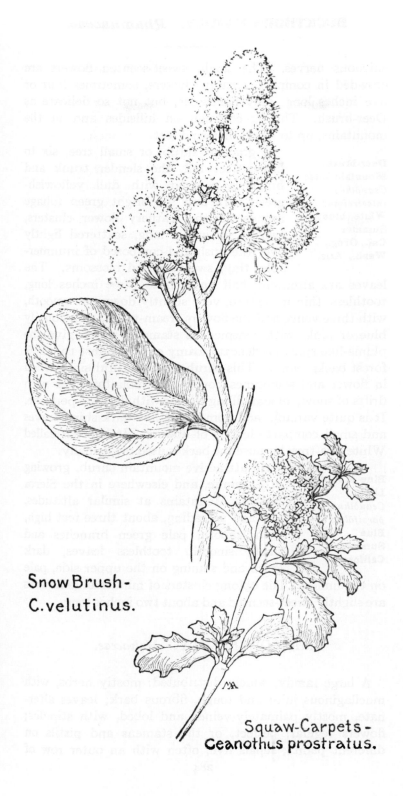

Snow Brush-
C. velutinus.

Squaw-Carpets-
Ceanothus prostratus.

spicuous nerves. The small, sweet-scented flowers are crowded in compact, creamy clusters, sometimes four or five inches long, very handsome, but not so delicate as Deer-brush. This is common on hillsides and in the mountains, up to seven thousand feet.

**Deer-brush,
Mountain Lilac
*Ceanòthus
integérrimus*
White, blue
Summer
Cal., Oreg.,
Wash., Ariz.**

A graceful shrub, or small tree, six to fifteen feet tall, the slender trunk and branches covered with dull yellowish-green bark and the bright green foliage setting off the feathery flower clusters, two to six inches long, scattered lightly over the bush and composed of innumerable, tiny, sweet-scented blossoms. The leaves are alternate, half an inch to three inches long, toothless, thin in texture, very slightly downy or smooth, with three veins, and the flowers cream-white, occasionally blue or pink, with conspicuous stamens, which give the plume-like sprays a delicate foamy effect against the dark forest background. This shrub is a beautiful sight when in flower and sometimes covers the mountainsides with drifts of snowy bloom, filling the air with delicate perfume. It is quite variable and sometimes has dark shiny leaves and small compact clusters of flowers. It is often called White Tea-tree, because the bark is used medicinally.

**Blue Mountain
Lilac
*Ceanòthus
parvifòlius*
Blue
Summer
California**

An attractive mountain shrub, growing in Yosemite, and elsewhere in the Sierra Nevada Mountains at similar altitudes, low and spreading, about three feet high, with smooth, pale green branches and small, smooth, toothless leaves, dark green and shining on the upper side, pale on the under. The oblong clusters of minute blue flowers are slightly sweet-scented and about two inches long.

MALLOW FAMILY. *Malvaceae.*

A large family, widely distributed; mostly herbs, with mucilaginous juice and tough, fibrous bark; leaves alternate, mostly palmately-veined and lobed, with stipules; flowers regular, perfect, or the stamens and pistils on different plants; sepals five, often with an outer row of

Deer Brush—
Ceanothus integerrimus.

Blue Mountain Lilac—
C. parvifolius.

MALLOW FAMILY. *Malvaceae.*

bracts below, resembling another calyx; petals five, their bases or claws united with each other and with the base of the stamen-tube; stamens numerous, united by their filaments into a column, forming a tube enclosing the pistils; fruit a capsule, breaking when ripe into several one-seeded parts, or splitting down the back of the valves, allowing the seeds to escape. The little fruits are commonly called "cheeses." True Mallows are introduced "weeds" in this country.

Arizona Wild Cotton
Thurbéria thespesioìdes
(*Ingenhouzia triloba*)
White
Summer
Arizona

The only kind, a fine shrub, from four to eight feet high, with smooth leaves, most of them with three lobes, and handsome cream-white flowers, tinged with pink on the outside and measuring two inches across. This grows in the mountains of southern Arizona and is beautiful under cultivation, often growing to a height of six or eight feet in a season.

There are a number of kinds of Sidalcea, difficult to distinguish; perennials; leaves round in general outline, variously cut and lobed; flowers showy, in terminal clusters; calyx with no outer bracts, or with only one; stamen-column double; stigmas threadlike, distinguishing them from Malvastrum and Sidalcea.

Rose Mallow
Sidálcea Califórnica
Pink
Spring
California

This has velvety leaves, those from the root much less deeply lobed than the others, and a slender, slightly hairy stalk, one to two feet tall, leaning to one side and bearing a loose raceme of rose-pink flowers, with petals about an inch long. Only one or two flowers are open at a time, but they are very pretty and conspicuous in open woods and along the edges of fields, around Santa Barbara, in May.

Oregon Mallow
Sidálcea Oregàna
Pink
Summer, autumn
Northwest

A pretty plant, with one or more smooth, pale, branching stems, about two feet tall, and dark green leaves, with conspicuous veins. The buds are downy and the flowers are about three-quarters of an inch across, with pale pink petals, prettily veined, shading to white at the center. The anthers are white and the pistil, when the stigmas have expanded, is prettily tipped with a tiny crimson brush.

Oregon Mallow—
Sidalcea Oregana.

Rose Mallow—
S. Californica.

MALLOW FAMILY. *Malvaceae.*

Checker-bloom
Sidálcea
malvaeflòra
Pink
Spring
California

A pretty perennial, with several leaning, hairy stems, one or two feet tall, and dark green leaves. Some plants have perfect flowers, an inch or more across, often very pale pink, and others have only rudimentary stamens and smaller flowers, usually deep pink in color, but the plant is very variable. This is common near the coast. It is sometimes called Wild Hollyhock.

Mallow
Sidálcea Neo-
Mexicàna
Pink
Summer
Ariz., Utah,
New Mex.,
Col., Wyo.

This is from one to three feet tall, with smooth, rather dark green leaves and very pretty, pale purplish-pink flowers with pale-yellow anthers and pinkish pistil. This grows in the mountains.

There are many kinds of Malvastrum, natives of America and Africa; perennial herbs or shrubs; the calyx often with three outer bracts; the stamen-column bearing anthers at the top; the stigmas with round heads. The name is from the Greek, meaning "star-mallow."

Spotted Mallow
Malvástrum
rotundifòlium
Pink
Spring
Southwest

A very pretty desert plant, from six to eight inches tall, the coloring of the flowers, stems, and leaves vivid and oddly contrasting, for the stems are bright red and hairy, and the leaves stiff, hairy, and bronze-green in color, while the lovely globe-shaped flowers, which are over an inch across, are delicately shaded from lilac to rose outside and paler inside, with conspicuous round blotches of orange-vermilion at the base of each petal within. The calyx and buds are very hairy, the petals each have a twist to one side, and the mauve stamens form a pretty cluster in the center. These flowers last a long time in water, closing at night and opening again in the morning.

Spotted
Mallow.

Malvastrum
rotundifolium.

Spotted   Tracaustrum
Mallow   rotundifolium

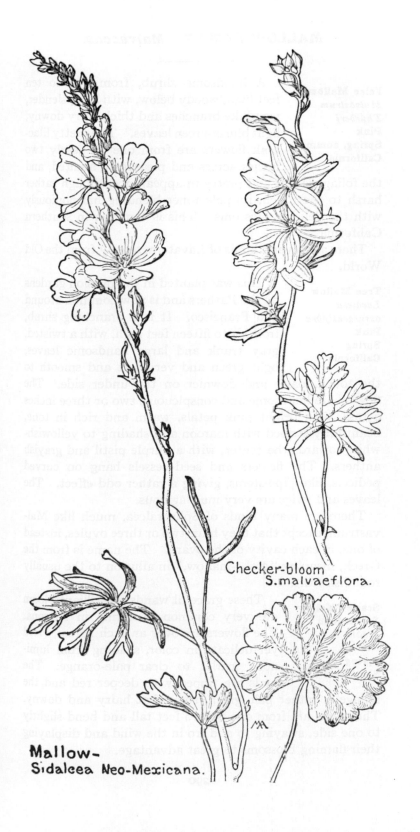

Checker-bloom
S. malvaeflora.

Mallow—
Sidalcea Neo-Mexicana.

MALLOW FAMILY. *Malvaceae.*

False Mallow
Malvástrum
Thúrberi
Pink
Spring, summer
California

A handsome shrub, from five to ten feet high, woody below, with long, slender, wandlike branches and thick, very downy, light bluish-green leaves. The pretty lilac-pink flowers are from one to nearly two inches across and pleasantly scented, and the foliage is soft and pretty in appearance, though rather harsh to the touch, its pale tones blending harmoniously with the delicate blossoms. This is common in southern California.

There are several kinds of Lavatera, mostly from the Old World.

Tree Mallow
Lavátera
assurgentiflóra
Pink
Spring
California

This was planted in the mission gardens by the Fathers and is now common around San Francisco. It is a branching shrub, from six to fifteen feet high, with a twisted, gray trunk and large handsome leaves, light green and very soft and smooth to the touch, paler and downier on the under side. The flowers are handsome and conspicuous, two or three inches across, with bright pink petals, warm and rich in tone, beautifully striped with maroon and shading to yellowish-white towards the center, with a purple pistil and grayish anthers. The flowers and seed-vessels hang on curved pedicels, like pipe-stems, giving a rather odd effect. The leaves and twigs are very mucilaginous.

There are many kinds of Sphaeralcea, much like Malvastrum, except that they have two or three ovules, instead of one, in each cavity of the ovary. The name is from the Greek, meaning "globe-mallow," in allusion to the usually roundish fruit.

Scarlet Mallow
Sphaerálcea
pedáta
Red
Spring
Southwest

These graceful wands of brilliant bloom are very common in spring in Arizona. The flowers are over an inch across, vivid yet delicate in color, shading from luminous scarlet to clear pale-orange. The buds are tipped with deeper red and the foliage is rather pale green, somewhat hairy and downy. The stems are from one to two feet tall and bend slightly to one side, swaying to and fro in the wind and displaying their flaming blossoms to great advantage.

Salmon Globe Mallow
Sphaeralcea pedata

Tree Mallow—
Lavatera
assurgentiflora

False Mallow—
Malvastrum
Thurberi.

ST. JOHN'S-WORT FAMILY. *Hypericaceae.*

Not a large family, mostly natives of temperate and warm regions. Ours are herbs, sometimes shrubby, without stipules, with opposite, toothless leaves, with clear or black dots; the flowers regular and complete, all the parts borne on the receptacle; the sepals and petals usually five; the stamens usually numerous, sometimes grouped in three to five clusters; the ovary superior; the fruit a capsule.

There are many kinds of Hypericum, widely distributed; the leaves without leaf-stalks, the flowers yellow, with three to six styles. This is the ancient Greek name. These plants bloom in June, about St. John's Day, and so tradition gives them magic properties, appropriate to the Eve of that day, when fairies and witches are abroad, and they are commonly called St. John's-wort.

St. John's-wort
Hypéricum concínnum
Yellow
Summer
California

This has very pretty flowers and grows from three to eighteen inches tall, with smooth stems, branching and woody at base, and smooth, rather bluish-green leaves, usually folded, not clasping at base, usually with only a few dots. The flowers are an inch or more across, with bright golden petals, with some black dots, and numerous stamens in three bunches, forming large, fuzzy, golden centers. This grows on dry hills and is supposed to be poisonous to sheep.

St. John's-wort
Hypéricum formósum var. Scoúleri
Yellow
Summer
West

A pretty plant, from six inches to three feet tall, with a stiff stem, often branching towards the top, and rather dull green leaves, blunt, oblong and clasping at base, about an inch long, thin in texture, with black dots on the margins. The flowers are from half an inch to an inch across, with bright yellow petals, dotted with black, and are very pretty, but not so handsome as the last. This grows in moist places, chiefly in the mountains, and is common in Yosemite.

Creeping St. John's-wort
Hypéricum anagalloìdes
Orange
Summer
Northwest

An attractive little plant, only a few inches tall, with many weak, slender, branching stems, spreading on the ground and rooting at the joints, and small, smooth, light yellowish-green leaves, often tinged with red. It grows in wet places

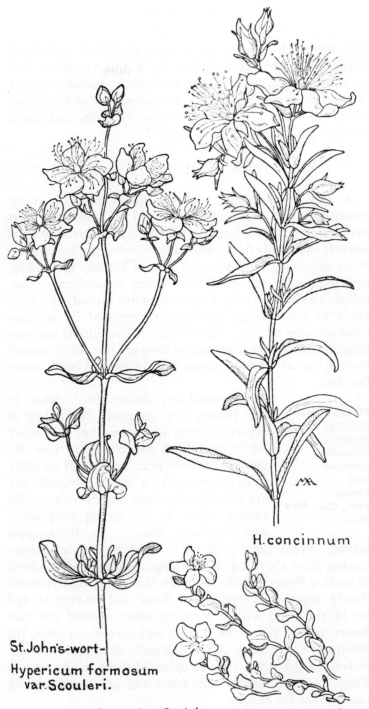

H. concinnum

St. John's-wort-
Hypericum formosum
var. Scouleri.

Creeping St. Johns-wort- H. anagalloides.

and forms close mats of foliage, sprinkled with light-orange or salmon-colored flowers, a quarter of an inch or more across, with fifteen to twenty, yellow stamens. The effect is something like Anagallis, Scarlet Pimpernel, hence the name. This is common in Yosemite and similar places, up to nine thousand feet.

FOUQUIERA FAMILY. *Fouquieriaceae.*

A very small family, with one genus and only a few species; natives of the Southwest and Mexico; the flowers are brilliant red, in terminal clusters; the sepals five, not united; the petals five, united into a tube, the lobes somewhat spreading; the stamens ten to fifteen, protruding, inserted under the pistil; the ovary imperfectly three-celled; the styles three, long, somewhat united; the seeds three to six, oblong, flattened, surrounded by a membranous wing or long, white hairs. These plants are very puzzling, but interesting, and as they are not nearly related they have at varicus times been classified with other families.

Flaming Sword, Ocotillo, Candle Flower
Fouquièra spléndens
Red
Spring
Ariz., Cal., New Mex.

A magnificent desert shrub, when in full bloom, but strangely forbidding in aspect in spite of its beauty. Its many stiff stems, from six to twenty feet tall, entirely without branches, stand up stiffly from the root, like a bunch of wands, and are armed their whole length with terrible thorns, which in the spring are masked with beautiful foliage, like little apple leaves. From the tip of each wand springs a glorious cluster, from six to ten inches long, composed of hundreds of scarlet flowers, each about an inch long, and crowded closely together, suggesting a flame and waving to and fro in the wind with a startling effect against the pale desert sand. When the flowers and leaves are gone, the clumps of dry, thorny sticks look quite dead and it is hard to believe that they were so splendid early in the season. They make an impenetrable fence and are much used by the Indians for hedges.

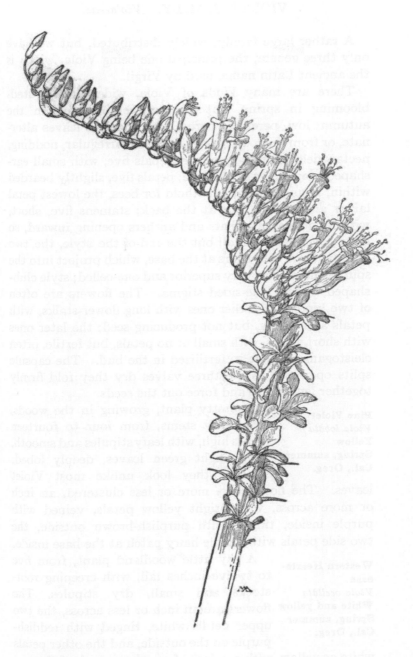

Flaming Sword—
Fouquiera splendens.

VIOLET FAMILY. *Violaceae.*

A rather large family, widely distributed, but we have only three genera, the principal one being Viola, which is the ancient Latin name, used by Virgil.

There are many kinds of Viola, widely distributed, blooming in spring, but often flowering again in the autumn; low, perennial herbs, with stipules; leaves alternate, or from the root; flowers complete, irregular, nodding, nectar-yielding, usually single; sepals five, with small ear-shaped projections at the base; petals five, slightly bearded within, so as to afford a foothold for bees, the lowest petal larger and with a spur at the back; stamens five, short, with broadened filaments and anthers opening inward, so as to cover the pistil all but the end of the style, the two lower anthers with spurs at the base, which project into the spur of the petal; ovary superior and one-celled; style club-shaped, with a one-sided stigma. The flowers are often of two kinds, the earlier ones with long flower-stalks, with petals and showy, but not producing seed; the later ones with short stalks, with small or no petals, but fertile, often cleistogamous, that is, fertilized in the bud. The capsule splits open and as the three valves dry they fold firmly together lengthwise and force out the seeds.

Pine Violet
Viola lobàta
Yellow
Spring, summer
Cal., Oreg.

A pretty plant, growing in the woods, with leafy stems, from four to fourteen inches high, with leafy stipules and smooth, rather light green leaves, deeply lobed, so that they look unlike most Violet leaves. The flowers are more or less clustered, an inch or more across, with bright yellow petals, veined with purple inside, tinged with purplish-brown outside, the two side petals with a little hairy patch at the base inside.

Western Hearts-ease
Viola ocellàta
White and yellow
Spring, summer
Cal., Oreg.

A shy little woodland plant, from five to twelve inches tall, with creeping root-stocks and small, dry stipules. The flowers are an inch or less across, the two upper petals white, tinged with reddish-purple on the outside, and the other petals white or yellow, with a splash of purple on each of the two side petals and the lower one veined with purple. This grows in shady woods.

296

Western Heartsease - Viola ocellata.

Pine Violet - V. lobata.

VIOLET FAMILY. *Violaceae.*

Yellow Mountain Violet
Vìola venòsa
Yellow
Spring
Northwest and Utah

An attractive kind, usually about three inches tall, with almost smooth leaves, often with purplish veins, with blunt tips and margins obscurely or coarsely toothed, or almost toothless, and with long leaf-stalks. The flowers are usually less than half an inch long, with clear yellow petals, more or less tinged with purple on the outside, the lower petal usually with several, purplish-black veins, the two side petals with one or two veins. This has no scent, the capsule is roundish and hairy, and the cleistogamous flowers are abundant. It grows on dry mountainsides and is very variable both as to flower and foliage and much smaller at great altitudes, the whole plant being not more than an inch high. The drawing is of a Utah plant.

Canada Violet
Vìola Canadénsis
Pale-violet, white
Spring, summer
West, etc., except Cal.

This is quite tall, the slender, rather weak stems being sometimes over a foot high, with smooth leaves, often with some hairs on the veins of the under side. The flowers, over half an inch across, with a short petal-spur, are almost white, delicately veined with purple, yellow in the throat and tinged with violet or purple on the outside. Occasionally they are pure-white all over and sometimes sweet-scented. The capsule is oval and smooth. This is common in eastern mountain woods, and to eastern eyes looked far from home when we found it in Walnut Canyon in Arizona.

Pale Mountain Violet
Vìola adúnca var. glàbra
Pale-blue
Spring, summer
Utah

This is small and low, about three inches high, with leafy stems, forming a clump of small, smooth, more or less toothed leaves, with blunt tips, dark green on the upper side and paler on the under, with two, quite large, fringed bracts at the bases of the leaf-stalks, and two, small, fringed bracts on the flower-stems, half an inch below the flower. The flowers are scentless, measure less than half an inch across, and are pale-blue or almost white, with veins of dark blue on the lower petal and tufts of white, fuzzy hairs inside, at the base of the side petals, the spur purplish. This grows in mountain canyons, at a height of five thousand to nine thousand feet, and is very small at great altitudes.

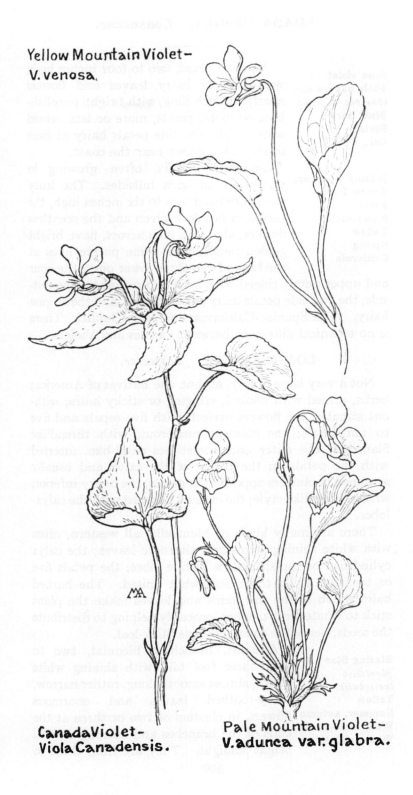

Yellow Mountain Violet—
V. venosa.

Canada Violet—
Viola Canadensis.

Pale Mountain Violet—
V. adunca var. glabra.

Blue violet
Vìola adûnca var.
lóngipes
Blue, purple
Spring
Cal., Oreg.

A pretty plant, two to four inches high, with slightly hairy leaves and flowers nearly an inch long, with bright purplish-blue or violet petals, more or less veined with purple, the side petals hairy at base inside. This grows near the coast.

Johnny Jump-up,
Yellow Pansy
Vìola
pedunculàta
Yellow
Spring
California

Charming flowers, often growing in quantities on open hillsides. The leafy stems are from two to six inches high, the leaves rather dark green and the scentless flowers, about an inch across, have bright golden petals, with some purple lines at the base of the three lower ones, the spur and upper petals tinged with brownish-purple on the outside, the two side petals hairy at base inside, and the stigma hairy. The Spanish-Californian name is Gallito. There is no technical difference between Pansies and Violets.

LOASA FAMILY. *Loasaceae.*

Not a very large family, all but one natives of America; herbs, armed with hooked, stinging or sticky hairs; without stipules; the flowers perfect, with five sepals and five to ten petals; the stamens numerous, with threadlike filaments, the outer ones sometimes petal-like, inserted with the petals on the throat of the calyx and usually arranged in clusters opposite the petals; the ovary inferior, with a threadlike style; the capsule crowned with the calyx-lobes.

There are many kinds of Mentzelia, all western, often with white shining stems and alternate leaves; the calyx cylindrical or top-shaped, with five lobes; the petals five or ten; the styles three, somewhat united. The barbed hairs which clothe the stems and leaves make the plant stick to whatever it touches, probably helping to distribute the seeds, hence the common name Stick-leaf.

Blazing Star
Mentzèlia
laevicàulis
Yellow
Summer, autumn
West, except
Wash. and Ariz.

A stout, branching biennial, two to over three feet tall, with shining white stems, almost smooth, long, rather narrow, wavy-toothed leaves and enormous flowers, in clusters of two or three at the ends of the branches and opening only in bright sunlight. They are from three to

Blue Violet-
V. adunca var. longipes.

Johnny Jump-up-
Viola pedunculata.

five inches across, with five, broad, light yellow petals and quantities of very long stamens, making a beautiful center. Five of the stamens have broadened filaments, resembling narrow petals, the style is three-cleft, and the capsule is oblong, containing many flat, winged seeds. These plants usually grow in dry stream-beds and are not rare, but through various accidents I have never been able to secure a drawing of either this or the next.

Evening Star
Mentzèlia Lìndleyi
Yellow Summer California

A more slender plant than the last, with magnificent flowers, two and a half inches across, which open in the evening and remain open during the following morning. They have five, broad petals, with pointed tips, bright golden-yellow, colored with vermilion at the base, and handsome yellow centers. The filaments are very slender, some of the outer ones slightly broadened at base, and the style is not cleft. This grows in the mountains. There is a drawing of it in Miss Parsons's *Wild Flowers of California*. It is called Buena Mujer, or Good Woman, by the Spanish Californians, because the leaves stick so tightly to one.

Mentzèlia multiflòra
Yellow Spring Southwest, Utah, etc.

An odd-looking plant, with very pale, straggling stems and thickish leaves, a pretty shade of pale green, all exceedingly disagreeable to touch. The buds are tipped with salmon-color and the flowers are an inch and a half to two inches across, with a long green calyx-tube with buff lobes, ten petals, bright yellow inside and pale buff outside, and pretty, fuzzy, yellow centers. They open in the evening, about five o'clock, and the plant would be pretty, in spite of its harsh foliage, if more of the flowers were out at one time. This is common along roadsides in the Southwest and in New Mexico and Colorado.

Mentzèlia gracilénta
Yellow Spring Southwest

This has several pale greenish or pinkish stems, from a few inches to a foot and a half tall, which look smooth but are very harsh to the touch, springing from a cluster of stiff, harsh, dull-green leaves, variously lobed or toothed. The flowers are nearly an inch across, with glossy, bright yellow petals and beautiful, fuzzy, yellow centers, and are very delicate and pretty.

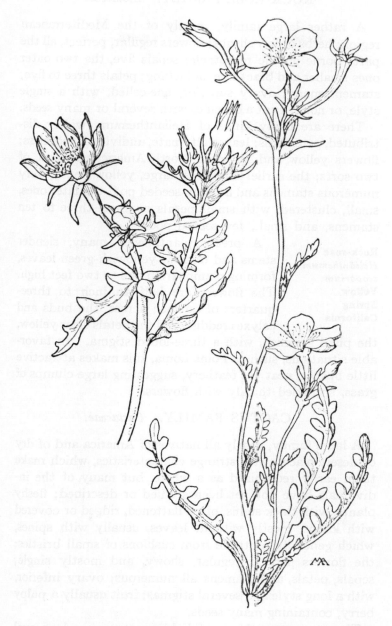

Mentzelia multiflora. **M. gracilenta.**

ROCK-ROSE FAMILY. *Cistaceae.*

A rather large family, mostly of the Mediterranean region; herbs or low shrubs; flowers regular, perfect, all the parts borne on the receptacle; sepals five, the two outer ones smaller and bract-like, or lacking; petals three to five; stamens many; ovary superior, one-celled, with a single style, or none; fruit a capsule, with several or many seeds.

There are many kinds of Helianthemum, widely distributed, perennials; leaves alternate, undivided, toothless; flowers yellow and, in most North American species, of two sorts; the earlier ones with large, yellow petals, very numerous stamens and a many-seeded pod; the later ones, small, clustered, with small petals or none, three to ten stamens, and small, few-seeded pods.

Rock-rose
Heliánthemum
scopàrium
Yellow
Spring
California

A pretty plant, with many, slender stems and narrow, yellowish-green leaves, forming clumps from one to two feet high. The flowers are half an inch to three-quarters of an inch across, the buds and calyxes reddish and the petals clear yellow, the pistil greenish, with a three-lobed stigma. In favorable situations, such as Point Loma, this makes attractive little bushes, neat yet feathery, suggesting large clumps of grass, sprinkled thickly with flowers.

CACTUS FAMILY. *Cactareae.*

A large family, nearly all natives of America and of dry or desert places, with strange characteristics, which make them easily recognized as a whole, but many of the individuals have not yet been studied or described; fleshy plants, with thick stems, often flattened, ridged or covered with knobs, mostly without leaves, usually with spines, which generally protrude from cushions of small bristles; the flowers perfect, regular, showy, and mostly single; sepals, petals, and stamens all numerous; ovary inferior, with a long style and several stigmas; fruit usually a pulpy berry, containing many seeds.

There are many kinds of Echinocactus, round or oval plants, mostly ribbed, with bunches of spines of several kinds, arranged in straight or spiral rows; the fruits scaly, though spineless.

304

Rock-rose —   Helianthemum scoparium.

CACTUS FAMILY. *Cactaceae.*

Barrel Cactus, Bisnaga
Echinocáctus Wislizèni
Yellow, reddish
Summer
Southwest

A common and useful kind, the shape and often the size of a barrel, covered with spines. The Indians cut off the top of the plant and pound the pulp with a stick into a soft mass, which they squeeze with their hands, extracting a large amount of watery juice, which is wholesome and not unpalatable and has often saved lives in the desert. Indians use the spines for fish-hooks, hence a common name, Fish-hook Cactus, and the celebrated cactus candy is made from it. The flowers are large.

There are many kinds of Echinocereus, oblong or cylindrical, spiny plants, generally a few inches tall, usually growing in clumps; stems ridged, or with spiny ribs; fruits spiny.

Hedgehog Cactus
Echinocèreus polyacánthus
Red
Spring
Ariz., New Mex.
Tex.

This forms a clump of several stems, each about the shape and size of a cucumber, and armed with bunches of long, stiff spines. The flowers are two or three inches long, with deep red petals, dull pink anthers, and a bright green pistil. This grows in the Grand Canyon.

There are many kinds of Opuntia, with jointed stems, cylindrical or flattened, armed with bristles, usually with spines. The fruits and fleshy joints are good for fodder, if the spines are removed, and hence there has been much inquiry into the economic value of these plants. It has been found that the spiny species are the most valuable for fodder, under extremely arid conditions, as the spines can be burned off, while the unarmed forms are subject to the attacks of so many animals that a crop cannot be secured without the protection of fences. The spines are removed either by singeing the growing plant with a torch, or the upper parts are cut off and thrown into a fire, or sometimes the plants are made into fodder by being chopped up, spines and all, in a machine. The Prickly Pears in Sicily and the Orient came from America.

Opúntia acanthocárpa
Yellow
Spring
Southwest

From three to six feet tall, resembling Cholla, with long, cylindrical joints and whitish spines. The pretty flowers are about two inches long, with orange-yellow petals and an ivory-white pistil. The

Hedgehog
Cactus.

Echinocereus polyacanthus.

Opuntia acanthocarpa.

fruits are spiny and become dry when ripe. This grows in the desert around Needles.

Cholla
Opúntia fúlgida
Red
Spring, summer
Arizona

A horrible shrub, or dwarf tree, four to six feet high, with a thick trunk and several, spreading, contorted branches, with cylindrical joints, twisting in awkward ways. The trunk and larger limbs are brownish-gray, starred with dead, dry spines, but the twigs are pale bluish-green, covered thickly with stars of pale-yellowish spines, each an inch or so long, with a barbed tip. From the numerous magenta flowers strange, yellowish, cup-shaped fruits develop, seeming to spring one out of the other in a haphazard way, hanging in long chains, awkward but rather ornamental, and remaining on the plants for several years without change, except that they grow slightly larger. The distant effect of this plant is a pale, fuzzy mass, attractive in color, giving no hint of its treacherous character—more like a wild beast than a plant! The joints suggest a very ferocious chestnut-burr and break off at a touch, thrusting their spines deeply into the flesh of the unwary passer-by, so that the Indian story, that this plant flings its darts at wayfarers from a distance, might almost as well be true, and the barbs making the extraction difficult and painful. The ground under the plants is strewn with fallen joints, which take root and propagate themselves. Small animals pile these around their holes for defense, several kinds of birds build in the thorny branches and are safe from enemies, and the fruits, being spineless and succulent, are valuable for fodder, so the Cholla is not entirely malevolent. The name is pronounced *Choya*. There are many similar kinds, some with very handsome rose-like flowers, others with bright scarlet fruits. They are curious and interesting inhabitants of the desert.

Prickly Pear
Opúntia basilàris
Pink
Spring
Arizona

Low plants, with no main stem, with spreading, flattened branches, the joints of which are flat disks, resembling fleshy, bluish-green leaves. These disks are half an inch to an inch thick and six inches long, more or less heart-shaped, sprouting one out of the other, at unexpected angles. The beautiful flower is about three inches across, like a tissue-paper rose, pale or very

Opuntia basilaris.

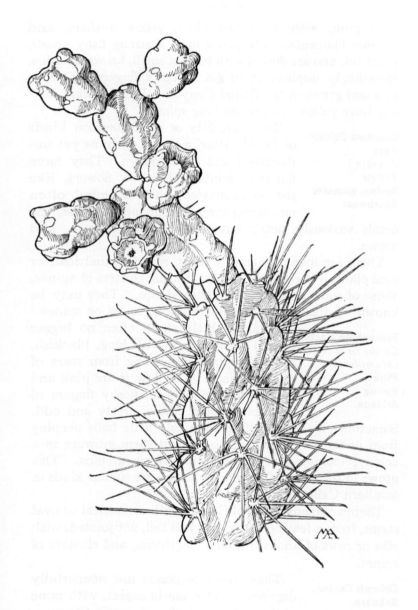

Cholla
(fruit)

Opuntia
fulgida.

deep pink, with a whitish pistil, yellow anthers, and crimson filaments. The joints have a strong fishy smell, when cut, and are dotted with tufts of small, brown bristles, exceedingly unpleasant to get in one's fingers. This is rare and grows at the Grand Canyon.· Prickly pears usually have yellow flowers and long spines.

Common Prickly Pear
Opúntia
Yellow
Spring, summer
Southwest

There are fifty or more common kinds of Prickly Pear, many of them as yet undescribed and little known. They have flattened joints and yellow flowers, like the one illustrated, which is typical, often measuring three or four inches across, the petals variously tinted outside with salmon, rose, and brown.

There are many kinds of Cactus, round, cylindrical, or oval plants, covered with knobs, bearing clusters of spines, those of some species having hooked tips. They may be known by their smooth fruits, without scales or spines.

Pincushion Cactus
Cáctus Gràhami
(Mamillaria)
Pink
Spring
Arizona

A quaint little plant, often no bigger than a billiard ball, with long, blackish, hooklike spines, projecting from stars of smaller spines. The flowers are pink and the berries are smooth, fleshy fingers of brightest scarlet, edible, pretty and odd. Sometimes we see one of these prickly little balls peeping from under a rock and again we find them growing in a colony, looking much like a pile of sea-urchins. This grows in the Grand Canyon, and there are similar kinds in southern California.

There are many kinds of Cereus, with cylindrical or oval stems, from a few inches to forty feet tall, not jointed, with ribs or rows of knobs, running lengthwise, and clusters of spines.

Column Cactus,
Sahuaro
Cèreus gigantèus
White
Spring, summer
Arizona

These tree-like plants are wonderfully dignified and solemn in aspect, with none of the grotesque or ferocious effect so common among their relations. They grow in numbers on the mountain slopes around Tucson and are easily recognized by their size and very upright form, rearing their thick, cylindrical branches straight up in the air, to a height of thirty or forty feet. They are smooth and light green, armed with

310

Pincushion Cactus.
Cactus Grahami.

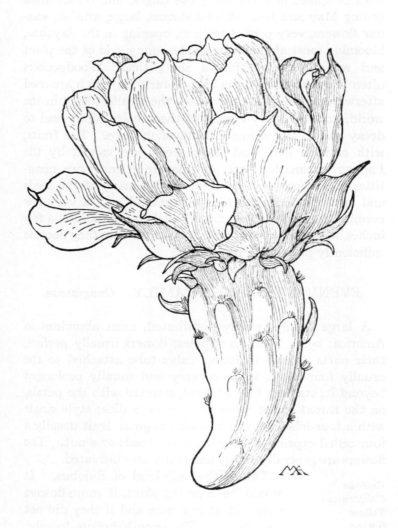

Common Prickly Pear-   Opuntia.

rows of spines in stars along the ridges, and ornamented during May and June with handsome, large, whitish, wax-like flowers, very perfect in form, opening in the daytime, blooming most abundantly on the sunny side of the plant and remaining open but a short time. Woodpeckers often make holes for nests in the branches, which are used afterwards by a little native owl, the smallest kind in the world, and by honey-bees, and these holes often lead to decay and to the ultimate death of the tree. The fruits, with crimson flesh and black seeds, are valued by the Papago Indians for food, and mature in enormous quantities in midsummer, but birds eat up many of the seeds and of the millions reaching the ground only a very few germinate and develop into odd, little round plants, a few inches high, often eaten by some animal before they become sufficiently prickly for protection.

EVENING PRIMROSE FAMILY. *Onagraceae.*

A large family, widely distributed, most abundant in America; herbs, with no stipules; flowers usually perfect, their parts usually in fours; calyx-tube attached to the usually four-celled, inferior ovary and usually prolonged beyond it; stamens four or eight, inserted with the petals, on the throat of the calyx-tube, or on a disk; style single with a four-lobed or round-headed stigma; fruit usually a four-celled capsule, containing small seeds or a nut. The flowers are generally showy and many are cultivated.

Eulòbus
Califórnicus
Yellow
Spring
Southwest

This is the only kind of Eulobus. It would be a pretty plant, if more flowers were out at one time and if they did not close so soon. The smooth, hollow, loosely-branching stem is from one to three feet tall, with a "bloom," the leaves are smooth, rather light dull-green, and the buds are erect. The flowers are about three-quarters of an inch across, with a very short calyx-tube, light-yellow petals, fading to reddish-pink, eight stamens, four of them smaller and shorter, and the light-green stigma with a round top. The slender pods are three inches long, smooth, cylindrical, and turning stiffly down, with many seeds. This grows in mountain canyons.

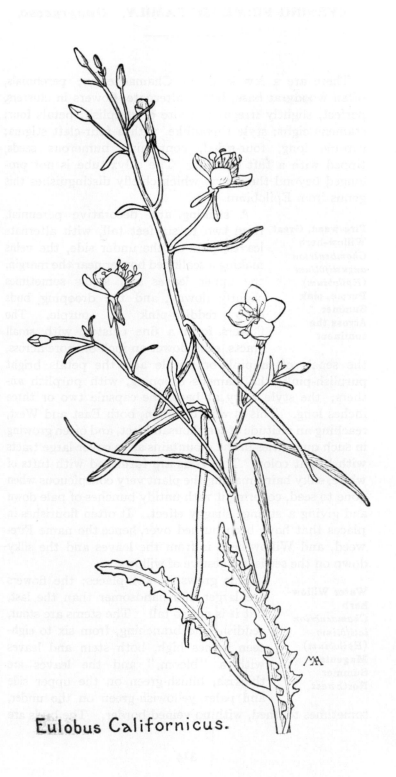

Eulobus Californicus.

There are a few kinds of Chamaenerion; perennials, often woody at base; leaves alternate; flowers in clusters, perfect, slightly irregular, white or purplish; petals four; stamens eight; style threadlike, with a four-cleft stigma; capsule long, four-sided, containing numerous seeds, tipped with a tuft of hairs. The calyx-tube is not prolonged beyond the ovary, which chiefly distinguishes this genus from Epilobium.

Fire-weed, Great Willow-herb
Chamaenèrion angustifòlium
(Epilobium)
Purple, pink
Summer
Across the continent

A striking and decorative perennial, from two to six feet tall, with alternate leaves, pale on the under side, the veins making a scalloped border near the margin, the upper leaves and stems sometimes slightly downy, and the drooping buds deep reddish-pink or purple. The flowers form a fine cluster, with small bracts, each flower an inch or more across, the sepals often pink or purple and the petals bright purplish-pink; the stamens drooping, with purplish anthers; the style hairy at base, the capsule two or three inches long. This is very common, both East and West, reaching an altitude of ten thousand feet, and often growing in such quantities in the mountains as to cover large tracts with bright color. The seeds are furnished with tufts of white, silky hairs, making the plant very conspicuous when gone to seed, covering it with untidy bunches of pale down and giving a strange shaggy effect. It often flourishes in places that have been burned over, hence the name Fire-weed, and Willow-herb is from the leaves and the silky down on the seeds, suggestive of willows.

Water Willow-herb
Chamaenèrion latifòlium
(Epilobium)
Magenta
Summer
Northwest

This grows in wet places; the flowers are larger and handsomer than the last, but it is not so tall. The stems are stout, reddish, and branching, from six to eighteen inches high, both stem and leaves with a "bloom," and the leaves are thickish, bluish-green on the upper side and paler yellowish-green on the under, sometimes toothed, with no veined border. The buds are

WaterWillow-herb.
Chamaenerion
latifolium.

Fire-weed.
C.angustifolium.

deep-red and the flowers form a handsomer cluster, shorter than the last, with leafy bracts, each flower from one to over two inches across, with reddish-pink sepals, deep-red outside, and magenta petals veined with deeper color, sometimes notched, one petal longer than the others; the anthers purplish; the pistil drooping and purplish, with a smooth style. This plant is also covered with tufts of white down when gone to seed. The contrasting purples and reds of the flowers give a very vivid effect, set off by the bluish-green foliage, especially when growing among the gray rocks of moraines, watered by icy glacier streams. It reaches an altitude of ten thousand feet, growing in the East and in Europe and Asia.

There are many kinds of Epilobium, differing from Chamaenerion chiefly in the calyx-tube, which is prolonged beyond the ovary.

Willow Herb
Epilòbium
Franciscànum
Pink
Spring
Northwest
A perennial, not especially pretty, with a stout, reddish stem, from one to three feet tall, slightly downy above, and dull green leaves, mostly smooth and the lower ones opposite. The flowers are less than half an inch across, with bright or pale, purplish-pink petals, deeply notched and not spreading. This grows in wet spots around San Francisco.

There are several kinds of Gayophytum; differing from Epilobium in the capsule and seeds, and easily distinguished from them by the hairy buds; leaves alternate, long, narrow, and toothless; flowers small; petals four, white or pink, with very short claws; stamens, with swinging anthers, eight, four shorter and usually sterile; capsule club-shaped. The species are difficult to distinguish, because of the smallness of the flowers.

Gayophỳtum
eriospèrmum
White
Summer
Cal., Oreg.
A delicate little plant, with smooth, purplish stems, exceedingly slender branches, dull green leaves, and pretty little flowers, an eighth of an inch to half an inch across, white, with a little yellow in the center, fading to pink. This grows in sandy soil, at rather high altitudes, in Yosemite.

**Willow-herb –
Epilobium Franciscanum.**

**Gayophytum
eriospermum.**

EVENING PRIMROSE FAMILY. *Onagraceae.*

There are numerous kinds of Godetia, variable and difficult to distinguish, not yet fully understood by botanists, all western and mostly Californian, with narrow, alternate leaves and handsome flowers, which close at night. They have four petals and resemble Onagra, but the flowers are never yellow and the anthers are not swinging, but fixed to the tips of the filaments by their bases; also resembling Clarkia, but the petals are without claws. The calyx is often colored, tube more or less funnel-form, lobes turned back, or more or less united and turned to one side; stamens eight, unequal, the shorter ones opposite the petals; style threadlike; stigma with four, short lobes; capsule four-sided, or cylindrical, mostly ribbed, rather leathery, splitting open, with four valves, containing many seeds. These plants bloom in late spring, hence the pretty name, Farewell-to-Spring.

Farewell-to-Spring
Godètia deflèxa
Pink
Summer
California

A branching plant, woody at base, two feet high, with smooth stems; smooth, toothed leaves; nodding buds and large handsome flowers. The petals are pale-pink, about an inch long, the pistil pink, and at a distance the effect of the flower is much like a Mallow. As is usual with Godetias, the sepals are stuck together and stand out at one side, giving the flower a quaint effect of having thrown back a little hood in order to look about. This grows in light shade.

Farewell-to-Spring
Godètia quadrivúlnera
Pink, lilac
Spring, summer
Northwest

This is common in the foothills of the Sierras and Coast Ranges and has a slender stem, about a foot tall, with more or less downy leaves, sometimes slightly toothed, and a few very pretty flowers, about an inch and a half across, with bright lilac-pink petals, usually splashed with carmine. This red spot gives a vivid effect and the delicate flowers look exceedingly gay and charming, as they sway in the wind among tall grasses on open hillsides.

Godètia Góddardii
var. capitàta
Pink
Spring, summer
California

From one to two feet tall, with a rather stout, more or less branching stem and soft, rather downy, dull green leaves. The flowers are about an inch across, with purplish-pink petals, often stained with crimson at the tips. This is found on dry hills in the Coast Ranges.

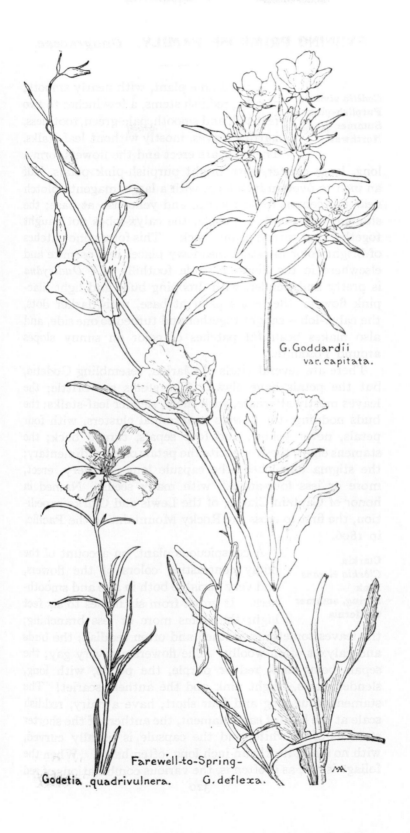

G. Goddardii
var. capitata.

Farewell-to-Spring-
Godetia quadrivulnera. G. deflexa.

Godètia vimínea
Purplish-pink
Summer
Northwest

A handsome plant, with nearly smooth, slender, reddish stems, a few inches to two feet tall, and smooth, pale-green, toothless, narrow leaves, mostly without leaf-stalks. The buds are erect and the flowers form a long, loose cluster, with bright purplish-pink petals, half an inch to over an inch long, with a large, magenta blotch near the center, or at the tip, and yellowish at base; the stamens and pistil all purple; the calyx-lobes not caught together, but turned primly back. This forms fine patches of bright color in rather meadowy places in Yosemite and elsewhere in the Sierra Nevada foothills. *G. Dudleyàna* is pretty and slender, with drooping buds and light lilac-pink flowers, the petals paler at base, with darker dots, the calyx-lobes caught together and turned to one side, and also makes beautiful patches of color on sunny slopes around Yosemite.

There are several kinds of Clarkia, resembling Godetia, but the petals have claws. The stems are brittle; the leaves mostly alternate, with short, slender leaf-stalks; the buds nodding; the flowers in terminal clusters, with four petals, never yellow, and four sepals, turned back; the stamens eight, those opposite the petals often rudimentary; the stigma four-lobed; the capsule long, leathery, erect, more or less four-angled, with many seeds. Named in honor of Captain Clarke, of the Lewis and Clarke expedition, the first to cross the Rocky Mountains to the Pacific, in 1806.

Clarkia
Clàrkia élegans
Pink
Spring, summer
California

A conspicuous plant, on account of the oddly contrasting colors of the flowers, and very variable both in size and smoothness. It grows from six inches to six feet high; the stems more or less branching; the leaves sometimes toothed and often reddish; the buds and calyxes often woolly. The flowers are very gay; the sepals being dark red or purple, the petals, with long, slender claws, bright pink and the anthers scarlet! The stamens, four long and four short, have a hairy, reddish scale at the base of each filament, the anthers of the shorter stamens often white, and the capsule is usually curved, with no stalk, nearly an inch long, often hairy. When the foliage is red, as it often is, the various combinations of red

Godetia viminea.   Clarkia elegans.

in the flowers and leaves are quite startling. This is common in the foothills of the Sierra Nevada and Coast Ranges and is often rather shabby looking, but in favorable situations is very handsome.

Clarkia
Clàrkia
rhomboìdea
Purple
Spring, summer
Northwest, Nev.,
Utah

Pretty and delicate and not nearly so conspicuous as the last, with a slender, smooth, branching stem, one to three feet tall, with smooth leaves, mostly alternate, nodding buds, and a few pretty flowers, about three-quarters of an inch across. The sepals are reddish-yellow; the petals pinkish-purple, often dotted with purple at base, with a short, broad, toothed claw; the stigma magenta; the filaments purple, with a whitish, hairy scale at the base of each; the anthers grayish, all perfect; the capsule four-angled, slightly curved, about an inch long. This grows in the foothills of the Sierra Nevada and Coast Ranges and is widely distributed in Yosemite, but nowhere very abundant.

Pink Fairies
Clàrkia pulchélla
Pink
Summer
Northwest

Odd and exceedingly charming flowers, with very slender, very slightly downy, purplish, branching stems, from six inches to a foot tall, and smooth leaves. The flowers are fantastic in form, the airiest and most fairy-like blossoms that can well be imagined, over two inches across, their delicate petals with long, toothed claws and three lobes, bright rose-pink, shading to a deeper tint at the base, the calyx slightly downy and reddish. Four of the stamens are perfect and four are rudimentary; the anthers are reddish; the pistil white; the capsule an inch long, eight-angled, with a spreading stalk. It is a pretty sight to see these gay flowers dancing in the wind on open mountain slopes. *C. concínna (Euchari-dium)*, of the Coast Ranges, is similar, equally beautiful and even more brilliant in coloring; the flowers sometimes in such quantities as to make patches of bright pink color, very effective when growing among yellow Sedums, Scarlet Larkspurs, and scarlet Indian Pinks, in shady mountain canyons.

Clarkia
rhomboidea.

Pirk Fairies-
C.pulchella.

EVENING PRIMROSE FAMILY. *Onagraceae.*

There are several kinds of Sphaerostigma; leaves alternate; flowers yellow, white or pink, turning green or reddish; stamens eight, with oblong, swinging anthers; style threadlike, with a round-top stigma; capsule four-celled, usually long and narrow, four-angled, often twisted, with no stalk.

Evening Primrose
Sphaerostigma
bistórta
(Oenothera)
Yellow
Spring
California

A common kind, very variable in its manner of growth, being tall and erect in moist, shady places and spreading flat on the ground in dry, sunny spots. The leaves are dull green, more or less downy and more or less toothed, and the flowers are three-quarters of an inch across, clear yellow, usually with a speck, or blotch, of reddish-brown at the base of each petal; the stamens and pistil also yellow; the pods reddish and very much twisted. Gravelly washes are often thickly sprinkled with these gay and charming flowers.

Sphaerostigma
Veitchiànum
(Oenothera)
Yellow
Spring
California

Much like the last, but the flowers are only a little over a quarter of an inch across. The pods are dark red and shiny, with a few hairs.

Beach Primrose
Sphaerostigma
viridéscens
(Oenothera
cheiranthifolia var.
suffriticosa)
Yellow
All seasons
California

A beautiful seashore plant, forming large, low clumps of reclining stems and pale gray, downy foliage, the twigs and younger leaves silvery-white. The flowers are about an inch and a quarter across, clear yellow, often with two, dark red dots at the base of each petal; the stamens and pistil also yellow of the same shade; the pods pinkish, downy, and much twisted. The flat masses of pale foliage, strewn with golden disks, are exceedingly effective, growing in drifting sand hills along the coast, from San Francisco south.

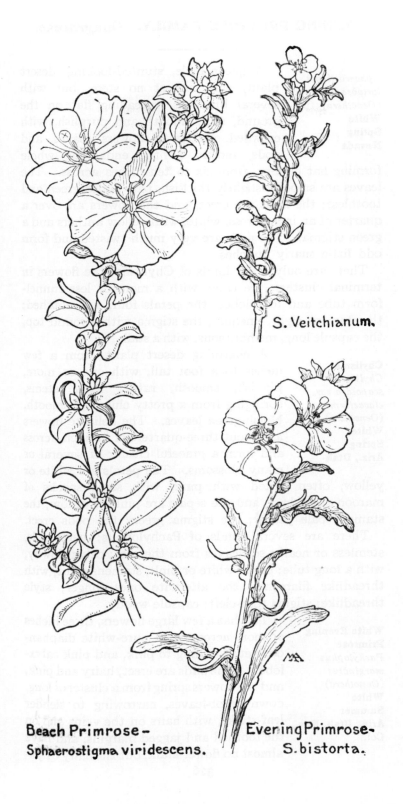

S. Veitchianum.

Beach Primrose –
Sphaerostigma viridescens.

Evening Primrose –
S. bistorta.

EVENING PRIMROSE FAMILY. *Onagraceae.*

Sphaerostigma tortuòsa.
(*Oenothera*)
White
Spring
Nevada

A queer little, stunted-looking, desert plant, with almost no stem, but with several branches, spreading flat on the ground, stiff, smooth and purplish, with crowded clusters of flowers, leaves, and pods, mostly at the ends, the whole forming flat clumps, from six to ten inches across. The leaves are smooth, slightly thickish, pale bluish-green and toothless; the buds are erect, and the flowers are over a quarter of an inch across, white, with yellow anthers and a green stigma. The pods are very much twisted and form odd little snarly bunches.

There are only a few kinds of Chylisma; the flowers in terminal clusters; the calyx with a more or less funnel-form tube and four lobes; the petals four, not notched; the stamens eight, unequal; the stigma with a round top, the capsule long, membranous, with a stalk.

Chylisma
Chylisma scapoìdea var. clavaefórmis
(*Oenothera*)
White
Spring
Ariz., Utah

A charming desert plant, from a few inches to a foot tall, with one or more, pinkish, smooth, rather leafy stems, springing from a pretty clump of smooth, bluish-green leaves. The delicate flowers are about three-quarters of an inch across and form a graceful cluster of several or many blossoms. The petals are white or yellow, often tinted with pink, with some specks of maroon at the base, and the sepals are pinkish-yellow; the stamens pale yellow; the stigma green; the pods erect.

There are several kinds of Pachylophus; perennials, stemless or nearly so; leaves from the root; calyx downy, with a long tube; petals white or pink; stamens eight, with threadlike filaments, the alternate ones longer; style threadlike; stigma four-cleft; capsule woody.

White Evening
Primrose
Pachýlophus marginàtus
(*Oenothera*)
White
Summer
Ariz., Utah, Nev.,
Col.

This has a few large flowers, three inches or more across, with pure-white diaphanous petals, fading to pink, and pink calyx-lobes. The buds are erect, hairy and pink, and the flowers spring from a cluster of long, downy root-leaves, narrowing to slender leaf-stalks, with hairs on the veins and on the toothed and jagged margins, and have almost no flower-stalk, but the hairy calyx-

White
Evening Primrose.

Pachylophus
marginatus.

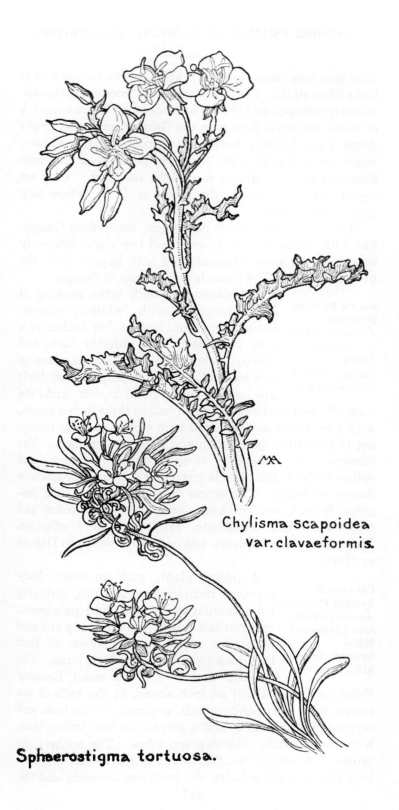

Chylisma scapoidea
var. clavaeformis.

Sphaerostigma tortuosa.

tube is so long, sometimes as much as seven inches, that it looks like a stalk. The root is thick and woody and the capsule is egg-shaped and ribbed, with no stem. There is a patch of these wonderful flowers in the Grand Canyon on Bright Angel trail, halfway between the rim and the plateau, where in a shaded spot beside a great rock the pure blossoms seem to shed a moonlight radiance. They are equally beautiful on the dry plains of Utah, where they grow in quantities.

There are several kinds of Anogra, resembling Onagra, but with white or pink flowers and the seeds differently arranged; the stems often clothed with papery bark; the buds drooping. The name is an anagram of Onagra.

Prairie Evening Primrose
Ánogra albicáulis.
(Oenothera)
White
Spring, summer
Southwest, etc.

A conspicuous kind, often growing in large patches, with whitish, downy, branching stems, from a few inches to a foot tall, often with shreddy bark, and downy, pale bluish-green leaves, more or less toothed. The drooping, downy buds are tinted with reddish-pink and the lovely flowers are from one and a half to three inches across, with pure white petals, tinted with yellow at base, changing to pink after pollination and fading to crimson. The stamens have cobwebby threads, white filaments, and yellow anthers, the pistil is green and the curved capsule is downy or hairy. The whole color scheme, of pale sea-green foliage, reddish buds, and white, rose-color, and crimson flowers, is delicate, harmonious, and effective. This grows in sandy places, and on the prairies from Dakota to Mexico.

Cut-leaved Evening Primrose
Ánogra coronopi-fòlia (Oenothera)
White
Summer, autumn
Ariz., Utah, etc.

A pretty plant, with an erect, leafy stem, six inches to two feet tall, springing from running rootstocks, and pale green, more or less downy, leaves, finely cut into numerous, small, narrow lobes, so that they look like rather dry little ferns. The delicate flowers are the usual Evening Primrose shape, about an inch across, in the axils of the leaves, with pure white petals, greenish at the base and turning pink in fading, and a calyx-tube two inches long, with turned-back, pinkish-green lobes. The anthers are brown, the pistil green, the throat of the corolla is closed by a fringe of white hairs, the buds are drooping and the

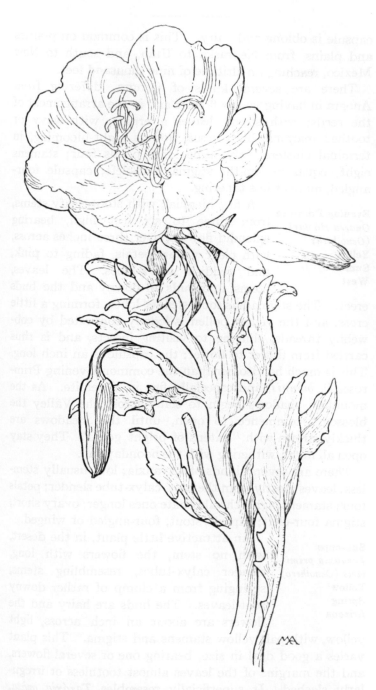

Prairie Evening Primrose – Anogra albicaulis.

capsule is oblong and hairy. This is common on prairies and plains, from Nebraska to Utah, and south to New Mexico, reaching an altitude of nine thousand feet.

There are several kinds of Onagra, differing from Anogra in having yellow flowers and in the arrangement of the seeds; with stems; leaves alternate, with wavy or toothed margins; buds erect; flowers night-blooming, in terminal clusters; calyx-tube long; petals four; stamens eight, equal in length; stigma four-cleft; capsule four-angled, more or less tapering.

Evening Primrose
Ónagra Hóokeri
(Oenothera)
Yellow
Summer
West

A fine biennial, with stout, leafy stems, from three to six feet high, bearing splendid flowers, over three inches across, with clear yellow petals, fading to pink, and reddish calyx-lobes. The leaves, stems, and buds all downy and the buds erect. The stigma has four, slender lobes, forming a little cross, and the yellow pollen is loosely connected by cobwebby threads, clinging to visiting insects, and is thus carried from flower to flower; the capsule is an inch long. This is much handsomer than the common Evening Primrose, *O. biénnis*, and especially fine in Yosemite. As the mountain shadows begin to slant across the Valley the blossoms commence to open, until the meadows are thickly strewn with "patens of bright gold." They stay open all night, withering with the noonday sun.

There are several kinds of Lavauxia; low, usually stemless; leaves mostly from the root; calyx-tube slender; petals four; stamens eight, the alternate ones longer; ovary short, stigma four-cleft; capsule stout, four-angled or winged.

Sun-cups
Lavaùxia primi-
vèris (Oenothera)
Yellow
Spring
Arizona

An attractive little plant, in the desert, with no stem, the flowers with long, slender calyx-tubes, resembling stems, springing from a clump of rather downy root-leaves. The buds are hairy and the flowers are about an inch across, light yellow, with pale yellow stamens and stigma. This plant varies a good deal in size, bearing one or several flowers, and the margins of the leaves almost toothless or irregularly slashed. It superficially resembles *Taráxia ovàta*, the Sun-cups so common on the southwestern coast, for the flowers have the same little fresh, sunny faces, but the latter has a round-topped stigma.

Evening Primrose -
Onagra Hookeri.

Sun-cups -
Lavauxia primiveris.

PARSLEY FAMILY. *Umbelliferae.*

A large family, widely distributed, not abundant in the tropics; usually strong-smelling herbs, remarkable for their aromatic oil, mostly with hollow, grooved stems; leaves alternate, compound, generally deeply cut, leaf-stalks often broadened at base; flowers very small, usually in broad, flat-topped clusters, generally with bracts; calyx usually a five-toothed rim around the top of the ovary; petals five, small, usually with tips curled in, inserted on a disk, which crowns the ovary and surrounds the base of the styles; stamens five, with threadlike filaments and swinging anthers, also on the disk; ovary two-celled, inferior, with two threadlike styles; fruit two, dry, seedlike bodies, when ripe separating from each other, and usually suspended from the summit of a slender axis, each body marked with ribs, usually with oil-tubes between the ribs. The examination of these oil-tubes in mature fruits, with a microscope, is necessary to determine most of the genera and species, so description of genera is omitted here, and botanists have added to the difficulties of the amateur by giving almost every genus more than one name. The flowers are much alike, yet the leaves often differ very much in the same genus. Many kinds are poisonous, although others, such as Parsley, Carrot, and Parsnip, are valuable food plants.

Peucédanum
Euryptèra
Yellow
Spring
California

A fine robust plant, a foot or more tall, with stout, purplish stems and smooth, crisp leaves, the lower ones with three leaflets, the upper with five, and the teeth tipped with bristles. The flowers are greenish-yellow and the main cluster measures four or five inches across, with no bracts at base, but the small clusters have bracts. The flowers are ugly, but the foliage is handsome and the seed vessels richly tinted with wine-color, making the plant decorative and conspicuous on the sea cliffs of southern California.

Turkey Peas
Orogènia
linearifòlia
White
Spring
Northwest and Utah

A quaint little plant, only about three inches high, with a tuberous root, spreading, slanting stems, and smooth leaves, all from the root, with three, long, narrow leaflets; a reddish, stiff, papery scale sheathing the stem at base. The minute, white flowers form a cluster less than an

332

**Turkey Peas -
Orogenia
linearifolia.**

**(fruit)
Peucedanum
Euryptera.**

inch across, without bracts, with a stout, ridged flower-stalk and composed of from two to ten smaller clusters, with small bracts; the anthers red. This grows in rich moist soil, in shady valleys, on mountain ridges; in the Wasatch Mountains, sometimes on the edge of the snow.

Pleýrxia Cali-fórnica
(Cymópterus)
Yellow
Summer
Cal., Oreg.

Over a foot tall, with very pretty, dark green foliage and rather ugly, dull yellow flowers, in flat-topped clusters, three inches across. The leaves are in a cluster at the root, with long leaf-stalks sheathing at base, very finely cut and toothed, with stiffish points; the main flower-cluster without bracts, but the smaller clusters with narrow bracts.

Whisk-broom
Parsley
Cogswéllia platy-càrpa (Peuce-danum simplex)
Yellow
Spring
Northwest and
Utah

An odd-looking plant, for the foliage looks like pieces of a whisk-broom stuck in the ground. It is six to fourteen inches tall, with a thickish root and minute, sulphur-yellow flowers, forming a flat-topped cluster, about two inches across, without bracts, and composed of three to fifteen smaller clusters, with small bracts; usually only the outermost flowers of both the large and small clusters are fertile. The stem and leaves are stiff and sage-green, the root-leaves with broad leaf-stems, reddish and papery at base, sheathing the stem, and all the leaves cut into narrow divisions, not much thicker than pine needles, folded together so that they appear to be cylindrical. This grows on dry gravelly hills, at an altitude of from six to eight thousand feet.

Leptotaènia
multifida
(Ferula)
Yellowish-green
Spring, summer
Northwest, Nev.,
Utah, New Mex.

A fine, stout plant, about two feet tall, with a thick, spindle-shaped root and dark, rich-green, feathery foliage; the large leaves, over a foot long, appearing smooth but really imperceptibly downy, finely cut and lobed, with long, stout leaf-stalks; the small flowers, yellowish-green or bronze-color, in flat-topped clusters, two or three inches across, with few or no bracts, with tall, stout flower-stalks, and composed of about eighteen, small clusters, forming round knobs, with many bracts, on slender pedicels of various lengths. This grows in rich soil and is conspicuous on account of its size and foliage.

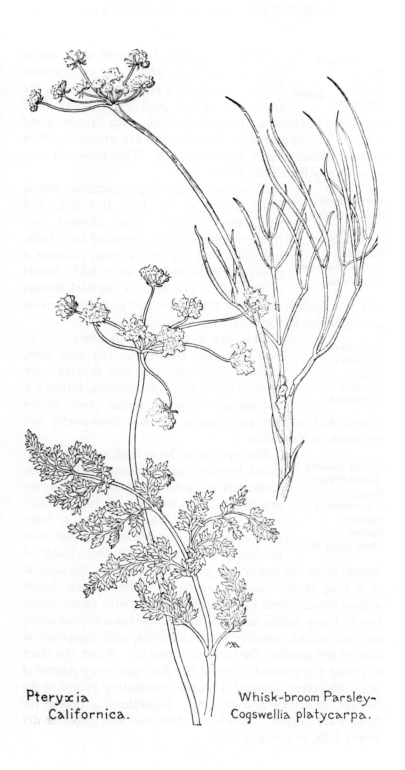

Pteryxia
Californica.

Whisk-broom Parsley-
Cogswellia platycarpa.

Velaèa argùta
Yellow
Spring
California

This has a stout, brownish stem, about eight inches tall, and fine, conspicuous foliage, mostly in a clump at the base, the leaves rich-green and very glossy, stiff and crisp in texture, though not thick, with bristle-tipped teeth. The rather ugly little flowers are greenish-yellow and the main cluster has no bracts. This grows in canyons in southern California.

Purple Sanicle,
Nigger-babies
Sanicula
bipinnatifida
Purplish
Spring, summer
Cal., Oreg.

This has branching, purplish stems, from six inches to three feet tall, and handsome foliage. The flowers are maroon-color and are crowded into balls, less than half an inch across, forming a loose, irregular cluster, with leafy bracts at the base. The effect of the dark flowers and fine foliage is rather attractive and it is common on grassy slopes in the hills.

Eulòphus
Bolánderi
White
Summer
Northwest

This has a smooth, stiff stem, one to two feet tall, the leaves cut into long, narrow divisions, and the flowers very small, cream-white or pinkish, forming a flat-topped cluster, about two inches across, with narrow, pale bracts. This is quite pretty and common in Yosemite.

Indian Parsnip
Aulospérmum
lóngipes
(*Cymopterus*)
Yellow
Spring
Utah, Col., Wyo.

Decorative in form and color and unusual looking, with smooth, pale bluish-green foliage, with a "bloom," the leaves prettily cut and lobed, with pinkish leaf-stalks, forming, when young, a large rosette, close to the ground, but the stem gradually lengthens until the cluster of leaves, after the flowers are gone, finds itself on the summit of a long stem, sheathed at base. The minute, bright yellow flowers form flat-topped clusters, with flower-stems two or three inches tall, not hollow, the main cluster about an inch across, usually without bracts, and composed of five to ten smaller clusters, with bracts. When the plant is young the general effect of the flat, pale gray rosette of fern-like leaves, spotted with the contrasting yellow of the flowers, is pretty and striking. Sometimes a few of the flowers are purple. This has a thick root and grows on dry sunny hills, in gravelly soil.

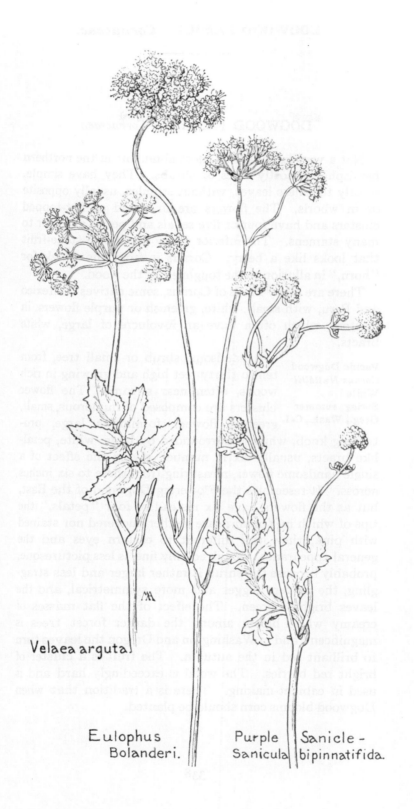

Velaea arguta

Eulophus
Bolanderi.

Purple Sanicle -
Sanicula bipinnatifida.

DOGWOOD FAMILY. *Cornaceae.*

Not a very large family, most abundant in the northern hemisphere, mostly trees or shrubs. They have simple, mostly toothless leaves, without stipules, usually opposite or in whorls. The flowers are in round or flat-topped clusters and have four or five sepals and petals and four to many stamens. The inferior ovary becomes a stone-fruit that looks like a berry. Cornus is from the Greek for "horn," in allusion to the toughness of the wood.

There are many kinds of Cornus, some natives of Mexico and Peru, with small, white, greenish or purple flowers, in clusters, which often have an involucre of large, white bracts.

Pacific Dogwood
Córnus Nuttóllii
White
Spring, summer
Oreg., Wash., Cal.
A handsome shrub or small tree, from ten to thirty feet high and growing in rich woods, often near streams. The flower clusters are composed of numerous, small, greenish flowers, forming a large, protruding knob, which is surrounded by large, white, petal-like bracts, usually six in number, giving the effect of a single handsome flower, measuring from three to six inches across. It resembles the Flowering Dogwood of the East, but as the flowers have six instead of four "petals," the tips of which in Yosemite are neither puckered nor stained with pink, they look different to eastern eyes and the general appearance, though equally fine, is less picturesque, probably because the shrub is rather larger and less straggling, the flowers bigger and more symmetrical, and the leaves brighter green. The effect of the flat masses of creamy white bloom among the darker forest trees is magnificent, and in Washington and Oregon the leaves turn to brilliant red in the autumn. The fruit is a cluster of bright red berries. The wood is exceedingly hard and is used in cabinet-making. There is a tradition that when Dogwood blooms corn should be planted.

Pacific Dogwood-   Cornus Nuttallii.

HEATH FAMILY. *Ericaceae.*

Red-osier Dogwood
Córnus stolonifera var. ripària
White
Spring, summer, autumn
Utah, Ariz., New Mex., Col.

A handsome shrub, five to eight feet high, with smooth, dark red branches and bright red twigs. The leaves are thin in texture, smooth and rich-green on the upper side, paler on the under, and the small, cream-white flowers, with long, yellow stamens, form handsome, flat-topped clusters, about two inches across, smelling pleasantly of honey; the berries are dull white. This is common.

Bunchberry
Córnus Canadénsis
White
Summer
West, except Ariz.

A charming little plant, about six inches high, growing in moist, cool woods and common in the East. The slender stem, with one or two pairs of small leaves, springs from creeping, woody shoots and is crowned by a circle of larger leaves, six, or rarely four, in number, smooth and bright green, setting off a pretty white blossom, with a slender flower-stalk. This looks like a single flower, measuring about an inch across, but it is really composed of a number of tiny, greenish flowers, forming a cluster in the center, and surrounded by four white bracts, which look like large petals. The flowers are succeeded by a bunch of red berries, insipid in flavor, but vivid scarlet in hue.

HEATH FAMILY. *Ericaceae.*

A large and interesting family, of very wide geographic distribution, in temperate and cold regions; herbs, shrubs, or trees; the leaves undivided, without stipules; the flowers mostly perfect; the calyx with four or five divisions; the corolla usually regular, with four or five, usually united, petals; the stamens inserted under the pistil, usually as many, or twice as many, as the petals; the ovary usually superior, with one style; the fruit a capsule, berry, or stone-fruit, usually with many small seeds.

There are many kinds of Gaultheria, mostly of the Andes; ours are evergreen shrubs, with alternate, aromatic leaves and nodding flowers; the calyx five-cleft; the corolla more or less urn-shaped, with five teeth; the stamens ten; the fruit a berry, composed of the fleshy calyx surrounding the ovary and containing many seeds. The Wintergreen, or Checkerberry, used for flavoring, belongs to this genus.

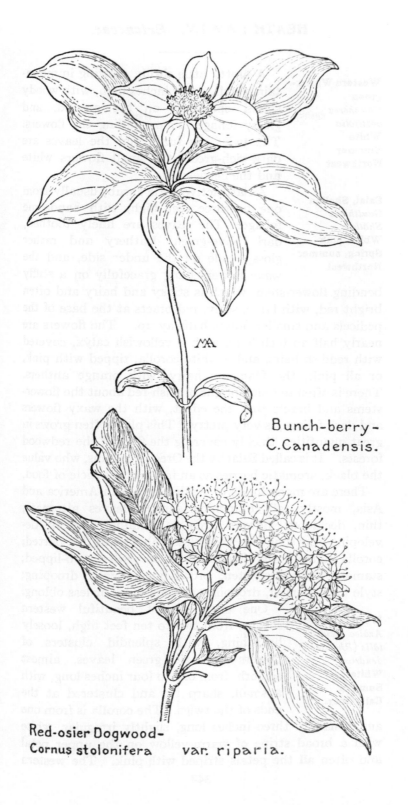

Bunch-berry—
C. Canadensis.

Red-osier Dogwood—
Cornus stolonifera   var. riparia.

HEATH FAMILY. *Ericaceae.*

Western Winter-green
Gaulthèria ovatifòlia
White
Summer
Northwest

A pretty little shrub, growing in mountain woods, a few inches high, with woody stems, spreading on the ground, and glossy foliage, almost hiding the flowers. The twigs are fuzzy and the leaves are dark rich-green, the small flowers white and the berries red.

Salal, Shallon
Gaulthèria Shállon
White, pink
Spring, summer
Northwest

An attractive little shrub, usually from one to three feet high, with handsome foliage. The leaves are finely toothed, dark olive-green, leathery and rather glossy, pale on the under side, and the waxy flowers hang gracefully on a stiffly bending flower-stem, which is sticky and hairy and often bright red, with large, scaly, red bracts at the base of the pedicels and smaller bracts halfway up. The flowers are nearly half an inch long, with a yellowish calyx, covered with reddish hairs, and a white corolla, tipped with pink, or all pink; the filaments hairy, with orange anthers. There is often so much bright pinkish-red about the flower-stems and bracts that the effect, with the waxy flowers and dark foliage, is very pretty. This plant often grows in great quantities, thickly covering the floor of the redwood forests. It is called Salál by the Oregon Indians, who value the black, aromatic berries as an important article of food.

There are many kinds of Azalea, of North America and Asia, mostly tall, branching shrubs; leaves alternate, thin, deciduous; flowers large, in terminal clusters, developing from cone-like, scaly buds; calyx small, five-parted; corolla funnel-form, five-lobed or somewhat two-lipped; stamens five, rarely ten, protruding, usually drooping; style long, slender, drooping; capsule more or less oblong.

Western Azalea
Azàlea occiden-tàlis (Rhodo-dendron)
White
Summer
Cal., Oreg.

One of the most beautiful western shrubs, from two to ten feet high, loosely branching, with splendid clusters of flowers and rich-green leaves, almost smooth, from one to four inches long, with a small, sharp tip and clustered at the ends of the twigs. The corolla is from one and a half to three inches long, slightly irregular, white with a broad stripe of warm-yellow on the upper petal and often all the petals striped with pink. The western

Western Azalea·
Azalea occidentalis·

Salal —
G. Shallon.

Western Wintergreen —
Gaultheria ovatifolia.

woodland streams are bordered with these wonderful blossoms, leaning over the water and filling the air with their delicious fragrance.

There are many kinds of Rhododendron, most abundant in Asia, resembling Azalea, but with evergreen, leathery leaves. The name is from the Greek, meaning "rose-tree."

California Rose Bay
Rhododéndron Califórnicum
Pink
Spring, summer
Northwest

A magnificent shrub, the handsomest in the West, from three to fifteen feet high, with a grayish trunk and fine, evergreen foliage. The leaves are from three to ten inches long, rich-green and leathery, smooth but not shiny, paler on the under side, spreading out around the large flower-clusters, so as to set them off to great advantage, and the flowers are over two inches across, scentless, with small, pale sepals and pink corollas, almost white at the base and shading to deep pink at the edges, which are prettily ruffled. The upper petal is freckled with golden-brown, or greenish spots and arrow-shaped markings, the pistil is crimson and the stamens, with pale pink filaments and pale yellow anthers, curve in, like little serpents' heads. The coloring of the flower clusters, mixed with the crimson-tipped buds, is a combination of delicate and brilliant tints and in such places as the redwood forests, along the Noyo River in California, where the shrub develops into a small tree, the huge clusters, glowing high above us among the dark forest trees, are a wonderful sight. This is the "State flower" of Washington.

There are a good many kinds of Arctostaphylos, mostly western; evergreen shrubs, with very crooked branches; smooth, dark red or brown bark; alternate leaves, and usually nodding, white or pink flowers, with bracted pedicels, in terminal clusters, the parts usually in fives; the corolla urn-shaped; the stamens usually ten, not protruding, the filaments hairy; the ovary raised on a disk on the receptacle; the fruit berry-like, several nutlets surrounded by soft pulp. The leaves, by a twisting of their stalks, assume a vertical position on the branches, a habit which enables many plants of dry regions to avoid unnecessary evaporation. These shrubs are often very abundant and with Chaparral Pea, Buck Brush, Scrub

California Rose Bay -
Rhododendron Californicum

Oak, etc., form the extensive brush thickets known as chaparral, so characteristic of the western mountain scenery. The Greek name means "bear-berry," as bears are fond of the berries, and Manzanita is from the Spanish for "little apple," as the fruits often resemble tiny apples. They are dry but pleasantly acid and are popular with Indians, bears, and chipmunks, and jelly can be made from them. The largest Manzanita tree known is one in Napa County, California, thirty-five feet high and as large across.

Green Manzanita
Arctostáphylos
pátula
Pink
Winter, spring
California

A decorative shrub, from four to six feet high, with spreading branches. The leaves are from one to two inches long, smooth, pale green, and leathery and the flowers are waxy, a quarter of an inch or more long, crowded in pretty, roundish clusters, of various shades of pink. The very smooth trunk and branches are picturesquely gnarled and twisted and, in fine contrast to the pale foliage, are rich mahogany-color, with here and there openings in the outer bark, showing the gray, under layer, as if the branches had been dipped in hot chocolate, which had melted off in some places. The berry is about a quarter of an inch across, smooth and fleshy. This forms most of the chaparral on the slopes around the Yosemite Valley, ranging from over four thousand to nine thousand feet in altitude, and is widely distributed in the Sierra Nevada Mountains.

Manzanita
Arctostáphylos
bicolor
Pink
Spring
California

A handsome shrub, three or four feet high, with rich-green leaves, very glossy on the upper side and covered with close white down on the under. The waxy flowers are a lovely shade of pink and the pretty fruit is about the size of a pea, like a tiny greenish-yellow apple, with a brownish-red cheek. This grows in the South near the coast.

Kinnikinic. Red
Bearberry
Arctostáphylos
Úva-Úrsi
White
Spring, summer
West, etc.

An attractive little shrub, with many trailing branches, creeping over the ground and often covering the rocks with a beautiful mat of evergreen foliage. The leaves are small, toothless, shining and leathery and the little white or pinkish, bell-shaped flowers hang in pretty little

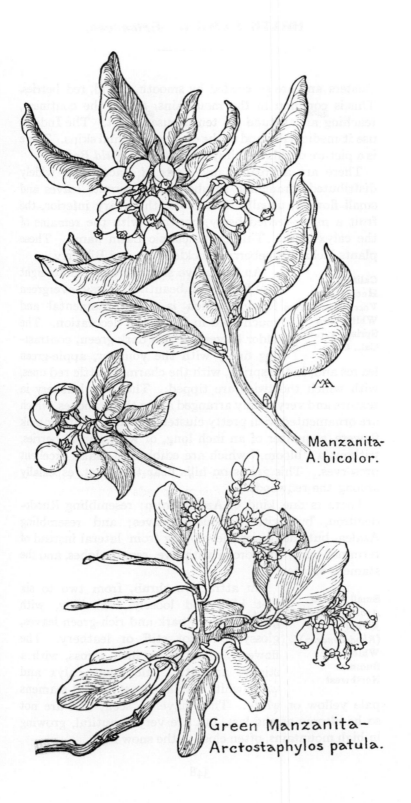

Manzanita–
A. bicolor.

Green Manzanita–
Arctostaphylos patula.

clusters and are succeeded by smooth, round, red berries. This is common in the mountains, across the continent, reaching an altitude of ten thousand feet. The Indians use it medicinally and in the curing of animal skins. There is a picture of this in Schuyler Mathews' *Field Book.*

There are a great many kinds of Vaccinium, widely distributed; branching shrubs, with alternate leaves and small flowers, usually in clusters; the ovary inferior, the fruit a many-seeded berry, crowned with the remains of the calyx-teeth. This is the classic Latin name. These plants include Blueberry, Huckleberry, and Bilberry.

California Huckleberry
Vaccinium ovàtum
White, pink
Spring, summer
Cal., Oreg.

An attractive shrub, from four to eight feet high, with beautiful, glossy, evergreen foliage, which is very ornamental and much used in household decoration. The older leaves are rich dark green, contrasting finely with the younger, apple-green leaves and, in the spring, with the charming little red ones, with which the twigs are tipped. They are leathery in texture and very neatly arranged along the branches, which are ornamented with pretty clusters of waxy, white or pink flowers, a quarter of an inch long, or with purple berries, without a "bloom," which are edible and make excellent preserves. This grows on hills near the coast, especially among the redwoods.

There is one kind of Azaleastrum; resembling Rhododendron, but with deciduous leaves; and resembling Azalea, but the flowers developing from lateral instead of terminal buds, the corolla with five, regular lobes, and the stamens shorter.

Small Azalea
Azaleàstrum albi-flòrum
(Rhododendron)
White
Summer
Northwest

An attractive shrub, from two to six feet high and loosely branching, with grayish-brown bark and rich-green leaves, glossy, but not stiff or leathery. The flowers are about an inch across, with a sticky, aromatic, pale green calyx and waxy-white corolla, the style and stamens pale yellow or white. They have no scent and are not so handsome as the last, but are very beautiful, growing in high mountains, often close to the snow line.

Small Azalea -
Azaleastrum
albiflorum.

California Huckleberry- Vaccinium ovatum.

There are several kinds of Kalmia, almost all of eastern North America, the flowers alike in form.

Swamp Laurel
Kálmia micro-phýlla (K. glauca var. microphylla)
Pink
Summer
Northwest, etc.

A very pretty little evergreen shrub, from a few inches to over a foot high, with glossy, leathery, rich-green leaves, whitish on the under side, with the margins rolled back. The flowers are single or in clusters, each about half an inch across, with five sepals and a bright purplish-pink, saucer-shaped corolla, with five lobes, which is prettily symmetrical and intricate in form. There are ten little pouches below the border and in these the tips of the ten anthers are caught, so that the filaments curve over from the center, and at the touch of a visiting insect they spring out of the pouches and dust the visitor's back with pollen, which is carried to another flower. The little, pointed buds, angled and deep in color, are also pretty and the capsule is roundish, with many small seeds. This grows in northern swamps, across the continent.

There are several kinds of Menziesia, some Japanese; branching shrubs, with alternate, deciduous, toothless leaves, and small, nodding flowers, in clusters, developing from scaly buds, their parts almost always in fours; stamens eight, not protruding; capsule more or less egg-shaped.

Fool's Huckle-berry
Menzièsia urceolària (M. ferruginea)
Yellowish, reddish
Summer
Northwest

A rather attractive little bush, from two to six feet high, with light brown bark, hairy twigs and slightly hairy leaves, with hairy margins. The flowers are less than half an inch long, with a hairy calyx and dull cream-colored corolla, tinged with dull-pink or red, and hang prettily in a circle, on drooping pedicels, which become erect as the capsules ripen. When crushed, the stems and foliage have a strong skunk-like smell.

There are only a few kinds of Ledum, all much alike.

Woolly Labrador Tea
Lèdum Groen-lándicum
White
Spring, summer
Northwest, etc.

A loosely-branching, evergreen shrub, from one to four feet high. The bark is reddish and the twigs are covered with reddish wool, the color of iron rust, and the leathery, dark green leaves, which are alternate, with rolled-back margins, are also covered with reddish wool on the

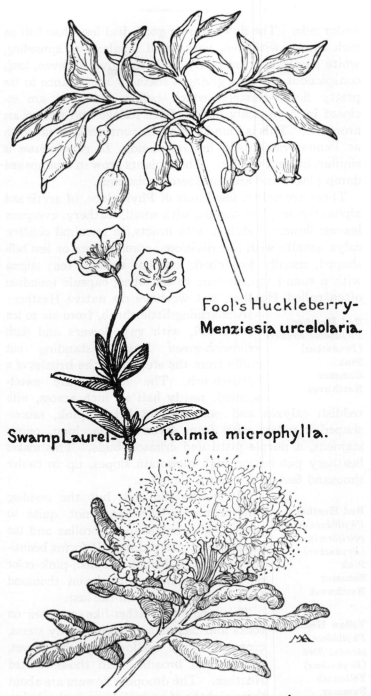

Fool's Huckleberry—
Menziesia urcelolaria.

Swamp Laurel— **Kalmia microphylla.**

Woolly Labrador Tea— **Ledum Groenlandicum.**

under side. The flowers are a good deal less than half an inch across, with five, very small sepals; five, spreading, white petals; a green ovary, and from five to seven, long, conspicuous stamens, giving a feathery appearance to the pretty flower-clusters, which before blooming are enclosed in large, scaly buds. Both foliage and flowers are aromatic. This is found across the continent, as far south as Pennsylvania, and in Greenland. *L. glandulòsum* is similar, but not woolly. These plants grow in swamps and damp places and are considered poisonous.

There are only a few kinds of Phyllodoce, of arctic and alpine regions; low shrubs, with small, leathery, evergreen leaves; flowers nodding, with bracts, in terminal clusters; calyx usually with five divisions; corolla more or less bell-shaped, usually five-lobed; stamens usually ten; stigma with a round top, or four to six lobes; capsule roundish: often called Heather, but we have no native Heather.

Red Heather
Phyllódoce Bréweri
(*Bryanthus*)
Pink
Summer
Northwest

A charming little shrub, from six to ten inches tall, with gay flowers and dark yellowish-green leaves, standing out stiffly from the stem, like the bristles of a bottle-brush. The flowers are sweet-scented, nearly half an inch across, with reddish calyxes and pedicels and bright pink, saucer-shaped corollas, with from seven to ten, long, purple stamens, a purple pistil and crimson buds. This makes heathery patches on high mountain slopes, up to twelve thousand feet in the Sierra Nevadas.

Red Heather
Phyllódoce empetrifórmis
(*Bryanthus*)
Pink
Summer
Northwest

Much like the last, but the nodding flowers are smaller and not quite so pretty, with bell-shaped corollas and the stamens not protruding. It forms beautiful patches of bright purplish-pink color on mountainsides, up to eleven thousand feet, farther north than the last.

Yellow Heather
Phyllódoce glanduliflòra
(*Bryanthus*)
Yellowish
Summer
Northwest

This makes heather-like patches on rocks and has many rough, woody stems, crowded with yellowish-green leaves, shorter and broader than those of Red Heather. The drooping flowers are about three-eighths of an inch long, with a hairy, greenish-yellow calyx and yellowish corolla,

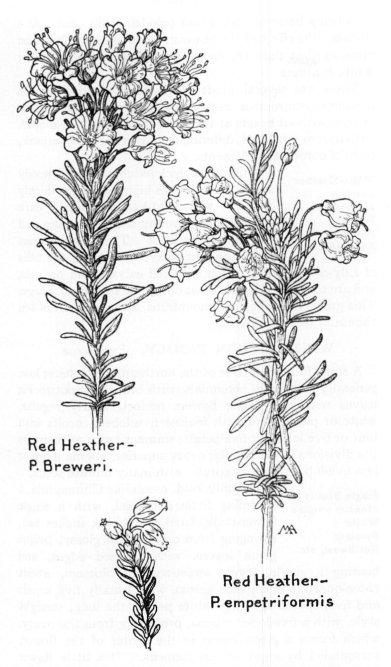

Red Heather—
P. Breweri.

Red Heather—
P. empetriformis

Yellow Heather— Phyllodoce glanduliflora.

---

something between cream and pale-lemon in color. At a distance the effect of the flowers is much more yellow than close by, but they are not so pretty as either the red or white heathers.

There are several kinds of Cassiope, named for the mother of Andromeda, resembling Heather; the sepals four or five, without bracts at the base; the corolla bell-shaped, with four or five lobes; differing from Phyllodoce in capsule, form of corolla and filaments.

White Heather
Cassiope
Mertensiàna
White
Summer
Northwest

This makes thick patches of many woody stems, a few inches high, the twigs thickly clothed with odd-looking, small, dark green leaves, overlapping like scales and ridged on the back. The single flowers are white and waxy, resembling the bells of Lily-of-the-valley, often with red calyxes and pedicels, and are pretty and delicate, set off by the stiff, dark foliage. This grows in the highest mountains, at an altitude of ten thousand feet and above.

WINTERGREEN FAMILY. *Pyrolaceae.*

A small family, natives of the northern hemisphere; low, generally evergreen, perennials, with branched rootstocks; leaves with leaf-stalks; flowers perfect, nearly regular, white or pink; calyx with four or five lobes; corolla with four or five lobes, or five petals; stamens twice as many as the divisions of the corolla; ovary superior, stigma more or less five-lobed; fruit a capsule, with many minute seeds.

Single Beauty
Monèses uniflòra
White
Summer
Northwest, etc.

The only kind, much like Chimaphila, a charming little perennial, with a single flower-stalk, from two to six inches tall, springing from a cluster of glossy, bright green leaves, with toothed edges, and bearing a single, lovely sweet-scented blossom, about three-quarters of an inch across, with usually five sepals and five, spreading, waxy-white petals; the long, straight style, with a five-lobed stigma, projecting from the ovary, which forms a green hump in the center of the flower, surrounded by eight or ten stamens. This little flower modestly turns its face down to the ground and we have to pick it to find how very pretty it is. It grows in wet, northern mountain woods, across the continent.

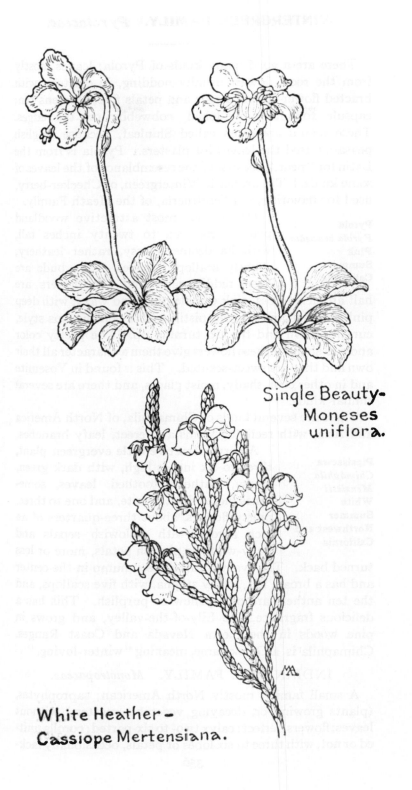

Single Beauty-
Moneses
uniflora.

White Heather-
Cassiope Mertensiana.

WINTERGREEN FAMILY. *Pyrolaceae.*

There are a good many kinds of Pyrola; leaves mostly from the root; flowers usually nodding, in clusters, with bracted flower-stalks; sepals and petals five; stamens ten; capsule roundish, five-lobed, cobwebby on the edges. These plants are often called Shinleaf, because English peasants used the leaves for plasters. Pyrola is from the Latin for "pear," because of the resemblance of the leaves of some kinds. The aromatic Wintergreen, or Checker-berry, used for flavoring, is a Gaultheria, of the Heath Family.

Pyrola
Pýrola bracteàta
Pink
Summer
California

One of our most attractive woodland plants, from six to twenty inches tall, with handsome, glossy, rather leathery, slightly scalloped leaves. The buds are deep reddish-pink and the flowers are half an inch across, pink or pale pink, and waxy, with deep pink stamens and a green pistil, with a conspicuous style, curving down and the tip turning up. The pretty color and odd shape of these flowers give them a character all their own and they are sweet-scented. This is found in Yosemite and in other cool, shady, moist places, and there are several similar kinds.

There are several kinds of Chimaphila, of North America and Asia, with reclining stems and erect, leafy branches.

Pipsissewa
Chimáphila
Menzièsii
White
Summer
Northwest and California

A very attractive little evergreen plant, three to six inches high, with dark green, glossy, leathery, toothed, leaves, sometimes mottled with white, and one to three, pretty flowers, about three-quarters of an inch across, with yellowish sepals and waxy-white or pinkish petals, more or less turned back. The ovary forms a green hump in the center and has a broad, flat, sticky stigma, with five scallops, and the ten anthers are pale yellow or purplish. This has a delicious fragrance, like Lily-of-the-valley, and grows in pine woods in the Sierra Nevada and Coast Ranges. Chimaphila is a Greek name, meaning "winter-loving."

INDIAN PIPE FAMILY. *Monotropaceae.*

A small family, mostly North American; saprophytes, (plants growing on decaying vegetable matter,) without leaves; flowers perfect; calyx two- to six-parted; corolla united or not, with three to six lobes or petals, occasionally lack-

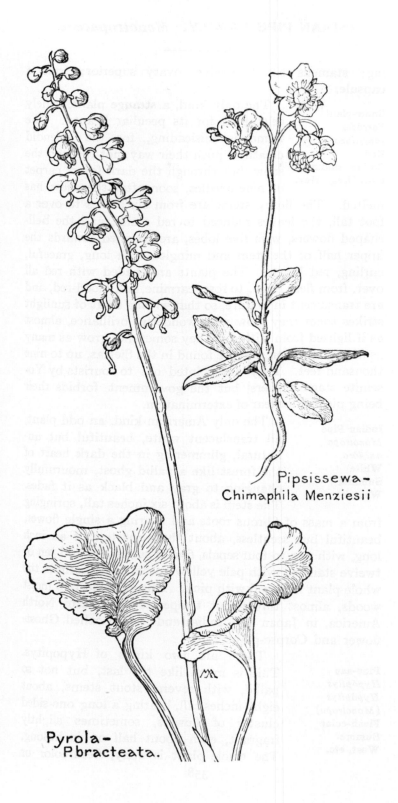

Pipsissewa-
Chimaphila Menziesii

Pyrola-
P.bracteata.

ing; stamens six to twelve; ovary superior; fruit a capsule.

Snow-plant
Sarcòdes
sanguinea
Red
Spring, summer
Cal., Oreg., Nev.

The only kind, a strange plant, widely celebrated for its peculiar beauty. The name is misleading, for the splendid creatures push their way, not through the snow, but through the dark forest carpet of pine-needles, soon after the snow has melted. The fleshy stems are from six inches to over a foot tall, the leaves reduced to red scales, and the bell-shaped flowers, with five lobes, are crowded towards the upper half of the stem and mingled with long, graceful, curling, red bracts. The plants are shaded with red all over, from flesh color, to rose, carmine, and blood-red, and are translucent in texture, so that when a shaft of sunlight strikes them they glow with wonderful brilliance, almost as if lighted from within. They sometimes grow as many as fifteen together, and are found in the Sierras, up to nine thousand feet. They are pointed out to tourists by Yosemite stage drivers, but the government forbids their being picked, for fear of extermination.

Indian Pipe
Monótropa
uniflòra
White
Summer
West, etc.

The only American kind, an odd plant, all translucent white, beautiful but unnatural, glimmering in the dark heart of the forest like a pallid ghost, mournfully changing to gray and black as it fades. The stem is about six inches tall, springing from a mass of fibrous roots and bearing a single flower, beautiful but scentless, about three-quarters of an inch long, with two to four sepals, five or six petals, and ten or twelve stamens, with pale yellow anthers. Sometimes the whole plant is tinged with pink. This grows in rich moist woods, almost throughout temperate and warm North America, in Japan and India, and is also called Ghost-flower and Corpse-plant.

Pine-sap
Hypópitys
Hypópitys
(Monotropa)
Flesh-color
Summer
West, etc.

There are two kinds of Hypopitys. This is much like the last, but not so pallid, with several stout stems, about eight inches tall, bearing a long one-sided cluster of flowers, sometimes slightly fragrant, each about half an inch long. The whole plant is waxy, flesh-color or

Snow Plant

Sarcodes
sanguinea

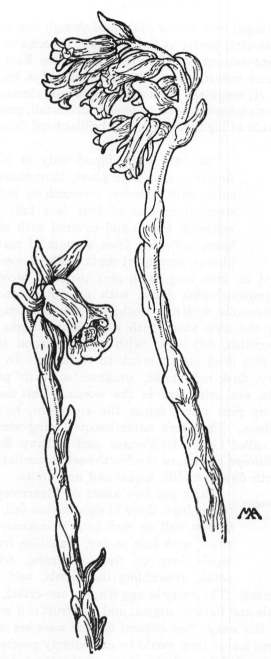

Indian Pipe—
Monotropa uniflora.

Pine Sap—
Hypopitys. Hypopitys.

yellowish, tinged with red or pink, and though interesting is not so delicately pretty as Indian Pipe. It seems to be a stouter plant around Mt. Rainier than in the East and grows in thick woods, across the continent and in Europe and Asia. *H. sanguínea* is a new kind, recently discovered in the Arizona mountains; six to twelve inches tall, growing in dense shade at high altitudes, and brilliant red throughout.

Pine-drops
Pteróspora
Andromedèa
White
Summer
Across the continent

The only kind, found only in North America, a strange plant, harmonious in color, with a fleshy, brownish or reddish stem, from one to four feet tall, with yellowish bracts and covered with sticky hairs, springing from a mass of matted, fibrous, astringent roots. The flowers are a quarter of an inch long, with pink pedicels, brownish bracts, a brownish-pink calyx, with five lobes, and an ivory-white corolla, with five teeth; the stamens ten, not protruding; the style short, with a five-lobed stigma; the capsule roundish, five-lobed, with many winged seeds. We often find dead insects stuck to the stem. In winter, the dry, dark red stalks, ornamented with pretty seed-vessels, are attractive in the woods. This usually grows among pine trees, across the continent, but nowhere common. The Greek name means "wing-seeded." It is also called Giant Bird's-nest and Albany Beech-drops. *Allótropa virgàta*, of the Northwest, is similar, but smaller, with five, roundish sepals and no corolla.

Flowering-fungus
Pleuricóspora
fimbriolàta
Flesh-color
Summer
California

There are two kinds of Pleuricospora; this is from three to eight inches tall, with flowers half an inch long, deliciously fragrant, with four or five, scale-like, fringed sepals, four or five, separate, fringed petals, resembling the sepals, and eight or ten stamens. The ovary is egg shaped, one-celled, with a thick style and flattish stigma, and the fruit is a watery berry. If the waxy, flesh-colored flowers were set off by proper green leaves they would be exceedingly pretty, but they are crowded on a fleshy stem, of the same color as themselves, mixed with fringed bracts, with brownish scales instead of leaves, and have an unnatural appearance. I found thirty of these curious plants, growing in a little

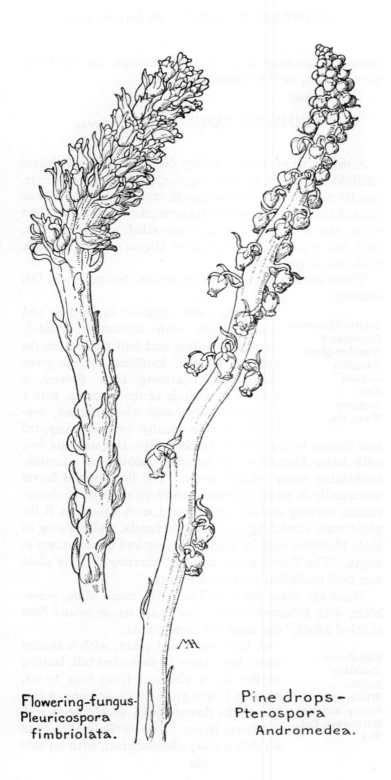

Flowering-fungus-
Pleuricospora
fimbriolata.

Pine drops-
Pterospora
Andromedea.

company, pushing their way up through the mold and pine-needles, in the Wawona woods.

PRIMROSE FAMILY. *Primulaceae.*

A rather large family, widely distributed; herbs; leaves undivided; flowers perfect, regular, parts usually in fives, corolla mostly with united petals, stamens on the base or tube of the corolla, opposite its lobes, sometimes with some extra, sterile filaments; ovary one-celled, mostly superior, with one style and round-headed stigma; fruit a capsule, with one or many seeds.

There are several kinds of Anagallis, not native in this country.

Scarlet Pimpernel
Poor-man's
Weather-glass
Anagállis
arvénsis
Red
Summer
West, etc.

A little weed, common in gardens and waste places, with smooth, four-sided, stems, branching and half trailing on the ground, smooth, toothless, bright green leaves and charming little flowers, a quarter of an inch or more across, with a five-lobed calyx and wheel-shaped, five-lobed corolla, usually bright orange-red and darker in the center, rarely white; the stamens five, with hairy filaments; the capsule smooth and roundish, containing many minute seeds. The flowers and leaves are usually in pairs, the seed-vessels on the tips of slender stems, curving around and toward each other, as if the plant were stretching out its little hands, and opening its little blossoms only in bright weather and closing them at night. The Greek name means "amusing." The plant was used medicinally by the ancients.

There are three kinds of Trientalis, much alike, perennials, with tuberous roots. The Latin name means "one third of a foot," the height of these plants.

Star-flower
Trientàlis
latifòlia
White, pink
Spring, summer
Northwest, Cal.,
Nev.

A little woodland plant, with a slender stem, from three to six inches tall, bearing at the top a circle of from four to six, smooth, bright green leaves and one or two, threadlike flower-stalks, each tipped with a delicate flower. The corolla is about half an inch across, wheel-shaped, with no tube

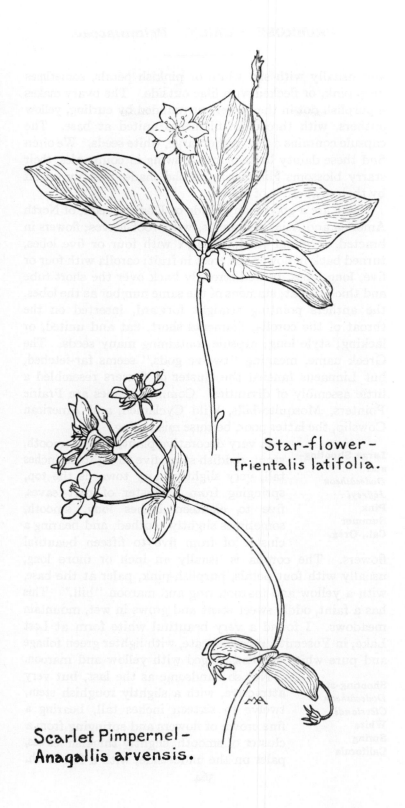

Star-flower-
Trientalis latifolia.

Scarlet Pimpernel-
Anagallis arvensis.

and usually with six, white or pinkish petals, sometimes deep pink, or flecked with lilac outside. The ovary makes a purplish dot in the center, surrounded by curling, yellow anthers, with threadlike filaments united at base. The capsule contains a few, rather large, white seeds. We often find these dainty little plants growing in companies, their starry blossoms glimmering in the shade, prettily set off by their neat circle of leaves.

There are a good many kinds of Dodecatheon, of North America and Asia; perennials, with root-leaves; flowers in bracted, terminal clusters; calyx with four or five lobes, turned back in flower but erect in fruit; corolla with four or five, long lobes, turned strongly back over the short tube and thick throat; stamens of the same number as the lobes, the anthers pointing straight forward, inserted on the throat of the corolla, filaments short, flat and united, or lacking; style long; capsule containing many seeds. The Greek name, meaning "twelve gods," seems far-fetched, but Linnaeus fancied the cluster of flowers resembled a little assembly of divinities. Common names are Prairie Pointers, Mosquito-bills, Wild Cyclamen, and American Cowslip, the latter poor, because misleading.

Large Shooting-star
Dodecátheon Jéffreyi
Pink
Summer
Cal., Oreg.

A very decorative plant, with a smooth, stout, reddish stem, five to eighteen inches tall, very slightly hairy towards the top, springing from a cluster of root-leaves, five to eighteen inches long, smooth, sometimes slightly toothed, and bearing a cluster of from five to fifteen beautiful flowers. The corolla is usually an inch or more long, usually with four petals, purplish-pink, paler at the base, with a yellow and maroon ring and maroon "bill." This has a faint, oddly sweet scent and grows in wet, mountain meadows. I found a very beautiful white form at Lost Lake, in Yosemite, more delicate, with lighter green foliage and pure white corollas, ringed with yellow and maroon.

Shooting-star
Dodecátheon Clèvelandi
White
Spring
California

Not so handsome as the last, but very attractive, with a slightly roughish stem, twelve to sixteen inches tall, bearing a fine crown of flowers and springing from a cluster of smooth, slightly thickish leaves, paler on the under side, with a few teeth.

**Large
Shooting Star -
Dodecatheon Jeffreyi**

MA

D.   Clevelandi.

OLIVE FAMILY. *Oleaceae.*

The sepals are slightly downy and the corollas are about three-quarters of an inch long, with pure-white petals, sometimes lilac-tinged, yellow at base, with a ring of maroon scallops and a dark purple "bill." The flowers are deliciously fragrant, like Clove Pinks. This grows in the south.

Small Shooting-star
Dodecàtheon pauciflòrum
Pink
Spring, summer
West

A charming little plant, growing in wet, rich mountain meadows, with a smooth reddish stem, about eight inches tall, bearing a bracted cluster of several delicate flowers, and springing from a loose clump of smooth leaves. The flowers are about three-quarters of an inch long, with bright purplish-pink petals, with a ring of crimson, a ring of yellow and a wavy line of red, where they begin to turn back; the stamens with united filaments and long purplish-brown anthers; the pistil white.

OLIVE FAMILY. *Oleaceae.*

A rather large family, widely distributed, including Olive, Lilac, and Privet; trees and shrubs; leaves mostly opposite; without stipules; flowers perfect or imperfect, with two to four divisions, calyx usually small or lacking, corolla with separate or united petals, sometimes lacking; stamens two or four, on the corolla, ovary superior, two-celled, with a short style or none; fruit a capsule, berry, stone-fruit, or wing-fruit.

There are many kinds of Fraxinus, almost all trees.

Flowering Ash, Fringe-bush
Fràxinus macropétala
White
Spring
Arizona

An odd and beautiful shrub, growing on Bright Angel trail, in the Grand Canyon, about as large as a lilac bush, with smooth, bright-green leaves, some of the leaflets obscurely toothed, and drooping plumes of fragrant white flowers. The calyx is very small, and the four petals are so long and narrow that the effect of the cluster is of a bunch of white fringe. The fruit is a flat winged-seed.

Small
Shooting Star

Dodecatheon
pauciflorum

Flowering Ash— Fraxinus macropetala.

GENTIAN FAMILY. *Gentianaceae.*

GENTIAN FAMILY. *Gentianaceae.*

A large family, widely distributed, most abundant in temperate regions; smooth herbs, with colorless, bitter juice; leaves toothless, usually opposite, without leafstalks or stipules; flowers regular; calyx four to twelve-toothed; corolla with united lobes, twisted or overlapping in the bud, of the same number as the calyx-teeth; stamens inserted on the tube or throat of the corolla, as many as its lobes, alternate with them; ovary superior, mostly one-celled, with a single style or none, and one or two stigmas; fruit a capsule, mostly with two valves, containing many seeds.   These plants were named for King Gentius of Illyria, said to have discovered their medicinal value.

There are several kinds of Frasera, North American, all but one western; herbs, with thick, bitter, woody roots; leaves opposite or in whorls; flowers numerous; corolla wheel-shaped, with four divisions, each with one or two fringed glands and sometimes also a fringed crown at base; stamens on the base of the corolla, with oblong, swinging anthers, the filaments often united at base; ovary egg-shaped, tapering to a slender style, with a small, more or less two-lobed, stigma; capsule leathery, egg-shaped, with flattish seeds.

Columbo, Deer's Tongue
Fràsera speciòsa
Greenish-white
Spring, summer, autumn
West, etc.

A handsome plant, though rather coarse, from two to six feet tall, with a pale glossy stem, very stout, sometimes over two inches across at the base, and very smooth, pale green leaves, in whorls of four and six, the lower ones sometimes a foot long. The flowers are mixed with the leaves all along the upper part of the stem, but mostly crowded at the top in a pyramidal cluster about six inches long, and are each nearly an inch and a half across, with a greenish or bluish-white corolla, the lobes bordered with violet and dotted with purple, and on each lobe two glands covered by a fringed flap, resembling a small petal, these fringes forming a sort of cross on the corolla.   The four stamens stand stiffly out between the corolla-lobes and the general effect of the flower is so symmetrical that it suggests an architectural or ecclesiastical ornament.   Though the flowers are not bright, this plant is decorative on account

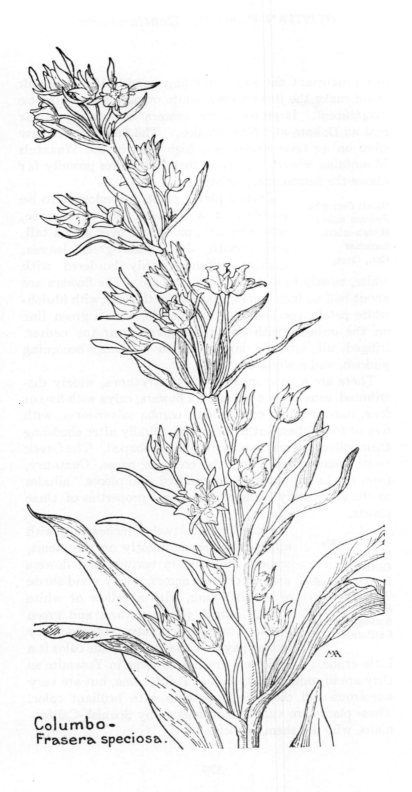

Columbo-
Frasera speciosa.

of its luxuriant size and pale foliage, and if Mr. Burbank could make the flowers clear white or purple it would be magnificent. It grows in the western mountains, as far east as Dakota and New Mexico. The finest I ever saw were on an open slope, in a high pass in the Wasatch Mountains, where they reared their pale spires proudly far above the surrounding herbage.

Small Columbo
Fràsera nitìda
Bluish-white
Summer
Cal., Oreg.

Quite a pretty plant, too colorless to be effective at a distance, but not coarse, with a smooth, pale stem, over a foot tall, and smooth, dull, bluish-green leaves, slightly stiffish, prettily bordered with white, mostly in a clump near the base. The flowers are about half an inch across, shaped like the last; with bluish-white petals, specked with dull-purple, with a green line on the outside, with one green gland near the center, fringed all around; large whitish anthers, becoming pinkish, and a white pistil.

There are a good many kinds of Erythræa, widely distributed, usually with red or pink flowers; calyx with five or four, narrow lobes, or divisions; corolla salver-form, with five or four lobes; anthers twisting spirally after shedding their pollen; stigmas two, oblong or fan-shaped. The Greek name means "red" and the common name, Centaury, from the Latin, meaning "a hundred gold pieces," alludes to the supposedly valuable medicinal properties of these plants.

Canchalagua,
California
Centaury
Erythraèa venústa
(Centaurium)
Pink
Spring, summer
California

From three to twelve inches tall, with apple-green leaves, mostly on the stems, smooth and thin in texture, and flowers an inch or more across, a very vivid shade of purplish-pink, with a yellow or white "eye," bright yellow anthers and green pistil. These are attractive, because they look so gay and cheerful, but the color is a little crude. The flowers are not so large in Yosemite as they are in some places, such as Point Loma, but are very numerous and cover large patches with brilliant color. These plants are called Canchalagua by Spanish-Californians, who use them medicinally.

Canchalagua·   Erythraea venusta·

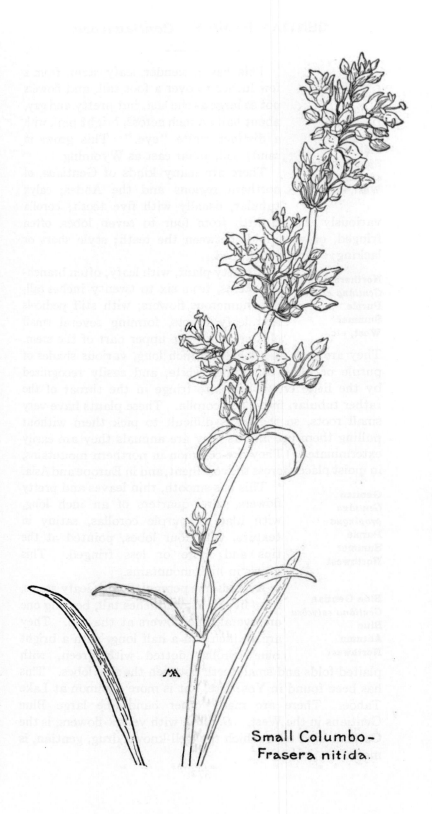

Small Columbo—
Frasera nitida.

GENTIAN FAMILY. *Gentianaceae.*

Tall Centaury
*Erythraèa
exaltàta (E.
Douglasii)
(Centaurium)*
Pink
Spring, summer,
autumn
West, etc.

This has a slender, leafy stem, from a few inches to over a foot tall, and flowers not so large as the last, but pretty and gay, about half an inch across, bright pink with a distinct white "eye." This grows in sandy soil, as far east as Wyoming.

There are many kinds of Gentiana, of northern regions and the Andes; calyx tubular, usually with five teeth; corolla variously shaped with from four to seven lobes, often fringed, or with folds between the teeth; style short or lacking; stigma two-lipped.

Northern Gentian
Gentiàna acùta
Purple
Summer
West, etc.

A pretty plant, with leafy, often branching stems, from six to twenty inches tall, and numerous flowers, with stiff pedicels and leafy bracts, forming several small clusters along the upper part of the stem. They are each about half an inch long, various shades of purple or blue, sometimes white, and easily recognized by the little crown of white fringe in the throat of the rather tubular, five-lobed corolla. These plants have very small roots, so that it is difficult to pick them without pulling them up, and as they are annuals they are easily exterminated. They are common in northern mountains, in moist places across the continent, and in Europe and Asia.

Gentian
*Gentiàna
propinqua*
Purple
Summer
Northwest

This has smooth, thin leaves and pretty flowers, three-quarters of an inch long, with lilac or purple corollas, satiny in texture, with four lobes, pointed at the tips and more or less fringed. This grows in high mountains.

Blue Gentian
Gentiàna calycòsa
Blue
Autumn
Northwest

A handsome perennial, with leafy stems, from five to fifteen inches tall, bearing one or several, fine flowers at the top. They are an inch and a half long, with a bright blue corolla, dotted with green, with plaited folds and small teeth between the five lobes. This has been found in Yosemite, but is more common at Lake Tahoe. There are many other handsome large Blue Gentians in the West. *G. lùtea*, with yellow flowers, is the German kind from which the well-known drug, gentian, is made.

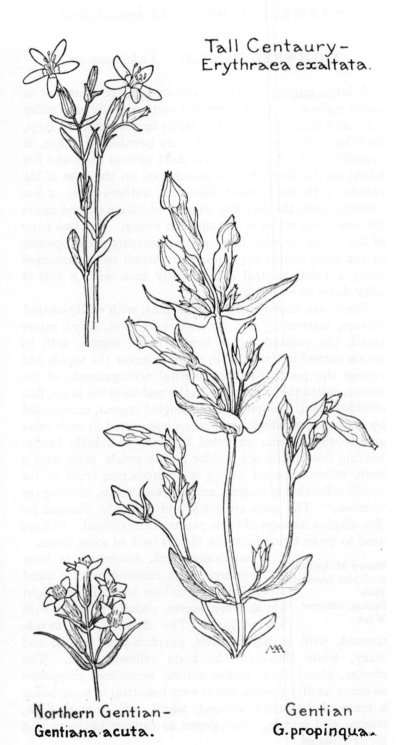

Tall Centaury –
Erythraea exaltata.

Northern Gentian –
Gentiana acuta.

Gentian
G. propinqua.

MILKWEED FAMILY. *Asclepiadaceae.*

A large family, widely distributed, most abundant in warm regions; ours are perennial herbs, usually with milky juice and tough fibrous inner bark; leaves generally large, toothless, without stipules; flowers peculiar in shape, in roundish clusters; calyx with a short tube or none and five lobes; corolla five-lobed; stamens five, on the base of the corolla, with short, stout filaments, anthers more or less united around the disk-like stigma, which covers and unites the two short styles of the superior ovary. The two parts of the ovary develop into two conspicuous pods, opening at the side, containing numerous flattish seeds, arranged along a thick, central axis, usually each with a tuft of silky down to waft it about.

There are many kinds of Asclepias, with oddly-shaped flowers, interesting and decorative in form; calyx rather small, the pointed sepals turned back; corolla with its petals turned entirely back, so as to cover the sepals and expose the peculiar-looking central arrangements of the flower, called the "crown." In the middle is the large, flat, shield-shaped, five-lobed or five-angled stigma, surrounded by the anthers, which are more or less united to each other and to the stigma, encircled by five, odd, little honey-bearing hoods, the same color as the petals, each with a horn, either enclosed within it or projecting from it, the whole collection of stigma, anthers, and hoods, forming the "crown." The pods are thick and pointed. Named for Æsculapius, as some of these plants are medicinal. Indians used to make twine from the fibrous bark of some kinds.

Showy Milkweed
Asclèpias speciòsa
Pink
Spring, summer
West

A handsome plant, decorative in form and harmonious in coloring, with a stout stem, from one to four feet tall, and light bluish-green leaves, usually covered with white down. The flowers are sweet-scented, with woolly pedicels, purplish-pink petals, and waxy, white "hoods," the buds yellowish-pink. The cluster, about three inches across, sometimes comprises as many as fifty flowers and is very beautiful in tone, being a mass of delicately blended, warm, soft tints of pink, cream, and purple. This grows in canyon bottoms and along streams.

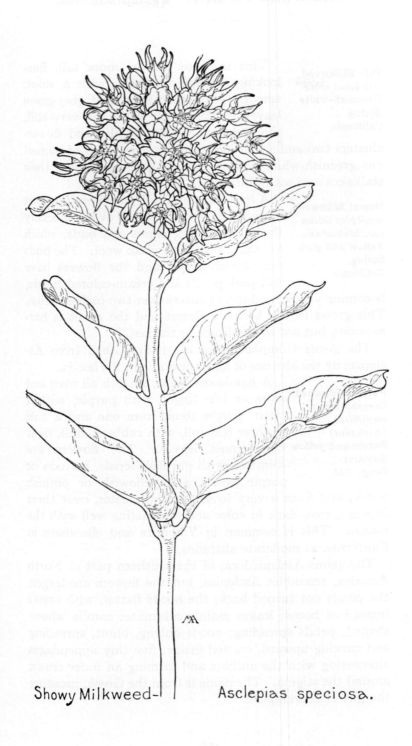

Showy Milkweed—　　　　Asclepias speciosa.

MILKWEED FAMILY. *Asclepiadaceae.*

Pale Milkweed
Asclèpias eròsa
Greenish-white
Spring
California

This is three feet or more tall, fine-looking, though too pale, with a stout, smooth, gray-green stem and gray-green leaves, mottled with white and very stiff, the under side white-woolly, and flower-clusters two and a half inches across, composed of numerous greenish-white flowers, each half an inch long, their stalks covered with white wool.

Desert Milkweed
Asclèpias vestìta
var. *Mohavénsis*
Yellow and pink
Spring.
California

A foot and a half tall, with very fragrant flowers, and very woolly all over, especially the upper leaves, stems and buds, which are thick with long white wool. The buds are pinkish-purple and the flowers have dull pink petals and cream-colored hoods, becoming yellow, and form clusters over two inches across. This grows in the Mohave Desert and the effect is harmonious, but not so handsome as the last.

The genus Gomphocarpus is distinguished from Asclepias by the absence of horns or crests in the hoods.

Purple Milkweed
Gomphocàrpus
cordifòlius
(*Asclèpias*)
Purple and yellow
Summer
Oreg., Cal.

A handsome plant, smooth all over and more or less tinged with purple, with a stout, purple stem, from one and a half to three feet tall, with rubbery, dull, light bluish-green leaves. The flowers are scentless, with purplish sepals, maroon or purple petals, and yellowish or pinkish hoods, and form a very loose graceful cluster, over three inches across, dark in color and contrasting well with the foliage. This is common in Yosemite and elsewhere in California, at moderate altitudes.

The genus Asclepiodora, of the southern part of North America, resembles Asclepias, but the flowers are larger, the petals not turned back, the hoods flatter, with crests instead of horns; leaves mainly alternate; corolla wheel-shaped; petals spreading; hoods oblong, blunt, spreading and curving upward, crested inside; five tiny appendages alternating with the anthers and forming an inner crown around the stigma. The name is from the Greek, meaning the gift of Æsculapius.

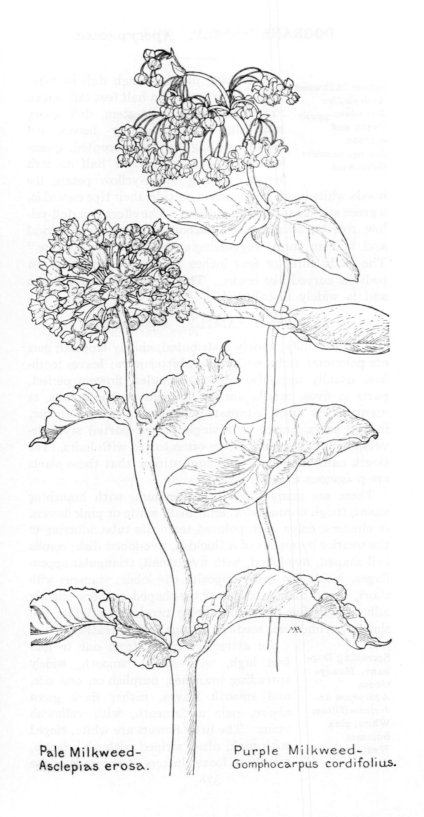

Pale Milkweed-
Asclepias erosa.

Purple Milkweed-
Gomphocarpus cordifolius.

DOGBANE FAMILY. *Apocynaceae.*

Spider Milkweed
Asclepiodòra
decúmbens
Green and maroon
Spring, summer
Southwest

A striking plant, though dull in color, from one to one and a half feet tall, with a rough, rather slanting stem, dull green, roughish, rather leathery leaves, and clusters of slightly sweet-scented, queer-looking flowers, each over half an inch across, with greenish-yellow petals, the hoods white inside and maroon outside, their tips curved in, a green stigma and brown anthers. The effect is a dull-yellow rosette, striped with maroon, curiously symmetrical and stiff in form, suggesting an heraldic "Tudor rose." The pods, three or four inches long, stand up stiffly, on pedicels curved like hooks. This grows on dry hillsides and is widely distributed.

DOGBANE FAMILY. *Apocynaceae.*

A large family, widely distributed, chiefly tropical; ours are perennial herbs, with milky, bitter juice; leaves toothless, usually opposite, without stipules; flowers perfect, parts in fives; corolla united; stamens on the corolla, as many as its lobes, alternate with them, ovary superior, in two parts, united by a single or two-parted style, developing into two pods; seeds often tufted with hairs. The Greek name alludes to the superstition that these plants are poisonous to dogs.

There are many kinds of Apocynum, with branching stems, tough fibrous bark, and small, white or pink flowers, in clusters; calyx with pointed teeth, its tube adhering to the ovaries by means of a thickish, five-lobed disk; corolla bell-shaped, five-lobed, with five, small, triangular appendages, inside the tube, opposite the lobes; stamens with short, broad filaments and arrow-shaped anthers, slightly adhering to the blunt, obscurely two-lobed stigma; pod slender, cylindrical; seeds numerous, small, feathery.

Spreading Dog-bane, Honey-bloom
Apócynum an-drosaemifòlium
White, pink
Summer
West, etc.

An attractive plant, from one to four feet high, with many, smooth, widely spreading branches, purplish on one side, and smooth leaves, rather dark green above, pale underneath, with yellowish veins. The little flowers are white, tinged with pink, often striped with pink inside, mainly in loose clusters at the ends of the

378

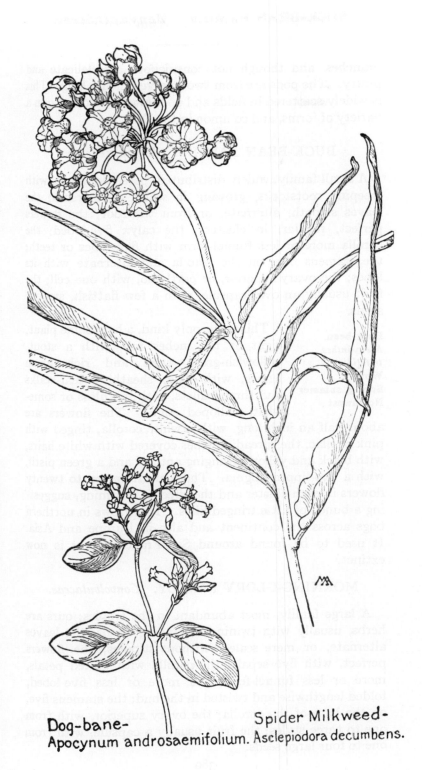

Dog-bane-
Apocynum androsaemifolium.

Spider Milkweed-
Asclepiodora decumbens.

branches, and though not conspicuous are delicate and pretty. The pods are from two to seven inches long. This is widely scattered in fields and open woods, occurring in a variety of forms, and common in the East.

BUCK-BEAN FAMILY. *Menyanthaceae.*

A small family, widely distributed; perennial herbs, with creeping rootstocks, growing in water or marshes; the leaves smooth, alternate, or from the root; the flowers perfect, regular, in clusters; the calyx five-lobed; the corolla more or less funnel-form with five lobes or teeth; the stamens five, on the corolla and alternate with its lobes; the ovary superior, or partly so, with one cell; the fruit usually an oval capsule, with a few flattish, smooth seeds.

Buck-bean
Menyánthes
trifoliàta
White
Spring, summer
Northwest

This is the only kind, a handsome plant, eight or ten inches tall, with a stout, yellowish-green stem and rich green leaves, with long, sheathing leaf-stalks and three leaflets, with toothless or somewhat scalloped edges. The flowers are about half an inch long, with a white corolla, tinged with pink or lilac, the spreading lobes covered with white hairs, with black and yellow, swinging anthers and a green pistil, with a two-lipped stigma. There are from ten to twenty flowers in each cluster and the effect is charming, suggesting a bunch of little fringed lilies. This grows in northern bogs across the continent and also in Europe and Asia. It used to be found around San Francisco, but is now extinct.

MORNING-GLORY FAMILY. *Convolvulaceae.*

A large family, most abundant in the tropics; ours are herbs, usually with twining or trailing stems; the leaves alternate, or mere scales, without stipules; the flowers perfect, with five sepals; the corolla with united petals, more or less funnel-form and more or less five-lobed, folded lengthwise and twisted in the bud; the stamens five, on the base of the corolla; the ovary superior, with from one to three styles; the fruit usually a capsule, with from one to four large seeds.

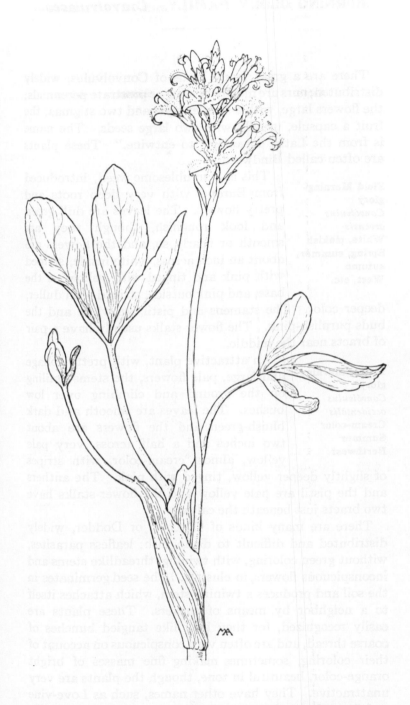

Buck-bean —   Menyanthes trifoliata.

There are a great many kinds of Convolvulus, widely distributed; ours are mostly twining or prostrate perennials; the flowers large, with a slender style and two stigmas; the fruit a capsule, usually with two large seeds. The name is from the Latin, meaning "to entwine." These plants are often called Bindweed.

Field Morning-glory
Convólvulus arvénsis
White, pinkish
Spring, summer, autumn
West, etc.

This is a troublesome weed, introduced from Europe, with very deep roots and pretty flowers. The leaves are dull green and look roughish, though they are smooth or nearly so, and the flowers are about an inch across, white inside, striped with pink and tinged with yellow at the base, and pink outside, striped with duller, deeper color. The stamens and pistil are white and the buds purplish-pink. The flower stalks usually have a pair of bracts near the middle.

Yellow Morning-glory
Convólvulus occidentàlis
Cream-color
Summer
Northwest

An attractive plant, with pretty foliage and large, pale flowers, the stems trailing on the ground and climbing over low bushes. The leaves are smooth and dark bluish-green and the flowers are about two inches and a half across, very pale yellow, almost cream-color, with stripes of slightly deeper yellow, tinged with pink. The anthers and the pistil are pale yellow and the flower-stalks have two bracts just beneath the calyx.

There are many kinds of Cuscuta, or Dodder, widely distributed and difficult to distinguish; leafless parasites, without green coloring, with twining, threadlike stems and inconspicuous flowers, in clusters. The seed germinates in the soil and produces a twining stem, which attaches itself to a neighbor by means of suckers. These plants are easily recognized, for they look like tangled bunches of coarse thread, and are often very conspicuous on account of their coloring, sometimes making fine masses of bright orange-color, beautiful in tone, though the plants are very unattractive. They have other names, such as Love-vine and Strangle-weed.

Field Morning-glory-
C. arvensis.

Yellow Morning-glory - Convolvulus occidentalis.

PHLOX FAMILY. *Polemoniaceae.*

Not a large family, most abundant in western North America, a few in Europe and Asia; sometimes slightly woody; the leaves without stipules; the flowers generally regular; the calyx with five united sepals; the corolla with five united petals, rolled up in the bud and often remaining more or less twisted to one side in the flowers; the stamens with slender filaments, with swinging anthers, often unequally inserted, on the tube or throat of the corolla and alternate with its lobes; the ovary superior, with a slender style and three-lobed stigma, but in immature flowers the three branches are folded together so that the style appears to have no lobes; the pod with three compartments, containing few or many seeds, which are sometimes winged and sometimes mucilaginous.

There are a good many kinds of Polemonium, growing in cool places, usually perennials; the leaves alternate, with leaflets, not toothed; the calyx not ribbed or angled, bell-shaped; the corolla more or less bell-shaped; the stamens equally inserted, but often of unequal lengths; the seeds mucilaginous when wet. This is the Greek name, used by Dioscorides.

Jacob's Ladder
Polemònium
occidentàle (P. coeruleum)
Blue
Summer
Northwest

A graceful plant, with attractive and unusual-looking foliage. The juicy stem and tender, bright green leaves are smooth or hairy and the pretty flowers are nearly three-quarters of an inch across, bright rather purplish blue, paler inside and delicately veined with blue, with a yellow "eye." The stamens are protruding, with white anthers, and the pistil is long and protruding, even in quite small buds. This is variable and grows in damp places in the mountains, across the continent and also in the Old World. The common name comes from the shape of the leaf and it is also called Greek Valerian. Another handsome sort is *P. carnèum*, with flowers varying in color from salmon to purple, growing in the mountains of California and Oregon, but rather rare.

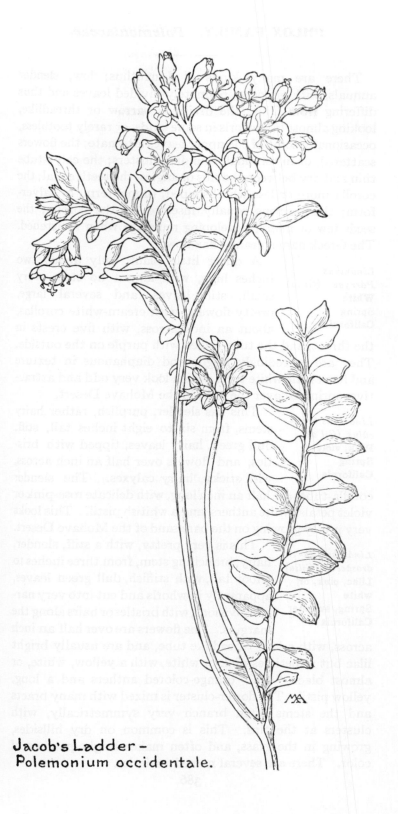

Jacob's Ladder –
Polemonium occidentale.

PHLOX FAMILY. *Polemoniaceae.*

There are many kinds of Linanthus; low, slender annuals, with opposite, palmately-divided leaves and thus differing from Gilia, the divisions narrow or threadlike, looking almost like whorls in some kinds, or rarely toothless, occasionally some of the upper leaves alternate; the flowers scattered, or in terminal, roundish clusters; the calyx-tube thin and dry between the ribs or angles, the teeth equal; the corolla more or less wheel-shaped, funnel-form, or salver-form; the stamens equally inserted on the corolla; the seeds few or many, developing mucilage when moistened. The Greek name means "flax flower."

Linánthus Párryae (Gilia)
White
Spring
California

A queer little plant, only about two inches high, with almost no stem, very small, stiff leaves, and several large, pretty flowers, with cream-white corollas, about an inch across, with five crests in the throat, and the tube tinged with purple on the outside. They are exceedingly fragile and diaphanous in texture and form little white tufts, which look very odd and attractive, sprinkled over the sand in the Mohave Desert.

Linánthus brevi-cùlus (Gil a)
Pink, violet
Spring
California

This has slender, purplish, rather hairy stems, from six to eight inches tall, stiff, dull green, hairy leaves, tipped with bristles, and flowers over half an inch across, with sticky, hairy calyxes. The slender corolla-tubes are half an inch long, with delicate rose-pink or violet petals, white anthers, and a whitish pistil. This looks very pretty growing on the bare sand of the Mohave Desert.

Linánthus an-drosàceus (Gilia)
Lilac, pink, or white
Spring, summer
California

This is very pretty, with a stiff, slender, hairy, branching stem, from three inches to a foot tall, with stiffish, dull green leaves, apparently in whorls and cut into very narrow divisions, with bristles or hairs along the margins. The flowers are over half an inch across, with a long threadlike tube, and are usually bright lilac but sometimes pink or white, with a yellow, white, or almost black "eye," orange-colored anthers and a long, yellow pistil. The flower-cluster is mixed with many bracts and the stems often branch very symmetrically, with clusters at the tips. This is common on dry hillsides, growing in the grass, and often makes bright patches of color. There are several named varieties.

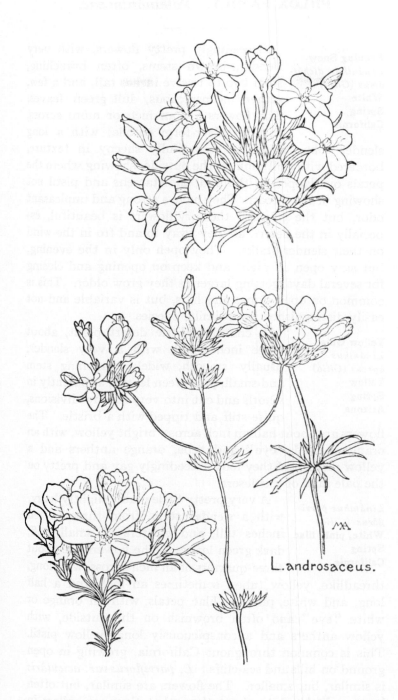

L.androsaceus.

L. Parryae.—   Linanthus breviculus.

PHLOX FAMILY. *Polemoniaceae.*

Evening Snow
Linánthus dichót-
omus (Gilia)
White
Spring
California

Exceedingly pretty flowers, with very slender, brown stems, often branching, from two to twelve inches tall, and a few, rather inconspicuous, dull green leaves. The flowers are an inch or more across, with a salver-form corolla, with a long slender tube, white and beautifully sheeny in texture, bordered with dull pink on the outside, showing where the petals overlapped in the bud; the stamens and pistil not showing in the throat. They have a strong and unpleasant odor, but the effect of the airy flowers is beautiful, especially in the desert, as they sway to and fro in the wind on their slender stalks. They open only in the evening, but stay open all night and keep on opening and closing for several days, getting larger as they grow older. This is common on open slopes and hills, but is variable and not easily distinguished from similar species.

Yellow Gilia
Linánthus
áureus (Gilia)
Yellow
Spring
Arizona

A charming little desert plant, about three inches tall, with a very slender, usually smooth, widely branching stem and small, pale green leaves, apparently in whorls and cut into very narrow divisions, quite stiff and tipped with a bristle. The flowers are about half an inch across, bright yellow, with an orange-colored "eye" and tube, orange anthers and a yellow pistil, and they look exceedingly gay and pretty on the pale sand of the desert.

Linánthus parvi-
flòrus (Gilia)
White, pink, lilac
Spring
California

A very pretty little plant, slightly hairy, with a slender stem, from three to ten inches tall, and clusters of small, stiff, dark green leaves. The flowers are about three-quarters of an inch across, with long, threadlike, yellow tubes, sometimes an inch and a half long, and white, pink, or lilac petals, with an orange or white "eye" and often brownish on the outside, with yellow anthers and a conspicuously long, yellow pistil. This is common throughout California, growing in open ground on hills and sea-cliffs. *L. parviflorus var. aciculàris* is similar, but smaller. The flowers are similar, but often have so little white about them that they are yellow in general effect, and are sometimes specked with crimson at the base of the petals. They grow in sandy places in southern California.

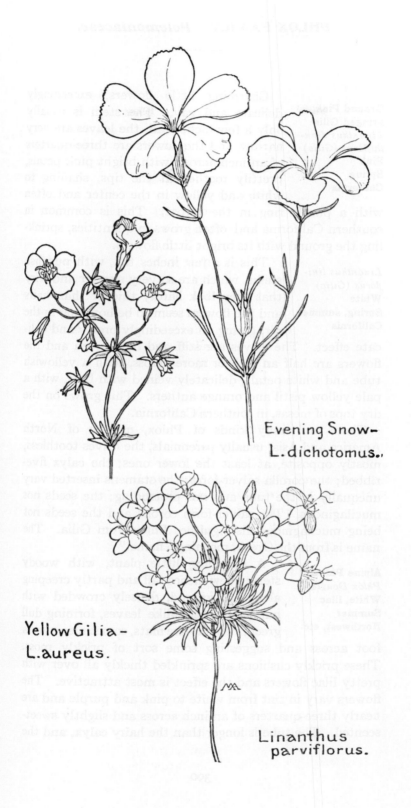

Evening Snow—
L. dichotomus.

Yellow Gilia—
L. aureus.

Linanthus
parviflorus.

Ground Pink,
Fringed Gilia
Linánthus dian-
thiflòrus (Gilia)
Pink
Spring
California

Charming little flowers, exceedingly delicate and gay. The stem is usually only a few inches tall, the leaves are very narrow, and the flowers are three-quarters of an inch across, with bright pink petals, prettily toothed at the tips, shading to white and yellow in the center and often with a purple ring in the throat. This is common in southern California and often grows in quantities, sprinkling the ground with its bright little flowers.

Linánthus lini-
flòrus (Gilia)
White
Spring, summer
California

This is a few inches tall, with purplish stems, which are so very slender and wiry that they look hardly thicker than hairs and the flowers seem to be hovering in the air, giving an exceedingly pretty and delicate effect. The leaves are stiff and dark green and the flowers are half an inch or more across, with a yellowish tube and white petals, delicately veined with blue, with a pale yellow pistil and orange anthers. This grows on the dry tops of mesas, in southern California.

There are many kinds of Phlox, natives of North America and Asia, usually perennials, the leaves toothless, mostly opposite, at least the lower ones; the calyx five-ribbed; the corolla salver-form; the stamens inserted very unequally in the tube and not protruding; the seeds not mucilaginous. The salver-form corolla and the seeds not being mucilaginous distinguishes Phlox from Gilia. The name is from the Greek, meaning "flame."

Alpine Phlox
Phlóx Douglásii
White, lilac
Summer
Northwest, etc.

A charming little plant, with woody stems a few inches tall and partly creeping along the ground, densely crowded with numerous needle-like leaves, forming dull green, cushion-like mats, sometimes over a foot across and suggesting some sort of prickly moss. These prickly cushions are sprinkled thickly all over with pretty lilac flowers and the effect is most attractive. The flowers vary in tint from white to pink and purple and are nearly three-quarters of an inch across and slightly sweet-scented. The tube is longer than the hairy calyx, and the

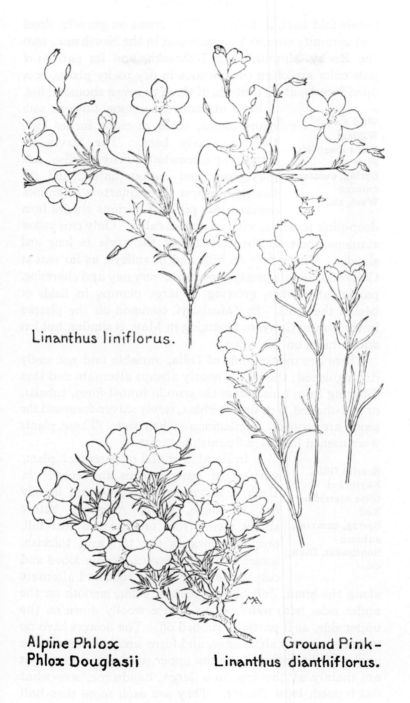

Linanthus liniflorus.

Alpine Phlox
Phlox Douglasii

Ground Pink-
Linanthus dianthiflorus.

petals fold back in fading. This grows on gravelly slopes and summits around Yosemite and in the Northwest, from the Rocky Mountains to Nebraska, and its patches of pale color are often conspicuous in dry rocky places, or in open forests, at an altitude of three to seven thousand feet.

Wild Sweet William
Phlóx longifòlia
Pink
Spring, summer, autumn
West, etc.

Very attractive common flowers, with many stems, three to eight inches high, from a woody base. The leaves are smooth or somewhat downy, stiffish, pale gray-green and rather harsh, and the flowers are over three-quarters of an inch across, clear pink, of various shades from deep-pink to white, with an angled calyx. Only two yellow stamens show in the throat and the style is long and slender. This grows on hills and in valleys, as far east as Colorado, and its pretty flowers are very gay and charming, particularly when growing in large clumps in fields or beside the road. *P. Stánsburyi*, common on the plateau in the Grand Canyon, blooming in May, is similar, but has sticky hairs on the calyx.

There are many kinds of Gilia, variable and not easily distinguished; the leaves nearly always alternate and thus differing from Linanthus; the corolla funnel-form, tubular, or bell-shaped, but, unlike Phlox, rarely salver-form and the seeds are usually mucilaginous when wet. These plants were named for Gil, a Spanish botanist.

Scarlet Gilia, Skyrocket
Gília aggregàta
Red
Spring, summer, autumn
Southwest, Utah, etc.

A brilliant biennial or perennial plant, varying in general form and color. In Utah it is somewhat coarse and usually has a single, leafy, roughish, rather sticky stem, from one to two feet tall, purplish towards the top, and thickish, somewhat sticky leaves, deeply lobed and cut, in a cluster at the root and alternate along the stem, dull bluish-green in color, smooth on the under side, with more or less sparse woolly down on the upper side, as if partially rubbed off. The flowers have no pedicels, or very short ones, and form small clusters in the angles of the leaves along the upper part of the stem, but are mainly at the top, in a large, handsome, somewhat flat-topped, loose cluster. They are each more than half an inch across, with a corolla of clear scarlet, the lobes

Scarlet Gilia.
G. aggregata.

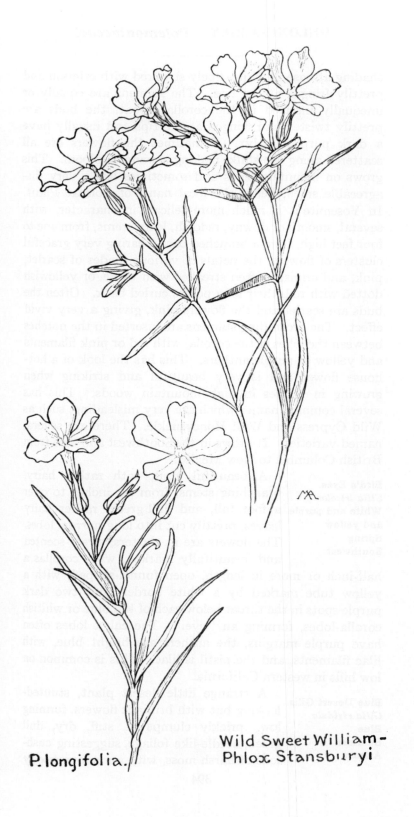

P. longifolia.

Wild Sweet William—
Phlox Stansburyi

shading at base to white, finely streaked with crimson and prettily fringed at the tips. The stamens are equally or unequally inserted in the corolla throat, the buds are prettily twisted and fringed at the tips and usually have a dark purplish calyx. Sometimes the flowers are all scattered along the stalk, making a wand of bloom. This grows on mountain sides and sometimes has a very disagreeable smell, hence the local name of Polecat Plant. In Yosemite it is much more delicate in character, with several, smooth or downy, reddish, leafy stems, from one to four feet high, from a branched base, bearing very graceful clusters of flowers, the petals of various shades of scarlet, pink, and crimson, often streaked with white, or yellowish dotted with red, their long points curled back. Often the buds are scarlet and the flowers pink, giving a very vivid effect. The protruding stamens are inserted in the notches between the lobes of the corolla, with red or pink filaments and yellow or purple anthers. This has the look of a hothouse flower and is very beautiful and striking when growing in masses in high mountain woods. This has several common names which are very misleading, such as Wild Cypress and Wild Honeysuckle. There are several named varieties. It grows in the Southwest and also from British Columbia to New Mexico.

Bird's Eyes
Gilia tricolor
White and purple and yellow
Spring
Southwest

A beautiful kind, with rather hairy, branching stems, from six inches to over a foot tall, and dull green, rather hairy leaves, prettily cut into long narrow lobes. The flowers are in clusters, sweet-scented and beautifully marked, with corollas a half-inch or more in length, open funnel-shaped, with a yellow tube marked by a white border, and two dark purple spots in the throat below each of the blue or whitish corolla-lobes, forming an "eye." The calyx lobes often have purple margins, the anthers are bright blue, with lilac filaments, and the pistil is lilac. This is common on low hills in western California.

Blue Desert Gilia
Gilia rigidula
Blue
Summer
Arizona

A strange little desert plant, stunted-looking but with brilliant flowers, forming low, prickly clumps of stiff, dry, dull green, needle-like foliage, suggesting cushions of harsh moss, with numerous woody

Blue Desert Gilia-
G. rigidula.

Bird's Eyes   Gilia tricolor.

stems, two or three inches high, and numbers of pretty flowers, half an inch across, deep bright blue, with a little yellow in the center; the stamens, with bright yellow anthers, projecting from the throat. This bravely opens its bright blue eyes in the desert wastes of the Petrified Forest.

Downy Gilia
Gilia floccòsa
Blue
Spring
Southwest

A little desert plant, about three inches tall, more or less downy all over, the upper leaves and buds covered with soft white down and the lower leaves dark green and stiff, tipped with a bristle. The tiny flowers have a blue corolla, varying from sky-blue to almost white, with a yellow throat and white stamens, and although they are too small to be conspicuous, the effect of the bits of blue on the desert sand is exceedingly pretty.

Small Prickly Gilia
Gilia púngens
White
Summer
California

This resembles Alpine Phlox in general effect, but the corolla is funnel-form instead of salver-form, for the lobes do not spread so abruptly. The many stems are woody below, a few inches high, and crowded with leaves, which are dull green, stiff, and cut into needle-like divisions, which look like single leaves, about half an inch long. The flowers are pretty and fragrant, half an inch across, white or pale pink, often with purplish streaks on the outside, with rounded lobes, the edge of each overlapping the next, and yellow anthers, not projecting from the throat of the corolla. This forms loose mats on rocky ledges, at high altitudes.

Gilia multicàulis
Lilac
Spring
California

A rather pretty little plant, about eight inches tall, with several slender, slightly hairy stems and leaves cut into very narrow divisions. The little flowers are pale lilac, quite delicate and pretty, though not conspicuous, and form clusters at the tips of the branches. This sometimes grows in quantities in the hills of southern California and is variable.

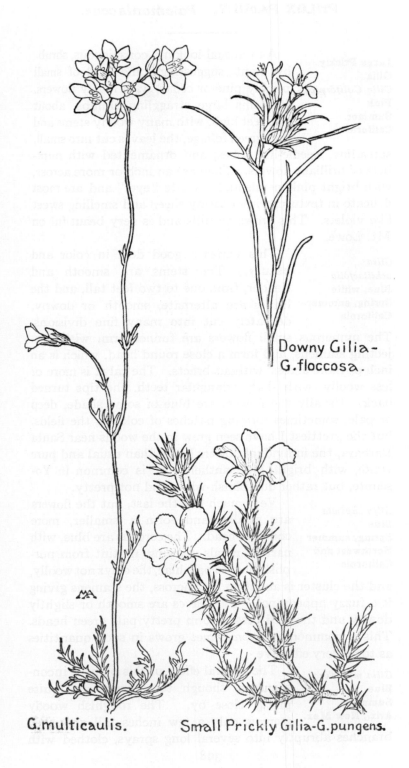

Downy Gilia–
G. floccosa.

G. multicaulis.

Small Prickly Gilia–G. pungens.

Large Prickly Gilia
Gilia Califórnica
Pink
Summer
California

An unusual-looking, conspicuous, shrubby plant, suggesting some kind of small prickly pine or cedar, with lovely flowers. It forms large straggling clumps, about two feet high, with many woody stems and rich-green foliage, the leaves cut into small, spreading, needle-like lobes, and ornamented with numbers of brilliant flowers. They are an inch or more across, with bright pink petals and a white "eye," and are most delicate in texture, with a satiny sheen and smelling sweet like violets. This grows on hills and is very beautiful on Mt. Lowe.

Gilia achillaefòlia
Blue, white
Spring, summer
California

This varies a good deal in color and beauty. The stems are smooth and slender, from one to two feet tall, and the leaves are alternate, smooth or downy, delicately cut into many fine divisions. The numerous small flowers are funnel-form, with projecting stamens, and form a close round head, which is an inch or more across, without bracts. The calyx is more or less woolly, with sharp triangular teeth, the tips turned back. Usually the flowers are blue of some shade, deep or pale, sometimes forming patches of color in the fields, but the prettiest I have seen grew in the woods near Santa Barbara, the individual flowers larger than usual and pure white, with bright blue anthers. It is common in Yosemite, but rather dull bluish-white and not pretty.

Gilia capitàta
Blue
Spring, summer
Northwest and California

Very much like the last, but the flowers are smaller and form a smaller, more compact head. The corollas are blue, with narrow petals, varying in tint from purplish-blue to pale lilac, the calyx not woolly, and the cluster is about an inch across, the stamens giving it a fuzzy appearance. The leaves are smooth or slightly downy and the seed-vessels form pretty pale green heads. This is common and sometimes grows in such quantities as to be very effective.

Gilia multiflòra
Blue
Summer
Ariz., New Mex.

The general effect of this plant is inconspicuous, though the flowers are quite pretty close by. The roughish woody stem is only a few inches tall and then branches abruptly into several long sprays, clothed with

Large
Prickly Gilia.

Gilia
Californica.

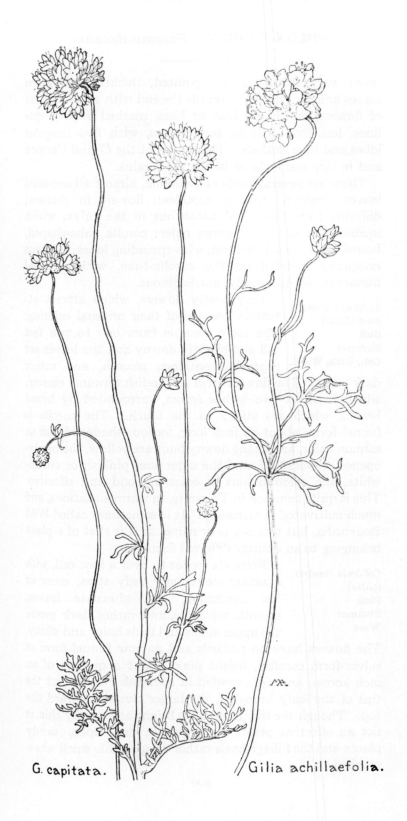

G. capitata.   Gilia achillaefolia.

many very small, narrow, pointed, thickish, dull green
leaves and ornamented towards the end with small clusters
of flowers, which are lilac or blue, marked with purple
lines, less than half an inch across, with five irregular
lobes and blue anthers. This grows at the Grand Canyon
and in dry open places in the mountains.

There are several kinds of Collomia, almost all annuals;
leaves alternate, usually toothless; flowers in clusters;
differing from Gilia and Linanthus in the calyx, which
increases in size as it grows older; corolla tube-shaped,
funnel-form, or salver-form, with spreading lobes; stamens
unequally inserted on the corolla-tube, with unequal
filaments; seeds usually mucilaginous.

Collòmia grandi-
flòra (Gilia)
Buff
Summer
Cal., Utah, Wash.

Very pretty flowers, which attract attention because of their unusual coloring.
The leafy stem is from one to two feet
tall and slightly downy and the leaves are
generally toothless, smooth, and rather
dark green. The flowers form a roundish terminal cluster,
which is about two inches across, surrounded by broad
bracts, which are sticky to the touch. The corolla is
funnel-form, about an inch long, various shades of buff or
salmon-color, and as the downy buds are yellow, the newly-
opened flowers buff, and the older ones pinkish or cream-
white, the combinations of color are odd and effective.
This is quite common in Yosemite, in warm situations, and
much cultivated in Germany. It is sometimes called Wild
Bouvardia, but this is a poor name, as it is that of a plant
belonging to an entirely different family.

Collòmia lineàris
(Gilia)
Pink
Summer
West

From six inches to over a foot tall, with
a rather stout, very leafy stem, more or
less branching, and alternate leaves,
smooth, toothless, and rather dark green,
the upper stems and buds hairy and sticky.
The flowers have no pedicels and narrow funnel-form or
salver-form corollas, bright pink, about a quarter of an
inch across, and are crowded in roundish clusters, at the
tips of the leafy branches, the larger clusters toward the
top. Though the tiny flowers are bright and pretty this is
not an effective plant. It grows in dry, open, sandy
places and the foliage has a rather disagreeable smell when
crushed.

Collomia
grandiflora.

C. linearis

WATERLEAF FAMILY. *Hydrophyllaceae.*

WATERLEAF FAMILY. *Hydrophyllaceae.*

Herbs or shrubs, mostly natives of western North America; often hairy; with no stipules; the leaves mainly alternate or from the root; the flowers chiefly blue or white, often in coiled clusters; the calyx with five united sepals; the corolla with five united petals; the stamens five, on the base of the corolla and alternate with its lobes, with thread-like filaments and usually with swinging anthers; the ovary superior, the styles two or two-cleft; the fruit a capsule, containing few or many seeds. The leaves were formerly supposed to have water-cavities in them, hence the misleading name. Some of this family resemble some of the Borages, but the stamens are long, the styles are two, at least above, and the ovary has not the four conspicuous lobes of the latter family.

There are many kinds of Phacelia, hairy plants, with no appendages between the sepals; resembling Hydrophyllum, except that the petals overlap in the bud, instead of being rolled up, and the seeds are different. The name is from the Greek, meaning "cluster."

Phacelia
Phacèlia lóngipes
Purple
Spring
California

This has pretty and rather unusual looking foliage, for the leaves are a peculiar shade of bluish-green, with purplish margins. They are somewhat sticky, soft and velvety, and although hairy are not disagreeable to touch. The hairy, purplish stems grow from a few inches to a foot tall and the pretty flowers are lilac or purple, with yellow anthers, and measure three-quarters of an inch across. This grows on sunny, sandy mountain slopes.

Phacelia
Phacèlia glecho-
maefòlia
Lilac, white
Summer
Ariz., Utah, Cal.

A low plant, partly creeping, with weak, brittle, sticky stems and soft, slightly thickish, very dull yellowish-green leaves, sticky and often dingy with dust. The flowers are usually violet, but sometimes pure white, about three-eighths of an inch across, with yellow stamens, and are rather pretty. I found this little plant growing under a huge red rock in the Grand Canyon, on apparently perfectly dry, bare soil. It has an aromatic and slightly unpleasant smell and is rare.

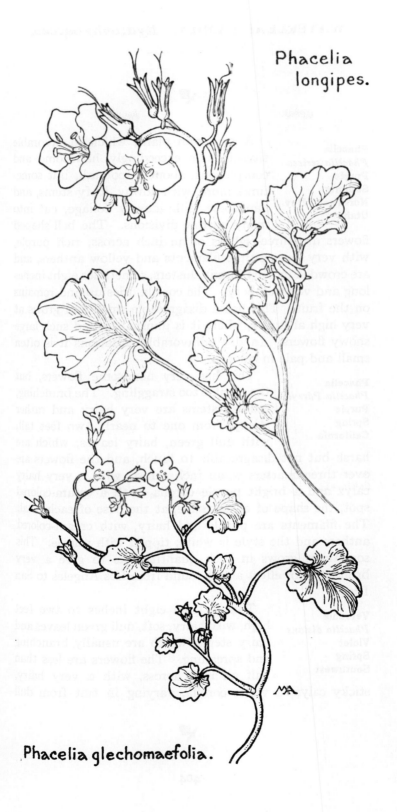

Phacelia
longipes.

Phacelia glechomaefolia.

Phacelia
Phacèlia serícea
Purple
Summer
Northwest, Nev.,
Utah

A mountain plant, which in favorable situations is exceedingly handsome and conspicuous, about a foot tall, but sometimes more, with downy, leafy stems, and handsome, silky-downy foliage, cut into many narrow divisions. The bell-shaped flowers are three-eighths of an inch across, rich purple, with very long, purple filaments and yellow anthers, and are crowded in magnificent clusters, sometimes eight inches long and very feathery. The corolla dries up and remains on the fruit. This has a disagreeable smell and grows at very high altitudes, where it is unusual to find such large showy flowers. In dry unfavorable situations it is often small and pale in color.

Phacelia
Phacèlia Párryi
Purple
Spring
California

This has very handsome flowers, but the plant is too straggling. The branching, reddish stems are very hairy and rather sticky, from one to nearly two feet tall, with dull green, hairy leaves, which are harsh but not disagreeable to touch, and the flowers are over three-quarters of an inch across, with a very hairy calyx and a bright purple corolla, with a cream-colored spot, the shape of a horseshoe, at the base of each petal. The filaments are purple and hairy, with cream-colored anthers and the style is white, tipped with purple. This sometimes grows in such quantities as to give a very brilliant color effect and is found from Los Angeles to San Diego.

Vervenia
Phacèlia dístans
Violet
Spring
Southwest

This is from eight inches to two feet high, with hairy, soft, dull green leaves and hairy stems, which are usually branching and spreading. The flowers are less than half an inch across, with a very hairy, sticky calyx, a violet corolla, varying in tint from dull

Mountain Phacelia.   Phacelia sericea.

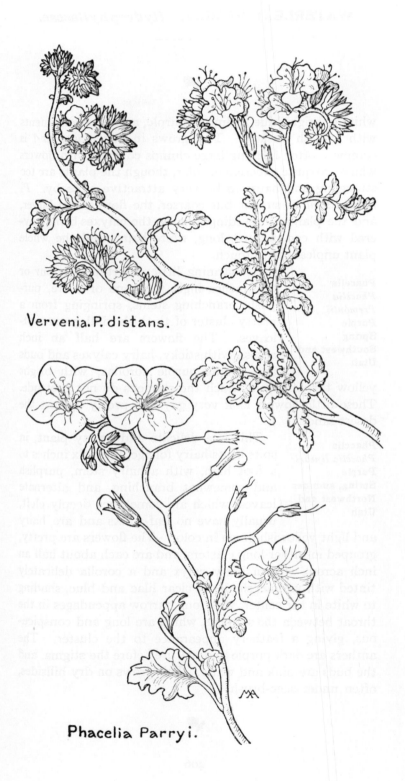

Vervenia. P. distans.

Phacelia Parryi.

white to bright blue, fading to purple, and purple filaments with whitish anthers. This grows in dry places and is common, often forming large clumps covered with flowers which are quite effective in color, though the plants are too straggling and hairy to be very attractive close by. *P. ramosíssima* is similar but coarser, the flowers are larger, and the plant is exceedingly hairy, the calyxes being covered with conspicuous, long, white hairs, and the whole plant unpleasant to touch.

Phacelia
Phacèlia
Fremónt·i
Purple
Spring
Southwest and
Utah

A charming little desert plant, four or five inches high, with one or more, purplish, branching stems, springing from a pretty cluster of thickish, dull green root-leaves. The flowers are half an inch across, with sticky, hairy calyxes and buds and bright purple corollas, with bright yellow throats, from which the stamens do not protrude. These little flowers look very gay and pretty against the desert sand.

Phacelia
Phacèlia linedris
Purple
Spring, summer
Northwest and
Utah

This is a delicate and pretty plant, in spite of its hairy foliage, from six inches to a foot high, with a hairy stem, purplish and somewhat branching, and alternate leaves, which are sometimes deeply cleft, usually have no leaf-stalks and are hairy and light yellowish-green in color. The flowers are pretty, grouped in rather long clusters, and are each about half an inch across, with a hairy calyx and a corolla delicately tinted with various shades of clear lilac and blue, shading to white in the center, with long narrow appendages in the throat between the stamens, which are long and conspicuous, giving a feathery appearance to the cluster. The anthers are dark purple and mature before the stigma, and the buds are pink and white. This grows on dry hillsides, often under sage-brush.

Phacelia linearis.

Phacelia   Fremontii.

Phacelia
Phacèlia
grandiflòra
Lilac
Summer
California

A very handsome kind, though rather coarse, and hairy and sticky all over, but with lovely, delicate flowers. The stems are from one to three feet tall and the dark green leaves are velvety on the upper side and hairy on the under. The flowers often measure two inches across, with a lilac or mauve corolla, shading to white in the center, flecked and streaked with brown, blue, or purple, and the stamens have purple filaments and pale yellow anthers. This plant is unpleasantly sticky, with a viscid fluid which stains everything with which it comes in contact, is poisonous to some people, and is found from Santa Barbara to San Diego.

Phacèlia viscida
var. albiflòra
White
Spring
California

This is a white variety, with pretty, delicate white flowers. *Phacelia viscida* is very much like *P. grandiflora*, and has about the same range, but is not so large a plant, usually about a foot tall, with smaller flowers, about an inch across. The corollas are blue, with purple or white centers.

Wild Canterbury-bell
Phacèlia
Whitlàvia
Purple
Summer
California

Charming flowers, though the foliage is rather too hairy. The stout, reddish stems are hairy, brittle, and loosely branching, about a foot tall, and the leaves dull green and hairy. The handsome flowers are in graceful nodding clusters, with a bell-shaped corolla, about an inch long, a rich shade of bluish-purple, the long conspicuous stamens and pistils giving an airy look to the blossoms. The filaments are purple and the anthers almost white and, as in other Phacelias, when the corolla drops off the long forked style remains sticking out of the calyx like a thread. This grows in light shade in rich moist soil in the hills.

Phacelia grandiflora.

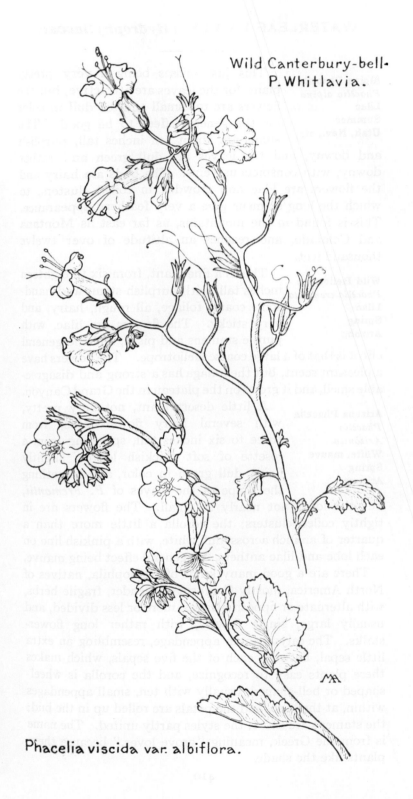

Wild Canterbury-bell-
P. Whitlavia.

Phacelia viscida var. albiflora.

WATERLEAF FAMILY.   *Hydrophyllaceae.*

Alpine Phacelia
Phacèlia alpìna
Lilac
Summer
Utah, Nev., etc.

This just misses being a very pretty plant, for the leaves are attractive, but the flowers are too small and too dull in color for the general effect to be good. The stems are about ten inches tall, purplish and downy, and the leaves are dull green and rather downy, with conspicuous veins. The buds are hairy and the flowers are lilac and crowded in coiled clusters, to which the long stamens give a very feathery appearance. This is found in the mountains, as far east as Montana and Colorado, and reaches an altitude of over twelve thousand feet.

Wild Heliotrope
Phacèlia crenulàta
Lilac
Spring
Arizona

This is a fine plant, from six to eighteen inches tall, with purplish stems and handsome coarse foliage, all rough, hairy, and very sticky. The flowers are lilac, with purple stamens and pistil, and the general effect is that of a large coarse Heliotrope. The flowers have a pleasant scent, but the foliage has a strong and disagreeable smell, and it grows on the plateau in the Grand Canyon.

Arizona Phacelia
Phacèlia
Arizònica
White, mauve
Spring
Arizona

A little desert plant, not very pretty, with several hairy flower-stalks, from three to six inches tall, springing from a rosette of soft thickish leaves, slightly hairy, dull green in color, and something the shape of the leaves of *P. Fremontii*, but the lobes not nearly so small. The flowers are in tightly coiled clusters; the corolla a little more than a quarter of an inch across, dull white, with a pinkish line on each lobe and lilac anthers, the general effect being mauve.

There are a good many kinds of Nemophila, natives of North America, mostly Californian, slender, fragile herbs, with alternate or opposite leaves, more or less divided, and usually large, single flowers, with rather long flower-stalks. The calyx has an appendage, resembling an extra little sepal, between each of the five sepals, which makes these plants easy to recognize, and the corolla is wheel-shaped or bell-shaped, usually with ten, small appendages within, at the base, and the petals are rolled up in the bud; the stamens are short; the styles partly united. The name is from the Greek, meaning "grove lover," because these plants like the shade.

Alpine
Phacelia-   P. alpina.

Wild Heliotrope-
Phacelia crenulata.

WATERLEAF FAMILY. *Hydrophyllaceae.*

Baby Blue-eyes, Mariana
Nemóphila insignis
Blue and white
Spring
California

These are exceedingly charming little plants, with slender, weak, hairy stems, varying a good deal in height, but usually low and spreading, and pretty, light green, soft, hairy foliage, sprinkled with many lovely flowers, an inch or more across, with hairy calyxes and sky-blue corollas, which are clear white in the center and more or less specked with brown, with ten hairy scales in the throat. The blue of their bright little faces is always wonderfully brilliant, but they are variable and are usually deeper in color and rather smaller in the South. This is one of the commonest kinds of Nemophila in California and it is a general favorite. It is called Mariana by the Spanish Californians.

Baby Blue-eyes
Nemóphila
intermèdia
Blue and white
Summer
California

This is much like the last, but it is a taller and more slender plant, usually about ten inches high. The lovely delicate flowers are less than an inch across, with light blue corollas, usually shading to white at the center and delicately veined with blue, or speckled with purple dots. This grows among the underbrush.

Spotted Nemophila
Nemóphila
maculàta
White and purple
Summer
California

These are charming flowers, their corollas oddly and prettily marked. The weak, hairy stems, from three to twelve inches long, are usually spreading and the leaves are opposite, hairy, and light green. The flowers are about an inch across, with hairy calyxes and white corollas, which are prettily dotted with purple and usually have a distinct indigo spot at the tip of each petal, which gives an unusual effect. The filaments are lilac and the anthers and pistil are whitish. This is common in meadows around Yosemite and in other places in the Sierras at moderate altitudes.

Baby
Blue-eyes

Nemophila
intermedia

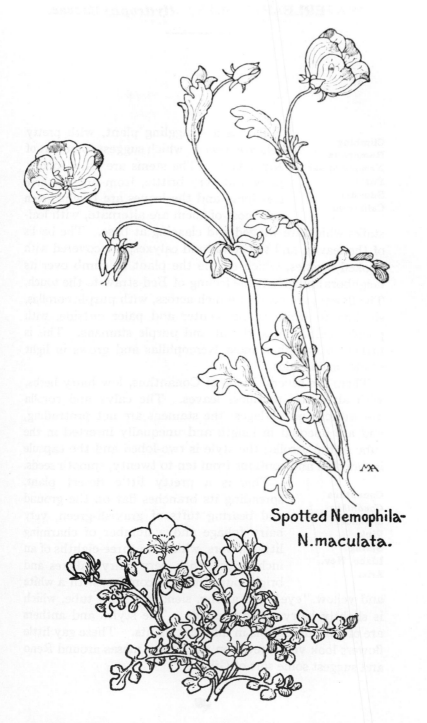

Spotted Nemophila-
N. maculata.

Baby Blue-eyes-   Nemophila insignis.

WATERLEAF FAMILY. *Hydrophyllaceae.*

Climbing Nemophila
Nemóphila aurìta
Purple
Summer
California

This is a straggling plant, with pretty delicate flowers, which suggest some sort of Nightshade. The stems are pale, square, juicy and very brittle, from one to three feet long, and the leaves are bright green and most of them are alternate, with leaf-stalks which are winged and clasping at base. The backs of the leaves, and the stems and calyxes, are covered with hooked bristles, which enable the plant to climb over its neighbors and give it the feeling of Bed-straw to the touch. The flowers are nearly an inch across, with purple corollas, shading to white in the center and paler outside, with purple scales in the throat and purple stamens. This is rather coarser than most Nemophilas and grows in light shade on hillsides.

There are several kinds of Conanthus, low hairy herbs, with alternate, toothless leaves. The calyx and corolla are without appendages; the stamens are not protruding, and are unequal in length and unequally inserted in the tube of the corolla; the style is two-lobed and the capsule is roundish and contains from ten to twenty, smooth seeds.

Conanthus
Conánthus aretioìdes
Pink
Spring
Idaho, Nev., Ariz.

This is a pretty little desert plant, spreading its branches flat on the ground and bearing tufts of grayish-green, very hairy foliage and a number of charming little flowers, which are three-eighths of an inch across, with very hairy calyxes and bright purplish-pink corollas, with a white and yellow "eye" and a long, slender, yellow tube, which is slightly hairy on the outside. The styles and anthers are of various lengths in different plants. These gay little flowers look very pretty on the dreary mesas around Reno and suggest some sort of Gilia.

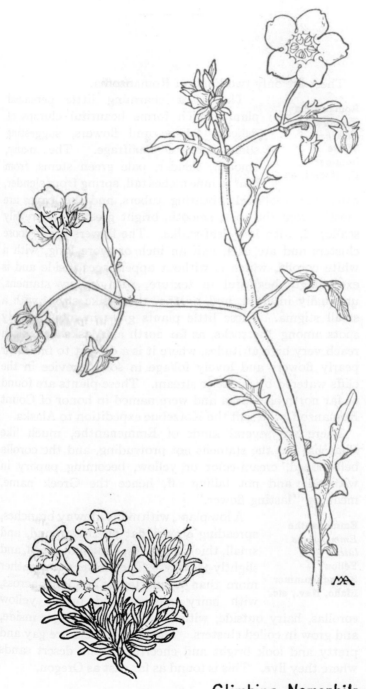

Climbing Nemophila-
N. aurita.

Conanthus aretioides.

WATERLEAF FAMILY. *Hydrophyllaceae.*

There are only two kinds of Romanzoffia.

Romanzoffia
Romanzóffia
sitchénsis
White
Summer
Northwest, etc.

This is a charming little perennial plant, which forms beautiful clumps of delicate foliage and flowers, suggesting some sort of Saxifrage. The many, smooth, slender, pale green stems, from four to nine inches tall, spring from slender, threadlike rootstocks, bearing tubers, and the leaves are mostly from the root, smooth, bright green, and prettily scalloped, with long leaf-stalks. The flowers are in loose clusters and are each half an inch or more long, with a white corolla, which is without appendages inside and is exceedingly beautiful in texture, with yellow stamens, unequally inserted, and a long, threadlike style, with a small stigma. These little plants grow in moist, shady spots among the rocks, as far north as Alaska and often reach very high altitudes, where it is a delight to find their pearly flowers and lovely foliage in some crevice in the cliffs watered by a glacier stream. These plants are found as far north as Alaska and were named in honor of Count Romanzoff, who sent the Kotzebue expedition to Alaska.

There are several kinds of Emmenanthe, much like Phacelia, but the stamens not protruding, and the corolla bell-shaped, cream-color or yellow, becoming papery in withering and not falling off, hence the Greek name, meaning "lasting flower."

Emmenanthe
Emmenánthe
lùtea
Yellow
Spring, summer
Idaho, Nev., etc.

A low plant, with many, downy branches, spreading almost flat on the ground, and small, thickish leaves, light dull green, and slightly downy. The flowers are rather more than a quarter of an inch across, with hairy calyxes, and bright yellow corollas, hairy outside, with ten little appendages inside, and grow in coiled clusters. The little flowers are gay and pretty and look bright and cheerful on the desert sands where they live. This is found as far east as Oregon.

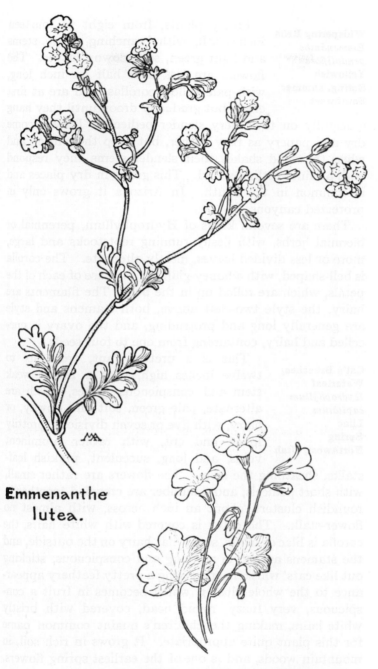

**Emmenanthe
lutea.**

Romanzoffia sitchensis.

WATERLEAF FAMILY. *Hydrophyllaceae.*

Whispering Bells
Emmenánthe
penduliflòra
Yellowish
Spring, summer
Southwest

Pretty plants, from eight to fourteen inches tall, with branching, hairy stems and light green, soft, downy leaves. The flowers are less than half an inch long, with pale yellow corollas, and are at first erect, but gradually droop until they hang gracefully on their very slender pedicels. They become dry and papery as they wither, but keep their form, and when the wind shakes their slender stems they respond with a faint rustling sound. This grows in dry places and is common in the South. In Arizona it grows only in protected canyons.

There are several kinds of Hydrophyllum, perennial or biennial herbs, with fleshy running rootstocks and large, more or less divided leaves, mostly alternate. The corolla is bell-shaped, with a honey-gland at the base of each of the petals, which are rolled up in the bud. The filaments are hairy, the style two-cleft above, both stamens and style are generally long and protruding, and the ovary is one-celled and hairy, containing from one to four seeds.

Cat's Breeches,
Waterleaf
Hydrophýllum
capitátum
Lilac
Spring
Northwest, Utah

This is a pretty plant, from six to twelve inches high, with a rather weak stem and conspicuous leaves, which are alternate, pale green, soft and downy, or hairy, with five or seven divisions, prettily lobed and cut, with rather prominent veins, and long, succulent, pinkish leaf-stalks, sheathing the stem. The flowers are rather small, with short pedicels, and a number are crowded together in roundish clusters, about an inch across, with almost no flower-stalk. The calyx is covered with white hairs, the corolla is lilac or white, somewhat hairy on the outside, and the stamens and style are long and conspicuous, sticking out like cats' whiskers and giving a pretty feathery appearance to the whole cluster, which becomes in fruit a conspicuous, very fuzzy, round head, covered with bristly white hairs, making the children's quaint common name for this plant quite appropriate. It grows in rich soil, in mountain woods, and is one of the earliest spring flowers. It is sometimes called Bear's Cabbage, but this name is far fetched, both as regards bears and cabbages!

**Cat's Breeches—
Hydrophyllum
capitatum.**

**Whispering Bells
Emmenanthe penduliflora.**

WATERLEAF FAMILY. *Hydrophyllaceae.*

There are several kinds of Eriodictyon, shrubs, with alternate, toothed, leathery, evergreen leaves, which are netted-veined, generally green and smooth on the upper side and whitish and downy on the under, with leaf-stalks; the flowers in coiled clusters; the corolla more or less funnel-form or salver-form, without appendages in the tube; the stamens and the two distinct styles not protruding; the capsule small, with few seeds. The name is from the Greek for "wool" and "net," in allusion to the netted wool on the under surface of the leaves.

Yerba Santa, Mountain Balm
Eriodictyon Califórnicum
White, lilac
Summer
Cal., Oreg., Wash.

A branching shrub, from two to six feet high, with thickish leaves, with toothed or wavy margins, from two to six inches long, dark and shiny on the upper side, pale with close down and netted-veined on the underside. The flowers are not especially pretty, about half an inch long, with white, lilac, or purple corollas, and are slightly sweet scented. The leaves are strongly and pleasantly aromatic when they are crushed and were used medicinally by the Indians, hence the Spanish name, meaning "holy herb." Cough-syrup is made from them and also substitutes for tobacco and hops. This grows on dry hills and is very variable, being sometimes a handsome shrub. There are intermediate forms between this and the next, *E. tomentosum*, which are difficult to distinguish.

Woolly Yerba Santa
Eriodíctyon tomentòsum
Lilac
Spring
California

A large leafy shrub, about five feet high and much handsomer than the last, with velvety, light green branches and very velvety, purplish twigs. The beautiful leaves are veined like chestnut leaves and made of the thickest, softest, sea-green or gray velvet, like a mullein leaf in texture, but much smoother and softer. The flowers are three-quarters of an inch long, with a pale pinkish-lilac corolla, shading to purple and white, downy on the outside, and form quite handsome clusters, mixed with pretty gray velvet buds, the lilac of the flowers harmonizing well with the gray foliage. This grows in quantities on Point Loma, and other places along the coast, from San Diego to Santa Barbara. There are several similar varieties.

Woolly Yerba Santa-
E. tomentosum.

YerbaSanta-
Eriodictyon | Californicum.

BORAGE FAMILY. *Boraginaceae.*

A large family, widely distributed, chiefly rough-hairy herbs, without stipules; usually with alternate, toothless leaves; flowers usually in coiled, one-sided clusters; calyx usually with five sepals; corolla usually symmetrical, with five united petals, often with crests or appendages in the throat; stamens five, inserted in the tube of the corolla, alternate with its lobes; ovary superior, with a single, sometimes two-cleft, style, and usually deeply four-lobed, like that of the Mint Family, forming in fruit four seed-like nutlets. Mature fruit is necessary to distinguish the different kinds. These plants superficially resemble some of the Waterleaf Family, but the four lobes of the ovary are conspicuous.

There are many kinds of Lappula, chiefly of the north-temperate zone; leaves narrow; corolla blue or white, salver-form or funnel-form, with a very short tube, the throat closed by five short scales, the stamens, with short filaments, hidden in the tube; ovary deeply four-lobed; style short; nutlets armed with barbed prickles, forming burs, giving the common name, Stickseed, and the Latin name, derived from "bur." Some of them resemble Forget-me-nots, but are not true Myosotis.

White Forget-me-not
Láppula subdecúmbens
White
Spring, summer
Northwest

Though the foliage is harsh, this plant is so graceful and has such pretty flowers that it is most attractive. It is from ten to eighteen inches tall, with several yellowish, hairy stems, springing from a perennial root and a cluster of root-leaves, the stem-leaves more or less clasping at base, all bluish-green, covered with pale hairs, with prominent veins on the back and sparse bristles along the edges. The flowers form handsome, large, loose clusters and the hairy buds are tightly coiled. The calyx is hairy, with blunt lobes, and the corolla, about half an inch across, is pure white, or tinged with blue, often marked with blue, with two ridges on the base of each petal, and the throat closed by five yellow crests, surrounded by a ring of fuzzy white down. This grows on dry plains and hillsides, sometimes making large clumps.

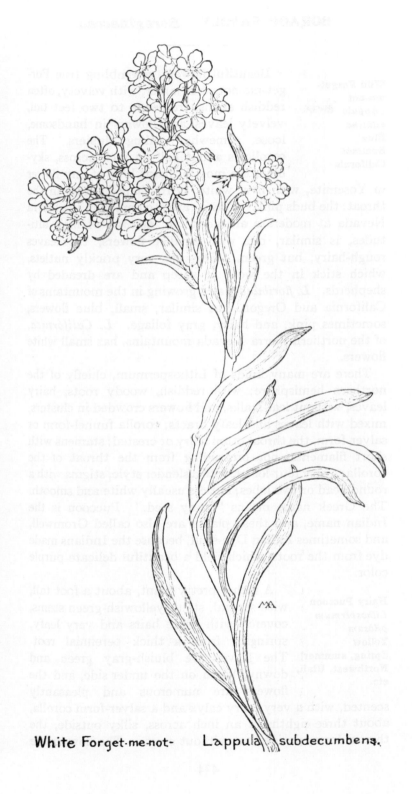

White Forget-me-not- **Lappula subdecumbens.**

BORAGE FAMILY. *Boraginaceae.*

Wild Forget-me-not
Láppula velùtina
Blue
Summer
California

Beautiful flowers, resembling true Forget-me-nots, but larger, with velvety, often reddish stems, from one to two feet tall, velvety leaves, and flowers in handsome, loose, somewhat coiling clusters. The corolla is about half an inch across, sky-blue, the most brilliant blue of any flower in Yosemite, with five, white, heart-shaped crests in the throat; the buds pink. This is rather common in the Sierra Nevada at moderate altitudes. *L. nervòsa,* of high altitudes, is similar, but with smaller flowers, the leaves rough-hairy, but green. This has very prickly nutlets, which stick in the wool of sheep and are dreaded by shepherds. *L. floribúnda,* also growing in the mountains of California and Oregon, has similar, small, blue flowers, sometimes pink, and hairy, gray foliage. *L. Califórnica,* of the northern Sierra Nevada mountains, has small white flowers.

There are many kinds of Lithospermum, chiefly of the northern hemisphere; with reddish, woody roots, hairy leaves, without leaf-stalks, and flowers crowded in clusters, mixed with leaves and leafy bracts; corolla funnel-form or salver-form, the throat often hairy or crested; stamens with short filaments, not protruding from the throat of the corolla; ovary four-lobed, with a slender style, stigma with a round head or two lobes; nutlets usually white and smooth. The Greek name means "stony seed." Puccoon is the Indian name, and these plants are also called Gromwell, and sometimes Indian Dye-stuff, because the Indians made dye from the roots, which yield a beautiful delicate purple color.

Hairy Puccoon
Lithospérmum pilòsum
Yellow
Spring, summer
Northwest, Utah, etc.

A rather pretty plant, about a foot tall, with several, stout, yellowish-green stems, covered with white hairs and very leafy, springing from a thick perennial root. The leaves are bluish-gray green and downy, harsh on the under side, and the flowers are numerous and pleasantly scented, with a very hairy calyx and a salver-form corolla, about three-eighths of an inch across, silky outside, the throat downy inside, but without crests. The flowers are

Hairy Puccoon-
Lithospermum pilosum.

Wild Forget-me-not-
Lappula velutina

yellow, an unusual shade of pale corn-color, and harmonize with the pale foliage, but are not conspicuous, and the flower cluster is so crowded with leaves and leafy bracts that it is not effective. This grows in dry fields, as far east as Nebraska, and sometimes makes pretty little bushes, over two feet across.

Pretty Puccoon
Lithospérmum
angustifòlium
Yellow
Spring
West, etc.

These are pretty flowers, but have a disagreeable smell. They are perennials, with a deep root and hairy or downy, branching stems, from six inches to two feet high, and hairy or downy leaves, which are rather grayish green. The flowers are in terminal leafy clusters and are of two sorts. The corollas of the earlier ones are very pretty, clear bright yellow, sometimes nearly an inch and a half long, with toothed lobes, which are charmingly ruffled at the edges, and with crests in the throat, but the later flowers are small, pale, and inconspicuous. This grows in dry places, especially on the prairies, and is very widely distributed in the western and west central states.

Gromwell
Lithospérmum
multiflòrum
Yellow
Summer
Ariz., Utah, etc.

This has a rough, hairy stem, about a foot tall, and dull green, rough, hairy leaves, with bristles along the edges. The yellow flowers are half an inch long and form rather pretty coiled clusters. This grows in open woods at the Grand Canyon, and is found as far east as New Mexico and Colorado.

There are a good many kinds of Amsinckia, natives of the western part of our country and of Mexico and South America. They are rather difficult to distinguish, rough, hairy or bristly, annual herbs, the bristles usually from a raised base, and with yellow flowers, in curved, rather showy, clusters. The corolla is more or less salver-form, without crests, but with folds; the stamens and pistil not protruding, the stigma two-lobed. In order to insure cross pollination by insects, in some kinds the flowers are of two types, as concerns the insertion of the stamens on the corolla and the length of the style. Several of these plants are valuable in Arizona for early spring stock feed, and the leaves of young plants are eaten by the Pima Indians for greens and salads.

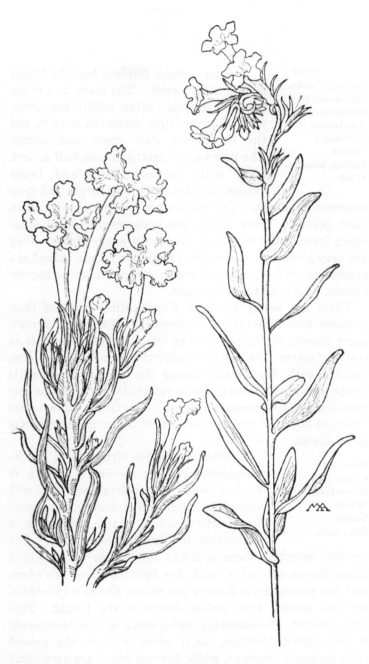

Pretty Puccoon –
Lithospermum angustifolium.

Gromwell –
L.multiflorum.

BORAGE FAMILY. *Boraginaceae.*

Saccato Gordo,
Fiddle-neck,
Buckthorn Weed
Amsinckia
intermèdia
Yellow
Spring, summer
West

This has bright flowers, but the foliage is dreadfully harsh. The stem is from one to three feet tall, often widely branching, with white bristles scattered over it, and the leaves are dull green and bristly. The flowers are pretty, about half an inch long, with narrow sepals and bright orange corollas, with five bright red spots between the lobes. The nutlets are roughened with short, hard points. These plants are very common and sometimes form rank thickets in fields and waste places. They are very abundant in southern Arizona and are valued as a grazing plant for stock and are therefore known as Saccato Gordo, which means "fat grass."

There are many kinds of Cryptanthe, most of them western and difficult to distinguish. They are slender, hairy plants, with small flowers, which are usually white, in coiled clusters; the calyx bristly; the corolla funnel-form, usually with five crests closing the throat; the nutlets never wrinkled. These plants resemble white Forget-me-nots and are sometimes so called. The Greek name means "hidden flower," perhaps because of the minute flowers of some kinds.

Nievitas
Cryptánthe
intermèdia
White
Spring
Cal., Ariz.

A rather attractive little plant, but inconspicuous except when it grows in patches, when it powders the fields with white, like a light fall of snow, and suggests the pretty Spanish name, which is a diminutive of "nieve," or snow. The slender, roughish stem is about ten inches tall, the light green leaves are hairy, with fine bristles along the edges, and the pretty little flowers are white, about a quarter of an inch across, with yellow crests in the throat. Popcorn Flower, *Plagiobòthrys nothofúlvus*, of the Northwest, is also called Nievitas, as it often whitens the ground with its small, fragrant, white flowers, which are very much like the last.

428

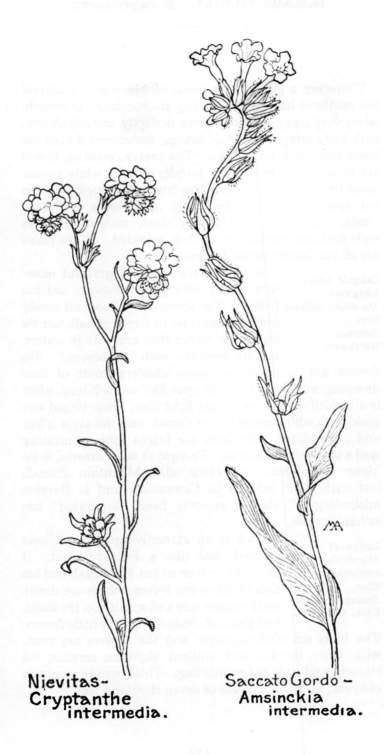

Nievitas–
Cryptanthe
intermedia.

Saccato Gordo –
Amsinckia
intermedia.

BORAGE FAMILY. *Boraginaceae.*

There are a good many kinds of Mertensia, natives of the northern hemisphere. They are handsome perennials, never very hairy and sometimes perfectly smooth all over, with leafy stems and broad leaves, sometimes dotted, the lower ones with leaf-stalks. The pretty, nodding flowers are in clusters and have a purple, blue, or white corolla, often turning pink, more or less trumpet-shaped, the lobes not spreading much, the throat open, with or without crests; the ovary deeply four-lobed, with a threadlike style and one stigma; the nutlets wrinkled. These plants are all commonly called Lungwort.

Languid Lady,
Lungwort
Merténsia Sibírica
Blue
Summer
Northwest

A very attractive and graceful mountain plant, with pretty flowers and fine foliage. The stems are hollow and usually smooth, from one to five feet tall, and the leaves are rather thin and soft in texture, usually smooth, with a "bloom." The flowers are in handsome loose clusters, most of them drooping, and have a corolla over half an inch long, which is a beautiful shade of bright light blue, often tinged with pink, with white crests in the throat, and the style is long and protruding. The buds are bright pink, contrasting well with the blue flowers. This grows near streams, in the higher mountains. It is often called Mountain Bluebell, but that name belongs to Campanula and is therefore misleading. (This has recently been "separated" into several species.)

Lungwort
Merténsia
brevístyla
Blue
Spring, summer
Utah, Col., Wyo.

This is an attractive plant and looks a good deal like a Forget-me-not. It grows from four to ten inches tall and has dull bluish-green leaves, which are downy on the upper side and smooth on the under, and graceful clusters of pretty little flowers. The buds are pinkish-purple and the flowers are small, with hairy calyxes and brilliant sky-blue corollas, the stamens and style not protruding. This grows in mountain canyons, up to an altitude of seven thousand feet.

Mertensia—
M. brevistyla.

Languid Lady—
Mertensia Sibirica.

BORAGE FAMILY. *Boraginaceae.*

There are many kinds of Heliotrope, widely distributed in temperate and tropical regions; ours have small, white or blue flowers, in coiled spikes; the corolla salver-form or funnel-form, without crests or hairs; the stamens not protruding, the filaments short or none, the anthers sometimes joined by their pointed tips; the ovary not four-lobed, but sometimes grooved, with a short style, the stigma cone-shaped or round.

Sea-side Helio-trope, Chinese Pusley
Heliotrópium Curassávicum
White
Summer, autumn
Cal., Oreg., etc.

This is not a pretty plant and is rather insignificant because of its dull coloring. It forms low, branching, straggling clumps, with thickish stems and leaves, which are succulent and perfectly smooth, with a "bloom," and the flowers are small, the corolla white or pale lilac, with a yellow "eye" which changes to purple, forming crowded coiled spikes, mostly in pairs, without bracts. The fruit consists of four nutlets. This is widely distributed, in moist, salty or alkaline places, growing also in the East and in South America and the Old World.

There are several kinds of Oreocarya, natives of western North America and Mexico, coarse, hairy, perennial or biennial herbs, with thick woody roots; the leaves narrow, alternate or from the root; the flowers small, mostly white, in clusters, with a funnel-form or salver-form corolla, usually with crests and folds in the throat; the stamens not protruding; the style usually short. The name is from the Greek, meaning "mountain-nut," which does not seem very appropriate.

Oreocarya
Oreocàrya multicâulis
White
Spring
Ariz., Utah, etc.

A rather pretty plant, about six inches tall, not rough and harsh like most kinds of Oreocarya, for the pale grayish-green stem and leaves are covered with white down. The flowers are quite pretty, about three-eighths of an inch across, with white corollas, with yellow crests in the throat. This is found as far east as southern Colorado and New Mexico. *O. setosíssima* is quite tall, growing in the Grand Canyon, and has a large cluster of small white flowers and is harsh and hairy all over, covered with such long stiff white hairs as to make it conspicuous and very unpleasant to touch.

Chinese
Pusley –
Heliotropium
Curassavicum.

Oreocarya multicaulis.

VERBENA FAMILY. *Verbenaceae.*

A large family, widely distributed; herbs and shrubs; leaves opposite, or in whorls; flowers perfect, in clusters; calyx with four or five lobes or teeth; corolla with four or five united lobes, almost regular or two-lipped; stamens on the corolla, usually four, in two sets; ovary superior, with one style and one or two stigmas, when ripe separating into from two to four, one-seeded nutlets.

There are many kinds of Verbena, chiefly American; perennials; calyx tubular, with five teeth; corolla usually salver-form, with five lobes, usually slightly two-lipped; stigmas with two lobes, only the larger lobe fertile; fruit four nutlets. This is the Latin name of some sacred plant.

Wild Verbena
Verbèna
Arizònica
Lilac
Spring
Arizona

This is very much like a garden Verbena, an attractive little plant, from four to six inches tall, with hairy stems and prettily shaped leaves, dull green, soft and hairy. The gay little flowers are about half an inch across, with a bright pinkish-lilac corolla, with a white or yellowish "eye," and a sticky-hairy calyx, and form a charming flat-topped cluster. This grows among the rocks, above the Desert Laboratory at Tucson and in similar places.

Common Vervain
Verbèna prostràta
Lilac
Spring, summer, autumn
California

A loosely-branching plant, from one to two feet tall, with dull green, hairy stems, dull green, soft, hairy leaves, and very small flowers in a long spike, too few open at one time to be effective. The corolla is lilac or bluish, often with a magenta tube and magenta "eye." This grows in dry open hill country.

MINT FAMILY. *Labiatae.*

A very large family, with distinctive characteristics; widely distributed. Ours are herbs or low shrubs, generally aromatic, with usually square and hollow stems; leaves opposite, with no stipules; flowers perfect, irregular, in clusters, usually with bracts; calyx usually five-toothed, frequently two-lipped; corolla more or less two-lipped, upper lip usually with two lobes, lower lip with three; stamens usually four, in pairs, on the corolla-tube, alter-

Wild Verbena - V. Arizonica.

Common Vervain - Verbena prostrata.

nate with its lobes; ovary superior, with four lobes, separating when ripe into four, small, smooth, one-seeded nutlets, surrounding the base of the two-lobed style, like the four nutlets of the Borage Family, but the flowers of the latter are regular. These plants are used medicinally and include many herbs used for seasoning, such as Sage, Thyme, etc.

There are a few kinds of Micromeria; trailing perennials; flowers small; calyx tubular, with five teeth; corolla two-lipped, with a straight tube; stamens four, all with anthers, not protruding. The Greek name means "small."

**Yerba Buena,
Tea-vine**
*Micromèria
Chamissònis*
(*M. Douglasii*)
**Lilac, white
Spring, summer
Cal., Oreg., Wash.**

An attractive little plant, resembling the little eastern Gill-over-the-ground, with slender trailing stems, slightly downy foliage, and lilac or whitish flowers, about a quarter of an inch long. The calyx and corolla are hairy on the outside; the corolla has an erect upper lip, sometimes notched, and a spreading, three-lobed lower lip, and the stamens are four, the lower pair shorter. This is common in shady places near the coast. It has a pleasant aromatic fragrance and was used medicinally by California Indians, so it was called "good herb" by the Mission Fathers, and is still used as a tea by Spanish-Californians, who call it Yerba Buena del Campo, "field herb," distinguishing it from Yerba Buena del Poso, "herb of the well," the garden mint.

There are several kinds of Monardella, fragrant herbs, all western, chiefly Californian; leaves mostly toothless; flowers small, in terminal heads, on long flower-stalks, with bracts, which are often colored; calyx tubular, with five, nearly equal teeth; corolla with erect upper lip, two-cleft, lower lip with three, nearly equal lobes; stamens four, protruding, sometimes the lower pair longer.

**Western Penny-royal, Mustang
Mint**
*Monardélla
lanceolàta*
**Lilac
Summer
California**

An attractive plant, pretty in color and form, with purplish, often branching stems, from six inches to over two feet high, smooth leaves, and small bright pinkish-lilac flowers, crowded in terminal heads, about an inch across, with purplish bracts. The outer ring of flowers blooms first and surrounds a knob of small green

Yerba Buena –
Micromeria Chamissonis.

Mustang Mint –   Monardella lanceolata.

---

buds, so that the effect of the whole flower-head slightly suggests a thistle. This has a strong, pleasant smell like Pennyroyal and is abundant in Yosemite, and elsewhere in the Sierra Nevada foothills.

There are several kinds of Ramona, abundant in southern California; shrubby plants, with wrinkled leaves and flowers like those of Salvia, except for differences in the filaments; stamens two. They are very important honey-plants, commonly called Sage, and by some botanists considered to be a species of Salvia.

Desert Ramona
Ramòna incàna
(Audibertia)
Blue
Spring
Southwest

A low desert shrub, from two to three feet high, varying very much in color. On the plateau in the Grand Canyon it is delicate and unusual in coloring, with pale gray, woody stems and branches and small, stiffish, gray-green, toothless leaves, covered with white down. The small flowers are bright blue, projecting from close whorls of variously tinted bracts, and have long stamens, protruding from the corolla-tube, with blue filaments and yellow anthers, and a blue style. The bracts are sometimes lilac, sometimes pale blue, or cream-color, but always form delicate pastelle shades, peculiar yet harmonizing in tone with the vivid blue of the flowers and with the pale foliage. This is strongly aromatic when crushed. In the Mohave Desert it is exceedingly handsome, but the coloring is often less peculiar, as the foliage is not quite so pale as in other places, such as the Grand Canyon, and the flowers vary from blue to lilac or white. It blooms in spring and when its clumps of purple are contrasted with some of the yellow desert flowers, clustered about the feet of the dark Joshua Trees which grow around Hesperia, the effect is very fine.

Humming-bird
Sage
Ramòna grandi-
flòra (Audibertia)
Red
Spring
California

This is a handsome and very decorative plant, though rather coarse and sticky, with a stout, bronze-colored stem, which is woody at base, from two to three feet tall, and velvety, wrinkled leaves, from three to eight inches long, with scalloped edges and white with down on the under side. The flowers are an inch and a half long, with crimson corollas of various fine shades, which project from the crowded whorls of broad, bronze or purplish bracts,

Ramona incana·

Humming-bird Sage-   *Ramona grandiflora*

arranged in tiers along the stem. Sometimes there are as many as nine of these clusters and the effect of the whole is dark and very rich, especially in shady places. This is common in the hills, from San Francisco south. Humming-birds are supposed to be its only visitors.

White Ball Sage
Ramòna nivea
(Audibertia)
Lilac
Spring
California

A very conspicuous, shrubby plant, much handsomer than Black Sage, from three to six feet high, with many, downy, stout, leafy stems, woody below, forming enormous clumps of pale foliage. The leaves are covered with pale down and are a delicate shade of sage-green and feel like soft thick velvet, and the mauve or lilac flowers, about three-quarters of an inch long, are arranged in a series of very round, compact balls along the stiff stalks. This is a honey-plant and smells strong of sage, and is common in the South, giving a beautiful effect of mingled mauve and gray.

White Sage
Ramòna poly-
stàchya (Audi-
bertia), (Salvia
apiana)
White, lilac
Spring
California

Not so handsome as the last, but a very conspicuous plant, on account of its size and the pale tint of its foliage, though the flowers are too dull in color to be striking. It is shrubby and has a number of stems, which form a loose clump from three to six feet high, with rather leathery, resinous leaves, all but the upper ones with scal-loped edges, and the whole plant is covered with fine white down, so that the general effect is pale gray, blending with the white or pale lilac flowers and purplish buds. The flowers are about half an inch long and are very queer in form, for the only conspicuous part is the lower lip, which is very broad with a ruffled edge and is turned straight up and backward, so as to conceal almost all the rest of the flower. The long jointed stamens, which are borne on the lower lip, stand out awkwardly like horns and from one side of the flower's face a long white pistil sticks out, with something the effect of a very long cigar hanging out of the corner of its mouth! All these eccentric arrangements are apparently for the purpose of securing cross-pollination from the bees, which frequent these flowers by the thou-

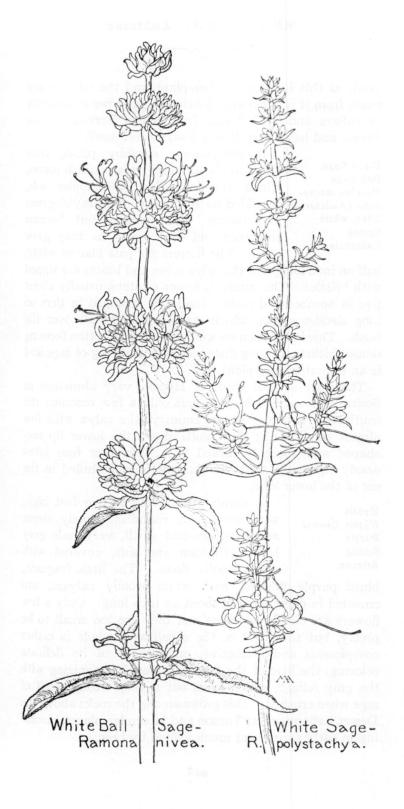

White Ball Sage-
Ramona nivea.

White Sage-
R. polystachya.

sand, as this is a famous bee-plant and the white honey made from it is peculiarly delicious. It grows abundantly in valleys and on hillsides, from Santa Barbara to San Diego, and has a very strong disagreeable smell.

**Black Sage,
Ball Sage**
*Ramòna stachy-
oìdes (Audibertia)*
**Lilac, white
Spring
California**

A conspicuous shrubby plant, from three to six feet high, with stiffish leaves, which are downy on the under side, wrinkled on the upper, and grayish-green and downy when young, but become smoother and dark green as they grow older. The flowers are pale lilac or white, half an inch long, and the calyx-lobes and bracts are tipped with bristles. The compact flower clusters, usually about five in number and rather small, are arranged in tiers on long slender stalks, which stand up stiffly all over the bush. This is common on southern hillsides, often forming dense thickets for long distances, smells strong of sage and is an important bee-plant.

There are several kinds of Hyptis, very abundant in South America and Mexico, but only a few reaching the southwestern border of our country; the calyx with five almost equal teeth; the corolla short, the lower lip sac-shaped and abruptly turned back, the other four lobes nearly equal and flat; the stamens four, included in the sac of the lower lobe.

Hyptis
Hỳptis Émoryi
**Purple
Spring
Arizona**

A shrub, from three to five feet high, with very pale, roundish, woody stems and branches and small, very pale gray leaves, thickish and soft, covered with white woolly down. The little fragrant, bluish-purple flowers, with white woolly calyxes, are crowded in close clusters about an inch long. Only a few flowers are out at one time and they are too small to be pretty, but the effect of the shrub as a whole is rather conspicuous and attractive, on account of its delicate coloring, the lilac of the flower-clusters harmonizing with the gray foliage, which gives out a very strong smell of sage when crushed. This grows among the rocks above the Desert Laboratory at Tucson and in similar places, blooming in early spring and much visited by bees.

442

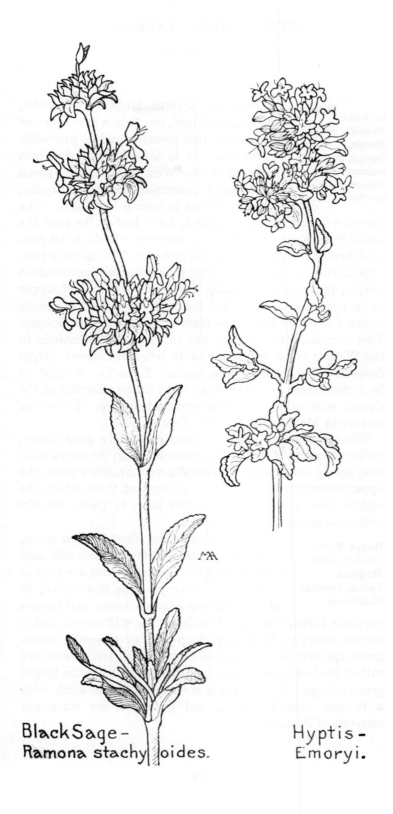

Black Sage—
Ramona stachyoides.

Hyptis—
Emoryi.

MINT FAMILY. *Labiatae.*

Self-heal
Prunélla vulgàris
Purple
Spring, summer,
autumn
Across the
continent
There are several kinds of Prunella, widely distributed, but this is the only one common in this country and is probably not native. It is abundant in dampish places, in the far West often staying green all winter, a perennial, sometimes hairy, from two inches to over a foot high. The leaves, often obscurely toothed, have leaf-stalks and the small flowers are crowded in a series of whorls, with purplish bracts and forming a spike or head. The calyx is two-lipped, with five teeth and often purplish, and the corolla is purple, pink, or occasionally white, with an arched upper lip, a spreading, three-lobed lower lip, and four stamens, under the upper lip of the corolla, the lower pair longer. This is usually not pretty, but in favorable situations in the West is often handsome, with brighter-colored, larger flowers. The name, often spelled Brunella, is said to be derived from an old German word for an affection of the throat, which this plant was supposed to cure. There is a picture in Mr. Mathews' *Field Book.*

There are many kinds of Stachys, widely distributed; herbs, often hairy, with a disagreeable smell; the calyx with five, nearly equal teeth; the corolla with a narrow tube, the upper lip erect, the lower lip spreading and three-lobed, the middle lobe longest; the stamens four, in pairs, usually under the upper lip of the corolla.

Hedge Nettle
Stàchys ciliàta
Magenta
Spring, summer
Northwest
This is a handsome plant, with a stout, rough, hairy stem, over two feet tall, and very bright green leaves, which are thin in texture but velvety. The flowers are in whorls, making a large cluster, and have a purplish calyx, smooth or with a few stiff hairs, and a corolla about an inch long, deep pink or magenta, sometimes spotted with white inside. Though the flowers are rather crude in color, they contrast finely with the bright green foliage. *S. coccínea* is a very handsome kind, with a tubular scarlet corolla, and grows in the mountain canyons of Arizona.

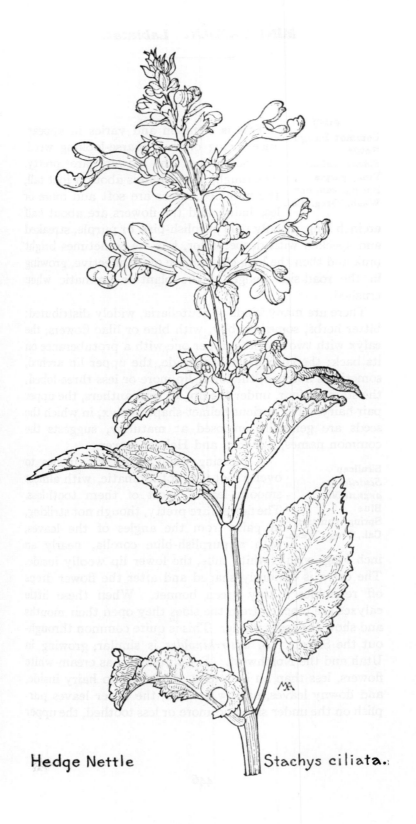

Hedge Nettle   Stachys ciliata.

Common Hedge Nettle
Stàchys bullàta
Pink, purple
Spring, summer
Wash., Oreg., Cal.

This is common and varies in appearance, being often a coarse-looking weed, but sometimes the flowers are pretty. The rough, hairy stem is about a foot tall, the wrinkled leaves are soft and more or less hairy, and the flowers are about half an inch long, usually pale purplish-pink or purple, streaked and specked with deeper color, but are sometimes bright pink and then the long clusters are quite effective, growing in the road-side hedges. The plant is aromatic when crushed.

There are many kinds of Scutellaria, widely distributed; bitter herbs, some shrubby, with blue or lilac flowers; the calyx with two lips, the upper one with a protuberance on its back; the corolla smooth inside, the upper lip arched, sometimes notched, the lower lip more or less three-lobed; the stamens four, under the lip, all with anthers, the upper pair hairy. The curious helmet-shaped calyx, in which the seeds are generally enclosed at maturity, suggests the common names, Skullcap and Helmet-flower.

Skullcap
Scutellària angustifòlia
Blue
Spring, summer
Cal., Oreg., Wash.

A pleasing plant, from six inches to over a foot tall, not aromatic, with almost smooth leaves, most of them toothless. The flowers are pretty, though not striking, in pairs from the angles of the leaves, with a purplish-blue corolla, nearly an inch long, with a white tube, the lower lip woolly inside. The calyx is curiously shaped and after the flower drops off resembles a tiny green bonnet. When these little calyxes are pinched from the sides they open their mouths and show the seeds inside. This is quite common throughout the Sierras. *S. antirrhinoìdes* is similar, growing in Utah and the Northwest. *S. Califórnica* has cream-white flowers, less than an inch long, the lower lip hairy inside, and downy leaves, narrow at base, the lower leaves purplish on the under side and more or less toothed, the upper

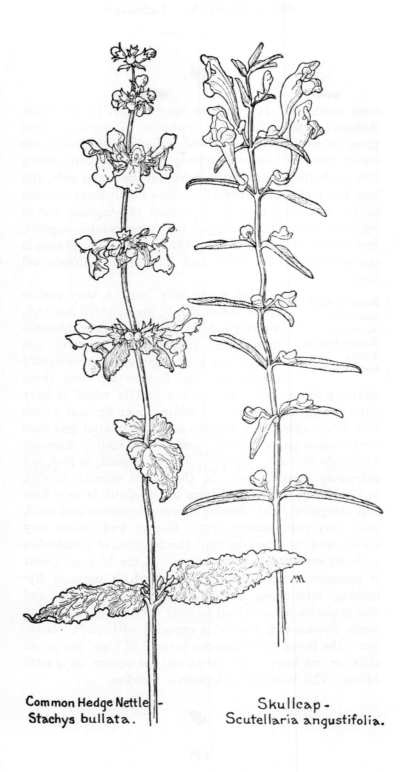

Common Hedge Nettle -
Stachys bullata.

Skullcap-
Scutellaria angustifolia.

ones toothless. It grows in open woods in the Coast Ranges and Sierra Nevada mountains. *S. tuberòsa* is from three to five inches high, with tuberous rootstocks; the leaves more or less oval, downy, thin in texture, with a few teeth, the lower ones purplish on the under side, with long leaf-stalks, the flowers dark blue, about three-quarters of an inch long, each pair, instead of standing out at opposite sides of the stem, generally turn sociably together, first to one side and then to the other. This blooms in spring and grows in the Coast Ranges of California and Oregon.

Bladder-bush
Salazària
Mexicàna
Blue and white
Spring
Southwest

This is the only kind, a very curious spiny desert shrub, about three feet high, varying a great deal in general appearance in different situations. The stems and foliage are gray-green and imperceptibly downy and the flowers are over three-quarters of an inch long, with a corolla which is hairy outside and has a lilac and white upper lip and a dark blue lower one. The calyxes become inflated and form very curious papery globes, over half an inch in diameter, very pale in color, tinged with yellow, pink, or lilac, and extremely conspicuous. In the desert around Needles, in California, the general form of the shrub is very loose and straggling, with slender twisting branches and small, pale gray-green leaves, both flowers and leaves very scanty and far apart, so that the bunches of bladder-like pods are exceedingly conspicuous. In the Mohave Desert it becomes a remarkably dense shrub, a mass of dry-looking, criss-cross, tangled branches, spiky twigs, and dull green leaves, speckled all over with the dark blue and white flowers and the twigs crowded with pods. Sometimes the flowers are magenta instead of blue, but are all alike on one bush. The stems are not square, as in most Mints. The drawing is of a plant at Needles.

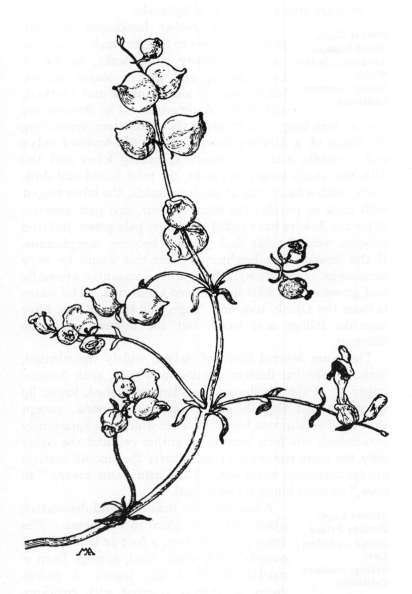

Bladder-bush —   **Salazaria Mexicana.**

MINT FAMILY. *Labiatae.*

There are only a few kinds of Sphacele.

**Pitcher Sage,
Wood-balm
Sphácele calycìna
White
Spring, summer
California**
This is a rather handsome shrubby plant, from two to five feet high, woody at base, with many stout, leafy, woolly or hairy stems, and rather coarse leaves, hairy, more or less wrinkled and toothed, and rather dark green. The flowers are over an inch long, in pairs along the upper stem, something the shape of a Monkey-flower, with a five-toothed calyx and a corolla with four, short, spreading lobes and the fifth lobe much longer and erect, the tube broad and dull-white, with a hairy ring at the base inside, the lobes tinged with pink or purple; the stamens four, one pair shorter. After the flowers have faded the large, pale green, inflated calyxes, veined with dull purple, become conspicuous. If the flowers were brighter in color this would be very handsome. It is strongly but rather pleasantly aromatic and grows on dry hills in southern California. The name is from the Greek, meaning "sage," as these plants have sage-like foliage and smell, but the flowers are quite different.

There are several kinds of Salvia, widely distributed, herbs or shrubs; flowers usually in whorls, with bracts; upper lip of the corolla erect, seldom two-lobed, lower lip spreading and three-lobed; resembling Ramona, except that the two stamens have filaments which are apparently two-forked, one fork bearing an anther cell and the other only the mere rudiment of an anther; the smooth nutlets are mucilaginous when wet. The Latin name means "to save," as some kinds are medicinal.

**Thistle Sage,
Persian Prince
Sálvia carduàcea
Lilac
Spring, summer
California**
A fantastically beautiful and decorative plant, very individual in character. The stout purplish stem, a foot or two tall and covered with white wool, springs from a rosette of thistle-like leaves of palest green, so thickly covered with cushions of white wool that they appear to be inflated, their teeth tipped with brown spines. The stem bears a series of flower-clusters, resembling large, round, pale balls of wool, pierced here and there by long prickles and encircled by lovely flowers, so etherial that they appear almost to hover in the air. They are each about an inch long, the corolla

Thistle
Sage.

Salvia
carduacea.

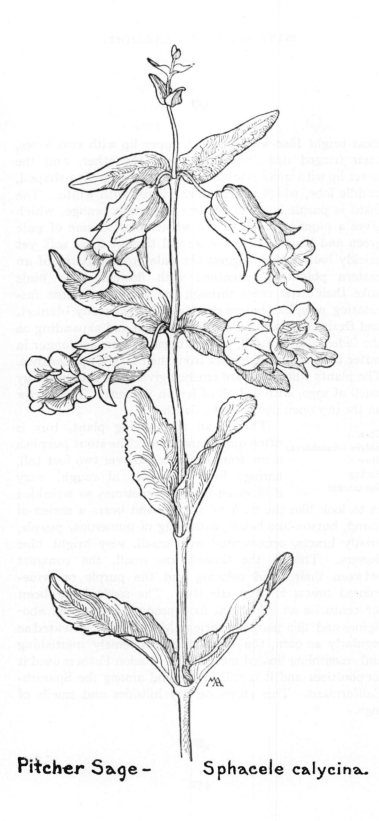

Pitcher Sage — Sphacele calycina.

clear bright lilac with an erect upper lip with two lobes, their fringed tips crossed one over the other, and the lower lip with small side lobes and a very large, fan-shaped, middle lobe, which is delicately fringed with white. The pistil is purple and the anthers are bright orange, which gives a piquant touch to the whole color scheme of pale green and lilac. There are several tiers of these soft yet prickly balls, which suggest the pale green turbans of an eastern potentate, wreathed with flowers. The buds poke their little noses through the wool, in a most fascinating way, like babies coming out of a woolly blanket, and fresh buds keep on coming through and expanding as the faded blossoms fall, so that these flowers last longer in water than we would expect from their fragile appearance. The plants when they are crushed give out a rather heavy smell of sage, with a dash of lemon verbena. They grow on the dry open plains of the South.

Chia
Sálvia columbàriae
Blue
Spring
Southwest
This is an odd-looking plant, but is often quite handsome. The stout purplish stem, from six inches to over two feet tall, springs from a cluster of rough, very dull green leaves, sometimes so wrinkled as to look like the back of a toad, and bears a series of round, button-like heads, consisting of numerous, purple, bristly bracts, ornamented with small, very bright blue flowers. Though the flowers are small, the contrast between their vivid coloring and the purple or wine-colored bracts is very effective. The seeds have been for centuries an important food product among the aborigines and this plant in ancient Mexico was cultivated as regularly as corn, the meal being extremely nourishing and resembling linseed meal. The Mission Fathers used it for poultices and it is still in demand among the Spanish-Californians. This grows on dry hillsides and smells of sage.

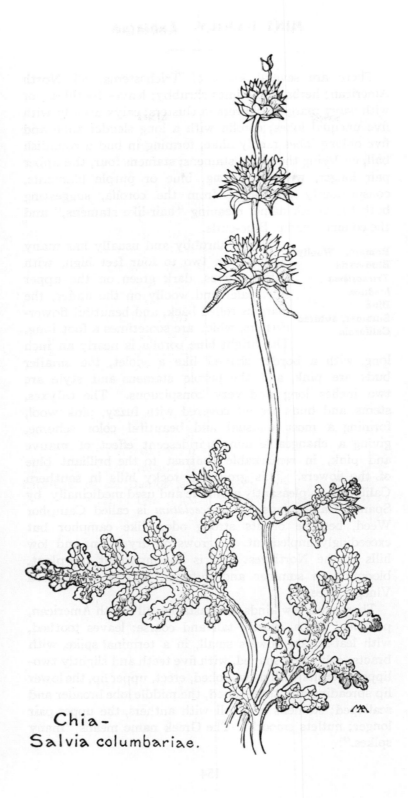

Chia-
Salvia columbariae.

MINT FAMILY. *Labiatae.*

There are several kinds of Trichostema, all North American; herbs, sometimes shrubby; leaves toothless, or with wavy margins; flowers in clusters; calyx usually with five unequal lobes; corolla with a long slender tube and five oblong lobes nearly alike, forming in bud a roundish ball, enclosing the coiled stamens; stamens four, the upper pair longer, with very long, blue or purple filaments, conspicuously protruding from the corolla, suggesting both the Greek name, meaning "hair-like stamens," and the common name, Blue-curls.

Romero, Woolly Blue-curls
Trichostèma lanàtum
Blue
Summer, autumn
California

This is shrubby and usually has many stems, from two to four feet high, with stiffish leaves, dark green on the upper side, paler and woolly on the under, the margins rolled back, and beautiful flower-clusters, which are sometimes a foot long. The bright blue corolla is nearly an inch long, with a border shaped like a violet, the smaller buds are pink, and the purple stamens and style are two inches long and very conspicuous. The calyxes, stems, and buds are all covered with fuzzy, pink wool, forming a most unusual and beautiful color scheme, giving a changeable almost iridescent effect of mauve and pink, in remarkable contrast to the brilliant blue of the flowers. This grows on rocky hills in southern California, is pleasantly aromatic and used medicinally by Spanish-Californians. *T. lanceolàtum* is called Camphor Weed, because of its strong odor, like camphor but exceedingly unpleasant. It grows on dry plains and low hills in the Northwest and is an important bee-plant, blooming in summer and autumn, and is also called Vinegar Weed.

There are a few kinds of Agastache, all North American, perennial herbs, mostly tall and coarse; leaves toothed, with leaf-stalks; flowers small, in a terminal spike, with bracts; calyx bell-shaped, with five teeth and slightly two-lipped; corolla with a two-lobed, erect, upper lip, the lower lip spreading and three-lobed, the middle lobe broader and scalloped; stamens four, all with anthers, the upper pair longer; nutlets smooth. The Greek name means "many spikes."

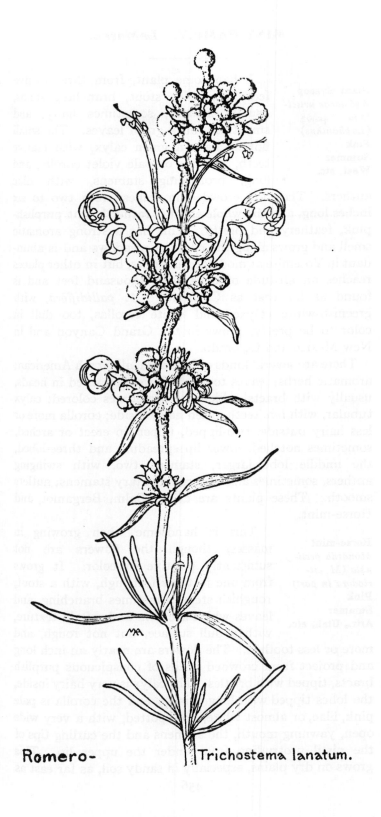

Romero— **Trichostema lanatum.**

MINT FAMILY. *Labiatae*.

Giant Hyssop
Agástache urtici-folia
(*Lophanthus*)
Pink
Summer
West, etc.

A handsome plant, from three to five feet high, with stout, branching stems, usually smooth, sometimes hairy, and smoothish, dark green leaves. The small flowers have a green calyx, with mauve teeth, a white or pale violet corolla, and long, protruding stamens, with lilac anthers. They are crowded in spikes, from two to six inches long, and the whole effect is rather bright purplish-pink, feathery and pretty. This has a strong aromatic smell and grows along the edges of meadows and is abundant in Yosemite at moderate altitudes, but in other places reaches an altitude of over eight thousand feet and is found as far east as Colorado. *A. pallidiflòra*, with greenish-white calyxes and white corollas, too dull in color to be pretty, grows in the Grand Canyon and in New Mexico and Colorado.

There are several kinds of Monarda, all North American; aromatic herbs; leaves toothed; flowers crowded in heads, usually with bracts, which are sometimes colored; calyx tubular, with five teeth, often hairy inside; corolla more or less hairy outside, two-lipped, upper lip erect or arched, sometimes notched, lower lip spreading and three-lobed, the middle lobe larger; stamens two, with swinging anthers, sometimes also two rudimentary stamens; nutlets smooth. These plants are called Balm, Bergamot, and Horse-mint.

Horse-mint
Monàrda pecti-nàta (*M. cit-riodora in part*)
Pink
Summer
Ariz., Utah, etc.

This is handsome when growing in masses, though the flowers are not sufficiently positive in color. It grows from one to three feet high, with a stout, roughish stem, sometimes branching, and leaves which are thin and soft in texture, with a dull surface, but not rough, and more or less toothed. The flowers are nearly an inch long and project from crowded heads of conspicuous purplish bracts, tipped with bristles. The calyx is very hairy inside, the lobes tipped with long bristles, and the corolla is pale pink, lilac, or almost white, not spotted, with a very wide open, yawning mouth, the stamens and the curling tips of the pistil protruding from under the upper lip. This grows on dry plains, especially in sandy soil, as far east as

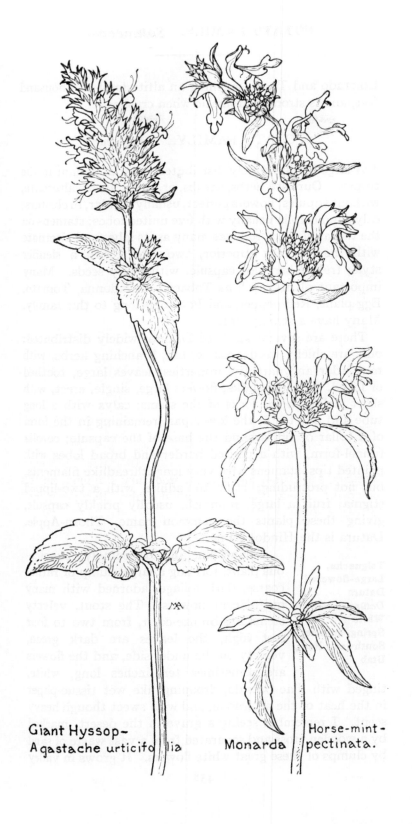

Giant Hyssop-
Agastache urticifolia

Monarda

Horse-mint-
pectinata.

Colorado and Texas, reaching an altitude of six thousand feet, and is strongly aromatic when crushed.

POTATO FAMILY. *Solanaceae.*

A large family, widely distributed, most abundant in the tropics. Ours are herbs, shrubs, or vines; leaves alternate, without stipules; flowers perfect, usually regular, in clusters; calyx and corolla usually with five united lobes; stamens on the throat of the corolla, as many as its lobes and alternate with them; ovary superior, two-celled, with a slender style; fruit a berry or capsule, with many seeds. Many important plants, such as Tobacco, Belladonna, Tomato, Egg-plant, Red-pepper, and Potato, belong to this family. Many have a strong odor.

There are several kinds of Datura, widely distributed; ours are chiefly weeds, coarse, tall, branching herbs, with rank odor and narcotic properties; leaves large, toothed or lobed, with leaf-stalks; flowers large, single, erect, with short stalks, in the forks of the stems; calyx with a long tube and five teeth, the lower part remaining in the form of a collar or rim around the base of the capsule; corolla funnel-form, with a plaited border and broad lobes with pointed tips; stamens with very long, threadlike filaments, but not protruding; style threadlike, with a two-lipped stigma; fruit a large, roundish, usually prickly capsule, giving these plants the common name, Thorn-Apple. Datura is the Hindoo name.

**Tolguacha,
Large-flowered
Datura**
Datùra meteloìdes
White
Spring, summer
Southwest, Nev.,
Utah

A handsome and exceedingly conspicuous plant, forming a large clump of rather coarse, dark foliage, adorned with many magnificent flowers. The stout, velvety stems are bronze-color, from two to four feet high, the leaves are dark green, velvety on the under side, and the flowers are sometimes ten inches long, white, tinged with lilac outside, drooping like wet tissue-paper in the heat of the afternoon, and with sweet though heavy scent. I remember seeing a grave in the desert, marked by a wooden cross and separated from a vast waste of sand by clumps of these great white flowers. It grows in valley

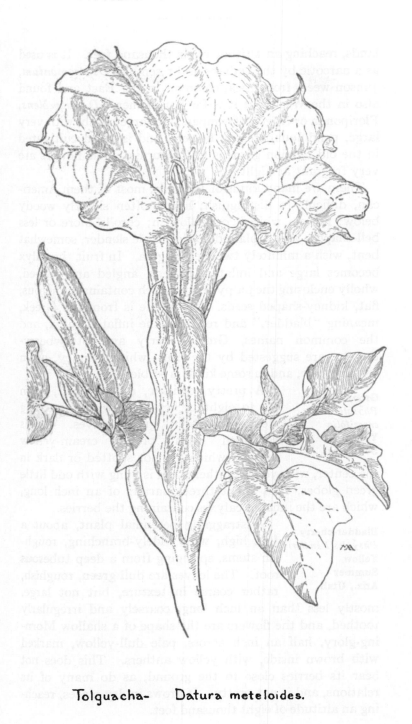

Tolguacha-   Datura meteloides.

lands, reaching an altitude of six thousand feet. It is used as a narcotic by the Indians and resembles *D. stramònium*, Jimson-weed, from Asia, common in the East and found also in the West, but it is far handsomer. *D. suaveòlens*, Floriponda or Angels' Trumpets, is a large shrub, with very large, pendulous, creamy flowers, and is often cultivated in the old mission gardens in California. The flowers are very fragrant at night.

There are many kinds of Physalis, most of them American, difficult to distinguish; herbs, often slightly woody below; flowers whitish or yellowish; corolla more or less bell-shaped, with a plaited border; style slender, somewhat bent, with a minutely two-cleft stigma. In fruit the calyx becomes large and inflated, papery, angled and ribbed, wholly enclosing the pulpy berry, which contains numerous, flat, kidney-shaped seeds. The name is from the Greek, meaning "bladder," and refers to the inflated calyx, and the common names, Ground-cherry and Strawberry-tomato, are suggested by the fruit, which is juicy, often red or yellow, and in some kinds is edible.

Ground-cherry
Phýsalis
crassifòlia
Yellow
Southwest

A pretty, delicate, desert plant, from six to eight inches high, with branching stems and light green leaves. It is sprinkled with pretty cream-yellow flowers, which are not spotted or dark in the center, with yellow anthers, and is hung with odd little green globes, each about three-quarters of an inch long, which are the inflated calyxes containing the berries.

Bladder-cherry
Phsýalis Féndleri
Yellow
Summer
Ariz., Utah

A straggling perennial plant, about a foot high, with widely-branching, roughish stems, springing from a deep tuberous root. The leaves are dull green, roughish, rather coarse in texture, but not large, mostly less than an inch long, coarsely and irregularly toothed, and the flowers are the shape of a shallow Morning-glory, half an inch across, pale dull-yellow, marked with brown inside, with yellow anthers. This does not bear its berries close to the ground, as do many of its relations, and is not pretty. It grows in dry places, reaching an altitude of eight thousand feet.

Ground-cherry—   Physalis crassifolia.

POTATO FAMILY. *Solanaceae.*

There are a great many kinds of Solanum, abundant in tropical America; herbs or shrubs, sometimes climbing; often downy; calyx wheel-shaped, with five teeth or lobes, corolla wheel-shaped, the border plaited, with five angles or lobes and a very short tube; anthers sometimes grouped to form a cone, filaments short; fruit a berry, either enclosed in the calyx or with the calyx remaining on its base. This is the Latin name of the Nightshade, meaning "quieting."

Purple Nightshade
Solànum Xánti
Purple
Spring, summer
California

This is much handsomer than most of the eastern Nightshades, hairy and sticky, with several spreading stems, from one to three feet high, springing from a perennial root, with thin, roughish leaves, more or less toothed. In favorable situations the flowers are beautiful, each about an inch across, and form handsome loose clusters. The corolla is saucer-shaped, bright purple, with a ring of green spots in the center, bordered with white and surrounding the bright yellow cone formed by the anthers. The berry is pale green or purple, the size of a small cherry. This is sometimes sweet-scented and is very fine on Mt. Lowe and elsewhere in southern California, but is paler and smaller in Yosemite. Blue Witch, *S. umbelliferum*, is very similar, more woody below, with deep green stems, shorter branches, smaller, thicker leaves, and a dull white or purplish berry. It grows in the foothills of the Coast Ranges and Sierra Nevada Mountains and flowers chiefly in summer, but more or less all through the year.

Nightshade
Solànum Douglásii
White
Spring, summer
Southwest

A branching plant, about two feet high and across, with roughish stems and thin, smooth or slightly hairy, dark green leaves, toothless, or the margins more or less coarsely toothed. The flowers are white, tinged with lilac, with a purplish ring surrounding the yellow cone formed by the anthers. In southern California the flowers are nearly half an inch across, but smaller elsewhere. The berries are black. This is common throughout California near the coast. *S. nìgrum*, the common Nightshade, is a weed in almost all countries, common in waste places and in cultivated soil, and has small white flowers and black berries, about as large as peas and said to be poisonous.

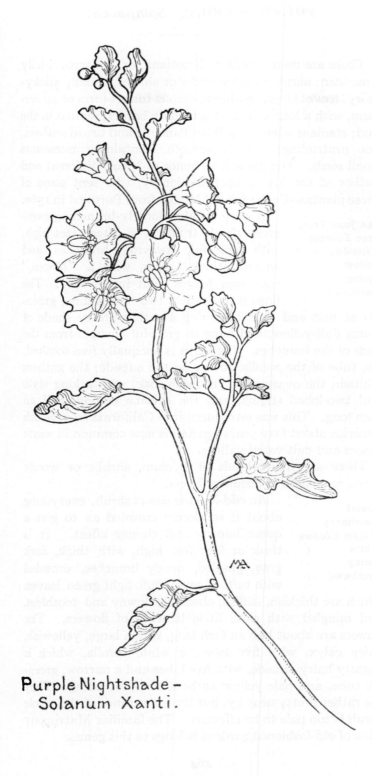

Purple Nightshade —
Solanum Xanti.

POTATO FAMILY. *Solanaceae.*

There are many kinds of Nicotiana, or Tobacco, chiefly American; acrid, narcotic herbs or shrubs, usually sticky-hairy; leaves large, toothless; corolla funnel-form or salver-form, with a long tube and spreading border, plaited in the bud; stamens with threadlike filaments and broad anthers, not protruding; capsule smooth, containing numerous small seeds. The name is in honor of Nicot, diplomat and author of the first French dictionary, who sent some of these plants to Catherine de' Medici from Portugal in 1560.

San Juan Tree,
Tree Tobacco
Nicotiàna glaùca
Yellow
Spring
Southwest

A very slender, loosely-branching ever-green shrub, from six to fifteen feet high, with graceful, swaying branches and smooth, thick leaves, with a "bloom," the lower leaves eight inches long. The flowers are nearly two inches long, green-ish at first and then becoming a rather pretty shade of warm dull-yellow, and hang in graceful clusters from the ends of the branches. The calyx is unequally five-toothed, the tube of the corolla downy on the outside; the anthers whitish; the ovary on a yellowish disk, with a long style and two-lobed stigma, and the capsule oblong, half an inch long. This was introduced into California from South America about fifty years ago and is now common in waste places and cultivated valleys.

There are many kinds of Lycium, shrubs or woody vines, named for the country Lycia.

Desert
Matrimony
L´cium Coòperi
White
Spring
Southwest

An odd-looking desert shrub, everything about it so closely crowded as to give a queer bunchy and clumsy effect. It is three or four feet high, with thick, dark gray, gnarled, woody branches, crowded with tufts of small, dull, light green leaves, which are thickish, stiffish, obscurely downy and toothless, and mingled with close little bunches of flowers. The flowers are about half an inch long, with a large, yellowish, hairy calyx, with five lobes, a white corolla, which is slightly hairy outside, with five lobes and a narrow, green-ish tube, and pale yellow anthers, not protruding. They are rather pretty near by, but the appearance of the whole shrub is too pale to be effective. The familiar Matrimony Vine of old-fashioned gardens belongs to this genus.

San Juan Tree—
Nicotiana glauca.

Desert Matrimony·   Lycium Cooperi.

FIGWORT FAMILY. *Scrophulariaceae.*

A large family, widely distributed, most of them natives of temperate regions; chiefly herbs, with bitter juice, sometimes narcotic and poisonous; without stipules; the flowers usually irregular; the calyx usually with four or five divisions, sometimes split on the lower or upper side, or on both sides; the corolla with united petals, nearly regular or two-lipped, two of the lobes forming the upper lip, which is sometimes beaklike, and three lobes forming the lower lip; the stamens on the corolla and alternate with its lobes, two or four in number, two long and two short, and sometimes also a fifth stamen which often has no anther, the anthers two-celled; the ovary superior, usually two-celled, the style slender, the stigma sometimes forked; the fruit a pod, splitting from the top into two parts and usually containing many seeds. This is a curious and interesting family, its members very dissimilar in appearance, having expressed their individuality in many striking and even fantastic forms.

There are several kinds of Maurandia, perennial herbs, climbing by their slender twisted leaf-stalks and occasionally also by their flower-stalks; the leaves triangular-heartshaped or halberd-shaped, only the lower ones opposite; the flowers showy, purple, pink, or white; the corolla with two lines or plaits, instead of a palate, which are usually bearded.

Snap-dragon Vine
Maurándia antir-rhìniflora (Antir-rhinum mauran-dioides)
Purple or pink and yellow
Spring
Ariz., New Mex.

This is a beautiful trailing or climbing vine, smooth all over, with charming foliage and twining stems, much like those of a Morning-glory, springing from a thickened, perennial root. The pretty flowers are over an inch long, with a purple or raspberry-pink corolla, with bright yellow blotches on the lower lip, forming an odd and striking combination of color. This blooms all through the spring and summer and may be found growing in the bottom of the Grand Canyon, near the river, where its delicate prettiness is in strange contrast to the dark and forbidding rocks over which it clambers and clothes with a mantle of tender green.

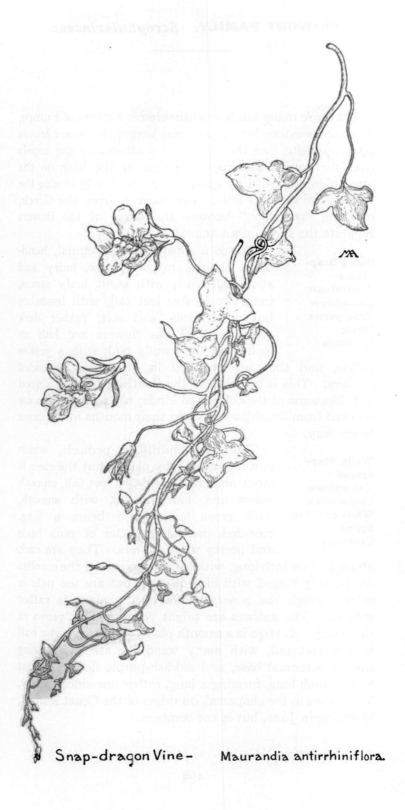

Snap-dragon Vine — Maurandia antirrhiniflora.

FIGWORT FAMILY. *Scrophulariaceae.*

There are many kinds of Antirrhinum, natives of Europe, Asia, and western North America; herbs; the lower leaves often opposite, and the upper ones alternate; the sepals five; the corolla two-lipped, swollen at the base on the lower side, but with no spur, the palate nearly closing the throat; the stamens four. The name is from the Greek, meaning "nose-like," because the shape of the flowers suggests the snout of an animal.

Sticky Snap-dragon
Antirrhìnum glandulòsum
Pink, purple
Spring
California

This is a conspicuous perennial, handsome though rather coarse, hairy and sticky all over, with stout leafy stems, from two to five feet tall, with branches but no tendrils, and soft, rather dark green leaves. The flowers are half an inch long, the corolla pink with a yellow palate, and they are crowded in fine, long, one-sided clusters. This is common in the South and looks a good deal like some of the cultivated kinds; when its flowers are pinched from the sides they open their mouths in the same funny way.

White Snap-dragon
Antirrhìnum Coulteriànum
White and lilac
Spring
California

This has tendril-like pedicels, which curl around nearby plants, but the stem is stout and erect, over two feet tall, smooth below and hairy above, with smooth, dark green leaves, and bears a long, crowded, one-sided cluster of pink buds and pretty white flowers. They are each about half an inch long, with hairy calyxes, and the corollas are prettily tinged with lilac or pink, but are too pale in color, though the general effect of the plant is rather striking. The anthers are bright yellow. This grows in the South. *A. vìrga* is a smooth plant, from two and a half to five feet tall, with many wand-like stems, springing from a perennial base, and reddish-purple flowers, about half an inch long, forming a long, rather one-sided cluster. This grows in the chaparral, on ridges of the Coast Ranges, blooming in June, but is not common.

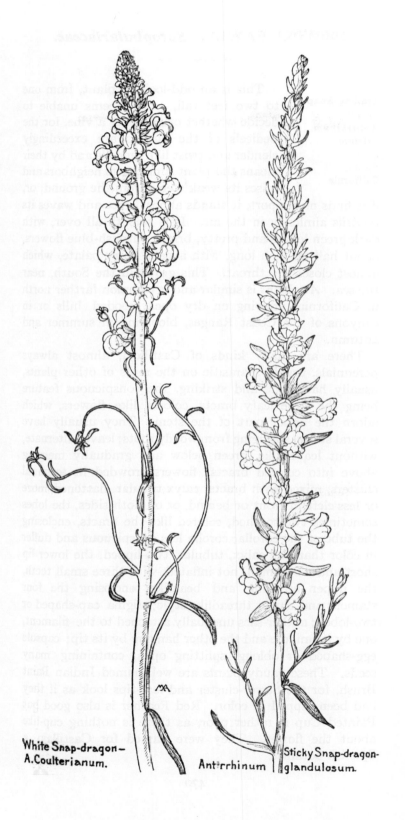

White Snap-dragon—
A. Coulterianum.

Antirrhinum

Sticky Snap-dragon-
glandulosum.

FIGWORT FAMILY. *Scrophulariaceae.*

Trailing Snap-
dragon
*Antirrhìnum
strictum*
Blue
Spring
California

This is an odd-looking plant, from one to two feet tall, which seems unable to decide whether or not it is a vine, for the pedicels of the flowers are exceedingly slender and twist like tendrils and by their means the plant clings to its neighbors and raises its weak stems from the ground, or, if it finds no support, it stands almost erect and waves its tendrils aimlessly in the air. It is smooth all over, with dark green leaves and pretty, bright purplish-blue flowers, about half an inch long, with a pale, hairy palate, which almost closes the throat. This grows in the South, near the sea. *A. vàgans* is similar and is common farther north in California, growing on dry open wooded hills or in canyons of the Coast Ranges, blooming in summer and autumn.

There are many kinds of Castilleja, almost always perennials, usually parasitic on the roots of other plants, usually handsome and striking, the conspicuous feature being the large leafy bracts, colored like flowers, which adorn the upper part of the stem. They usually have several stems, springing from woody roots; leaves alternate, without leaf-stalks, green below and gradually merging above into colored bracts; flowers crowded in terminal clusters, mixed with bracts; calyx tubular, flattened, more or less cleft in front or behind, or on both sides, the lobes sometimes two-toothed, colored like the bracts, enclosing the tube of the corolla; corolla less conspicuous and duller in color than the calyx, tubular, two-lipped, the lower lip short and very small, not inflated, with three small teeth, the upper lip long and beaklike, enclosing the four stamens and single threadlike style; stigma cap-shaped or two-lobed; anther-sacs unequally attached to the filament, one by its middle and the other hanging by its tip; capsule egg-shaped or oblong, splitting open, containing many seeds. These gaudy plants are well named Indian Paint Brush, for the flower-cluster and leaf-tips look as if they had been dipped in color. Red Feather is also good but Painted Cup is rather poor, as there is nothing cup-like about the flower. They were named for Castillejo, a Spanish botanist.

470

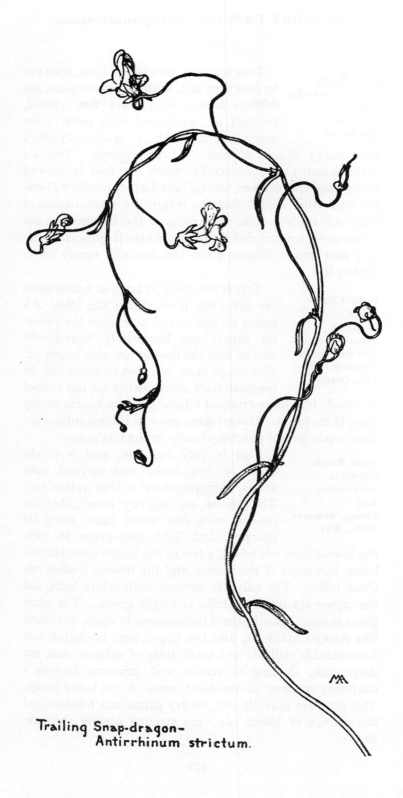

Trailing Snap-dragon—
Antirrhinum strictum.

FIGWORT FAMILY. *Scrophulariaceae.*

Paint Brush
Castillèja miniàta
Red
Summer
Northwest
This is a very handsome kind, from two to four feet tall, with a smooth stem, and smooth leaves, which are not crinkled, toothed, or lobed, and with more or less hairy bracts, which are beautifully tinted with many shades of pink, red, and purple. This is a magnificent plant, especially when we find it growing along irrigation ditches, among blue Lupines, yellow Mimulus and other bright flowers, where the combinations of color are quite wonderful, and it is the handsomest and commonest sort around Yosemite, where it grows in meadows and moist places, from the foothills nearly up to timber-line.

Scarlet Paint Brush
Castillèja pinetòrum
Red and yellow
Summer
Cal., Oreg.
This is not quite so large or handsome as the last, but gives much the effect of a brush dipped in red paint, for the yellowish bracts are beautifully tipped with scarlet and the flowers are also bright red. The rough stem is a foot or more tall, the roughish dark green leaves are not toothed or lobed, but have crinkled edges, and the bracts usually have three lobes. These plants grow in the mountains and often make bright patches of color in the landscape.

Paint Brush
Castillèja angustifòlia
Red
Spring, summer
Utah., Nev.
This is very variable, and is usually about a foot high, with several hairy stems, springing from a long yellow root. The leaves are slightly rough, but not coarse, with fine white hairs along the margins, and light gray-green in color, the lowest ones not lobed, a few of the upper ones with two lobes, but most of the leaves, and the bracts, slashed into three lobes. The calyx is covered with white hairs, and the upper lip of the corolla is bright green. The whole plant is most beautiful and harmonious in color, not coarse like many Castillejas, and the upper part is clothed with innumerable delicate yet vivid tints of salmon, rose, and deep pink, shading to scarlet and crimson, forming a charming contrast to the quiet tones of the lower foliage. This grows in gravelly soil, on dry plains and hillsides, and the clumps of bloom are very striking among the sagebrush.

Indian
Paint Brush.
Castilleja miniata.

Indian
Paint Brush
Castilleja miniata.

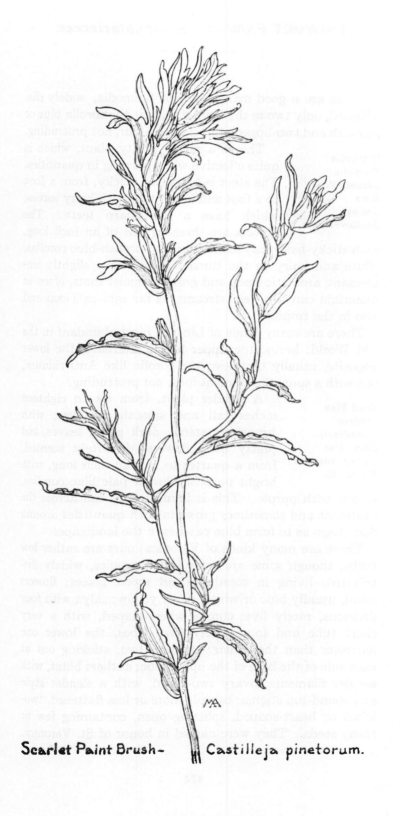

Scarlet Paint Brush—   Castilleja pinetorum.

FIGWORT FAMILY. *Scrophulariaceae.*

There are a good many kinds of Stemodia, widely distributed, only two in the United States; the corolla blue or purplish and two-lipped; the stamens four, not protruding.

Stemodia
Stemòdia
durantijòlia
Blue
Spring
Southwest, etc.

This is a rather pretty plant, which is quite effective when growing in quantities. The stem is hairy and sticky, from a foot to a foot and a half tall, with hairy leaves, which have a few sharp teeth. The flowers are three-eighths of an inch long, with sticky-hairy calyxes and bright purplish-blue corollas, white and hairy in the throat. This has a slightly unpleasant, aromatic smell and grows in moist spots, often in mountain canyons near streams, as far east as Texas and also in the tropics.

There are many kinds of Linaria, most abundant in the Old World; herbs; the upper leaves alternate, the lower opposite, usually toothless; the corolla like Antirrhinum, but with a spur; the stamens four, not protruding.

Toad Flax
Linària
Canadénsis
Blue, lilac
Spring, summer
West, etc.

A slender plant, from six to eighteen inches tall and smooth all over, with branching stems, dark green leaves, and pretty little flowers, delicately scented, from a quarter to half an inch long, with bright purplish-blue or pale lilac corollas, veined with purple. This is found in dry soil across the continent and sometimes grows in such quantities around San Diego as to form blue patches in the landscape.

There are many kinds of Veronica; ours are rather low herbs, though some are trees in the tropics, widely distributed, living in meadows and moist places; flowers small, usually blue or white, never yellow; calyx with four divisions, rarely five; corolla wheel-shaped, with a very short tube and four, rarely five, lobes, the lower one narrower than the others; stamens two, sticking out at each side of the base of the upper lobe; anthers blunt, with slender filaments; ovary two-celled, with a slender style and round-top stigma; capsule more or less flattened, two-lobed or heart-shaped, splitting open, containing few or many seeds. They were named in honor of St. Veronica.

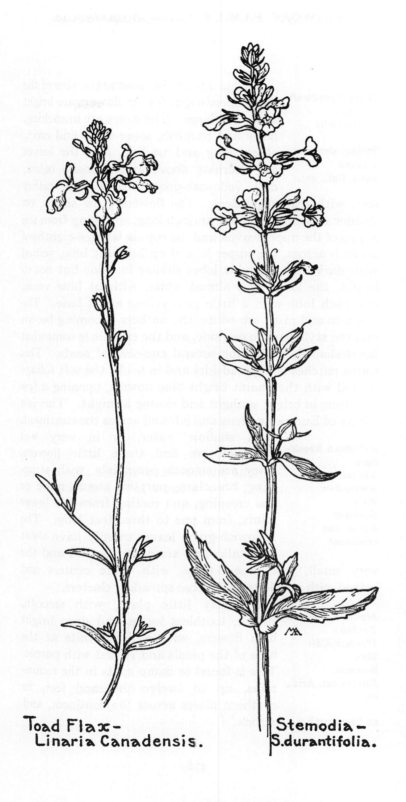

Toad Flax—
Linaria Canadensis.

Stemodia—
S. durantifolia.

FIGWORT FAMILY. *Scrophulariaceae.*

Hairy Speedwell
Verónica
Tournefórtii
Blue
Spring, summer,
autumn
Utah, Cal., etc.

This is one of the most attractive of the little Speedwells, for its flowers are bright and quite large. The stems are branching, hairy and purplish, some short and erect, others long and trailing, and the leaves are alternate above and opposite below, dull yellowish-green, hairy and rather soft, with scalloped edges. The flowers grow singly, on slender flower-stalks over an inch long, springing from the angles of the upper leaves, and the corolla is three-eighths of an inch across, the upper lobe deep brilliant blue, veined with dark blue, the side lobes similar in color but not so bright, the lower lobe almost white, without blue veins, and each lobe with a little pale yellow at its base. The stamens and pistil are white, the anthers becoming brown and the style bent to one side, and the capsule is somewhat heart-shaped, containing several cup-shaped seeds. This forms patches along roadsides and in fields, the soft foliage dotted with the quaint bright blue flowers, opening a few at a time in bright sunlight and closing at night. This is a native of Europe and Asia and is found across the continent.

American Brook-lime
Verónica
Americàna
Blue
Summer
Across the
continent

In shallow water, or in very wet meadows, we find these little flowers. They are smooth perennials, with straggling, branching, purplish stems, more or less creeping, and rooting from the lower joints, from one to three feet long. The yellowish-green leaves usually have short leaf-stalks and are often toothed and the very small, pale blue flowers, with white centers and veined with purple, grow in loose spreading clusters.

Alpine Speedwell
Verónica
Wormskjòldii
Blue
Summer
Northwest, Ariz.,
etc.

A pretty little plant, with smooth, stiffish, toothless leaves and deep bright blue flowers, with a little white at the base of the petals and veined with purple. This is found in damp spots in the mountains, up to twelve thousand feet, in northern places across the continent, and as far south as Arizona.

476

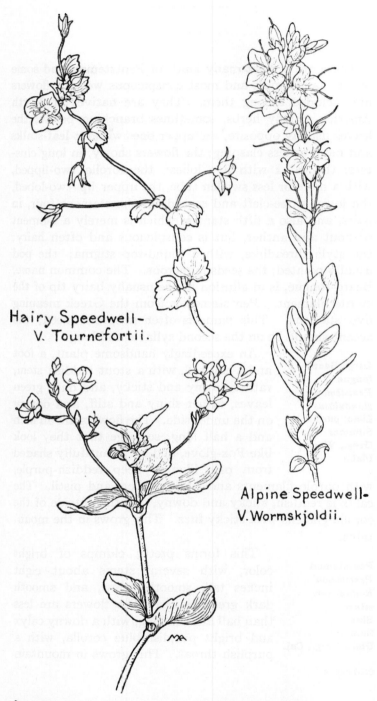

Hairy Speedwell—
V. Tournefortii.

Alpine Speedwell—
V. Wormskjoldii.

American Brooklime—   Veronica Americana

FIGWORT FAMILY. *Scrophulariaceae.*

There are a great many kinds of Pentstemon and some of our handsomest and most conspicuous western flowers are included among them. They are natives of North America, chiefly herbs, sometimes branching below; the leaves usually opposite, the upper ones without leaf-stalks and more or less clasping; the flowers showy, in long clusters; the calyx with five lobes; the corolla two-lipped, with a more or less swollen tube, the upper lip two-lobed, the lower three-cleft and spreading; the stamens four, in pairs, and also a fifth stamen, which is merely a filament without any anther, but is conspicuous and often hairy; the style threadlike, with a round-top stigma; the pod usually pointed; the seeds numerous. The common name, Beard-tongue, is in allusion to the usually hairy tip of the sterile filament. Pentstemon is from the Greek meaning five stamens. This name is often mispronounced; the accent should be on the second syllable and long.

Large Beard-tongue
Pentstèmon glandulòsus
Lilac, purple
Summer
Oreg., Wash., Idaho

An exceedingly handsome plant, a foot and a half tall, with a stout reddish stem, rather downy and sticky, and dark green leaves, rather shiny and stiff, and downy on the under side. The flowers are an inch and a half long, so large that they look like Fox-glove, and are beautifully shaded from pale lilac to deep reddish-purple, with purple filaments and white anthers and pistil. The calyx is reddish, sticky and downy, and the outside of the corolla glistens with sticky fuzz. This grows in the mountains.

Pentstemon
Pentstèmon Rattáni var. mìnor
Blue
Summer
Utah, Oreg., Cal.

This forms pretty clumps of bright color, with several stems about eight inches tall, smooth below, and smooth dark green leaves. The flowers are less than half an inch long, with a downy calyx and bright purplish-blue corolla, with a purplish throat. This grows in mountain canyons.

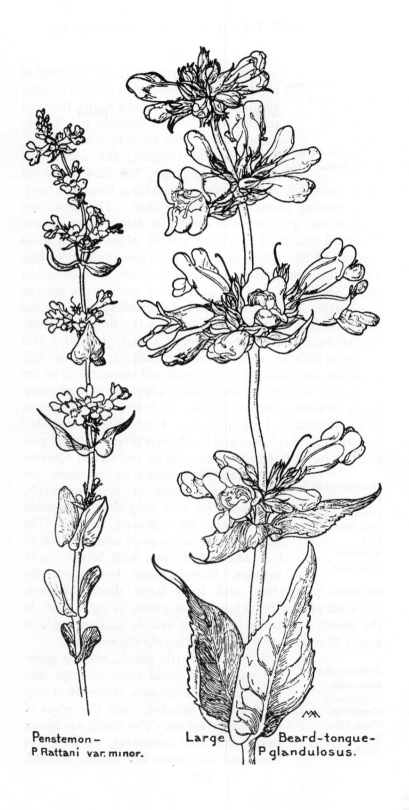

Penstemon –
P. Rattani var. minor.

Large   Beard-tonque–
        P glandulosus.

FIGWORT FAMILY. *Scrophulariaceae.*

Blue Pentstemon, Beard-tongue
Pentstèmon cyanánthus
Blue
Spring, summer
Utah, Ariz., Wyo.

This is perhaps the most beautiful of all the Pentstemons, with several smooth, stoutish, pale green, leafy stems, from one to two feet tall and smooth, pale bluish-green leaves, with more or less "bloom," toothless and thickish, the upper ones somewhat clasping. The flowers are not hairy or sticky, and are over an inch long, forming a handsome cluster about eight inches long. The sepals are narrow and pointed, the corolla is tinted with various beautiful shades of blue and purple, often with a white throat and blue lobes, or with a pink throat and deep blue lobes, the sterile filament has a thickened, more or less hairy, yellow tip, and the pale yellow anthers are more or less hairy. This plant is beautiful in every way, for the foliage is fine in form and color and the flowers are brilliantly variegated, yet harmonious and graceful. This grows on hillsides and in mountain valleys, at rather high altitudes, and used to be common and conspicuous on the "benches" around the Salt Lake Valley, but it is gradually being exterminated by sheep. It thrives and improves when transplanted into gardens. *P. acuminátus* is similar, but the cluster is looser and the flowers often pink and purple. It forms fine patches of color at the Grand Canyon.

Honeysuckle Pentstemon
Pentstèmon cordifólius
Red
Summer
California

A handsome shrub, with much the general appearance of a Honeysuckle, woody below, with long slender branches and pretty heart-shaped leaves. The flowers are often in pairs and are each an inch and a half long, with bright scarlet corollas, conspicuously two-lipped, the stamens protruding, and form large clusters towards the ends of the branches. This grows in light shade in the woods and trails its long branches and garlands of bright flowers over the neighboring shrubs and trees.

Pride-of-the-mountain
Pentstèmon Newbérryi
Pink, lilac
Summer
California

A beautiful little shrub, making splendid patches of vivid color on high bare rocks in the mountains, where it is very conspicuous, hanging over the edges of inaccessible ledges. The stems are woody below and very branching, about a foot high, and the leaves are usually toothed,

480

Penstemon
cyananthus.

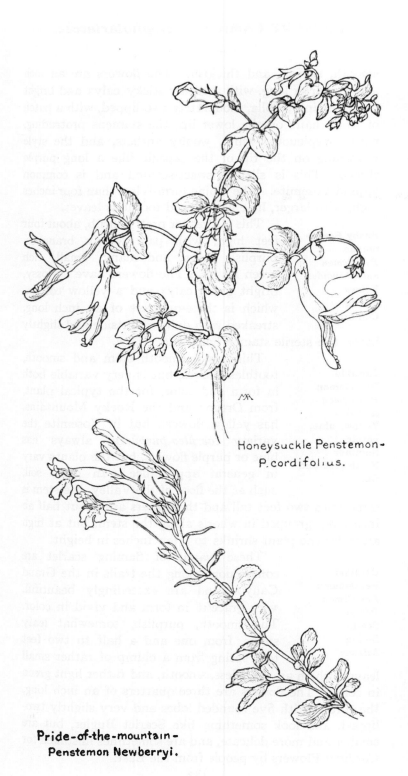

Honeysuckle Penstemon-
P. cordifolius.

Pride-of-the-mountain-
Penstemon Newberryi.

smooth, stiffish, and thickish. The flowers are an inch and a quarter long, with a rather sticky calyx and bright carmine-pink corolla, moderately two-lipped, with a patch of white hairs on the lower lip; the stamens protruding, with conspicuous, white, woolly anthers, and the style remaining on the tip of the capsule like a long purple thread. This is slightly sweet-scented and is common around Yosemite. The alpine form is less than four inches high, with larger, lilac flowers and toothless leaves.

**Bushy Beard-
tongue**
*Pentstèmon
antirrhinoìdes*
Yellow
Spring
California

This is a rather pretty shrub, about four feet high, with pale woody branches, purplish twigs, and many, small, rich green leaves. The flowers have a glossy, bright green calyx and a yellow corolla, which is three-quarters of an inch long, streaked with dull-red outside and slightly hairy, the sterile stamen hairy and yellow.

**Variable
Pentstemon**
*Pentstèmon
confèrtus*
**Yellow, blue,
purple**
Summer
**Northwest and
Cal.**

This has a smooth stem and smooth, toothless leaves, but is very variable both in form and color, for the typical plant, from Oregon and the Rocky Mountains, has yellow flowers, but in Yosemite the variety *caerùleo-purpùreus* always has blue or purple flowers, but the plants vary in general appearance. In good soil, such as the floor of the Valley, the stem is sometimes two feet tall and the flowers are about half an inch long, grouped in whorls along the stem, but at high altitudes the plant shrinks to a few inches in height.

**Cardinal
Pentstemon**
*Pentstèmon
Pàrryi*
Scarlet
Spring
Arizona

These wands of flaming scarlet are conspicuous along the trails in the Grand Canyon and are exceedingly beautiful, very graceful in form and vivid in color. The smooth, purplish, somewhat leafy stems, from one and a half to two feet tall, spring from a clump of rather small leaves, which are toothless, smooth, and rather light green in color. The flowers are three-quarters of an inch long, the corolla with five rounded lobes and very slightly two-lipped, and look something like Scarlet Bugler, but are smaller and more delicate, and are sometimes mistaken for Cardinal Flowers by people from the East.

Penstemon Parryi.

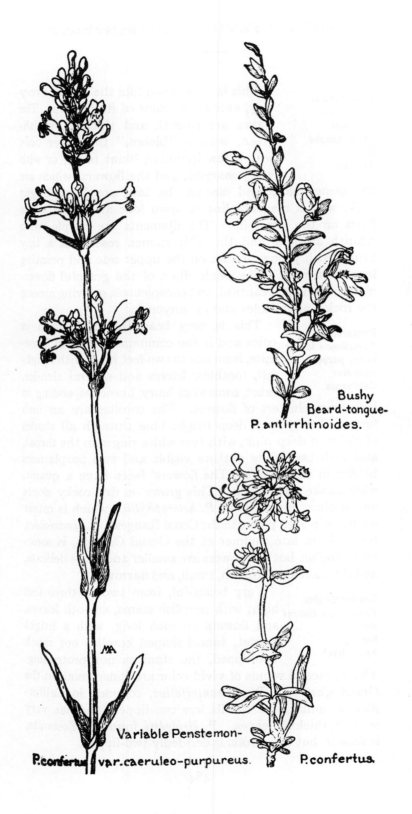

Bushy
Beard-tongue-
P. antirrhinoides.

Variable Penstemon-
P. confertus var. caeruleo-purpureus.   P. confertus.

FIGWORT FAMILY. *Scrophulariaceae.*

Pentstemon
Pentstémon
Wrìghtii
Pink, purple
Spring
Arizona

This is very much like the last in every way, except the color of its flowers. The leaves are smooth and thickish, bluish-green, with a "bloom," the lower ones with a few irregular, blunt teeth, or with wavy margins, and the flowers, which are the same shape and size as the last, are deep, bright pink, with a magenta line on each lobe and some white hairs on the lower lip. The filaments are purple, with whitish anthers, and the fifth stamen resembles a tiny brush, with yellow bristles on the upper side and pointing into the throat. The whole effect of the graceful flower-cluster is bright, beautiful, and conspicuous, growing among the rocks, on hillsides and in canyons.

Pentstemon
Pentstémon laètius
Blue, purple
Summer
California

This is very beautiful and varied in color and is the commonest kind in Yosemite, from one to two feet high, with roughish, toothless leaves and several slender, erect, somewhat hairy branches, ending in long loose clusters of flowers. The corollas are an inch long, and vary from deep bright blue through all shades of violet to deep pink, with two white ridges in the throat, and with two white anthers visible and two purple ones hidden in the throat. The flowers' faces have a quaint, wide-awake expression. This grows on dry rocky slopes and is often mistaken for *P. heterophýllus*, which is rather common in open places in the Coast Ranges. *P. linarioìdes*, blooming in late summer at the Grand Canyon, is somewhat similar, but the flowers are smaller and more delicate, and the leaves are smooth, small, and narrow.

Scarlet Bugler
Pentstémon Èatoni
Red
Spring
Ariz., Utah

Very beautiful, from two to three feet high; with purplish stems, smooth leaves, and flowers an inch long, with a bright scarlet, funnel-shaped corolla, not much two-lipped, the stamens not protruding. These graceful wands of vivid color are conspicuous in the Grand Canyon. *P. centranthifòlius*, common in California, is similar, the corolla less two-lipped, and has very smooth, thickish leaves. *P. Bridgésii*, found in Yosemite, is similar, but the corolla is decidedly two-lipped.

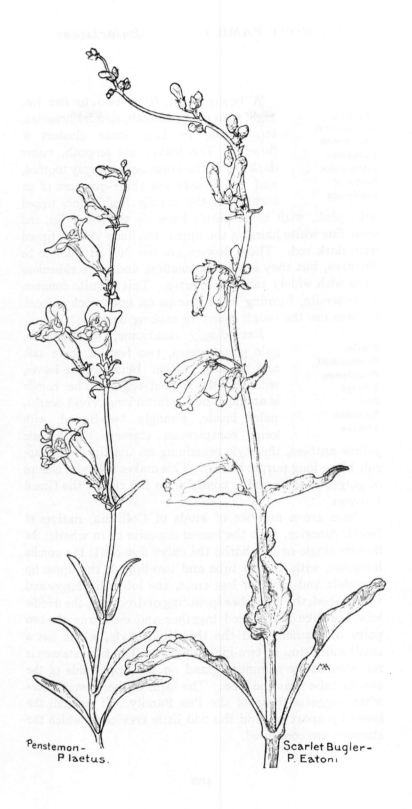

Penstemon-
P laetus.

Scarlet Bugler-
P. Eatoni.

FIGWORT FAMILY. *Scrophulariaceae.*

Yawning Pentstemon *Pentstèmon breviflòrus* **Flesh-color Summer California**

A bushy plant, from two to five feet high, with many smooth, slender branches, terminating in long loose clusters of flowers. The leaves are smooth, rather dark green, the lower ones sharply toothed, and the flowers are three-quarters of an inch long; the corolla flesh-color, tipped with pink, with some purple lines on the lower lip, and some fine white hairs on the upper; the buds yellow, tipped with dark red. These flowers are too dull in color to be effective, but they are sweet-smelling and have ridiculous faces with widely yawning mouths. This is quite common in Yosemite, forming large clumps on open rocky slopes. Indians use the tough stems for making baskets.

Scarlet Pentstemon *Pentstèmon Tórreyi* **Red Summer Arizona**

Exceedingly handsome, with smooth, pale green stems, two feet or more tall, and smooth, rather bluish-green leaves, with slightly rippled edges. The corolla is an inch and a quarter long, vivid scarlet, paler inside, strongly two-lipped, with long, conspicuous stamens, with pale yellow anthers, the style remaining on the tip of the capsule like a long purple thread. This makes splendid clumps of gorgeous color and is common on the rim of the Grand Canyon.

There are a number of kinds of Collinsia, natives of North America, with the leaves opposite or in whorls; the flowers single or in whorls; the calyx five-cleft; the corolla irregular, with a short tube and two-lipped; the upper lip two-cleft and more or less erect, the lower lip larger and three-lobed, the side lobes spreading or drooping, the middle lobe keel-like and folded together and enclosing the two pairs of stamens and the threadlike style, which has a small round-top or two-lobed stigma. The fifth stamen is represented by a minute gland on the upper side of the corolla tube near the base. The form of the flowers somewhat suggests those of the Pea Family. If we pull the lower lip apart we find the odd little crevice in which the stamens are concealed.

486

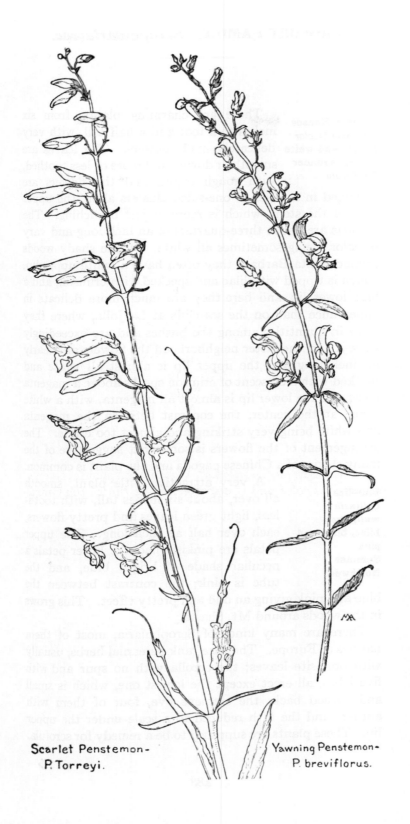

Scarlet Penstemon—
P. Torreyi.

Yawning Penstemon—
P. breviflorus.

FIGWORT FAMILY. *Scrophulariaceae.*

Chinese Houses
Collinsia bicolor
Purple and white
Spring, summer
California

These are charming plants, from six inches to a foot and a half tall, with very delicately made flowers. The leaves are smooth or downy and more or less toothed, with rough edges, and the flowers are arranged in a series of one-sided clusters along the upper part of the stem, which is more or less branching. The corollas are about three-quarters of an inch long and vary in color, being sometimes all white. In the shady woods around Santa Barbara they often have a white upper lip, which is tipped with lilac and specked with crimson, and a lilac lower lip, and here they are much more delicate in appearance than on the sea-cliffs at La Jolla, where they grow in quantities among the bushes and are exceedingly showy. In the latter neighborhood the flowers are nearly an inch long and the upper lip is almost all white and marked with a crescent of crimson specks above a magenta base, and the lower lip is almost all magenta, with a white stripe at the center, the contrast between the magenta and white being very striking and almost too crude. The arrangement of the flowers is somewhat suggestive of the many stories of a Chinese pagoda and the plant is common.

Blue-lips
Collinsia
multiflòra
Lilac, blue, and pink
Summer
Northwest

A very attractive little plant, smooth all over, about six inches tall, with toothless, light green leaves and pretty flowers, each over half an inch long. The upper petals are pinkish-lilac, the lower petals a peculiar shade of bright blue, and the tube is pink; the contrast between the blue and pink giving an odd and pretty effect. This grows in the woods around Mt. Shasta.

There are many kinds of Scrophularia, most of them natives of Europe. They are rank perennial herbs, usually with opposite leaves; the corolla with no spur and with five lobes, all erect except the lowest one, which is small and turned back; the stamens five, four of them with anthers and the fifth reduced to a scale under the upper lip. These plants are supposed to be a remedy for scrofula.

488

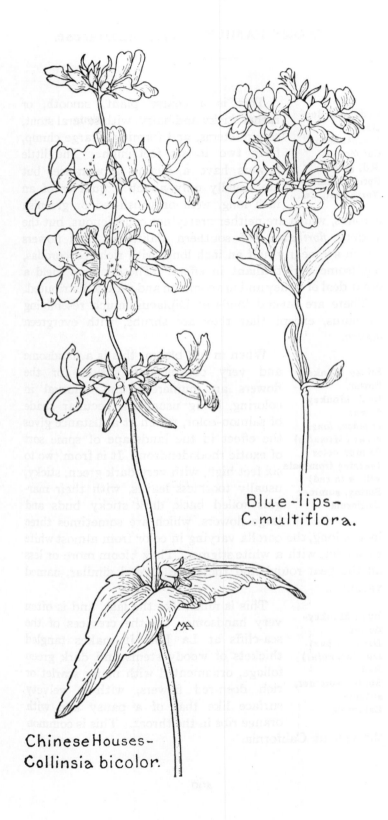

Blue-lips–
C. multiflora.

Chinese Houses–
Collinsia bicolor.

FIGWORT FAMILY. *Scrophulariaceae.*

California Bee-plant
Scrophulària Califórnica
R d, green
Spring, summer
Northwest, Cal.

This is a coarse plant, smooth, or rather sticky and hairy, with several stout, square stems, and forming a large clump, from two to six feet high. The little flowers have a quaint appearance, but are usually only about a quarter of an inch long, with brownish-red or greenish corollas, which are neither pretty nor conspicuous, but the variety *floribúnda*, of southern California, has flowers which are nearly half an inch long, with rich red corollas, handsome and brilliant in effect. These plants yield a great deal of honey and are common and widely distributed.

There are several kinds of Diplacus, much resembling Mimulus, except that they are shrubs, with evergreen leaves.

Sticky Monkey-flower,
Bush Monkey-flower
Diplácus longi-flòrus (Mimulus)
Salmon-color
(varying from pale yellow to red)
Spring, summer
California

When in full bloom, this is a handsome and very conspicuous shrub, for the flowers are numerous and unusual in coloring, being usually a peculiar shade of salmon-color, which at a distance gives the effect in the landscape of some sort of exotic rhododendron. It is from two to six feet high, with very dark green, sticky, usually toothless leaves, with their margins rolled back, dark sticky buds and large flowers, which are sometimes three inches long, the corolla varying in color from almost white to scarlet, with a white stigma. They bloom more or less all the year round and there are several similar, named varieties.

Bush Monkey-flower
Diplácus puni-ceus (Mimulus)
Red
Spring, summer, autumn
California

This is much like the last, and is often very handsome. In the crevices of the sea-cliffs at La Jolla it makes tangled thickets of woody stems and dark green foliage, ornamented with many scarlet or rich deep-red flowers, with a velvety surface like that of a pansy and with orange ribs in the throat. This is common throughout California.

Bush
Monkey-flower.

Diplacus
longiflorus.

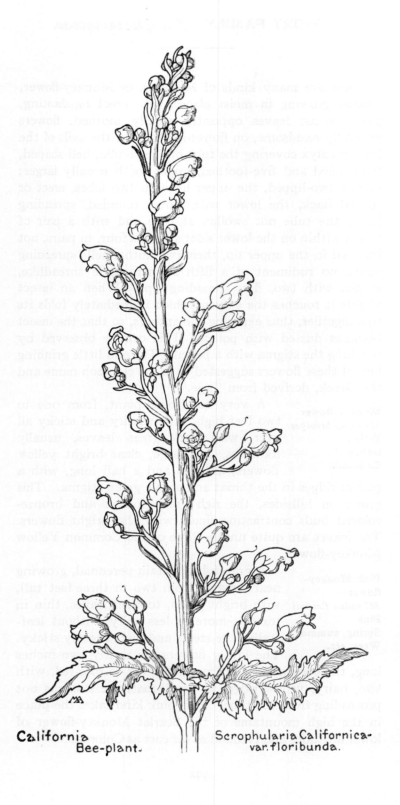

California
Bee-plant.

Scrophularia Californica-
var. floribunda.

FIGWORT FAMILY. *Scrophulariaceae.*

There are many kinds of Mimulus, or Monkey-flower, usually growing in moist places, with erect or slanting, juicy stems; leaves opposite, usually toothed; flowers generally handsome, on flower-stalks from the axils of the leaves; calyx covering the tube of the corolla, bell-shaped, five-angled and five-toothed, upper tooth usually larger; corolla two-lipped, the upper lip with two lobes, erect or turned back, the lower with three, rounded, spreading lobes, the tube not swollen at base and with a pair cf ridges within on the lower side; stamens four, in pairs, not inclosed in the upper lip, their two anther-cells spreading apart, no rudiment of a fifth stamen; style threadlike, stigma with two, flat, spreading tips. When an insect alights it touches the stigma, which immediately folds its tips together, thus exposing the anthers, so that the insect becomes dusted with pollen. This can be observed by touching the stigma with a pencil. The odd little grinning face of these flowers suggested both the common name and the Greek, derived from "ape."

Monkey-flower
Mimulus brévipes
Yellow
Spring
California

A very handsome plant, from one to two feet high, rather hairy and sticky all over, with dark green leaves, usually toothless, and large, clear bright yellow flowers, an inch and a half long, with a pair of ridges in the throat and a pale green stigma. This grows on hillsides, the rich green foliage and bronze-colored buds contrasting finely with the bright flowers. The leaves are quite unlike those of the Common Yellow Monkey-flower.

Pink Monkey-flower
Mimulus Lewisii
Pink
Spring, summer
West, etc.

A graceful mountain perennial, growing near streams, from two to three feet tall, with bright green, toothed leaves, thin in texture, more or less hairy, without leaf-stalks; the stems and buds slightly sticky. The lovely flowers are nearly two inches long, the corolla varying from pale pink to rose-red, with two, hairy, yellow ridges in the throat, the stamens not protruding from the tube. This pink kind takes the place in the high mountains of the Scarlet Monkey-flower of lower altitudes and is found as far east as Colorado.

492

Pink
Monkey-flower.

Mimulus
Lewisii.

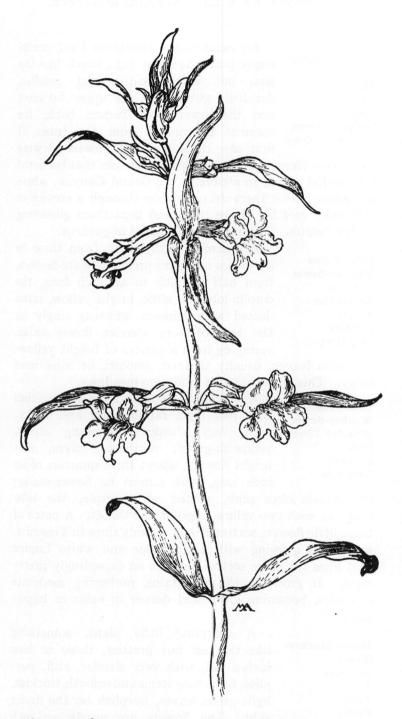

Monkey-flower-   **Mimulus brevipes**

FIGWORT FAMILY. *Scrophulariaceae.*

Scarlet Monkey-flower
Mimulus cardinàlis
Red
Spring, summer
Southwest. Oreg.

An exceedingly handsome kind, sometimes nearly five feet high, much like the last, but with vivid scarlet corollas, decidedly two-lipped, the upper lip erect and the lower lobes turned back, the stamens protruding from the tube. I first saw these gorgeous flowers glcwing like bits of flame among the ferns and grasses that bordered a beautiful spring in a cave in the Grand Canyon, where icy water fell on them drcp by drop through a crevice in the rocky roof far above them and kept them glistening with moisture. This is often cultivated in gardens.

Little Yellow Monkey-flower
Mimulus primuloìdes
Yellow
Summer
Cal., Oreg.

A charming little plant, from three to six inches tall, with pretty delicate flowers, from half an inch to an inch long, the corolla-lobes all alike, bright yellow, often dotted with crimson, growing singly on the tips of very slender flower-stalks, springing from a cluster of bright yellowish-green leaves, usually toothed, smooth, or sometimes hairy. This grows in moist mountain meadows.

Little Pink Monkey-flower
Mimulus Tórreyi
Pink
Summer
California

A delicate little plant, from three inches to a foot high, rather hairy and sticky, with very slender branching stems, yellowish-green, toothless leaves, and bright flowers, about three-quarters of an inch long, with almost no flower-stalks; the corolla-lobes pink, veined with purple, the tube crimson, with two yellow ridges in the throat. A patch of these little flowers scattered over a sandy slope in Yosemite, sometimes growing with a tiny blue and white Lupine that likes the same sort of place, is an exceedingly pretty sight. It grows in the mountains, preferring moderate altitudes, becoming lower and deeper in color in higher places.

Desert Monkey-flower
Mimulus Fremóntii
Pink
Spring
California

A charming little plant, something like the last but prettier, three or four inches tall, with very slender, stiff, purplish, branching stems and smooth, thickish, light green leaves, purplish on the under side. The flowers are nearly an inch across, with a hairy calyx and bright

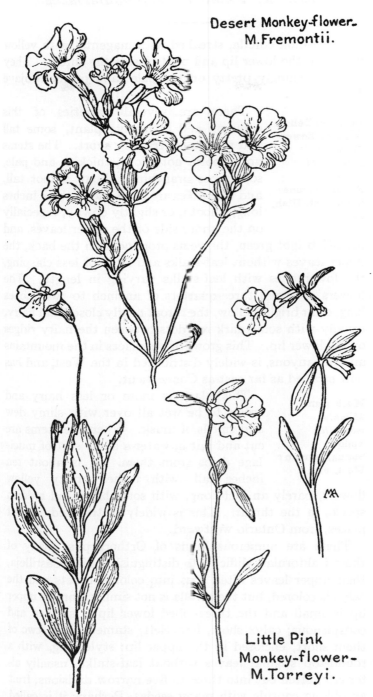

Desert Monkey-flower.
M.Fremontii.

Little Pink
Monkey-flower-
M.Torreyi.

Little Yellow Monkey-flow-er-
Mimulus primuloides.

purplish-pink corolla, streaked with magenta, with yellow ridges on the lower lip and plaits inside the throat. They look exceedingly pretty on the pale sand of the Mojave Desert.

Common Yellow Monkey-flower
Mimulus Langsdórfii
Yellow
Spring, summer
Southwest, Utah, etc.

There are several varieties of this common and attractive plant, some tall and robust, others very short. The stems are smooth, not sticky, thickish and pale, sometimes branching, about a foot tall, and the leaves are from one to three inches long, smooth, or slightly downy, especially on the under side of the upper leaves, and usually bright green, the veins prominent on the back, the upper leaves without leaf-stalks and more or less clasping, the lower ones with leaf-stalks varying in length. The flowers are from three-quarters of an inch to two inches long, clear bright yellow, the throat nearly closed and hairy, usually with some dark red dots between the hairy ridges on the lower lip. This grows in wet places in the mountains and in canyons, is widely distributed in the West, and has now strayed as far east as Connecticut.

Musk-plant
Mimulus moschátus
Yellow
Spring, summer
West, etc.

This plant is more or less hairy and seems to be wet all over with slimy dew and smells of musk. When the stems are cut and put in water a slimy sort of mucilage drips from them. It is about ten inches tall, with rather pretty yellow flowers, barely an inch long, with some hairs and reddish specks in the throat. This is widely distributed, in wet places, from Ontario westward.

There are numerous kinds of Orthocarpus, many of them Californian, difficult to distinguish. Like Castilleja, their upper leaves often pass into colored bracts and the calyx is colored, but the corolla is not similar, for the upper lip is small and the three-lobed lower lip is swollen and conspicuous; calyx short, four-cleft; stamens four, two of them short, enclosed in the upper lip; style long, with a round-top stigma; leaves without leaf-stalks, usually alternate, often cut into three to five narrow divisions; fruit an oblong capsule with many seeds. Perhaps it is called Owl's-clover because, in some kinds, the flowers look like the faces of owls.

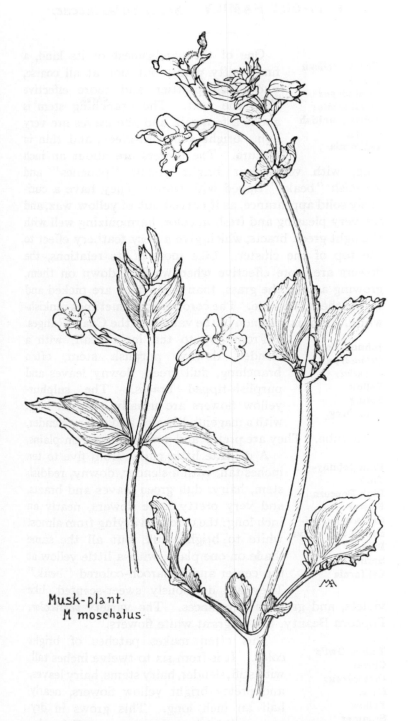

Musk-plant.
M moschatus

Common Yellow Monkey-flower—Mimulus Langsdorfii.

FIGWORT FAMILY. *Scrophulariaceae.*

Yellow Pelican Flower
Orthocárpus faucibarbátus
Yellow, whitish
Spring
California

One of the handsomest of its kind, a fine thrifty plant, but not at all coarse, and much prettier and more effective than the next. The branching stem is about a foot tall, and the leaves are very light, bright yellowish-green, and thin in texture. The flowers are about an inch long, with very clear bright yellow "pouches" and greenish "beaks" tipped with white. They have a curiously solid appearance, as if carved out of yellow wax, and are very pleasing and fresh in color, harmonizing well with the light green bracts, which give a very feathery effect to the top of the cluster. Like most of its relations, the flowers are more effective when we look down on them, growing among the grass, than when they are picked and we see them in profile. The corollas are sometimes pinkish-white. This is common in the valleys of the Coast Ranges.

Johnny-Tuck
Orthocárpus eriánthus
Yellow
Spring
Cal., Oreg.

From five to ten inches tall, with a slender, downy, purplish stem, often branching, dull green, downy leaves and purplish-tipped bracts. The sulphur-yellow flowers are usually an inch long. with a magenta "beak" and a very slender, white tube. They are pretty and very common on plains.

Pink Johnny-Tuck,
Pink Popcorn Flower
Orthocárpus eriánthus var. roséus
Pink
Spring
California

A delicate little plant, from five to ten inches tall, with a slender, downy, reddish stem, hairy, dull green leaves and bracts, and very pretty little flowers, nearly an inch long; the corollas varying from almost white to bright pink, but all the same shade on one plant, with a little yellow at the center and a maroon-colored "beak." They are deliciously sweet-scented, like violets, and grow in dry places. The variety *versicolor,* Popcorn Beauty, has fragrant white flowers.

Yellow Owl's Clover
Orthocárpus lúteus
Yellow
Summer
West, etc.

This often makes patches of bright color. It is from six to twelve inches tall, with stiff, slender, hairy stems, hairy leaves, and pretty bright yellow flowers, nearly half an inch long. This grows in dry sunny places as far east as Colorado. reaching an altitude of ten thousand feet.

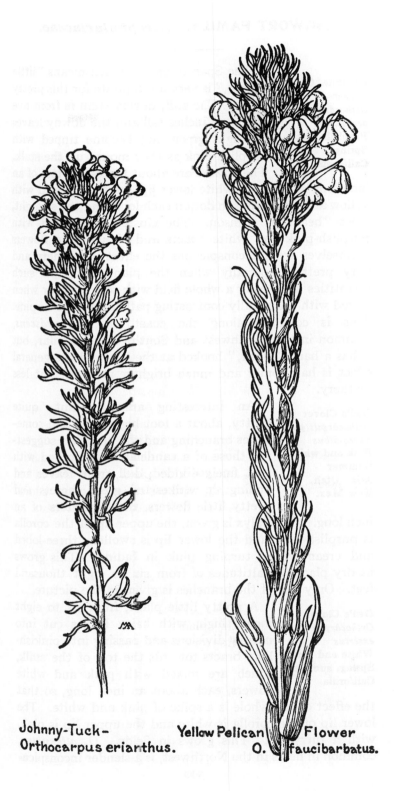

Johnny-Tuck —
Orthocarpus erianthus.

Yellow Pelican Flower
O. faucibarbatus.

FIGWORT FAMILY. *Scrophulariaceae.*

Escobita, Owl's Clover
Orthocàrpus densiflòrus
Purplish-pink
Spring
California

The Spanish name, which means "little broom," is very appropriate for this pretty plant. The stiff, downy stem is from five to fifteen inches tall and the downy leaves are light green and become tipped with purplish-pink as they mount up the stalk. The flowers are about three-quarters of an inch long and have a white lower lip, which is tipped with yellow and has a crimson dot on each lobe, and the straight, erect "beak" is crimson. The cluster is crowded with purplish-pink and white bracts and though the flowers themselves are not conspicuous the effect is feathery and very pretty, especially when the plants grow in such quantities as to color a whole field with soft pink, or when mixed with beautifully contrasting patches of blue Lupine. This is common along the coast. *O. purpuráscens*, common in the Northwest and Southwest, is similar, but it has a hairy "beak," hooked at the tip, and the general effect is handsomer and much brighter in color, but less feathery.

Owl's Clover
Orthocàrpus pur-pureo-álbus
Pink and white
Summer
Ariz., Utah, New Mex.

An interesting annual plant, quite pretty, about a foot high, the stem sometimes branching and the branches suggesting those of a candelabrum, clothed with soft, finely divided, dull green leaves and ending in spikes of green bracts and pretty little flowers, three-quarters of an inch long. The calyx is green, the upper lip of the corolla is purplish-pink and the lower lip is swollen, three-lobed and cream-white, turning pink in fading. This grows in dry places at altitudes of from six to eight thousand feet. Only one of the branches is given in the picture.

Owl's Clover
Orthocàrpus exsértus
White and pink
Spring, summer
California

A pretty little plant, from six to eight inches high, with hairy leaves cut into narrow divisions and passing into pinkish-lilac bracts towards the top of the stalk, which are mixed with pink and white flowers, each about an inch long, so that the effect of the whole is a spike of pink and white. The lower lip of the corolla is white and the upper lip is pink, with a furry tip. This grows in fields. *O. attenuàtus*, common in fields in the Northwest, is a slender inconspicu-

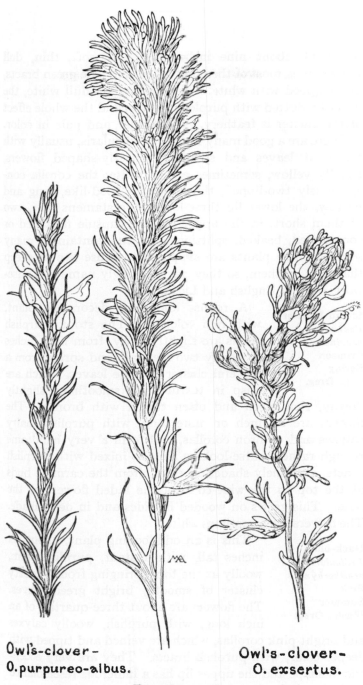

Owl's-clover—
O. purpureo-albus.

Owl's-clover—
O. exsertus.

Escobita—
Orthocarpus densiflorus.

ous kind, about nine inches tall, with soft, thin, dull green leaves, most of them not lobed, and pale green bracts, often tipped with white. The corollas are dull white, the lower lip dotted with purple or yellow, and the whole effect of the cluster is feathery, very slender, and pale in color.

There are a good many kinds of Pedicularis, usually with finely-cut leaves and spikes of queerly-shaped flowers, usually yellow, sometimes red or white; the corolla conspicuously two-lipped, the upper lip hood-like, long and narrow, the lower lip three-lobed; the stamens four, two of them short, in the upper lip; the capsule flattened or compressed, beaked, splitting open, and containing many seeds. These plants are supposed to cause lice in sheep that feed on them, so they have the ugly name of Lousewort, both in English and Latin.

Indian Warrior
Pediculàris
densiflòra
Crimson
Spring
Cal., Oreg.

A robust and very decorative plant, with rich coloring. The stout, purplish stems are slightly hairy, from nine inches to nearly two feet tall, and spring from a graceful cluster of large leaves, which are crisp in texture and smooth or slightly downy, rich green and often tinged with bronze. The flowers are an inch or more long, with purplish, hairy calyxes and crimson corollas, and form a very handsome though rather coarse-looking cluster, mixed with purplish bracts, and finely shaded in color, from the carmine buds at the top to the wine-color of the faded flowers at the base. This grows on wooded hillsides and in deep shade. The flowers are sometimes white.

Duck-bill
Pediculàris
ornithorhýncha
Pink
Summer
Wash., Oreg.

This is an odd-looking plant, about six inches tall, with a stout, purplish stem, woolly at the top, springing from a pretty cluster of smooth, bright green leaves. The flowers are about three-quarters of an inch long, with purplish, woolly calyxes and bright pink corollas, which are veined and tipped with deeper color, with purplish bracts. They are very eccentric in shape and the upper lip has a ludicrous resemblance to the head of a duck. This grows in the mountains.

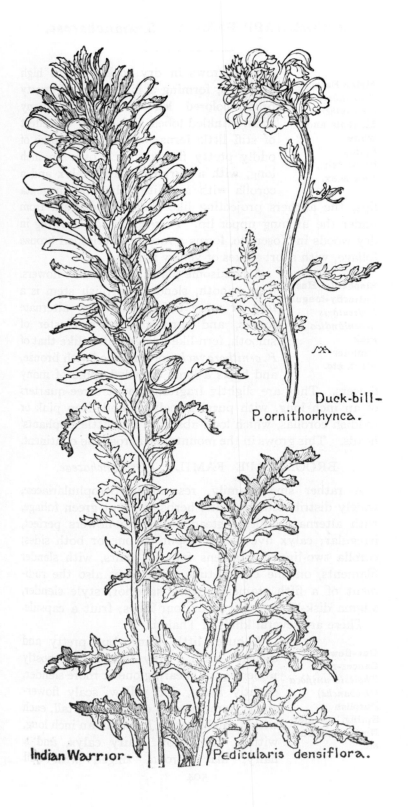

Duck-bill—
P. ornithorhynca.

Indian Warrior—   Pedicularis densiflora.

BROOM-RAPE FAMILY. *Orobanchaceae.*

Alpine Betony
Pediculàris
centranthèra
Magenta and
white
Spring
Utah, Ariz.,
New Mex.

This grows in dry rocky soil at high altitudes, forming a low clump of pretty bronze-colored leaves, cut into many small crinkled lobes, and giving the effect of stiff little ferns, with a short spike of oddly pretty flowers, each over an inch long, with a purplish, hairy calyx and a corolla with a white tube and magenta lips, the anthers projecting like sharp little teeth from under the arching upper lip. *P. semibarbàta*, growing in dry woods in Yosemite, forms a rosette of crinkled bronze foliage, with short spikes of yellow flowers.

Elephants' Heads,
Butterfly-tongue
Pediculàris
Groenlàndica
Pink
Summer
West, etc.

A handsome plant, with quaint flowers. The smooth, slender, purplish stem is a foot or more tall, with a few alternate leaves, and springs from a cluster of smooth, fern-like foliage, much like that of *P. ornithorhyncha*, often tinged with bronze, and bears a long, crowded spike of many flowers. They are slightly fragrant, about three-quarters of an inch long, with purplish calyxes and deep pink or reddish corollas, which look absurdly like little elephants' heads. This grows in the mountains, across the continent.

BROOM-RAPE FAMILY. *Orobanchaceae.*

A rather small family, resembling Scrophulariaceæ, widely distributed; parasitic herbs, without green foliage, with alternate scales instead of leaves; flowers perfect, irregular; calyx five-cleft, or split on one or both sides; corolla two-lipped; stamens four, in pairs, with slender filaments, on the corolla-tube (sometimes also the rudiment of a fifth stamen); ovary superior, style slender, stigma disk-like, with two or four lobes; fruit a capsule.

There are several kinds of Thalesia.

One-flowered
Cancer-root
Thalèsia uniflòra
(Orobanche)
Purplish
Spring, summer
Northwest, Utah,
etc.

A queer little thing, but pretty and delicate, with a very short stem, mostly underground, bearing one or more slender, slightly hairy, dull yellow, scaly flower-stems from three to eight inches tall, each with a single flower, less than an inch long, with a dull yellow, hairy calyx, and a hairy, lilac corolla, tinged with dull

Alpine Betony
Pedicularis centranthera.

Elephants' Heads-
P. Groenlandica.

One-flowered Cancer-root-
Thalesia uniflora.

yellow and veined with purple, with two yellow ridges in the throat. This is not common and is found across the continent.

MADDER FAMILY. *Rubiaceae.*

A large family, widely distributed, chiefly tropical. Ours are herbs, or shrubs; leaves opposite or in whorls; flowers regular, usually perfect; calyx with four teeth or none; corolla with four or five united lobes, often hairy inside; stamens on the corolla, as many as its lobes and alternate with them; ovary inferior, with one or two styles; fruit a capsule, berry, or stone-fruit. Coffee, Quinine, and Madder, used for dye, belong to this family. I am told that the latter plant is escaping around Salt Lake and is well established there. The Latin name means "red."

There are many kinds of Houstonia, North American, usually growing in tufts, leaves opposite; flowers small; calyx four-lobed; corolla funnel-form or salver-form, four-lobed; style slender, with two long stigmas; fruit a capsule. Sometimes the flowers are perfect, but usually they are of two kinds, one kind with high anthers and short pistil, the other kind with long pistil and anthers inside the corolla-tube; visiting insects carry pollen from the high anthers of the one to the high stigmas of the other, and from the low anthers to the low stigmas, thus ensuring cross-pollination.

Desert Innocence
Houstònia rùbra
Pink and white
Summer
Arizona

A pretty little desert plant, about two inches high, forming close tufts of sage-green foliage, like harsh moss, with stiff needle-like leaves and woody stems, sprinkled with charming little pink and white flowers. The corolla is three-eighths of an inch across, with a long slender tube, the stamens lilac, and the odd little nodding capsules have two round lobes. This grows in the dreadful sandy wastes of the Petrified Forest.

Kelloggia
Kellóggia
galioìdes
Spring, summer
White, pink,
yellowish
West, etc.

The only kind, a slender little plant, from six inches to a foot tall, usually with smooth leaves, with small stipules. The tiny flowers are white, pink, or greenish-yellow, with a bristly calyx, and the corolla usually has four petals, but sometimes five or three; the stigmas two. The fruit is covered with hooked bristles. This

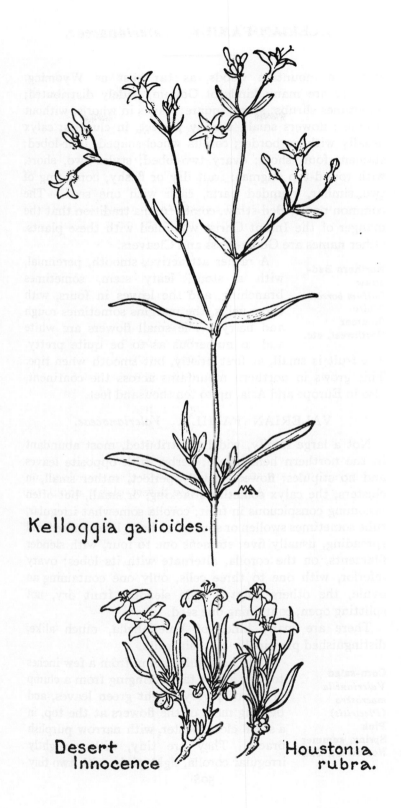

Kelloggia galioides.

Desert
Innocence

Houstonia
rubra.

---

grows in mountain woods, as far east as Wyoming.

There are many kinds of Galium, widely distributed; sometimes shrubs; stems square; leaves in whorls, without stipules; flowers small, usually perfect, in clusters; calyx usually with no border; corolla wheel-shaped, four-lobed; stamens four, short; ovary two-lobed; styles two, short, with round-top stigmas; fruit dry or fleshy, consisting of two similar, rounded parts, each with one seed. The common name, Bed-straw, comes from a tradition that the manger of the Infant Christ was filled with these plants. Other names are Goose-grass and Cleavers.

Northern Bed-straw
Gàlium boreàle
White
Summer
Northwest, etc.

A rather attractive, smooth, perennial, with a stout, leafy stem, sometimes branching, and the leaves in fours, with three veins, the margins sometimes rough and hairy. The small flowers are white and so numerous as to be quite pretty. The fruit is small, at first bristly, but smooth when ripe. This grows in northern mountains across the continent, also in Europe and Asia, up to ten thousand feet.

VALERIAN FAMILY. *Valerianaceae.*

Not a large family, widely distributed, most abundant in the northern hemisphere; herbs, with opposite leaves and no stipules; flowers usually perfect, rather small, in clusters; the calyx sometimes lacking, or small, but often becoming conspicuous in fruit; corolla somewhat irregular, tube sometimes swollen or spurred at base, lobes united and spreading, usually five; stamens one to four, with slender filaments, on the corolla, alternate with its lobes; ovary inferior, with one to three cells, only one containing an ovule, the others empty; style slender; fruit dry, not splitting open, containing one seed.

There are many kinds of Valerianella, much alike, distinguished principally by their fruits.

Corn-salad
Valerianélla macrosèra
(Plectritis)
Pink
Spring, summer
Northwest, Cal.

This has a juicy stem, from a few inches to over a foot tall, springing from a clump of smooth, very bright green leaves, and bearing most of the flowers at the top, in a small close cluster, with narrow purplish bracts. They are tiny, with a slightly irregular corolla, light pink, with two tiny

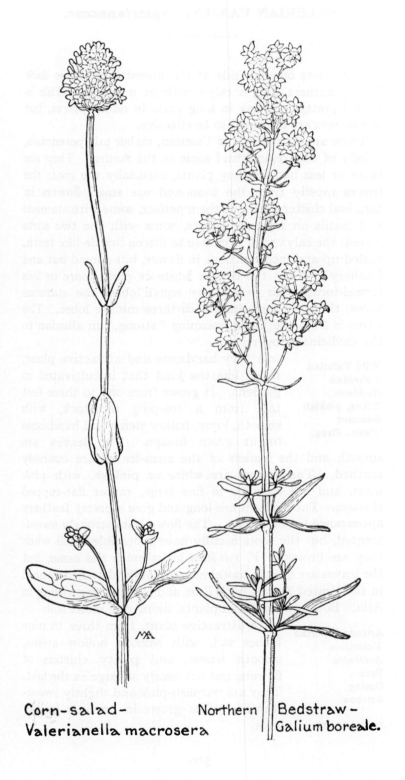

Corn-salad-
Valerianella macrosera

Northern Bedstraw-
Galium boreale.

crimson dots on each side of the lowest lobe, three dark brown anthers, and a calyx without a border. This is rather pretty, growing in long grass in damp places, but the flowers are too small to be effective.

There are many kinds of Valerian, rather tall perennials, chiefly of cool regions and some in the Andes. They are more or less bad-smelling plants, especially the root; the leaves mostly from the base and the small flowers in terminal clusters, some of them perfect, some with stamens and pistils on separate plants, some with the two sorts mixed; the calyx with from five to fifteen bristle-like teeth, curled up and inconspicuous in flower, but spread out and feathery in fruit; the corolla white cr pink, more or less funnel-form, with five nearly equal lobes; the stamens three; the style sometimes with three minute lobes. The name is from the Latin, meaning "strong," in allusion to the medicinal properties.

Wild Valerian
Valeriàna
sitchénsis
White, pinkish
Summer
Wash., Oreg.

A very handsome and attractive plant, much like the kind that is cultivated in gardens. It grows from one to three feet tall, from a creeping rootstock, with smooth, juicy, hollow stems and handsome bright green foliage. The leaves are smooth and the leaflets of the stem-leaves are coarsely toothed. The flowers are white or pinkish, with pink buds, and are crowded in fine large, rather flat-topped clusters. The stamens are long and give a pretty feathery appearance to the cluster. The flowers are strongly sweet-scented, but the roots usually have a horrible smell when they are broken. *V. sylvática* looks much the same, but the leaves are mostly toothless, and it is widely distributed in the United States, both East and West, also growing in Asia. Both are woodland plants, liking rich moist soil.

Arizona Valerian
Valeriàna
Arizònica
Pink
Spring
Arizona

An attractive plant, from three to nine inches tall, with smooth hollow stems, smooth leaves, and pretty clusters of flowers, but not nearly so large as the last. They are purplish-pink and slightly sweet-scented. This grows in crevices in the rocks in moist places.

White Valerian·

Valeriana sitchensis·

Arizona
Valerian -

Valeriana
Arizonica.

HONEYSUCKLE FAMILY. *Caprifoliaceae.*

Not a large family, mostly of the northern hemisphere; herbs, shrubs, shrubby vines or trees; leaves opposite, usually without stipules; flowers perfect, regular or irregular; calyx with three to five divisions; corolla usually with five united lobes, sometimes two-lipped; stamens on the corolla tube, usually as many as its lobes and alternate with them; ovary inferior, with one style; fruit a berry, stone-fruit, or capsule.

There are many kinds of Lonicera, shrubs, or twining woody vines; leaves usually without teeth or lobes, the upper ones sometimes united around the stem; flowers usually irregular; calyx with five, minute teeth; corolla more or less funnel-shaped, often two-lipped, four lobes forming the upper lip and one lobe the under, tube often swollen at base; stamens five; style with a cap-like stigma; fruit berrylike.

Orange Honeysuckle
Lonicèra ciliòsa
Orange and scarlet
Summer
Northwest

A climbing or trailing shrub, with brilliant flowers, set off by bright green leaves, thin in texture, with pale "bloom" on the under side and usually hairy margins, the lower ones with short leaf-stalks, the upper usually united and forming a disk. The flowers are scentless, about an inch and a quarter long, with smooth, trumpet-shaped corollas, bright orange at base, shading to scarlet above, with a bright green stigma and crimson or brownish anthers. This lives in the woods and sometimes climbs to the tops of quite tall trees, ornamenting them with its splendid clusters of flowers and sprinkling the forest floor with its fallen blossoms in a shower of scarlet and gold.

Black Twinberry
Lonicèra involucràta
Yellow
Spring, summer
West

A bush, from three to seven feet high, with thick, woody, pale gray stems and bright green leaves, glossy and thin in texture, or rather coarse and hairy, with fine hairs along the margins. The flower-stalks each bear a pair of flowers, without scent, emerging from an involucre of two bracts. The corolla is rather hairy and sticky, half an inch or more long, a pretty shade of warm dull yellow, sometimes

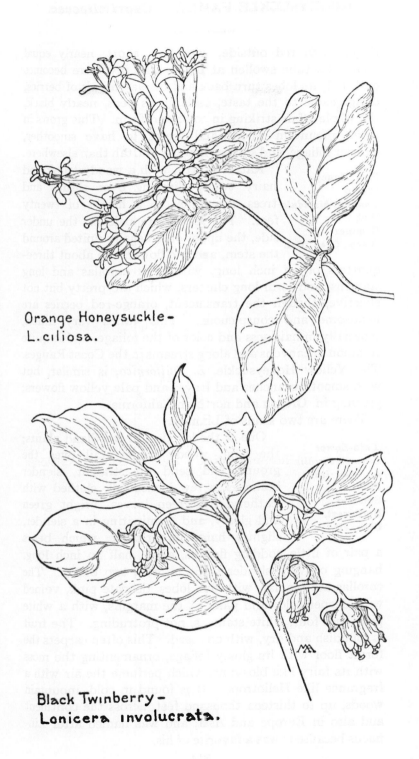

Orange Honeysuckle-
L. ciliosa.

Black Twinberry-
Lonicera involucrata.

tinged with red outside, with five, short, nearly equal lobes, the tube swollen at base. The involucre becomes dark red, its lobes turn back and display a pair of berries, disagreeable to the taste, as large as peas, nearly black, the whole affair striking in color and form. This grows in moist mountain woods and seems to have smoother, glossier foliage, and smaller flowers, in Utah than elsewhere.

Pink Honey-suckle
Lonicèra hispídula
Pink
Summer
Wash., Oreg., Cal.

Rather pretty, with a woody trunk and hairy twigs, climbing over shrubs and trees, sometimes to a height of twenty feet. The leaves are pale on the under side, the upper ones usually united around the stem, and the flowers are about three-quarters of an inch long, with pink corollas and long stamens, and form long clusters, which are pretty but not effective, though the translucent, orange-red berries are handsome and conspicuous. This varies very much, especially in hairiness and color of the foliage, and is quite common in canyons and along streams in the Coast Ranges. The Yellow Honeysuckle, *L. Califórnica*, is similar, but with smooth branches and leaves and pale yellow flowers; growing in Oregon and northern California.

There are two kinds of Linnaea.

Twin-flower
Linnaèa boreàlis
var. Americàna
Pink
Summer
Northwest,
Utah, etc.

One of the loveliest of woodland plants; the long, woody stems trail over the ground and send up straight, slender branches, a few inches tall, clothed with leathery, evergreen leaves, bright green and glossy, and terminating in a slender, slightly hairy flower-stalk, which bears a pair of little nodding flowers, about half an inch long, hanging on very slender pedicels, with two bracts. The corollas are regular, with five lobes, delicate pink, veined with deeper color and paler at the margins, with a white pistil and four, white stamens, not protruding. The fruit is roundish and dry, with one seed. This often carpets the forest floor with its glossy foliage, ornamenting the moss with its fairy-like blossoms, which perfume the air with a fragrance like Heliotrope. It is found in cold, mountain woods, up to thirteen thousand feet, across the continent and also in Europe and Asia, and was named after Linnaeus because it was a favorite of his.

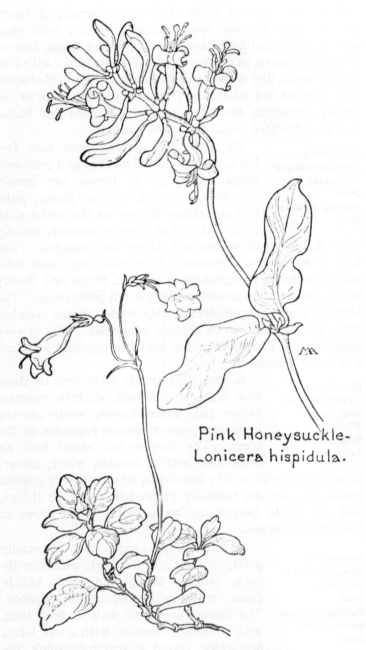

Pink Honeysuckle-
Lonicera hispidula.

Twin-flower- Linnaea borealis var.Americana.

HONEYSUCKLE FAMILY. *Caprifoliaceae.*

. There are several kinds of Symphoricarpos, of North America and Mexico; low, branching shrubs, with small leaves, scaly leaf-buds, and small, pink or white flowers, with two bracts, in clusters; the calyx roundish, with four or five teeth; the corolla regular, more or less bell-shaped, with four or five lobes; the fruit a roundish, white or red berry, containing two bony seeds. We often find Snowberries cultivated in old-fashioned gardens.

Snowberry
Symphoricàrpos
racemòsus
Pink
Spring, summer
U. S.

An attractive shrub, about four feet high, with slender branches and yellowish twigs. The pretty leaves are mostly smooth, rich green, but not glossy, paler and sometimes downy on the under side, thin, but rather crisp in texture, usually with a few shallow scallops along the margins. The flowers are about a quarter of an inch long, with bell-shaped corollas, purplish-pink outside, white and woolly in the inside, the stamens and style not protruding. The berry is large and pure-white, with white, almost tasteless pulp, which is said to be slightly poisonous. This is very common in California, in the hill country, and is found across the continent.

Snowberry
Symphoricàrpos
longiflòrus
White
Summer
Arizona
.

A straggling shrub, from two to three feet high, with small, slightly velvety, rather pale green leaves, white on the under side, sometimes set edgewise on the stem. The flowers are about half an inch long, with a slender, white, salverform corolla, with widely separating lobes and very smooth inside, the anthers partially protruding from the throat, and the pretty berries are waxy-white. This grows at the Grand Canyon.

Snowberry
Symphoricàrpos
oreóphilus
Pink
Spring, summer
Idaho, Utah,
Ariz.

A branching shrub, not especially pretty, about three feet high, with shreddy bark, pinkish twigs, and light, bluish-green, toothless leaves, usually smooth. The flowers are about half an inch long, with a tubular corolla, with short lobes, flesh-color, tinged with purplish-pink, the stamens and style not protruding and the buds purplish-pink. This grows in the mountains, up to eight or ten thousand feet.

516

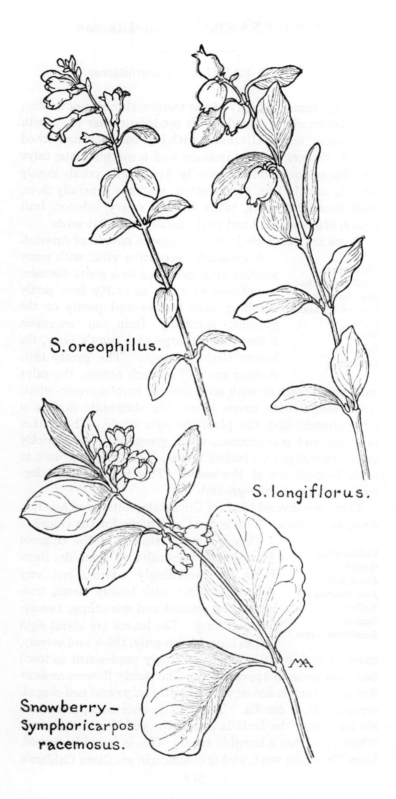

S. oreophilus.

S. longiflorus.

Snowberry —
Symphoricarpos
racemosus.

GOURD FAMILY. *Cucurbitaceae.*

A large family, chiefly of the tropics, climbing or trailing, herbaceous vines, usually with tendrils, rather juicy, with no stipules; leaves alternate, with leaf-stalks, usually lobed or cut; flowers some staminate and some pistillate; calyx bell-shaped or tubular, usually five-lobed; petals mostly united, usually five, on the calyx; stamens generally three, with short filaments, often united; ovary inferior; fruit fleshy, often with a hard rind, usually with flat seeds.

There are many kinds of Micrampelis, natives of America.

**Chilicothe,
Wild Cucumber**
*Micrámpelis
fabácea (Echino-
cystis)*
**White
Summer
California**

A graceful, decorative vine, with many tendrils and spreading to a great distance, sometimes as much as thirty feet, partly climbing over bushes and partly on the ground, springing from an enormous bitter root as large as a man's body, the leaves slightly rough. The pretty little flowers are half an inch across, the calyx with small teeth or with none and the corolla cream-white, with from five to seven lobes; the staminate flowers in loose clusters and the pistillate ones single. The fruit is peculiar and conspicuous, a big green ball, very prickly and measuring two inches across. The Indians used to make hair-oil out of the seeds. This is also called Big-root and Man-in-the-ground.

There are several kinds of Cucurbita, natives of America, Asia, and Africa. This is the Latin name for the Gourd.

**Calabazilla,
Gourd**
*Cucúrbita
foetidíssima*
**Yellow
Spring
Southwest, etc.**

This is a near relation of the common Pumpkin and Squash and resembles them. It is an exceedingly coarse, but very decorative vine, with bristly stems, trailing on the ground and sometimes twenty-five feet long. The leaves are about eight inches long, bluish-gray, thick and velvety, covered with bristles and exceedingly unpleasant to touch but handsome in appearance. The gaudy flowers measure five or six inches across, with a bristly calyx and bell-shaped, orange-yellow corolla. The root is enormous, sometimes six feet long, the fruit is a smooth, yellow gourd, and the whole plant has a horrible smell. This is found in dry soil, from Nebraska west, and is common in southern California

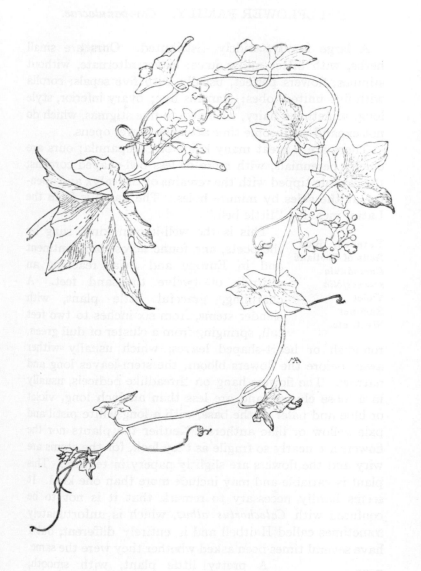

Chilicothe
Micrampelis fabacea

BELLFLOWER FAMILY. *Campanulaceae.*

A large family, widely distributed. Ours are small herbs, with bitter milky juice; leaves alternate, without stipules; flowers perfect, usually with five sepals; corolla with five united lobes; stamens five; ovary inferior, style long, sometimes hairy, with two to five stigmas, which do not expand until some time after the flower opens.

There are a great many kinds of Campanula; ours are chiefly perennials, with more or less bell-shaped corollas; the capsule tipped with the remains of the calyx and opening at the sides by minute holes. The name is from the Latin, meaning "little bell."

Harebell, Blue Bells of Scotland
Campánula rotundifòlia
Violet
Summer
West, etc.

This is the well-known kind, sung by the poets, and found across our continent and in Europe and Asia, reaching an altitude of twelve thousand feet. A charming, graceful little plant, with slender stems, from six inches to two feet tall, springing from a cluster of dull green, roundish or heart-shaped leaves, which usually wither away before the flowers bloom; the stem-leaves long and narrow. The flowers hang on threadlike pedicels, usually in a loose cluster, and are less than an inch long, violet or blue and paler at the base, with a long white pistil and pale yellow or lilac anthers. Neither the plants nor the flowers are nearly so fragile as they look, for the stems are wiry and the flowers are slightly papery in texture. This plant is variable and may include more than one kind. It seems hardly necessary to remark that it is not to be confused with *Calochortus albus*, which is unfortunately sometimes called Hairbell and is entirely different, but I have several times been asked whether they were the same.

Bellflower
Campánula Scoúleri
White, lilac
Summer
Northwest, Cal.

A pretty little plant, with smooth, slender stems, from six to eight inches tall, and smooth, toothed leaves. The flowers are in a loose cluster and are more the shape of little Lilies than of Blue Bells, white tinged with lilac, or pale blue, with yellow anthers and a long pistil with three pink stigmas. The California Harebell, *C. prenanthoìdes*, has blue flowers, similar in shape.

Bell-flower -
Campanula Scouleri.

Harebell -
C. rotundifolia.

SUNFLOWER FAMILY. *Compositae.*

SUNFLOWER FAMILY. *Compositae.*

The youngest and largest plant family, comprising about seven hundred and fifty genera and ten thousand species, highly specialized for insect pollination, easily recognized as a whole, but many of its members difficult to distinguish. Some tropical kinds are trees; ours are usually herbs, sometimes shrubs, without stipules; the leaves opposite, alternate or from the root; the flowers all small and crowded in heads, on the enlarged top of the flower-stalk, which is called the "receptacle," and surrounded by a common involucre of separate bracts, few or many, arranged in one or more rows; the receptacle also sometimes having scale-like or bristle-like bracts among the flowers, its surface smooth, or variously pitted and honey-combed. The flowers are sometimes perfect, or with only pistils, or only stamens, or with stamens and pistils on different plants, or all kinds mixed. The calyx-tube is sometimes a mere ring, or its margin consists of hairs, bristles or scales, called the "pappus." The corollas are chiefly of two sorts; they are tubular and usually have five lobes or teeth, but often the flowers around the margin of the head are strap-shaped, that is, the border of the corolla is expanded into what is called a "ray." For instance, the yellow center, or "disk," of a Daisy is composed of a crowded mass of tiny tube-shaped flowers, which is surrounded by a circle of white, strap-shaped flowers, or rays, which look like petals. A Thistle, on the other hand, has no rays and the head is made up of tube-shaped flowers only. Stamens usually five, on the corolla-tube, alternate with its lobes, anthers usually united into a tube surrounding the style, which has two branches in fertile flowers, but usually undivided in sterile flowers; ovary inferior, one-celled, maturing into an akene, often tipped with hairs from the pappus to waft it about, or with hooks or barbs to catch in fur of animals. (Descriptions of genera have been omitted as too technical.)

There are many kinds of Carduus (Cnicus) (Cirsium), widely distributed; with tubular flowers only.

Thistle
Càrduus Cóulteri
Pink, crimson
Spring, summer
California

A strikingly handsome, branching plant, from three to seven feet high, with light green leaves, very decorative in form, more or less downy on the upper side and pale with down on the under. The flower-

522

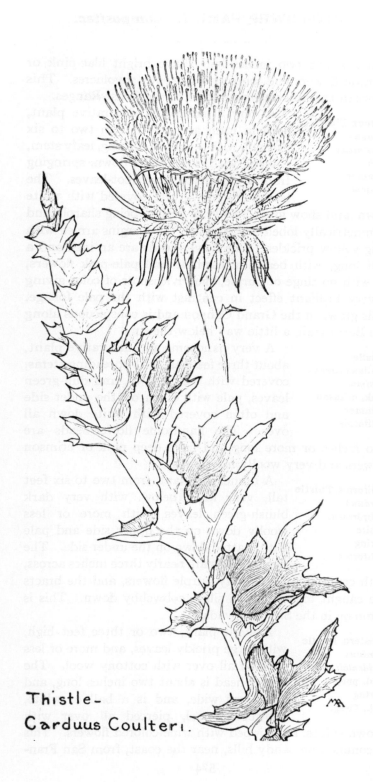

Thistle-
Carduus Coulteri.

heads, about two inches long, have bright lilac-pink or crimson flowers and more or less woolly involucres. This grows in the hills and mountains of the Coast Ranges.

Arizona Thistle
Càrduus
Arizònicus
Pink
Summer
Arizona

A very striking and decorative plant, both in form and color, from two to six feet tall, with a pale, branching, leafy stem, covered with close, white down, springing from a cluster of large root-leaves. The leaves are gray-green, covered with white down, and show great beauty of design, being sharply and symmetrically lobed and toothed, the margins armed with long yellow prickles. The flower-heads are an inch and a half long, with beautiful carmine and pale-pink flowers, all with no tinge of purple, the vivid spots of color giving a very brilliant effect in contrast with the pale foliage. This grows in the Grand Canyon and is conspicuous along the Berry trail, a little way below the rim.

Thistle
Càrduus canda-
dìssimus
Pink, crimson
Summer
California

A very handsome and decorative plant, about three feet tall, with spreading stems, covered with white down, and dull-green leaves, pale with down on the under side and often covered with white down all over. The handsome flower-heads are two inches or more long and have deep pink or crimson flowers and very woolly involucres.

California Thistle
Càrduus
Califórnicus
White
Spring
California

A branching plant, from two to six feet tall, very leafy below, with very dark bluish-green leaves, with more or less woolly down on the upper side and pale with matted down on the under side. The flower-heads are nearly three inches across, with cream-white or rarely purple flowers, and the bracts are caught together with silky, cobwebby down. This is common in the Sierra Nevada.

Western Thistle
Càrduus
occidentàlis
Red, purple
Spring
Cal., Oreg.

A stout plant, two or three feet high, with large prickly leaves, and more or less covered all over with cottony wool. The flower-head is about two inches long, and nearly as wide, and is a ball of white, cobwebby wool, pierced all over with brown spines, and tipped with wine-colored flowers. This is common on sandy hills, near the coast, from San Fran-

Arizona
Thistle.

Carduus
Arizonicus

Carduus
Arizonicus

Arizona
Thistle

Thistles.

Carduus Californicus.   **C. candadissimus.**

cisco south. Yellow-spined Thistle, *C. ochrocéntrus,* found
in Nevada and Arizona and as far east as Colorado, has
purple flowers and leaves deeply slashed and armed with
long yellow spines. This grows at the Grand Canyon.

There are a good many kinds of Anaphalis, natives of the
north temperate zone, but only one in North America.

Pearly Everlasting
Anáphalis
margaritàcea
White
Summer
U. S., etc.
This is the prettiest of the Everlastings,
from one to three feet tall, with a leafy
stem, covered with white wool, and alternate, toothless leaves, which are rather
long and narrow, gray-green and more or
less woolly on the upper side, pale and
woolly on the under. The flower-heads are numerous,
forming close, roundish clusters. The heads are without
rays, but the tiny, yellow, tubular flowers are surrounded
by many small, white, papery bracts, resembling petals,
making the involucre the conspicuous feature and forming
a pretty little, round, white head. This is common in dry
places, East and West, and found in Asia. There is a
picture in Mathews' *Field Book.* Rosy Everlasting,
Antennària ròsea, has the same general appearance, but
the bracts are pink, giving a pretty pink tint to the flower-
cluster, and is found in the Northwest at high altitudes.
Another kind of Everlasting is *Gnaphàlium microcéphalum,*
Cudweed, a mountain plant of the Northwest and California, with similar foliage, but with larger, looser clusters of
cream-white flowers, conspicuous at a distance, though
not pretty close by. There is a picture of a similar species
in Mathews' *Field Book.*

There are several kinds of Encelia.

Encelia
Encèlia
eriocéphala
Yellow
Spring
Southwest
A handsome, desert plant, with rough,
purplish stems, a foot and a half tall, dull-
green, hairy leaves, and flowers over an
inch across, in loose clusters, with bright
golden-yellow rays, yellow centers, and
woolly involucres. This makes fine
conspicuous clumps of bright color on the pale desert sand.

Golden Hills,
Brittle-bush
Encèlia farinòsa
Yellow
Spring
Arizona
A conspicuous shrubby plant, from two
to four feet high, with many stout, branch-
ing stems, grayish, downy twigs, and large
clumps of downy, gray-green leaves,
from which spring the long, slender flower-
stalks, bearing loose clusters of handsome

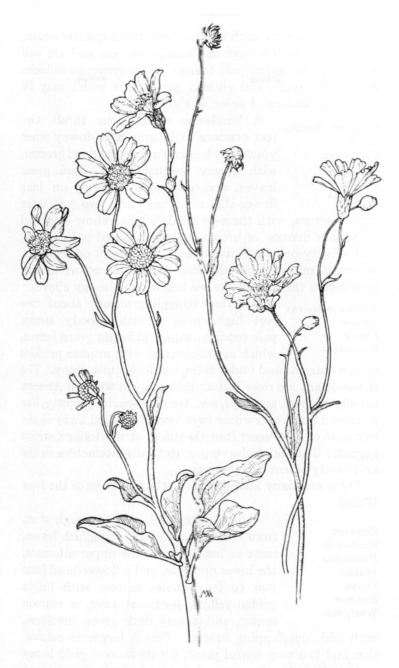

Golden Hills -
Encelia farinosa.

Encelia -
E. eriocephala.

flowers. They are each over an inch and a quarter across, with bright yellow rays and orange centers and are well set off by the rather pale foliage. This grows on hillsides among the rocks and gives a golden hue which may be seen at a distance of seven or eight miles.

California Encelia
Encèlia
Califórnica
Yellow
Spring
California

A handsome conspicuous shrub, two feet or more high, gray and downy when young but becoming smoother and greener, with downy, reddish twigs, dark green leaves, and numerous flowers, on long flower-stalks. They are two or three inches across, with three-toothed, bright yellow rays and very dark maroon or brown centers, specked with yellow, and velvety or hairy involucres. This grows on sea-cliffs, where it makes very effective masses of color, in fine contrast to the blue of the sea below and the sky above.

Encèlia frutéscens
Yellow
Spring
Southwest

A rather straggling shrub, about two feet high, with whitish, woody stems, pale reddish twigs, and bright green leaves, which are roughened with minute prickles on the margins and under sides, but look quite shiny. The flower-heads are over half an inch long, in western Arizona usually without any rays, and are not especially pretty, like a starved Sunflower whose rays have shrivelled away in the dry heat of the desert, but the effect of the foliage, which suggests little apple leaves, is decidedly attractive in the arid sandy places it frequents.

There are many kinds of Helianthus, natives of the New World.

Common
Sunflower
Heliánthus
ánnuus
Yellow
Summer
West, etc.

A handsome kind, with a rough stem, from two to ten feet tall, roughish leaves, more or less toothed, the upper alternate, the lower opposite, and a flower-head from two to four inches across, with bright golden-yellow, toothless rays, a maroon center, and a very dark green involucre, with stiff, overlapping bracts. This is larger in cultivation and is a very useful plant, for its flowers yield honey and a yellow dye, its seeds oil and food, the leaves are good for fodder, and the stalks for textile fiber. It is common nearly everywhere along roadsides, as far east as Missouri, and is found as a stray in the East.

California Encelia.
E. Californica.

Encelia frutescens. Common Sunflower.
Helianthus annuus.

SUNFLOWER FAMILY. *Compositae.*

Sunflower
Heliánthus fasciculàris
Yellow
Spring
Nev., Ariz., etc.

A handsome kind, forming a clump from two to four feet high, with several leafy, rough stems and harsh, rather shiny leaves. The fine flowers measure four inches across, with bright yellow rays, deeper yellow centers, and bronze, rough, rather resinous involucres. This is common around Reno and grows in dry mountain valleys as far east as Colorado.

Hairy Golden Aster
Chrysópsis villòsa
Yellow
Summer
Arizona, etc.

A striking plant, quite handsome, with a hairy, pale, leafy stem, from six inches to two feet tall, and gray-green, rather velvety leaves, generally toothless. The flowers are an inch or more across, with bright golden-yellow rays and centers of the same shade, growing singly, or in a more or less crowded cluster at the top of the stalk. This is common in open ground and dry hills, up to an altitude of ten thousand feet, as far east as Alabama, and there are many varieties. The Greek name means "golden aspect."

Velvet-rosette
Psathyròtes ánnua
Yellow
Spring
Southwest

A curious and pretty little desert plant, that looks as if it were trying to protect itself from cold rather than heat, as its pretty foliage and stems seem all made of silvery, gray velvet, forming a symmetrical rosette, dotted with the small, rayless, yellow flower-heads, like fuzzy buttons. The rosette is decorative in form, about a foot across, spreading flat and close to the ground, and is conspicuous on the bare sand of the desert. Only one of the branches is given in the picture.

Easter Daisy,
Ground Daisy
Townséndia exscàpa
Pink
Spring
Ariz., New Mex.
to Saskatchewan

This is a charming and quaint little plant, with close, downy rosettes of small, gray-green leaves and two or three, pretty, daisy-like flowers, all crowded together close to the ground. The flowers are over an inch across, with numerous, pale-pink rays, deeper pink on the under side, and a bright yellow center, and when they bloom in early spring, on bare rocky soil, they are exceedingly attractive.

There are a great many kinds of Erigeron, widely distributed, most abundant in the New World, easily confused with Asters, but usually with numerous and finer rays, so that the effect is more delicate.

530

Easter
Daisy.

Townsendia
exscapa.

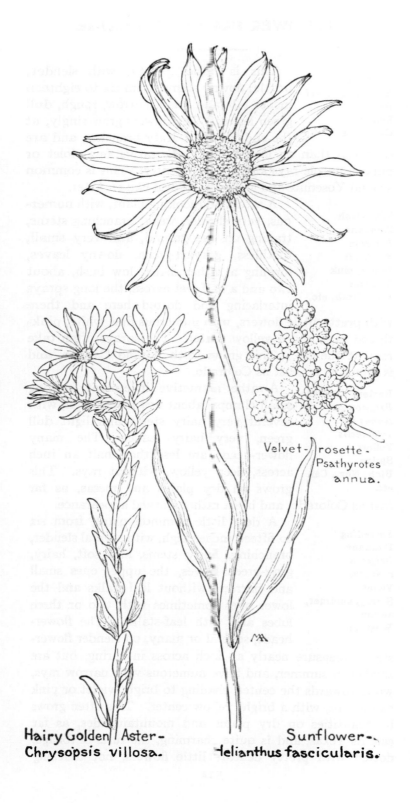

Velvet-rosette-
Psathyrotes
annua.

Hairy Golden Aster-
Chrysopsis villosa.

Sunflower-.
Helianthus fascicularis.

SUNFLOWER FAMILY. *Compositae.*

Fleabane
Erigeron Bréweri
Purple
Summer
California

This is rather pretty, with slender, brittle, downy stems, from six to eighteen inches tall, and small, narrow, rough, dull green leaves. The flowers grow singly, at the ends of short leafy branches, and are each less than an inch across, with rather few violet or pinkish-purple rays and a yellow center. This is common around Yosemite and looks a good deal like an Aster.

Whip-lash
Fleabane
Erigeron
flagellàris
White, pink
Summer
Ariz., Utah, etc.

A rather odd-looking plant, with numerous, very slender, weak, branching stems, trailing on the ground, and very small, toothless, grayish-green, downy leaves, forming a rather dense, low bush, about two and a half feet across, the long sprays interlacing and dotted here and there with pretty little flowers, with numerous fine, white, pink-tipped rays and a yellow center. The sprays often take root at the tip. This grows in the Grand Canyon, and is found as far east as Colorado.

Rayless Fleabane
Erigeron con-
cinnus var.
aphanáctis
Yellow
Spring
Utah, Nev., Cal.
etc.

A rather attractive little plant, forming small clumps, about five inches high, with several very hairy stems and light dull green, very hairy leaves. The many flower-heads are less than half an inch across, deep yellow, without rays. This grows on dry plains and mesas, as far east as Colorado, and has a rather starved appearance.

Spreading
Fleabane
Erigeron
divérgens
Violet
Spring, summer,
autumn
West, etc.

A dear little common plant, from six to fifteen inches high, with several slender, branching, hairy stems, and soft, hairy, gray-green leaves, the upper ones small and narrow, without leaf-stalks and the lower ones sometimes with two or three lobes and with leaf-stalks. The flower-heads, several or many, on slender flower-stalks, measure nearly an inch across in spring, but are smaller in summer, and have numerous very narrow rays, white towards the center, shading to bright violet or pink at the tips, with a bright yellow center. This often grows in quantities on dry plains and mountain-sides, as far east as Texas, and is quite charming, the tufts of foliage, dotted with pretty delicate little flowers, not touching

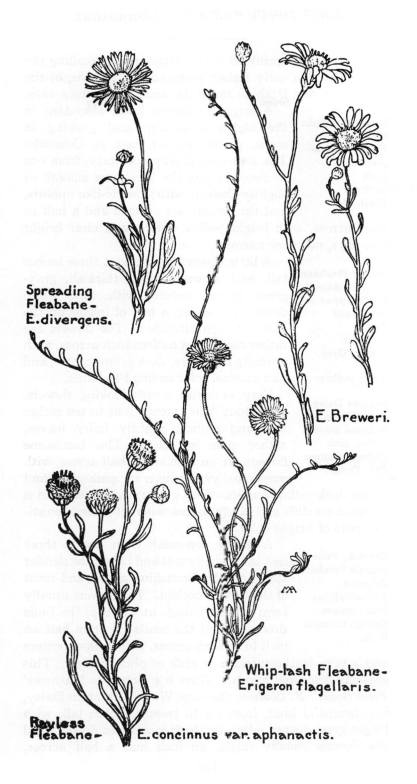

Spreading
Fleabane-
E.divergens.

E.Breweri.

Whip-lash Fleabane-
Erigeron flagellaris.

Rayless
Fleabane-   E. concinnus var. aphanactis.

each other, but sprinkled over a large space, recalling the little flowers in early Italian pictures. *E. pùmilis,* of the Northwest and Utah, is much the same, with white rays.

Large Mountain Fleabane
Erígeron salsuginòsus
Lilac
Summer
West, etc.

A large, handsome kind, abundant in the higher mountains and growing in moist places, as far east as Colorado. The stems are downy and leafy, from one to two feet tall, the leaves are smooth or slightly hairy, with bristle-like points, and the flowers are an inch and a half or more across, with bright yellow centers and clear bright lilac rays, not very narrow.

Yellow Fleabane
Erígeron àureus
(Aplopappus Brandegei)
Yellow
Summer
Wash., Oreg.

A little alpine plant, about three inches tall, with downy stems, thickish, gray-green leaves, covered with close white down and forming a mat of foliage on the rocks at high altitudes. The flowers are rather more than half an inch across, with a woolly involucre, dark yellow center, and deep yellow rays, an unusual color among Fleabanes.

Seaside Daisy,
Beach Aster
Erígeron glàucus
Violet, pink
Spring, summer
Cal., Oreg.

Very cheerful, sturdy-looking flowers, with stout, hairy stems, four to ten inches tall, and stiffish, slightly hairy leaves, rather pale in color. The handsome flowers are an inch and a half across, with numerous violet, lilac, or pink rays and rather dark yellow centers. This grows near the sea and is common on cliffs and sandy shores, where it makes beautiful spots of bright color.

Skevish, Philadelphia Fleabane
Erígeron Philadélphicus
Pink, mauve
Spring, summer
U. S.

A pretty perennial, from one to three feet tall, usually soft and hairy, the slender stems usually branching above and most of the leaves toothed. The flowers usually form a loose cluster at the top, the buds drooping, and the heads are from half an inch to an inch across, with yellow centers and a very feathery fringe of pink or pinkish rays. This grows in fields and woods. There is a picture in Mathews' *Field Book. E. Còulteri,* the large White Mountain Daisy, is a beautiful kind, from six to twenty inches tall, with bright green leaves, often toothed, sometimes downy, and the flowers usually single, an inch and a half across,

Yellow Fleabane—E. aureus.

Seaside
Daisy
Erigeron glaucus.

Large Mountain
Fleabane—
E. salsuginosus.

usually with pure white rays. This grows in Yosemite meadows and similar mountain places, in Utah, California, and Colorado. *E. compósitus* is a little Alpine plant, forming dense leafy mats, easily recognized by the broad tips of the leaves being cut into lobes, usually three. The flowers are an inch or more across, with violet or white rays. This grows on the granite peaks around Yosemite, and in other Alpine regions, as far east as Colorado.

Ptilonella
Ptilonélla scábra
(Blepharipappus)
White
Spring
Oreg., Ida.,
Nev., Cal.

A charming little desert plant, graceful and airy in character, with stiff, very slender, branching, roughish stems, about ten inches tall, and dull green leaves, very rough to the touch, with the edges rolled back. The delicate little flowers are an inch across, with pure white rays, and with white centers, which are specked with black and pink. This is common on the mesas around Reno and looks much like some kinds of Madia.

Desert Holly
Perèzia nàna
Pink
Spring
Ariz., Tex.

An odd little desert plant, only two or three inches high, with stiff, smooth, dull bluish-green leaves, with prickly edges, like holly leaves but not so stiff, and one quite pretty, light purplish-pink flower, the head about an inch long, with purplish bracts. The effect of the whole plant is of a little sprig stuck into the sand.

Brown-foot
Perèzia Wrìghtii
Pink
Spring
Ariz., Tex.

Much like the last, but more commonplace looking, for the flowers are smaller and the plant much larger. It is about a foot high and grows among rocks, and the general effect of dull mauve is rather pretty, though not bright in color. The common name alludes to the plant being covered with a mass of brown hairs at the base.

There are several kinds of Gutierrezia, all American.

Brown-weed
Gutierrèzia Saró-
thrae (G.
Euthamiae)
Yellow
Summer, autumn
West, etc.

A bushy plant, resinous, smooth or nearly so, from six inches to two feet high, with many stiff, upright branches and alternate, toothless, narrow leaves, an inch or so long. The flowers have yellow centers and small yellow rays, forming clusters at the ends of the branches, and though very small are so numerous as to make effective clumps of bright color. This grows at the Grand Canyon, and in dry rocky places, as far east as the Central States.

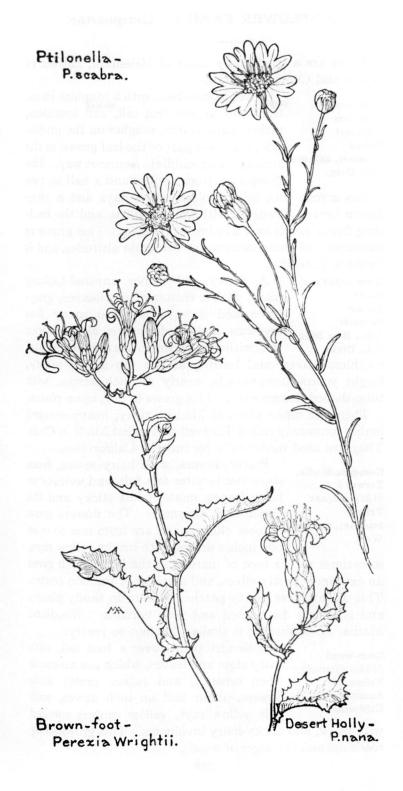

Ptilonella -
P. scabra.

Brown-foot -
Perezia Wrightii.

Desert Holly -
P. nana.

There are a good many kinds of Helenium, natives of North and Central America.

Sneeze-weed
Helènium
Bigelòwii
Yellow
Summer, autumn
Cal., Oreg.

A handsome plant, with a roughish stem, from two to four feet tall, and toothless, rather coarse leaves, rougher on the underside, the lower part of the leaf grown to the stem along its middle in a curious way. The flowers are from an inch and a half to two inches across, with bright golden-yellow rays and a rich-brown center, powdered with yellow pollen, and the budding flower heads look like brown buttons. This grows in meadows and along streams, at moderate altitudes, and is found in Yosemite.

Hymenopáppus
lùteus
Yellow
Summer
Ariz., New Mex.,
Col., Utah

A pretty and rather unusual-looking plant, with a cluster of root-leaves, gray-green and downy, cut into many fine divisions, and slender stems, about a foot tall, with two or three, narrow, alternate, toothless leaves, and bearing at the top a few pretty, bright yellow flower-heads, nearly an inch across, with tube-shaped flowers only. This grows in dry, open places.

There are many kinds of Madia, sticky, heavy-scented herbs, commonly called Tarweed and called Madi in Chili. They are used medicinally by Spanish-Californians.

Common Madia,
Tarweed
Màdia élegans
Yellow
Summer, autumn
West

Pretty flowers, with hairy stems, from six inches to three feet tall, and velvety or hairy leaves, more or less sticky and the upper ones alternate. The flowers grow in loose clusters and are from one to over two inches across, with bright yellow rays, sometimes with a spot of maroon at the base which gives an extremely pretty effect, and a yellow or maroon center. This often makes pretty patches of color in sandy places, and is widely distributed and very variable. Woodland Madia, *M. madioìdes,* is similar, but not so pretty.

Gum-weed
Màdia dissitiflòra
Yellow
Summer
California

A slender plant, over a foot tall, with hairy stem and leaves, which are aromatic when crushed, and rather pretty little flowers, about half an inch across, with pale yellow rays, yellow centers specked with black, and sticky-hairy involucres. This grows along roadsides and the edges of woods.

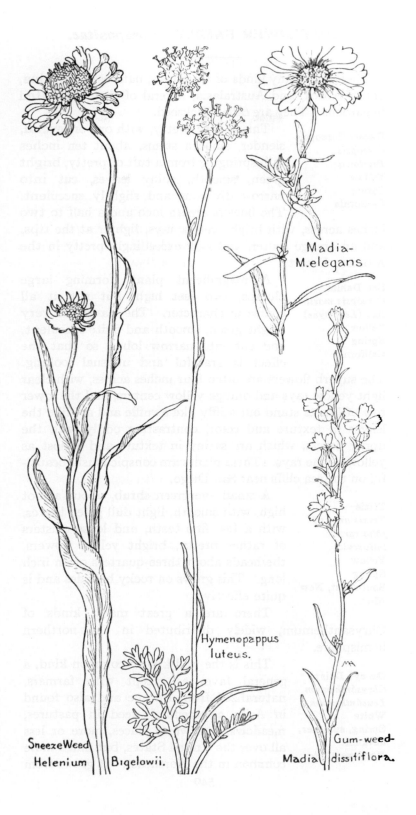

Madia-
M.elegans

Hymenopappus
luteus.

SneezeWeed
Helenium   Bigelowii.

Gum-weed-
Madia dissitiflora.

There are many kinds of Coreopsis, natives of America, South Africa, and Australasia, several of them cultivated in gardens. They are called Tickseed.

Desert Coreopsis
Coreópsis Bigelòwii
Yellow
Spring
California

This is very pretty, with one or several, slender, smooth stems, about ten inches tall, springing from a tuft of pretty, bright green, smooth, shiny leaves, cut into narrow divisions and slightly succulent. The flowers are an inch and a half to two inches across, with bright yellow rays, lighter at the tips, and an orange center, and look exceedingly pretty in the Mohave Desert.

Sea Dahlia
Coreópsis marit-ima (Leptosyne)
Yellow
Spring
California

A magnificent plant, forming large clumps, two feet high, but not at all coarse in character. The leaves are very bright green, smooth and quite succulent, and cut into narrow lobes, so that the effect is graceful and unusual looking. The superb flowers are often four inches across, with clear light yellow rays and orange-yellow centers, and the lower row of bracts stand out stiffly like a ruffle and are like the leaves in texture and color, contrasting oddly with the upper bracts, which are satiny in texture and almost as yellow as the rays. These plants are conspicuously beautiful on the sea cliffs near San Diego.

Trixis
Trixis angusti-fòlia var. latiúscula
Yellow
Spring
Southwest, New Mex.

A small evergreen shrub, about a foot high, with smooth, light dull green leaves, with a few fine teeth, and loose clusters of rather pretty, bright yellow flowers, the heads about three-quarters of an inch long. This grows on rocky hillsides and is quite effective.

There are a great many kinds of Chrysanthemum, widely distributed in the northern hemisphere.

Ox-eye Daisy
Chrysánthemum Leucánthemum
White
Spring, summer, autumn
Northwest, etc.

This is the well known common kind, a general favorite, except with farmers, naturalized from Europe and also found in Asia; a perennial weed in pastures, meadows, and waste places, more or less all over the United States, but much more common in the Northeast. It grows from

540

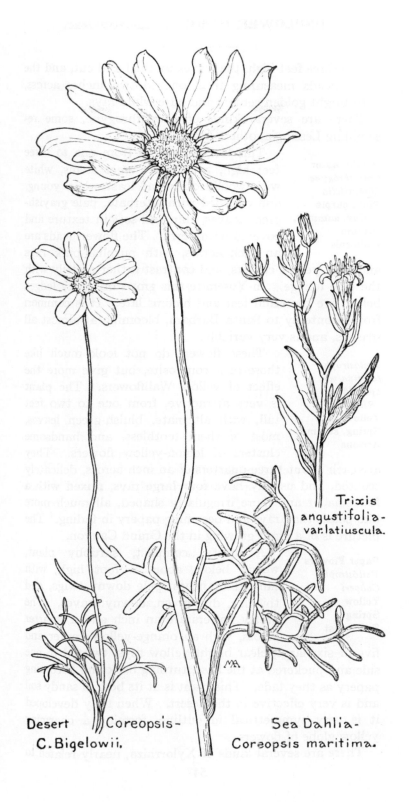

Trixis
angustifolia-
var. latiuscula.

Desert Coreopsis-
C. Bigelowii.

Sea Dahlia-
Coreopsis maritima.

one to three feet high, the leaves toothed and cut, and the
flower-heads measuring from one to two inches across,
with bright golden centers and pure white rays.

There are several kinds of Coreothrogyne, some resembling Lessingia, others Aster.

Woolly Aster
Coreothrógyne
filaginifòlia
Pink, purple
Spring, summer,
autumn
California

This forms a clump from one to three
feet high, with many erect stems, white
with woolly down, at least when young,
and crowded with alternate, pale grayish-
green leaves, thin and soft in texture and
covered with down. The flower-heads are
an inch across, with purplish-pink rays
and dark yellow centers, and contrast rather prettily with
the pale foliage. In Yosemite this grows on rocky ledges
below five thousand feet and blooms late. It is common
from Monterey to Santa Barbara, blooming at almost all
seasons, and is very variable.

Psilóstrophe
tagelìna var.
sparsiflòra
(Riddellia)
Yellow
Spring, summer
Arizona

These flowers do not look much like
those of a composite, but give more the
effect of yellow Wallflowers. The plant
is very attractive, from one to two feet
tall, with alternate, bluish-green leaves,
most of them toothless, and handsome
clusters of lemon-yellow flowers. They
are each about three-quarters of an inch across, delicately
scented, and usually have four large rays, mixed with a
few smaller and more irregularly shaped, all much more
like petals than rays and becoming papery in fading. The
picture is of a plant growing in the Grand Canyon.

Paper Flowers
Psilóstrophe
Coòperi
Yellow
Spring
Southwest

A pretty, compact, shrubby plant,
woody below, about a foot high, with
tangled branches, pale downy twigs, and
thickish, dull green, downy leaves. The
pretty flowers are an inch and a quarter
across, with an orange-yellow center and
five or six, large, clear bright yellow rays, twisted to one
side and puckered at the base, turning back and becoming
papery as they fade. This plant is at its best in sandy soil
and is very effective in the desert. When fully developed
it is very symmetrical in outline, forming a charming
yellow globe of flowers.

There are several kinds of Xylorrhiza, nearly related to

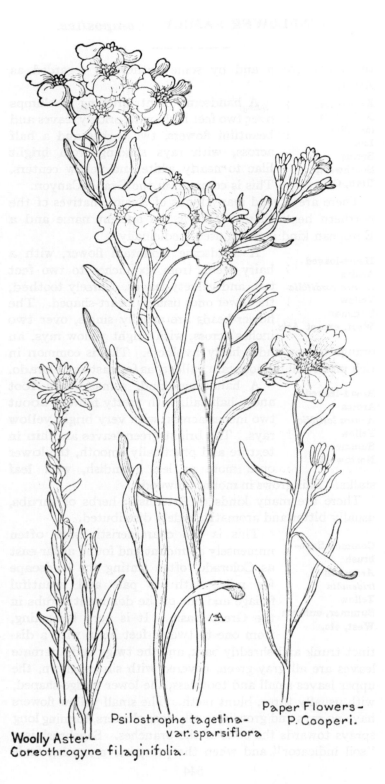

Woolly Aster—
Coreothrogyne filaginifolia.

Psilostrophe tagetina—
var. sparsiflora

Paper Flowers—
P. Cooperi.

the Aster group and by some authorities regarded as Asters.

Xylorrhiza
Xylorrhiza tortifòlia
Lilac
Spring
Southwest,
Utah, Col.

A handsome plant, growing in clumps over two feet high, with prickly leaves and beautiful flowers, two inches and a half across, with rays shading from bright lilac to nearly white and yellow centers. This is common in the Grand Canyon.

There are a good many kinds of Arnica, natives cf the northern hemisphere. This is the ancient name and a European kind is much used medicinally.

Heart-leaved
Arnica
Árnica cordifòlia
Yellow
Summer
West, except Ariz.

A handsome mountain flower, with a hairy stem, from six inches to two feet tall, and velvety leaves, coarsely toothed, the lower ones usually heart-shaped. The flower-heads are usually single, over two inches across, with bright yellow rays, an orange center, and a hairy involucre. This is common in rich moist soil in mountain valleys, as far east as Colorado.

Broad-leaved
Arnica
Árnica latifòlia
Yellow
Summer
Northwest

A handsome kind, sometimes a foot and a half tall, with pretty flowers, about two inches across, with very bright yellow rays. The bright green leaves are thin in texture and practically smooth, the lower ones more or less roundish, with leaf stalks. This grows in mountain woods.

There are many kinds of Artemisia; herbs or shrubs, usually bitter and aromatic, widely distributed.

Common Sage-brush
Artemisia tridentàta
Yellow
Summer, autumn
West, etc.

This is the characteristic sort, often immensely abundant and found as far east as Colorado, often tinting the landscape for miles with its pale and beautiful foliage and one of the dominant shrubs in the Great Basin. It is very branching, from one to twelve feet high, with a distinct trunk and shreddy bark, and the twigs and alternate leaves are all gray-green, covered with silvery down, the upper leaves small and toothless, the lower wedge-shaped, with usually three, blunt teeth. The small yellow flowers have no rays and grow in small, close clusters, forming long sprays towards the ends of the branches. Sagebrush is a "soil indicator" and when the prospective rancher finds

Xylorrhiza
tortifolia.

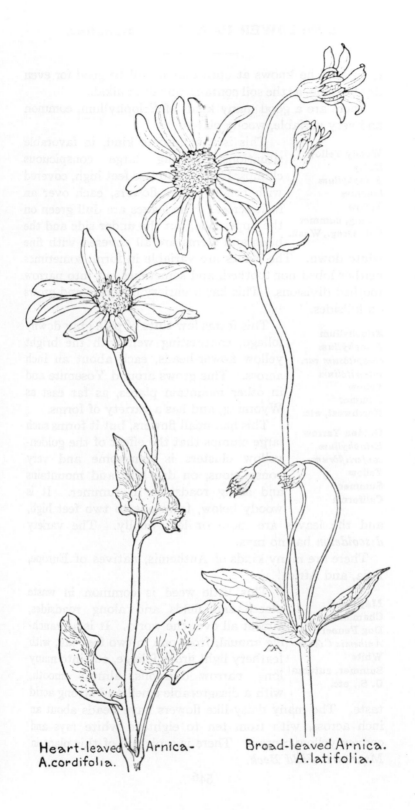

Heart-leaved Arnica-
A.cordifolia.

Broad-leaved Arnica.
A.latifolia.

SUNFLOWER FAMILY. *Compositae.*

it on land he knows at once that it will be good for even dry farming, as the soil contains no salt or alkali.

There are a good many kinds of Eriophyllum, common and very variable, woolly plants.

Woolly Yellow Daisy
Eriophýllum landtum
Yellow
Spring, summer
Cal., Oreg., Wash.

This is a handsome kind, in favorable situations forming large conspicuous clumps, from one to two feet high, covered with bright golden flowers, each over an inch across. The leaves are dull green on the upper side, but the under side and the buds and stems are all covered with fine white down. The leaves are variable in form, sometimes neither lobed nor toothed, and sometimes cut into narrow toothed divisions. This has a variety of forms and grows on hillsides.

Eriophyllum
Eriophýllum caespitòsum var. integrifòlium
Yellow
Summer
Northwest, etc.

This forms low tufts of pale gray downy foliage, contrasting well with the bright yellow flower-heads, each about an inch across. This grows around Yosemite and in other mountain places, as far east as Wyoming, and has a variety of forms.

Golden Yarrow
Eriophýllum confertiflòrum
Yellow
Summer
California

This has small flowers, but it forms such large clumps that the effect of the golden-yellow clusters is handsome and very conspicuous, on dry hills and mountains and along roadsides in summer. It is woody below, from one to two feet high, and the leaves are more or less woolly. The variety *discoídeum* has no rays.

There are many kinds of Anthemis, natives of Europe, Asia, and Africa.

Mayweed, Chamomile, Dog Fennel
Ánthemis Cótula
White
Summer, autumn
U. S., etc.

This little weed is common in waste places and fields and along roadsides, almost all over the world. It is a branching annual, from one to two feet tall, with feathery light green foliage, cut into many long, narrow divisions, almost smooth, with a disagreeable smell and strong acrid taste. The many daisy-like flowers have heads about an inch across, with from ten to eighteen white rays and convex yellow centers. There is a picture of this plant in Mathews' *Field Book.*

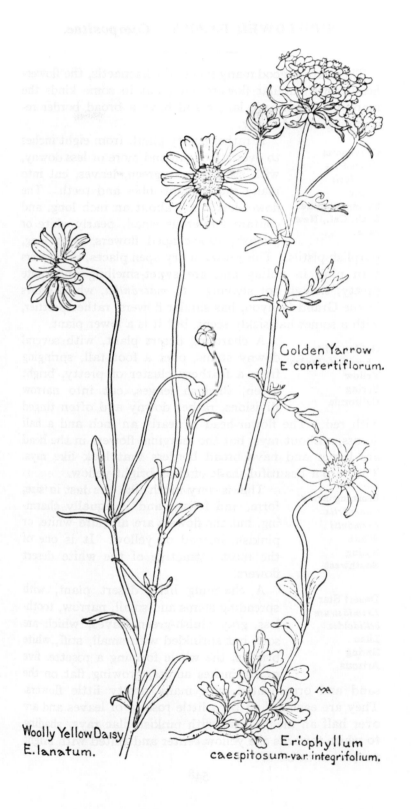

Golden Yarrow
E. confertiflorum.

Woolly Yellow Daisy
E. lanatum.

Eriophyllum
caespitosum·var integrifolium.

SUNFLOWER FAMILY. *Compositae.*

There are a good many kinds of Chaenactis, the flower-heads with tubular flowers only, but in some kinds the marginal flowers are larger and have a broad border resembling a kind of ray.

Chaenactis
Chaenáctis
Douglásii
White
Spring, summer
Utah, Cal., New Mex.

A rather pretty plant, from eight inches to over a foot tall and more or less downy, with stiffish, gray-green, leaves, cut into many short, blunt lobes and teeth. The flower-heads are about an inch long, and contain numerous small, pearly-white or pinkish, tube-shaped flowers, with long, purplish pistils. This grows in dry open places, the flowers turn pink in fading and are sweet-smelling and quite pretty, though not striking. *C. macrántha*, which grows in the Grand Canyon, has similar flowers, rather prettier, with a somewhat sickly scent, but it is a lower plant.

Golden Girls
Chaenáctis lanósa
Yellow
Spring
California

A charming desert plant, with several downy stems, over a foot tall, springing from a feathery cluster of pretty, bright green, thickish leaves, cut into narrow divisions, rather downy and often tinged with red. The flower-head is nearly an inch and a half across, without rays, but the marginal flowers in the head are larger and have broad borders that look like rays. They are a beautiful shade of clear bright yellow.

Morning Bride
Chaenáctis
Fremóntii
White
Spring
Southwest

This is very much like the last in size, form, and foliage and is equally charming, but the flowers are all pure white, or pinkish, instead of yellow. It is one of the most attractive of the white desert flowers.

Desert Star
Erimiástrum
bellidoídes
Lilac
Spring
Arizona

A charming little desert plant, with spreading stems and small, narrow, toothless, gray bluish-green leaves, which are soft, but sprinkled with small, stiff, white bristles, the whole forming a rosette, five or six inches across, growing flat on the sand and ornamented with many pretty little flowers. They are each set off by a little rosette of leaves and are over half an inch across, with pinkish-lilac rays, shading to white towards the yellow center and tinted with bright purple on the back.

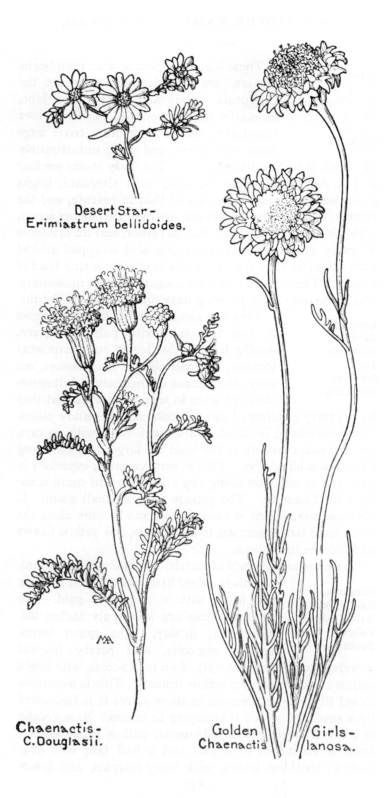

Desert Star —
Erimiastrum bellidoides.

Chaenactis —
C. Douglasii.

Golden
Chaenactis

Girls —
lanosa.

Venegasia
Venegásia
carpesioìdes
Yellow
Summer
California

These big, leafy plants, with their bright flowers, are a splendid feature of the California woods and canyons in June, especially on the slopes of the Santa Inez mountains, where they often cover large areas with green and gold; unfortunately the smell is rather disagreeable. The leafy stems are four or five feet high, nearly smooth, with alternate, bright green leaves, almost smooth and thin in texture, and the flowers, resembling Sun-flowers, are over two inches across, with clear yellow rays, an orange center, and an involucre of many green scales, overlapping and wrapped around each other, so that the bud looks much like a tiny head of lettuce. This was named for Venegas, a Jesuit missionary, and is the only kind, growing near the coast in the South.

Lessingia
Lessingia
leptóclada
Lilac
Summer
California

This is a slender plant, from six inches to two feet tall, with pale gray-green, woolly leaves, the lower ones somewhat toothed, and pale pinkish-lilac flowers, not very conspicuous in themselves, but sometimes growing in such quantities that they form pretty patches of soft pinkish color in sandy places. The flower-head is about half an inch long, with no rays, but the outer flowers in the head are larger and have long lobes resembling rays. This is very variable, especially in size, and is common along dry roadsides and quite abundant in Yosemite. The picture is of a small plant. *L. Germanдrum*, which is common on sandy hills along the coast from San Francisco to San Diego, has yellow flowers and blooms in autumn.

There are many kinds of Baeria, not easily distinguished.

Sunshine,
Gold Fields
Baéria grácilis
Yellow
Southwest

This is a dear little plant, often covering the fields with a carpet of gold. The slender stems are about six inches tall, with soft, downy, light green leaves, usually opposite, and pretty fragrant flowers, about three-quarters of an inch across, with bright yellow rays and darker yellow centers. This is sometimes called Fly Flower, because in some places it is frequented by a small fly, which is annoying to horses. *B. macrántha* is a much larger plant, a biennial, with a tuberous root, from seven inches to a foot and a half tall, with long, narrow, toothless leaves, with hairy margins, and flower-

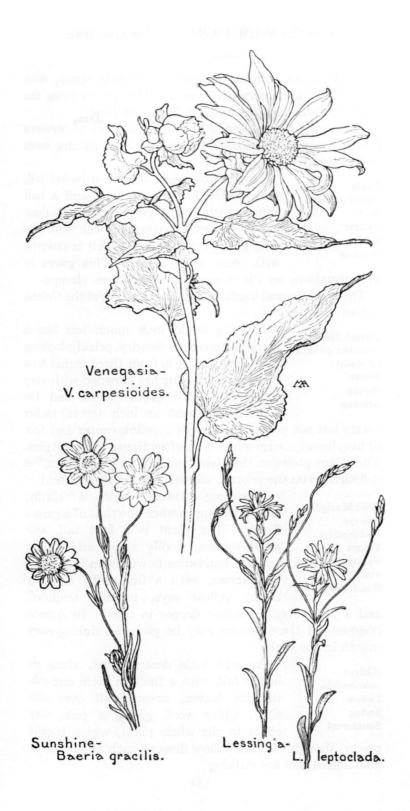

Venegasia—
V. carpesioides.

Sunshine—
Baeria gracilis.

Lessing'a-
L.) leptoclada.

heads from an inch to an inch and a half across, with yellow rays and hairy involucres. This grows along the coast in California, blooming in May and June.

There are several kinds of Bahia, natives of western North America, Mexico, and Chile, herbs or shrubs, more or less woolly.

Bahia
Bàhia absinthi-
fòlia
Yellow
Spring
Arizona

This is from eight to fifteen inches tall, with pretty flowers, an inch and a half across, with bright yellow rays and deep yellow centers, contrasting well with the pale gray-green foliage, which is covered with close white down. This grows in arid situations on the mesas and often forms clumps.

There are several kinds of Crassina, natives of the United States and Mexico.

Desert Zinnia
Crassìna pùmila
(Zinnia)
White
Spring
Arizona

Nothing could look much less like a garden Zinnia than this dry, prickly-looking dwarf shrub. It is from three inches to a foot high, the branches crowded with very small, stiff, dull green leaves, and the flowers are about an inch across, rather pretty but not conspicuous, with a yellow center and four or five, broad, cream-white rays, often tinged with dull pink. This plant grows on the plains and is a "soil-indicator," as it flourishes on the poorest, stoniest, and most arid land.

Wild Marigold
Bàileya
multiradiàta
Yellow
Spring, summer,
etc.
Southwest, Tex.

Charming flowers, with a thrifty, cultivated appearance like that of a garden flower. The plant is a foot tall, with grayish-green, woolly stems and foliage, and the handsome flower is an inch and a half across, with a fine ruffle of many bright yellow rays, prettily scalloped, and a yellow center, rather deeper in color. In Arizona bouquets of these flowers may be gathered during every month in the year.

Bàileya
pauciradiàta
Yellow
Spring
Southwest

An odd little desert plant, about six inches tall, with a thickish stem and soft, thickish leaves, covered all over with silky, white wool, giving a pale, silky effect to the whole plant, which is quite pretty, though the pale yellow flowers, each about half an inch across, are not striking.

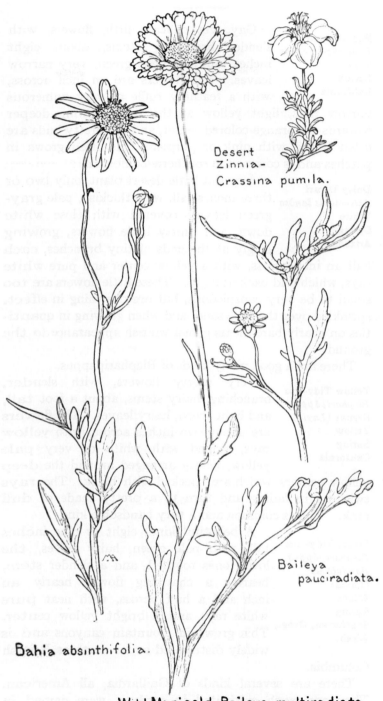

Desert
Zinnia-
Crassina pumila.

Baileya
pauciradiata.

Bahia absinthifolia.

Wild Marigold-Baileya multiradiata..

SUNFLOWER FAMILY. *Compositae.*

Pentachaeta
Pentachaèta àurea
Yellow
Spring
California

Gay, yet delicate little flowers, with slender branching stems, about eight inches tall, and light green, very narrow leaves. The flowers are an inch across, with a feathery ruffle of very numerous narrow rays, light yellow at the tips, growing deeper towards the orange-colored center, and the pretty buds are often tinged with pink or purple. This often grows in patches and is common in southern California.

Daisy Dwarf
Actinolèpis lanòsa
White
Spring
Arizona

A quaint little desert plant, only two or three inches tall, with thickish, pale gray-green leaves, covered with close white down, and pretty little flowers, growing singly at the ends of tiny branches, each half an inch across, with a yellow center and pure white rays, which fold back at night. These little flowers are too small to be very conspicuous, but are charming in effect, sprinkled over the bare sand, and when growing in quantities on nearly bare mesas give a whitish appearance to the ground.

There are a good many kinds of Blepharipappus.

Yellow Tidy-tips
Blepharipáppus
élegans (Layia)
Yellow
Spring
California

Very pretty flowers, with slender, branching, hairy stems, about a foot tall, and light green, hairy leaves. The flowers are about two inches across, with yellow rays, tipped with white or very pale yellow, neatly arranged around the deep yellow centers, which are specked with black. The rays twist up in fading and turn to a pretty shade of dull pink. This is common and a very handsome kind.

White Tidy-tips
Blepharipáppus
glandulòsus
(Layia)
White
Spring
Southwest, Oreg.,
Wash.

A beautiful kind, eight or nine inches tall, with pale green, hairy leaves, the lower ones toothed, and a slender stem, bearing a charming flower, nearly an inch and a half across, with neat pure white rays and a bright yellow center. This grows in mountain canyons and is widely distributed as far north as British Columbia.

There are several kinds of Gaillardia, all American. They are much cultivated in gardens, were named in honor of Gaillard de Merentonneau, a French botanist.

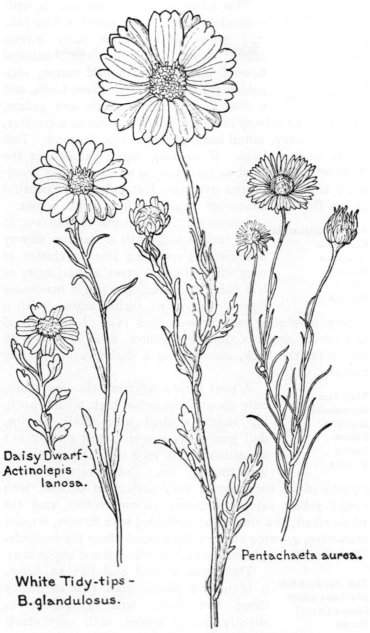

Daisy Dwarf-
Actinolepis
lanosa.

White Tidy-tips-
B. glandulosus.

Pentachaeta aurea.

Yellow Tidy-tips-
Blepharipappus elegans.

SUNFLOWER FAMILY. *Compositae.*

Blanket-flower,
Gaillardia
Gaillàrdia
pinnatifida
Yellow
Summer
Ariz., Col., Tex.

This is handsome and conspicuous, with a slender, rough stalk, about a foot tall, dull green, stiff, rather hairy leaves, mostly from the root, and beautiful flowers, an inch and a half across, with golden-yellow rays, with three teeth, and a center of shaded maroon and yellow, which is very velvety and pretty and becomes an attractive, purplish, fuzzy, round head when the rays drop off. This grows on the plains. *G. aristàta*, found throughout the West and as far east as Colorado, is an exceedingly handsome kind, sometimes over two feet tall, with beautiful yellow flowers, sometimes measuring four inches across.

Arizona Gaillardia
Gaillàrdia
Arizònica
Yellow
Spring
Arizona

A pretty little desert plant, from four to eight inches tall, with a slender, downy flower-stalk, springing from a cluster of roughish, light dull green leaves, more or less hairy and bearing a single handsome flower, nearly two inches across, with a downy involucre and three-toothed rays of an unusual and pretty shade of dull light yellow, finely veined with brown on the back, surrounding a darker yellow, fuzzy center.

Tiny Tim
Hymenathèrum
Hartwègi
Yellow
Spring
Arizona

A neat little evergreen, shrubby plant, only about three inches high, with branching stems, clothed with small, narrow, dull green leaves, which look prickly but are actually not very stiff, though tipped with tiny bristles. The flowers are three-eighths of an inch across, very perfect in outline, with bright yellow rays and deeper yellow centers, and the whole effect, of a tiny shrub sprinkled with flowers, is quite attractive, growing on very dry ground along the roadside. The plant has a pronounced smell, which is not unpleasant.

Tall Purple Aster
Machaeranthèra
incàna (Aster)
Purple
Spring
Southwest, Utah,
New Mex.

This looks a good deal like an Aster, a branching plant, from two to nearly three feet high, with grayish-green, slightly downy leaves, with very sharp teeth. The flowers are an inch and a half across, with narrow, bright violet rays and bright yellow centers. This grows abundantly in valleys.

556

Purple Aster-
Machaeranthera
incana.

Tiny Tim-
Hymenatherum Hartwegi.

Blanket-flower-
Gaillardia pinnatifida.

Arizona Gaillardia
G. Arizonica

*Laphàmia
biselòsa*
Yellow Summer
Ariz., New Mex.,
Tex.

An insignificant plant, except that it grows on the sides of bare, red rocks or head-downward on the under side of overhanging ledges, apparently needing little or no soil, and is therefore noticeable. It forms round clumps, one or two feet across, with many slender stems, about six inches high, small, pale yellowish-green, roughish leaves, and small yellow flower-heads, without rays. This is rare and grows in the Grand Canyon.

There are several kinds of Grindelia, common in the West, recommended as a remedy for Poison Oak.

Gum Plant
*Grindèlia
latifòlia*
Yellow
Spring
California

Coarse but rather effective flowers, with smooth, stiff, branching stems, about three feet high, and dark dull green leaves. The flower-heads are over an inch and a half across, with bright yellow rays and centers and very resinous, shiny buds.

There are several kinds of Balsamorrhiza. Both the Latin and common names allude to the aromatic roots.

Arrow-leaf
Balsam-root, Big
Root
*Balsamorrhìza
sagittàta*
Yellow
Spring
Utah, Ida., Cal.,
Nev., Col.

A very handsome plant, the contrast between the gray-velvet leaves and the great yellow flowers being very striking. It forms large clumps, about a foot and a half high, with slightly downy flower-stalks and heart-shaped or arrow-shaped, toothless leaves, pale gray-green and velvety, covered with silvery down, whiter on the under side. The flowers are over three inches across, with clear bright yellow rays, and a deeper yellow center, fuzzy and greenish-yellow in the middle. The involucre is almost white, thickly covered with silvery, silky wool, and the flowers are pleasantly sweet-smelling. This grows on dry hillsides.

Cut-leaved Bal-
sam-root
*Balsamorrhìza
macrophylla*
Yellow
Spring, summer
Utah, Wyo.

A strikingly handsome plant, forming clumps even larger than the last, with similar flowers, but with quite different foliage. The leaves are rich-green, and decorative in form, more or less slashed into lobes and very sticky, with hairy margins and leaf-stalks, and are nearly as tall as the hairy, sticky flower-stems, from one to two feet high. This grows in rich soil in mountain valleys.

Cut-leaved
Balsam
Root.

Balsamorrhiza
macrophylla.

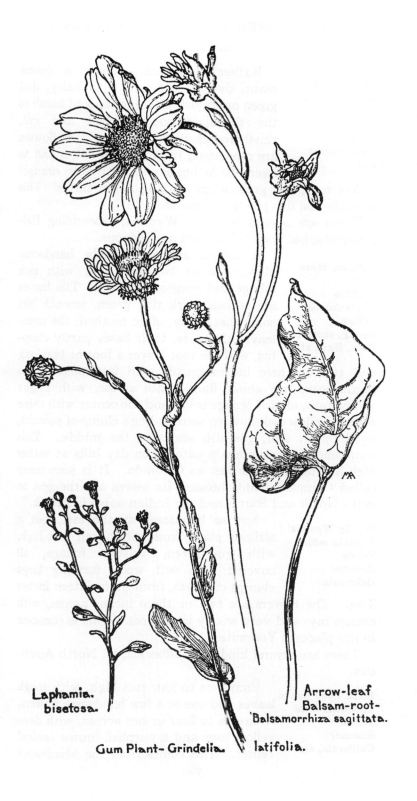

Laphamia.
bisetosa.

Arrow-leaf
Balsam-root-
Balsamorrhiza sagittata.

Gum Plant- Grindelia.   latifolia.

SUNFLOWER FAMILY. *Compositae:*

Balsam-root
Balsamorrhiza Hóokeri
Yellow
Spring
West, except Ariz.

Rather handsome, though a coarse plant, over a foot tall, with hairy, dull green or grayish leaves, crisp and harsh to the touch, variously lobed and cut, chiefly in a clump at the root. The flowers are numerous, from an inch and a half to over two inches across, with deep orange-yellow rays, and grow singly on long flower-stalks. This flourishes on dry plains and mesas.

There are several kinds of Wyethia, resembling Balsam-roots, but their thick roots not resinous.

Yellows, Mule-ears
Wyéthia amplexicáulis
Yellow
Spring, summer
Utah, Nev., etc.

A robust and exceedingly handsome plant, one or two feet tall, with rich foliage and gorgeous flowers. The leaves are stiffish, dark rich green, smooth but somewhat sticky, often toothed; the stem-leaves alternate, their bases partly clasping, and the root-leaves a foot or two long and two or three inches broad, with leaf-stalks. The flower-heads are about four inches across, with bright yellow rays, almost orange color, and the center with three rows of yellow disk-flowers, surrounding a clump of pointed, overlapping, stiff, greenish scales in the middle. This sometimes forms immense patches on dry hills at rather high altitudes, as far east as Colorado. It is sometimes called Compass Plant, because its leaves are thought to point North and South, and the Indian name is "Pe-ik."

Woolly Wyethia
Wyéthia móllis
Yellow
Summer
California

Not so handsome as the last, but a striking plant, from one to four feet high, with gray-green, velvety foliage, all covered with soft wool, forming large clumps of leaves, from six to fifteen inches long. The flowers are two or three inches across, with orange rays and very woolly involucres. This is common in dry places in Yosemite.

There are several kinds of Rudbeckia, all North American.

Black Eyed Susan
Rudbéckia hírta
Yellow
Summer
California, etc.

From one to four feet high, with rough leaves and one or a few handsome flowers, from one to four inches across, with deep yellow rays and a purplish-brown conical center. This comes from the Mississippi

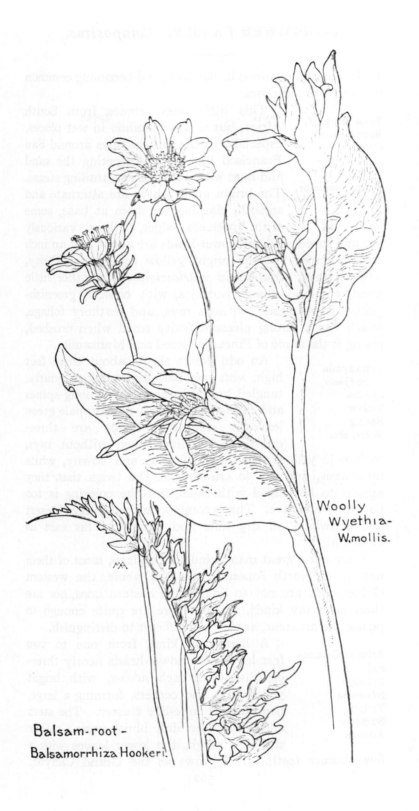

Woolly
Wyethia-
W. mollis.

MA

Balsam-root -
Balsamorrhiza Hookeri.

Valley, is very common in the East, and becoming common in Yosemite meadows.

Brass Buttons, Butter-heads
Cótula coronopifólia
Yellow
Spring, summer, autumn
Cal., Oreg.

This little weed comes from South Africa, but is now common in wet places, especially in the salt marshes around San Francisco Bay, often carpeting the sand and mud with its succulent, trailing stems. The bright green leaves are alternate and smooth, clasping the stem at base, some with toothless edges, others variously cut and lobed, and the flower-heads are about half an inch or less across, like the bright yellow center of a Daisy, without rays. *Matricària matricarioìdes* is another little weed, common along roadsides, with conical, greenish-yellow flower-heads, without rays, and feathery foliage, which has a strong pleasant fruity smell when crushed, giving it the name of Pineapple-weed and Manzanilla.

Tetradymia
Tetradỳmia spinòsa
Yellow
Spring
West, etc.

An odd desert shrub, about three feet high, with gray bark and crooked, gnarly, tangled branches, armed with long spines and clothed with small, downy, pale green leaves. The flower-heads are three-quarters of an inch long, without rays, with pale yellow tube-shaped flowers and downy, white involucres, and are so crowded on the twigs that they appear to be loaded with them, but the coloring is too pale to be effective. This is common in the Mohave Desert and elsewhere on dry hills and plains, as far east as Colorado.

There are a great many kinds of Solidago, most of them natives of North America. On the whole, the western Golden-rods are not so fine as the eastern ones, nor are there so many kinds, though there are quite enough to puzzle the amateur, as they are difficult to distinguish.

Arizona Golden-rod
Solidàgo trinervàta
Yellow
Summer
Arizona

A handsome kind, from one to two feet high, with flower-heads nearly three-eighths of an inch across, with bright yellow rays and centers, forming a large, handsome, plume-like cluster. The stem and leaves are dull bluish-green, rather stiff and rough, the lower leaves with a few obscure teeth. This grows at the Grand Canyon.

Tetradimia spinosa.

Arizona Golden-rod-
Solidago trinervata.

Brass Buttons-
Cotula coronopifolia.

S. occidentàlis, Western Golden-rod, is smooth all over, with leafy stems, from three to five feet tall, toothless leaves, and flat-topped clusters of small, yellow, sweet-scented flowers. This grows in marshes and along the banks of streams, in California, Oregon, and Washington, blooming in summer and autumn. *S. Califórnica,* California Golden-rod, is from two to four feet high, with grayish-green, roughish leaves, the lower ones toothed, and small yellow flowers, forming dense pyramidal clusters, from four to thirteen inches long. This grows on dry plains and hillsides and in the mountains, throughout California and in Oregon, blooming in the autumn. It is called Orojo de Leabre by the Spanish-Californians.

There are probably over a thousand different kinds of Senecio, very widely distributed. The name is from the Latin for "old man," in allusion to the long white hairs of the pappus, when "gone to seed." Our kinds have many common names, such as Groundsel, Ragwort, and Squaw-weed.

Ragwort
Senècio perplèxus
var. dispar
Yellow
Spring, summer
Utah, Idaho

A conspicuous plant and quite hand-some, though its flowers are rather untidy-looking, for, like many other Senecios, the rays do not come out evenly. It is about two feet high, with a stout, hollow, ridged stem, sparsely woolly, and dark green, thickish leaves, with shallow and uneven teeth and covered with sparse, fine, white woolly hairs, as if partially rubbed off. The flowers are over an inch across, with bright yellow rays, curling back in fading, an orange center, fading to brown, and the bracts of the involucre tipped with black. This grows in moist rich soil, in mountain valleys.

Creek Senecio
Serècio Douglàsii
Yellow
Spring, summer,
autumn
Southwest

A handsome bush, about three feet high, covered with many flowers, on slender flower-stalks, sticking up out of a mass of rather delicate foliage, which is often covered with white cottony wool. The flowers are an inch and three-quarters across, with bright light yellow, rather untidy rays and yellow centers. This grows in dry stream beds and on warm slopes in the foothills.

Creek Senecio—
S. Douglasii.

Squaw-weed—
S. perplexus
var dispar.

SUNFLOWER FAMILY. *Compositae.*

Senècio Lémmoni
Yellow
Spring
Arizona

This is quite effective, with attractive flowers and foliage, growing among rocks on hillsides and forming large clumps over a foot high. The stems are slender and often much bent, the leaves are dark green and thin in texture with toothed edges, rolled back, and the numerous flowers are an inch across, with bright yellow rays and deep yellow centers. This plant blossoms both as an annual and as a perennial.

White Squaw-
weed
Senècio cordàtus
White
Summer
Northwest

A rather handsome plant, with a stout stem, about two feet tall; the upper leaves more or less downy and the root-leaves rather thick and soft, covered with whitish hairs on the under side. The flower-heads are about three-quarters of an inch across, with a fuzzy, pale yellow center and white rays. This grows in open woods, at rather high altitudes.

Senècio Riddéllii
Yellow
Spring, winter
Arizona

A rather showy plant, from six inches to two feet tall, blossoming both as an annual and as a biennial, after which it dies. The whole plant is smooth and the foliage is green or bluish-green, rather delicate and pretty. The flowers are an inch to an inch and a half across and they begin to appear in winter when there is little else to brighten the desert mesas. This plant is abundant in valley lands, though it has a wide range.

S. multilobàtus
Yellow
Summer
Ariz., Utah, etc.

A rather pretty plant, about a foot tall, with a few small leaves on the slightly woolly stem, but most of them in a rosette at the base. They are smooth, thickish and slightly stiff, about an inch and a half long, and neatly cut into small, toothed lobes. The few flowers are in a loose cluster at the top of the stem and have heads about three-quarters of an inch across, with pale yellow rays and brighter yellow centers. This grows at the Grand Canyon and on the dry plains of Utah and Colorado, at altitudes of about seven thousand feet.

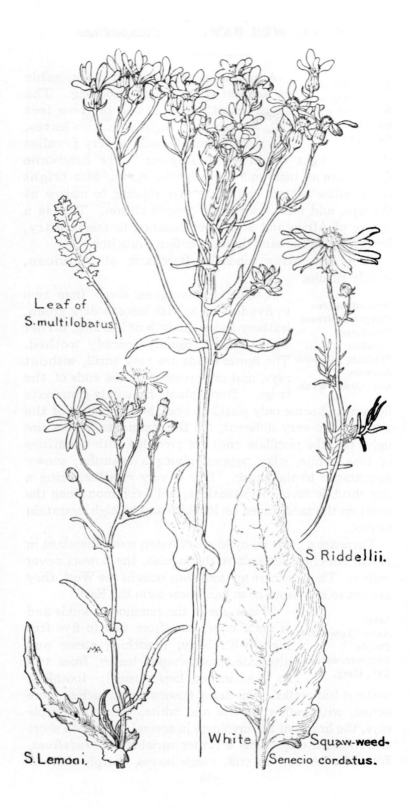

Leaf of
S.multilobatus

S Riddellii.

S.Lemoni.

White
Squaw-weed-
Senecio cordatus.

SUNFLOWER FAMILY. *Compositae.*

African Senecio
Senècio élegans
White and mauve
Spring
California
A handsome plant, which is noticeable on account of its unusual coloring. The stout, smooth stem is two or three feet tall, with smooth, slightly thickish leaves, the margins rolled back, a very peculiar shade of light bright yellowish-green. The handsome flowers are an inch and three-eighths across, with bright deep yellow centers and white rays shading to mauve at the tips, and form a large flat-topped cluster. This is a native of Africa and is not yet common in this country, but grows on the sand dunes near San Francisco.

There are many kinds of Baccharis, all American, chiefly shrubs.

Groundsel-tree
Chaparral Broom
Báccharis
pilulàris
Whitish, yellowish
Autumn
Cal., Oreg., Wash.
A branching evergreen shrub, from two to five feet high, with smooth dark green, leathery leaves, an inch or less long, rather wedge-shaped, usually coarsely toothed. The flower-heads are very small, without rays, and are crowded at the ends of the twigs. Some plants have only staminate flowers and some only pistillate ones, and the effect of the two sorts is very different, for the staminate flowers are ugly, but the pistillate ones are provided with quantities of long, white, silky pappus, giving a beautiful, snowy appearance to the shrub. This is very variable, being a fine shrub in favorable situations, and is common along the coast on the sand dunes, on low hills and on high mountain slopes.

There are a great many kinds of Aster, most abundant in North America, difficult to distinguish, the flowers never yellow. Though there are some fine ones in the West, they are not so numerous or so handsome as in the East.

Aster
Áster Chamissónis
Purple
Summer, autumn
Cal., Oreg.
This is one of the commonest kinds and is quite handsome, from two to five feet high, with leafy, branching stems and alternate, lance-shaped leaves, from two to five inches long, usually toothless, without leaf-stalks. The many flowers are an inch or more across, with yellow centers and white, violet, or purple rays, the bracts of the involucre in several rows, with short and rounded tips. This is rather variable. *A. radulìnus,* Broad-leaf Aster, has stiff, rough leaves, sharply toothed

568

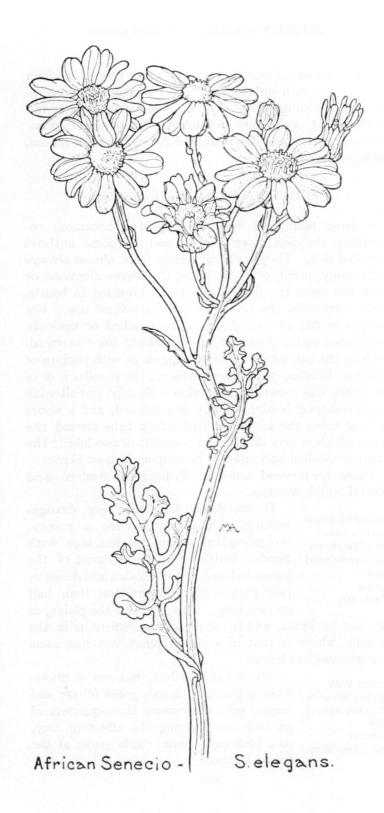

African Senecio — S. elegans.

---

towards the broad tips, and usually many flowers, an inch
or so across, with whitish rays. This is rather common on
dry hills in California and Oregon, blooming in summer and
autumn. *A. Andersóni*, of Yosemite, has toothless, grass-
like root-leaves and one beautiful flower, an inch across,
with purple rays.

CHICORY FAMILY. *Cicoriaceae.*

A large family, of wide geographic distribution, resembling the Sunflower Family and by some authors
included in it. They are herbs, rarely trees, almost always
with milky, acrid, or bitter juice; the leaves alternate or
from the root; the flowers small and crowded in heads,
with involucres, the bracts in one or several rows; the
receptacle flat or flattish, sometimes naked or smooth,
sometimes scaly, pitted or honeycombed; the flowers all
perfect; the calyx-tube without pappus, or with pappus of
scales or bristles, sometimes feathery; the corollas not of
two sorts, like those of the Sunflower Family, but all with
a strap-shaped border, usually five-toothed, and a short
or long tube; the anthers united into a tube around the
style, which is very slender and two-cleft or two-lobed; the
ovary one-celled and inferior, developing into an akene.

There are several kinds of Ptiloria, of western and
central North America.

Flowering-straw
*Ptilòria pauci-
flòra (Stephano-
meria runcinata)*
Pink
Spring
West, etc.
In the desert this is a very strange-
looking, pale plant, forming a scanty,
straggling bush, about two feet high, with
slender, brittle, gray stems, most of the
leaves reduced to mere scales, and delicate,
pale pinkish-lilac flowers, less than half
an inch long. This grows on the plains, as
far east as Texas, and is not always so leafless as in the
picture, which is that of a desert plant, but has some
coarsely-toothed leaves.

Desert Pink
*Ptilòria Wrìghtii
(Stephanomeria)*
Pink
Summer
Ariz., New Mex.
Much like the last, but not a queer-
looking plant, with pale green foliage and
larger, prettier flowers, three-quarters of
an inch long, giving the effect of tiny,
pale pink carnations. This grows at the
Grand Canyon.

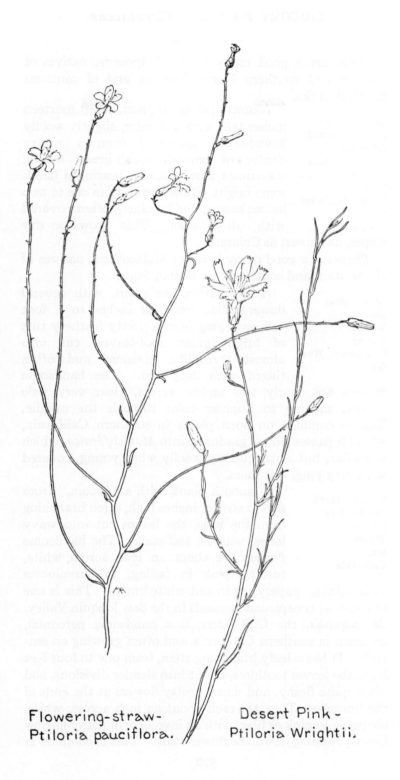

Flowering-straw-
Ptiloria pauciflora.

Desert Pink -
Ptiloria Wrightii.

CHICORY FAMILY. *Cicoriaceae.*

There are a good many kinds of Agoseris, natives of western and southern North America and of southern South America.

**Goat Chicory,
Large-flowered
Agoseris**
Agóseris glàuca
**Yellow
Spring
Utah, Ida., Wash.,
etc.**

A pretty perennial plant, about fourteen inches tall, with a slender, slightly woolly flower-stem, springing from a pretty cluster of smooth bluish-green leaves, sometimes toothless, and bearing a handsome bright yellow flower, from one to two inches across, the involucre often covered with white wool. This grows on dry slopes, as far east as Colorado.

There are a good many kinds of Malacothrix, natives of the western and southwestern United States.

*Malácothrix
glabràta*
**Yellow
Spring
Southwest, Nev.,
Utah**

A very attractive plant, with several flower-stalks, from six inches to a foot tall, springing from a pretty feathery tuft of bright green root-leaves, cut into almost threadlike divisions and often tinged with deep red. The handsome flowers are nearly two inches across, clear very pale yellow, shading to brighter color towards the middle. This is common on open plains in southern California, where it passes almost gradually into *M. Califórnica*, which is similar, but conspicuously woolly when young, covered with very long, soft hairs.

Snake's Head
*Malácothrix
Còulteri*
**White
Spring
California**

A smooth plant, with a "bloom," from five to sixteen inches high, often branching from the base, the leaves cut into wavy lobes, with no leaf-stalk. The handsome flowers are about an inch across, white, turning pink in fading, the involucres with shining, papery, green and white bracts. This is one of the most conspicuous annuals in the San Joaquin Valley. *M. saxàtilis*, the Cliff Aster, is a handsome perennial, common in southern California and often growing on sea-cliffs. It has a leafy branching stem, from one to four feet high, the leaves toothless, or cut into slender divisions, and often quite fleshy, and many pretty flowers at the ends of the branches. They are each about an inch across, white, changing to pink or lilac, with an involucre of many narrow bracts, running down the flower-stalk. This is common in

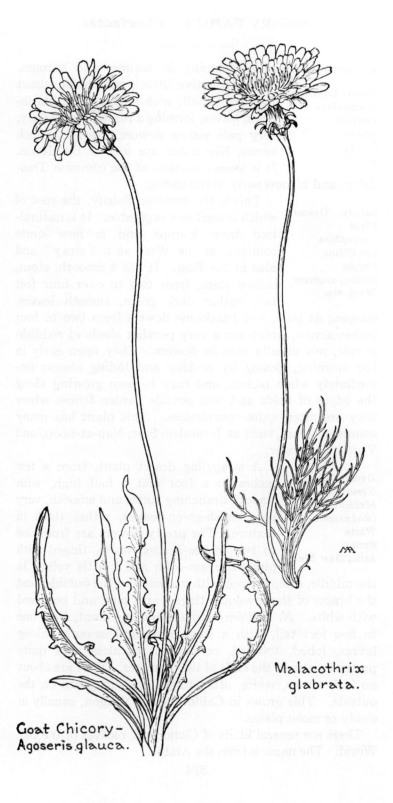

Malacothrix
glabrata.

Goat Chicory—
Agoseris glauca.

CHICORY FAMILY. *Cicoriaceae.*

southern California, blooming in summer and autumn.

Desert Dandelion
Malácothrix
Féndleri
Yellow
Spring
Arizona

An attractive little desert plant, about five inches tall, with stiffish, pale bluish-green leaves, forming a rosette, and pretty, very pale yellow flowers, nearly an inch across, like a delicate sort of Dandelion. It is a near relation of the common Dandelion and blooms early in the spring.

Salsify, Oyster
Plant
Tragopògon
porrifòlius
Purple
Spring, summer
West, etc.

This is the common Salsify, the root of which is used as a vegetable. It is naturalized from Europe and is now quite common in the West as a "stray" and also in the East. It has a smooth, stout, hollow stem, from two to over four feet tall, rather dark green, smooth leaves, clasping at base, and handsome flowers from two to four inches across, which are a very peculiar shade of reddish-purple, not usually seen in flowers. They open early in the morning, closing by midday and fading almost immediately when picked, and may be seen growing along the edges of fields and just outside garden fences where they are often quite conspicuous. This plant has many common names, such as Jerusalem Star, Nap-at-noon, and Vegetable Oyster.

Desert Chicory
Nemosèris Neo-
Mexicàna
(Rafinesquia)
White
Spring
Ariz., New Mex.

A straggling desert plant, from a few inches to a foot and a half high, with smooth branching stems and smooth, very pale bluish-green leaves, rather thick in texture. The pretty flowers are from one to two inches across, white, tinged with pink or cream-color and a little yellow in the middle, often striped with magenta on the outside, and the bracts of the involucre tinged with pink and bordered with white. *N. Califórnica* is a branching plant, from one to five feet tall, with a stout stem and smooth oblcng leaves, lobed, toothed, or almost toothless, and quite pretty flowers at the ends of the branches. They are about an inch across, white, often tinged with magenta on the outside. This grows in California and Oregon, usually in shady or moist places.

There are several kinds of Cichorium, natives of the Old World. The name is from the Arabic.

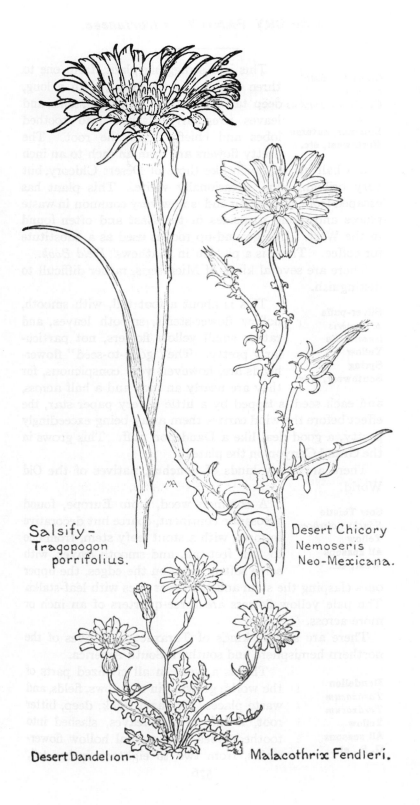

Salsify–
Tragopogon
porrifolius.

Desert Chicory
Nemoseris
Neo-Mexicana.

Desert Dandelion–

Malacothrix Fendleri.

CHICORY FAMILY. *Cicoriaceae.*

Chicory, Blue Sailors
Cichòrium Íntybus
Blue
Summer, autumn
Northwest, etc.

This is a straggling plant, from one to three feet tall, a perennial, with a long, deep tap-root, stiff, branching stems, and leaves irregularly slashed into toothed lobes and chiefly from the root. The pretty flowers are from an inch to an inch and a half across, much like those of Desert Chicory, but very brilliant blue, occasionally white. This plant has escaped from cultivation and is now very common in waste places and along roadsides in the East and often found in the West. The ground-up root is used as a substitute for coffee. There is a picture in Mathews' *Field Book*.

There are several kinds of Microseris, rather difficult to distinguish.

Silver-puffs
Microsèris linearifòlia
Yellow
Spring
Southwest, Nev.

This is about a foot tall, with smooth, hollow flower-stems, smooth leaves, and rather small yellow flowers, not particularly pretty. The "gone-to-seed" flower-heads are, however, very conspicuous, for they are nearly an inch and a half across, and each seed is tipped by a little silvery paper star, the effect before the wind carries them away being exceedingly pretty, a good deal like a Dandelion puff. This grows in the Grand Canyon on the plateau.

There are many kinds of Sonchus, natives of the Old World.

Sow Thistle
Sónchus oleràceus
Yellow
All seasons
West, etc.

A common weed, from Europe, found across the continent, coarse but decorative in form, with a stout leafy stem, from one to four feet tall, and smooth leaves, with some soft prickles on the edges, the upper ones clasping the stem and the lower ones with leaf-stalks. The pale yellow flowers are three-quarters of an inch or more across.

There are several kinds of Taraxacum, natives of the northern hemisphere and southern South America.

Dandelion
Taráxacum Taráxacum
Yellow
All seasons
U. S., etc.

This is a weed in all civilized parts of the world, growing in meadows, fields, and waste places. It has a thick, deep, bitter root, a tuft of root-leaves, slashed into toothed lobes, and several hollow flower-stalks, from two to eighteen inches tall,

576

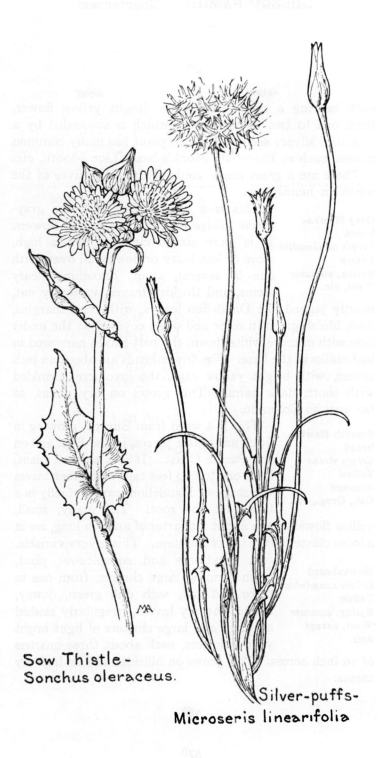

Sow Thistle -
Sonchus oleraceus.

Silver-puffs -
Microseris linearifolia

each bearing a single, handsome, bright yellow flower, from one to two inches across, which is succeeded by a beautiful silvery seed puff. This plant has many common names, such as Blow-ball, Monk's-head, Lion's-tooth, etc.

There are a great many kinds of Crepis, natives of the northern hemisphere.

Gray Hawks-beard
Crèpis occidentàlis
Yellow
Spring, summer
West, etc.

This is a pretty plant, for the gray-green foliage sets off the yellow flowers. It is from six to eighteen inches high, more or less hairy or downy all over, with one or several, stout, branching, leafy stems, and thickish leaves, variously cut, mostly jagged like Dandelion leaves, with crisp margins, dark bluish-green in color and often covered on the under side with obscure white down, the root-leaves narrowed to leaf-stalks at the base. The flower-heads are about an inch across, with bright yellow rays, the involucre sprinkled with short, dark hairs. This grows on dry plains, as far east as Colorado.

Smooth Hawks-beard
Crèpis vìrens
Yellow
Summer
Cal., Oreg., etc.

This is a weed from Europe, growing in fields and waste places, in the East and on the Pacific Coast. It is a smooth plant, from one to two feet tall, with green leaves the shape of Dandelion leaves, chiefly in a bunch at the root. The many, small, yellow flowers, each about a quarter of an inch long, are in a loose cluster at the top of the stem. This is very variable.

Hawksbeard
Crèpis acuminàta
Yellow
Spring, summer
West, except Ariz.

A handsome and conspicuous plant, often forming large clumps, from one to three feet tall, with dull green, downy, rather leathery leaves, irregularly slashed and cut, and large clusters of light bright yellow flowers, each about three-quarters of an inch across. This grows on hillsides and on high dry mesas.

Gray Hawksbeard-
C.occidentalis.

Hawksbeard- Crepis acuminata.

INDEX.

Abronia, 102.
Abronia latifolia, 106.
Abronia maritima, 104.
Abronia salsa, 104.
Abronia umbellata, 104.
Abronia villosa, 104.
Achlys triphylla, 156.
Aconitum, 136.
Aconitum Columbianum, 136.
Actaea, 140.
Actaea arguta, 140.
Actaea viridiflora, 140.
Actinolepis lanosa, 554.
Adam and Eve, 28.
Adder's tongue, 28.
Adenostoma, 228.
Adenostoma fasciculatum, 228.
Adenostoma sparsifolium, 228.
Aesculus, 280.
Aesculus Californica, 280.
Agastache, 454.
Agastache pallidiflora, 456.
Agastache urticifolia, 456.
Agoseris, 572.
Agoseris glauca, 572.
Agoseris, Large-flowered, 572.
Aizoaceae, 108.
Alfalfa, 242.
Alfilerilla, 276.
Alismaceae, 2.
Allionia, 106.
Allionia linearis, 106.
Allium, 14.
Allium acuminatum, 14.
Allium bisceptrum, 14.
Allium serratum, 14.
Allotropa virgata, 360.
Alpine Avens, 232.
Alsine, 118.
Alsine longipes, 118.
Alumroot, 200, 202.
Amapola, 164.
Amaranthus albus, 98.
Amelanchier, 214.
Amelanchier alnifolia, 216.
Amole, 12.
Amsinckia, 426.
Amsinckia intermedia, 428.
Anagallis, 362.
Anagallis arvensis, 362.
Anaphalis, 526.
Anaphalis margaritacea, 526.
Anemone, 142, 144.
Anemone deltoidea, 144.
Anemone occidentalis, 146.
Anemone parviflora, 144.
Anemone quinquefolia var. Grayi,
    144.

Anemone sphenophylla, 144.
Anemone, Canyon, 144.
Anemone, Northern, 144.
Anemone, Three-leaved, 144.
Anemone, Western, 146.
Anemone, Wood, 144.
Anemopsis Californica, 80.
Angels' Trumpets, 460.
Anisolotus, 242.
Anisolotus argyraeus, 242.
Anisolotus decumbens, 244.
Anisolotus formosissimus, 242.
Anisolotus glaber, 244.
Anisolotus strigosus, 244.
Anisolotus Wrightii, 244.
Anogra, 328.
Anogra albicaulis, 328.
Anogra coronopifolia, 328.
Antennaria rosea, 526.
Anthemis, 546.
Anthemis Cotula, 546.
Anthericum, 4.
Anthericum Torreyi, 4.
Antirrhinum, 468.
Antirrhinum Coulterianum, 468.
Antirrhinum glandulosum, 468.
Antirrhinum maurandioides, 466.
Antirrhinum strictum, 470.
Antirrhinum vagans, 470.
Antirrhinum virga, 468.
Apache Plume, 218.
Aplopappus Brandegei, 534.
Apocynaceae, 378.
Apocynum, 378.
Apocynum androsaemifolium,
    378.
Apple Family, 214.
Apple, 214.
Aquilegia, 134.
Aquilegia leptocera, 134.
Aquilegia truncata, 134.
Arabis, 176.
Arabis Fendleri, 176.
Arabis, Fendler's, 176.
Arctostaphylos, 344.
Arctostaphylos bicolor, 346.
Arctostaphylos patula, 346.
Arctostaphylos Uva-Ursi, 346.
Arenaria, 112.
Arenaria Fendleri, 112.
Argemone, 162.
Argemone hispida, 162.
Argentina, 232.
Argentina Anserina, 232.
Aristolochiaceae, 84.
Arnica, 544.
Arnica cordifolia, 544.
Arnica latifolia, 544.

Arnica, Broad-leaved, 544.
Arnica, Heart-leaved, 544.
Arrowhead, 2.
Arrow-leaf, 558.
Artemisia, 544.
Artemisia tridentata, 544.
Aruncus, 226.
Aruncus sylvester, 226.
Asarum Hartwegi, 84.
Asclepiadaceae, 374.
Asclepias, 374, 376.
Asclepias erosa, 376.
Asclepias speciosa, 374.
Asclepias vestita var. Mohavensis, 376.
Asclepiodora, 376.
Asclepiodora decumbens, 378.
Ash, Flowering, 366.
Aster, 532, 542, 544, 556, 568.
Aster Andersoni, 570.
Aster Chamissonis, 568.
Aster radulinus, 568.
Aster, Beach, 534.
Aster, Broad-leaf, 568.
Aster, Cliff, 572.
Aster, Hairy Golden, 530.
Aster, Tall Purple, 556.
Aster, Woolly, 542.
Astragalus, 256.
Astragalus MacDougali, 260.
Astragalus Menziesii, 256.
Astragalus nothoxys, 258.
Astragalus pomonensis, 258.
Astragalus Utahensis, 258.
Atragene, 150.
Atragene occidentalis, 150.
Audibertia, 438, 440, 442.
Aulospermum longipes, 336.
Azalea, 342.
Azalea occidentalis, 342.
Azalea, Small, 348.
Azalea, Western, 342.
Azaleastrum, 348.
Azaleastrum albiflorum, 348.
Azulea, 70.

Baby Blue-eyes, 412.
Baccharis, 568.
Baccharis pilularis, 568.
Baeria, 550.
Baeria gracilis, 550.
Baeria macrantha, 550.
Bahia, 552.
Bahia absinthifolia, 552.
Baileya multiradiata, 552.
Baileya pauciradiata, 552.
Balm, 456.
Balm, Mountain, 420.
Balsam-root, 558, 560.
Balsam-root, Cut-leaved, 558.
Balsamorrhiza, 558.
Balsamorrhiza Hookeri, 560.
Balsamorrhiza macrophylla, 558.
Balsamorrhiza sagittata, 558.
Baneberry, 140.
Barberry Family, 152.
Barberry, 154.
Barberry, Trailing, 154.
Barrenwort, 152.
Bean, 242.

Bearberry, Red.
Bear's Cabbage, 418.
Bear-clover, 222.
Bear Grass, 44.
Bear-mat, 222.
Beard-tongue, 478, 480.
Beard-tongue, Bushy, 482.
Beard-tongue, Large, 478.
Bedstraw, Northern, 508.
Beech-drops, Albany, 360.
Bee-plant, 188.
Bee-plant, California, 490.
Beet, 98.
Belladonna, 458.
Bellflower Family, 520.
Bellflower, 520.
Betony, Alpine, 504.
Berberidaceae, 152.
Berberis, 154.
Berberis aquifolium, 154.
Berberis Fendleri, 154.
Berberis repens, 154.
Bergamot, 456.
Berry, Salmon, 236, 238.
Berry, Thimble, 238.
Bicuculla, 168.
Bicuculla chrysantha, 170.
Bicuculla formosa, 168.
Bicuculla uniflora, 170.
Big Root, 558.
Bilberry, 348.
Bird's Eyes, 394.
Bird-foot, 242, 244.
Bird-foot, Pretty, 242.
Bird-of-paradise, 264.
Birthroot, 42.
Birthwort Family, 84.
Biscutella, 178.
Bishop's Cap, 204.
Bisnaga, 306.
Blackberry, 236.
Blackberry, Common, 236.
Black-eyed Susan, 560.
Bladder-bush, 448.
Bladder-cherry, 460.
Bladderpod, 184, 190.
Bladderpod, White, 184.
Bladderpod, Yellow, 184.
Blanket-flower, 556.
Blazing Star, 300.
Bleeding Heart Family, 168.
Bleeding Heart, 168.
Blepharipappus, 536, 554.
Blepharipappus elegans, 554.
Blepharipappus glandulosus, 554.
Bloomeria, 22.
Bloomeria aurea, 22.
Bloomeria Clevelandi, 22.
Blow-ball, 578.
Bluebell, Mountain, 430.
Blue Bells of Scotland, 520.
Blueberry, 348.
Blue-curls, 454.
Blue-curls, Woolly, 454.
Blue Dicks, 16.
Blue-eyes, Baby, 412.
Blue-eyed Grass, 70.
Blue-lips, 488.
Blue Sailors, 576.
Blue-weed, 136.

Blue Witch, 462.
Boraginaceae, 422.
Borage Family, 422.
Borage, 402.
Bottle-plant, 90.
Bouvardia, Wild, 400.
Brass Buttons, 562.
Brassica, 184.
Brassica nigra, 184.
Brevoortia, Ida-Maia, 26.
Brittle-bush, 526.
Brodiaea, 16.
Brodiaea capitata, 16.
Brodiaea capitata var. pauciflora, 16.
Brodiaea coccinea, 26.
Brodiaea congesta, 16.
Brodiaea Douglasii, 24.
Brodiaea grandiflora, 18.
Brodiaea lactea, 24.
Brodiaea minor, 18.
Brodiaea volubilis, 20.
Brodiaea, Golden, 22.
Brodiaea, Harvest, 18, 24.
Brodiaea, Twining, 20.
Brodiaea, White, 24.
Bronze Bells, 38.
Brooklime, American, 476.
Broom, Chaparral, 568.
Broom, Scotch, 264.
Broom-rape Family, 504.
Brown-foot, 536.
Brown-weed, 536.
Brunella, 444.
Brussels Sprouts, 184.
Bryanthus, 352.
Buck-bean Family, 380.
Buck-bean, 246, 380.
Buckbrush, 282.
Buckeye Family, 280.
Buckeye, California, 280.
Buckthorn Family, 282.
Buckthorn Weed, 428.
Buckwheat Bush, 94.
Buckwheat Family, 86.
Buckwheat, Wild, 96.
Buena Mujer, 302.
Bugbane, False, 142.
Bunchberry, 340.
Butter Balls, 92.
Buttercup Family, 126.
Buttercup, 38, 234.
Buttercup, Common Western, 126.
Butter-heads, 562.
Butterfly-tongue, 504.
Butterfly Tulip, 62.

Cabbage, 184.
Cactaceae, 304.
Cactus Family, 304.
Cactus, 310.
Cactus Grahami, 310.
Cactus, Barrel, 306.
Cactus, Column, 310.
Cactus, Fish-hook, 306.
Cactus, Hedgehog, 306.
Cactus, Pincushion, 310.
Calabazilla, 518.
Calliandra, 266.

Calliandra eriophylla, 266.
Calochortus, 56.
Calochortus albus, 58.
Calochortus amabilis, 56.
Calochortus Benthami, 60.
Calochortus Kennedyi, 64.
Calochortus luteus, 62.
Calochortus luteus var. citrinus, 62.
Calochortus luteus var. oculatus, 62.
Calochortus Maweanus, 60.
Calochortus nudus, 60.
Calochortus Nuttallii, 64.
Calochortus venustus, 62.
Caltha, 146.
Caltha leptosepala, 146.
Caltha palustris, 146.
Caltrop Family, 268.
Calycanthaceae, 158.
Calycanthus, 158.
Calycanthus occidentalis, 158.
Calyptridium, 124.
Camass, 48.
Camass, Death, 8, 48.
Camassia, 48.
Camassia quamash, 48.
Campanulaceae, 520.
Campanula, 520.
Campanula prenanthoides, 520.
Campanula rotundifolia, 520.
Campanula Scouleri, 520.
Camphor Weed, 454.
Campion, Moss, 114.
Cancer-root, One-flowered, 504.
Canchalagua, 370.
Candle Flower, 294.
Candle, Our Lord's 40.
Candytuft, 174.
Candytuft, Wild, 178.
Canterbury Bell, Wild, 408.
Caper Family, 186.
Caper, 186.
Capnoides, 170.
Capnoides aureum, 172.
Capnoides Scouleri, 172.
Capparidaceae, 186.
Caprifoliaceae, 512.
Cardinal Flower, 482.
Carduus, 522.
Carduus Arizonicus, 524.
Carduus Californicus, 524.
Carduus candadissimus, 524.
Carduus Coulteri, 522.
Carduus occidentalis, 524.
Carduus ochrocentrus, 524.
Carolina Allspice, 158.
Carpet-weed Family, 108.
Carrot, 332.
Caryophyllaceae, 112.
Cassiaceae, 264.
Cassia, 264.
Cassia armata, 266.
Cassia, Golden, 266.
Cassiope, 354.
Cassiope Mertensiana, 354.
Castilleja, 470.
Castilleja angustifolia, 472.
Castilleja miniata, 472.
Castilleja pinetorum, 472.

Catchfly, 112.
Cat's Breeches, 418.
Cat's-clover, 242.
Cauliflower, 184.
Cavalier's Spur, 128.
Ceanothus, 282.
Ceanothus integerrimus, 284.
Ceanothus parvifolius, 284.
Ceanothus prostratus, 282.
Ceanothus velutinus, 282.
Centaurium, 370, 372.
Centaury, California, 370.
Centaury, Tall, 372.
Cephalanthera, 72.
Cephalanthera Austinae, 72.
Cerastium, 118.
Cerastium arvense, 118.
Cereus, 310.
Cereus giganteus, 310.
Chaenactis, 548.
Chaenactis Douglasii, 548.
Chaenactis Fremontii, 548.
Chaenactis lanosa, 548.
Chaenactis macrantha, 548.
Chamaebatia foliolosa, 222.
Chamaebatiaria, 230.
Chamaebatiaria millefolium, 230.
Chamaenerion, 314.
Chamaenerion angustifolium, 314.
Chamaenerion latifolium, 314.
Chamise, 228.
Chamomile, 546.
Chatter-box, 74.
Checkerberry, 340, 356.
Checker-bloom, 288.
Chenopodiaceae, 96.
Cherry, 216.
Cherry, Holly-leaved, 216.
Chia, 452.
Chickweed, 112.
Chickweed, Field, 118.
Chickweed, Mouse-ear, 118.
Chickweed, Tall, 118.
Chicorium, 574.
Chicorium Intybus, 576.
Chicory Family, 570.
Chicory, 576.
Chicory, Desert, 574.
Chicory, Goat, 572.
Chilicothe, 518.
Chimaphila, 356.
Chimaphila Menziesii, 356.
Chinese Houses, 488.
Chinese Pusley, 432.
Chlorogalum pomeridianum, 12.
Cholla, 308.
Chorizanthe, 86.
Chorizanthe fimbriata, 86.
Chorizanthe staticoides, 86.
Christmas-horns, 132.
Christmas-rose, 138.
Chrysanthemum, 540.
Chrysanthemum leucanthemum, 540.
Chrysopsis villosa, 530.
Chylisma, 326.
Chylisma scapoidea var. clavae-formis, 326.
Cicoriaceae, 570.
Cinquefoil, 126, 234.

Cinquefoil, Arctic, 234.
Cinquefoil, Silky, 234.
Cinquefoil, Shrubby, 234.
Cirsium, 522.
Cistaceae, 304.
Clarkia, 320, 322.
Clarkia concinna, 322.
Clarkia elegans, 320.
Clarkia pulchella, 322.
Clarkia rhomboidea, 322.
Claytonia, 120, 122.
Claytonia lanceolata, 122.
Cleavers, 508.
Cleistoyucca, 40.
Cleistoyucca arborescens, 40.
Clematis, 126, 148, 150.
Clematis lasiantha, 148.
Clematis, Lilac, 151.
Clematis, Purple, 150.
Cleome, 188.
Cleome platycarpa, 190.
Cleome serrulata, 188.
Cleome, Yellow, 190.
Cleomella, 186.
Cleomella longipes, 186, 190.
Cliff Rose, 226.
Clintonia, 50.
Clintonia Andrewsiana, 50.
Clintonia uniflora, 50.
Clintonia, Red, 50.
Clintonia, White, 50.
Clocks, 276.
Clover, 242, 260, 262.
Clover, Sour, 262.
Cnicus, 522.
Cogswellia platycarpa, 334.
Coffee, 506.
Coleogyne ramosissima, 230.
Collinsia, 486.
Collinsia bicolor, 488.
Collinsia multiflora, 488.
Collomia, 400.
Collomia grandiflora, 400.
Collomia linearis, 400.
Columbine, Blue, 134.
Columbine, Scarlet, 134.
Columbine, White, 134.
Columbo, 368.
Columbo, Small, 370.
Comandra, 82.
Comandra pallida, 82.
Comandra, Pale, 82.
Compass Plant, 560.
Compositae, 522.
Conanthus, 414.
Conanthus aretioides, 414.
Convolvulaceae, 380.
Convolvulus, 382.
Convolvulus arvensis, 382.
Convolvulus occidentalis, 382.
Copa de Oro, 164.
Coral-root, 76.
Corallorrhiza, 76.
Corallorrhiza Bigelowii, 76.
Corallorrhiza multiflora, 76.
Coreopsis, 540.
Coreopsis Bigelowii, 540.
Coreopsis maritima, 540.
Coreopsis, Desert, 540.
Coreothrogyne, 542.

INDEX

Coreothrogyne filaginifolia, 542.
Cornaceae, 338.
Cornus, 338.
Cornus Canadensis, 340.
Cornus Nuttallii, 338.
Cornus stolonifera var. riparia, 340.
Corn-salad, 508.
Corpse-plant, 358.
Corydalis, 172.
Corydal, Golden, 172.
Corydalis, Pink, 172.
Cotton, Arizona Wild, 286.
Cotula coronopifolia, 562.
Cotyledon, 194.
Covena, 16.
Covillea glutinosa, 268.
Cowania Stansburiana, 226.
Cow-herb, 116.
Cowslip, American, 364.
Crane's-bill, 274.
Crane's-bill, Long-stalked, 276.
Crassina, 552.
Crassina pumila, 552.
Crassulaceae, 192.
Cream-cups, 166.
Creosote-bush, 268.
Crepis, 578.
Crepis acuminata, 578.
Crepis occidentalis, 578.
Crepis virens, 578.
Crimson-beak, 268.
Crocus, 38.
Crown Imperial, 38.
Crowtoes, 242.
Cruciferae, 174.
Cryptanthe, 428.
Cryptanthe intermedia, 428.
Cucurbitaceae, 518.
Cucurbita, 518.
Cucurbita foetidissima, 518.
Cucumber, Wild, 518.
Cudweed, 526.
Currant, Black, 212.
Currant, Buffalo, 214.
Currant, Golden, 214.
Currant, Missouri, 214.
Currant, Sierra, 212.
Cuscuta, 382.
Cyclamen, Wild, 364.
Cycloloma, 98.
Cycloloma atriplicifolium, 98.
Cymopterus, 334, 336.
Cypress, Wild, 394.
Cypripedium, 78.
Cypripedium Californicum, 78.
Cypripedium montanum, 78.
Cypripedium parviflorum, 78.
Cytisus, 264.
Cytisus scoparius, 264.

Dahlia, Sea, 540.
Daisy, 522.
Daisy Dwarf, 554.
Daisy, Easter, 530.
Daisy, Ground, 530.
Daisy, Ox-eye, 540.
Daisy, Seaside, 534.
Daisy, White Mountain, 534.
Daisy, Woolly Yellow, 546.

Dalea, 248.
Dandelion, 576.
Dandelion, Desert, 574.
Dasiphora fruticosa, 234.
Datura, 458.
Datura meteloides, 458.
Datura stramonium, 460.
Datura suaveolens, 460.
Datura, Large-flowered, 458.
Deer-brush, 284.
Deer-foot, 156.
Deer-weed, 244.
Deer's Tongue, 368.
Delphinium, 128.
Delphinium cardinale, 132.
Delphinium bicolor, 130.
Delphinium Hanseni, 128.
Delphinium nudicaule, 132.
Delphinium Parryi, 130.
Delphinium scaposum, 128.
Delphinium variegatum, 132.
Dendromecon, 156.
Dendromecon rigida, 166.
Dentaria, 174.
Dentaria Californica, 174.
Desert Holly, 536.
Desert Star, 548.
Desert Zinnia, 552.
Deutzia, 206.
Dicentra, 168, 170.
Diplacus, 490.
Diplacus longiflorus, 490.
Diplacus puniceus, 490.
Disporum, 54.
Disporum Hookeri, 54.
Disporum trachycarpum, 54.
Dithyrea, 178.
Dithyrea Wislizeni, 178.
Dock, 86, 88.
Dock, Sand, 88.
Dodder, 382.
Dodecatheon, 364.
Dodecatheon Clevelandi, 364.
Dodecatheon Jeffreyi, 364.
Dodecatheon pauciflorum, 366.
Dogbane Family, 378.
Dogbane, Spreading, 378.
Dog Fennel, 546.
Dog-tooth Violet, 28.
Dogwood Family, 338.
Dogwood, Flowering, 338.
Dogwood, Pacific, 338.
Dogwood, Red-osier, 340.
Dormidera, 164.
Drops of Gold, 54.
Drupaceae, 216.
Dryas, 232.
Dryas octopetala, 232.
Dryopetalon runcinatum, 182.
Duck-bill, 502.
Dudleya, 194.
Dudleya Nevadensis, 194.
Dudleya pulverulenta, 194.
Dutchman's Breeches, 168, 172.

Easter Bells, 28, 30.
Echeveria, 194.
Echinocactus, 304.
Echinocactus Wislizeni, 306.
Echinocereus, 306.

Echinocereus polyacanthus, 306.
Echinocystis, 518.
Egg-plant, 458.
Elephants' Heads, 504.
Emmenanthe, 416.
Emmenanthe lutea, 416.
Emmenanthe penduliflora, 418.
Encelia, Californica, 528.
Encelia eriocephala, 526.
Encelia farinosa, 526.
Encelia frutescens, 528.
Encelia, California, 528.
Epilobium, 314, 316.
Epilobium Franciscanum, 316.
Epipactis, 74.
Ericaceae, 340.
Erigeron, 532.
Erigeron aureus, 534.
Erigeron Breweri, 532.
Erigeron compositus, 536.
Erigeron concinnus var. aphan-actis, 532.
Erigeron Coulteri, 534.
Erigeron divergens, 532.
Erigeron flagellaris, 532.
Erigeron glaucus, 534.
Erigeron Philadelphicus, 534.
Erigeron pumilis, 532.
Erigeron salsuginosus, 534.
Erimiastrum bellidoides, 548.
Eriodictyon, 420.
Eriodictyon Californicum, 420.
Eriodictyon tomentosum, 420.
Eriogonum, 90.
Eriogonum Bakeri, 94.
Eriogonum compositum, 92.
Eriogonum elatum, 90.
Eriogonum fasciculatum, 94.
Eriogonum flavum, 94.
Eriogonum incanum, 94.
Eriogonum inflatum, 90.
Eriogonum orthocaulon, 92.
Eriogonum racemosum, 96.
Eriophyllum, 546.
Eriophyllum caespitosum var. integrifolium, 546.
Eriophyllum confertiflorum, 546.
Eriophyllum confertiflorum var. discoideum, 546.
Eriophyllum lanatum, 546.
Erodium, 276.
Erodium cicutarium, 276.
Erodium moschatum, 276.
Erysimum, 176.
Erysimum asperum, 176.
Erysimum asperum var. perenne, 178.
Erysimum capitatum, 178.
Erythraea, 370.
Erythraea Douglasii, 372
Erythraea exaltata, 372.
Erythraea venusta, 370.
Erythronium, 26.
Erythronium grandiflorum, 28.
Erythronium montanum, 28.
Erythronium parviflorum, 28.
Eschscholtzia, 164.
Eschscholtzia Californica, 164.
Escobita, 500.
Espuela del caballero, 128.

Eucharidium, 322.
Eulobus Californicus, 312.
Eulophus Bolanderi, 336.
Evening Primrose Family, 312.
Evening Primrose, 324, 330.
Evening Primrose, Cut-leaved, 328.
Evening Primrose, Prairie, 328.
Evening Primrose, White, 326.
Evening Snow, 388.
Evening Star, 302.
Everlasting, Pearly, 526.
Everlasting, Rosy, 526.

Fabaceae, 242.
Fairy Bells, 54.
Fairy Dusters, 266.
Fallugia paradoxa, 218.
Farewell-to-Spring, 318.
Fendlera, 206.
Fendlera rupicola, 206.
Fern-bush, 230.
Ferula, 334.
Fig-marigold, 110.
Figwort Family, 466.
Fiddle-neck, 428.
Filaree, Red-stem, 276.
Filaree, White-stem, 276.
Fire-cracker Flower, 26.
Fire-weed, 314.
Flag, Western Blue, 66.
Flaming Sword, 294.
Flat-top, 94.
Flax Family, 270.
Flax, Blue, 270.
Fleabane, 532.
Fleabane, Large Mountain, 534.
Fleabane, Philadelphia, 534.
Fleabane, Rayless, 532.
Fleabane, Spreading, 532.
Fleabane, Whip-lash, 532.
Fleabane, Yellow, 534.
Fleur-de-lis, 66.
Floerkia, 278.
Floerkia Douglasii, 278.
Floriponda, 460.
Flower-de-luce, 66.
Flowering-fungus, 360.
Flowering-straw, 570.
Fly Flower, 550.
Forget-me-not, 422, 430.
Forget-me-not, White, 422, 428.
Forget-me-not, Wild, 424.
Fouquieriaceae, 294.
Fouquiera Family, 294.
Fouquiera splendens, 294.
Four-o'clock Family, 100.
Four o'clock, 100.
Four-o'clock, California, 102.
Fragaria, 240.
Fragaria bracteata, 240.
Fragaria Chiloensis, 240.
Frasera, 368.
Frasera nitida, 370.
Frasera speciosa, 368.
Fraxinus, 366.
Fraxinus macropetala, 366.
Friar's cap, 136.
Fried-eggs, 162.
Fringe-bush, 366.

Fritillaria, 38.
Fritillaria atropurpurea, 38.
Fritillaria pudica, 38.
Fritillary, Brown, 38.
Fritillary, Yellow, 38.
Fumariaceae, 168.

Gaillardia, 556.
Gaillardia aristata, 556.
Gaillardia Arizonica, 556.
Gaillardia pinnatifida, 556.
Gaillardia, Arizona, 556.
Galium, 508.
Galium boreale, 508.
Gallito, 300.
Gaultheria, 340, 356.
Gaultheria ovatifolia, 342.
Gaultheria Shallon, 342.
Gayophytum, 316.
Gayophytum eriospermum, 316.
Gentianaceae, 368.
Gentiana, 372.
Gentiana acuta, 372.
Gentiana calycosa, 372.
Gentiana lutea, 372.
Gentiana propinqua, 372.
Gentian Family, 368.
Gentian, 372.
Gentian, Blue, 372.
Gentian, Northern, 372.
Geraniaceae, 274.
Geranium, 274.
Geranium columbinum, 276.
Geranium Fremontii, 274.
Geranium furcatum, 274.
Geranium incisum, 274.
Geranium Family, 274.
Geranium, Wild, 274.
Ghost Tree, 246.
Ghost-flower, 358.
Giant Bird's-nest, 360.
Gilia, 386, 388, 390, 392, 400.
Gilia achillaefolia, 398.
Gilia aggregata, 392.
Gilia Californica, 398.
Gilia capitata, 398.
Gilia floccosa, 396.
Gilia multicaulis, 396.
Gilia multiflora, 398.
Gilia pungens, 396.
Gilia rigidula, 394.
Gilia tricolor, 394.
Gilia, Blue Desert, 394.
Gilia, Downy, 396.
Gilia, Fringed, 390.
Gilia, Large Prickly, 398.
Gilia, Scarlet, 392.
Gilia, Small Prickly, 396.
Gilia, Yellow, 388.
Ginger, Wild, 84.
Globe-flower, 142.
Globe Tulip, White, 58.
Globe Tulip, Yellow, 56.
Gnaphalium microcephalum, 526.
Goat's Beard, 226.
Godetia, 318.
Godetia deflexa, 318.
Godetia Dudleyana, 320.
Godetia Goddardii var. capitata, 318.

Godetia quadrivulnera, 318.
Godetia viminea, 320.
Golden Eardrops, 170.
Golden-eyed Grass, 70.
Golden Girls, 548.
Golden Hills, 526.
Golden Stars, 22.
Golden-rod, Arizona, 562.
Golden-rod, California, 564.
Golden-rod, Western, 564.
Gold Fields, 550.
Gomphocarpus, 376.
Gomphocarpus cordifolius, 376.
Gooseberry Family, 210.
Gooseberry, Canyon, 210.
Gooseberry, Fuchsia-flowered, 210.
Gooseberry, Wild, 210.
Goose-grass, 508.
Gourd Family, 518.
Gourd, 518.
Grass Nuts, 16.
Grass of Parnassus, 196.
Grayia, 98.
Grayia polygaloides, 98.
Grayia spinosa, 98.
Greasewood, 228.
Greek Valerian, 384.
Grindelia, 558.
Grindelia latifolia, 558.
Gromwell, 424, 426.
Grossulariceae, 210.
Grossularia, 210.
Grossularia Menziesii, 210.
Grossularia Roezli, 210.
Grossularia speciosa, 210.
Ground-cherry, 460.
Groundsel, 564.
Groundsel-tree, 568.
Gum Plant, 558.
Gum-weed, 538.
Gutierrezia, 536.
Gutierrezia Euthamiae, 536.
Gutierrezia Sarothrae, 536.

Hairbell, 58, 520.
Harebell, 58, 520.
Harebell, California, 520.
Hardhack, 230.
Hastingsia, 10.
Hastingsia alba, 10.
Hawksbeard, 578.
Hawksbeard, Gray, 578.
Hawksbeard, Smooth, 578.
Hawthorn, 214.
Heartsease, Western, 296.
Heath Family, 340.
Heather, 352.
Heather, Red, 352.
Heather, White, 354.
Heather, Yellow, 352.
Hediondilla, 268.
Hedysarum, 260.
Hedysarum pabulare, 260.
Helenium, 538.
Helenium Bigelowii, 538.
Helianthemum, 304.
Helianthemum scoparium, 304.
Helianthus, 528.
Helianthus annuus, 528.

Helianthus fascicularis, 530.
Heliotropium, 432.
Heliotropium Curassavicum, 432.
Heliotrope, Sea-side, 432.
Heliotrope, Wild, 410.
Hellebore, 8.
Hellebore, False, 10.
Helmet-flower, 446.
Hen-and-Chickens, 194.
Hesperocallis undulata, 30.
Hesperonia, 100.
Hesperonia Californica, 102.
Hesperonia glutinosa, 102.
Hesperonia glutinosa var. gracilis, 102.
Heuchera, 200.
Heuchera micrantha, 200, 202.
Heuchera rubescens, 202.
Hippocastanaceae, 280.
Hog's Potato, 8.
Hog-onion, 16.
Holly, Desert, 536.
Hollyhock, Wild, 288.
Holly-leaved Cherry, 216.
Holodiscus, 236.
Honey-bloom, 378.
Honey-locust, 264.
Honeysuckle Family, 512.
Honeysuckle, Pink, 514.
Honeysuckle, Orange, 512.
Honeysuckle, Yellow, 514.
Honeysuckle, Wild, 394.
Hookera coronaria, 18.
Horkelia, 224.
Horkelia fusca, 224.
Horse Chestnut, 280.
Horse-mint, 456.
Horse-radish, 174.
Hosackia, 242, 244.
Houstonia, 506.
Houstonia rubra, 506.
Huckleberry, 348.
Huckleberry, California, 348.
Huckleberry, Fool's, 350.
Hyacinth, Indian, 24.
Hyacinth, Wild, 16, 48.
Hydrangeaceae, 206.
Hydrangea Family, 206.
Hydrangea, 206.
Hydrophyllaceae, 402.
Hydrophyllum, 418.
Hydrophyllum capitatum, 418.
Hymenatherum Hartwegi, 556.
Hymenopappus luteus, 538.
Hypericaceae, 292.
Hypericum, 292.
Hypericum anagalloides, 292.
Hypericum concinnum, 292.
Hypericum formosum var. Scouleri, 292.
Hypopitys Hypopitys, 358.
Hypopitys sanguinea, 360.
Hyptis, 442.
Hyptis, Emoryi, 442.
Hyssop, Giant, 456.

Ice-plant, 108.
Incense-shrub, 212.
Indian Dye-stuff, 424.
Indian Pipe Family, 356.

Indian Pipe, 358.
Indian Warrior, 502.
Ingenhouzia triloba, 286.
Innocence, Desert, 506.
Inside-out Flower, 152.
Iridaceae, 66.
Iris, 66.
Iris Douglasiana, 68.
Iris Hartwegi, 68.
Iris macrosiphon, 68.
Iris Missouriensis, 66.
Iris Family, 66.
Iris, Douglas, 68.
Iris, Ground, 68.
Iris, Hartweg's, 68.
Islay, 216.
Isomeris arborea, 190.
Ithuriel's Spear, 18, 24.
Ivesia, 224.

Jacob's Ladder, 384.
Jerusalem Star, 574.
Jimson-weed, 460.
Johnny Jump-up, 300.
Johnny-Tuck, 498.
Johnny-Tuck, Pink, 498.
Joshua Tree, 40.
Judas Tree, 264.
June-berry, 216.

Kalmia, 350.
Kalmia glauca var. microphylla, 350.
Kalmia microphylla, 350.
Kelloggia galioides, 506.
Kentucky Coffee-tree, 264.
Kinnikinic, 346.
Kittikit, 222.
Kit-kit-dizze, 222.
Knot-weed, 96.
Krameriaceae, 268.
Krameria Grayi, 268.
Krameria Family, 268.

Labiatae, 434.
Labrador Tea, Woolly, 350.
Lady's Slipper, Mountain, 78.
Lamb's Quarters, 98.
Languid Lady, 430.
Lantern of the Fairies, 58.
Laphamia bisetosa, 558.
Lappula, 422.
Lappula Californica, 424.
Lappula floribunda, 424.
Lappula nervosa, 424.
Lappula subdecumbens, 422.
Lappula velutina, 424.
Larkspur, 128.
Larkspur, Blue, 128, 130.
Larkspur, Foothills, 129.
Larkspur, Sacramento, 132.
Larkspur, Scarlet, 132.
Larrea Mexicana, 268.
Lathyrus, 254.
Lathyrus graminifolius, 254.
Lathyrus splendens, 256.
Lathyrus Utahensis, 254.
Laurel, Swamp, 350.
Lavatera, 290.

INDEX

Lavatera assurgentiflora, 290.
Lavauxia, 330.
Lavauxia primiveris, 330.
Layia, 554.
Ledum, 350.
Ledum glandulosum, 352.
Ledum Groenlandicum, 350.
Leptasea, 196.
Leptasea austromontana, 198.
Leptaxis Menziesii, 200.
Leptosyne, 540.
Leptotaenia multifida, 334.
Lesquerella, 184, 190.
Lesquerella Arizonica, 184.
Lesquerella Gordoni, 184.
Lesquerella purpurea, 184.
Lessingia, 542, 550.
Lessingia Germanorum, 550.
Lessingia leptoclada, 550.
Lettuce, Indian, 122.
Lilac, Blue Mountain, 284.
Lilac, Mountain, 282, 284.
Liliaceae, 4.
Lilium, 32.
Lilium Columbianum, 36.
Lilium pardalinum, 36.
Lilium Parryi, 34.
Lilium parvum, 32.
Lilium rubescens, 36.
Lilium Washingtonianum, 34.
Lily Family, 4.
Lilies, 32.
Lily, Amber, 4.
Lily, Avalanche, 28.
Lily Bell, Golden, 56.
Lily, Chamise, 28.
Lily, Chaparral, 36.
Lily, Cluster, 16.
Lily, Desert, 30.
Lily, Fawn, 28.
Lily, Glacier, 28.
Lily, Indian Pond, 156.
Lily, Lemon, 34.
Lily, Leopard, 36.
Lily, Ruby, 36.
Lily, Sego, 64.
Lily, Shasta, 34.
Lily, Small Tiger, 32.
Lily, Tiger, 36.
Lily-of-the-valley, Wild, 44.
Lily, Washington, 34.
Lily, Water, 156.
Limnanthaceae, 278.
Limnanthes, 278.
Limnorchis, 78.
Limnorchis leucostachys, 78.
Linaceae, 270.
Linanthus, 386.
Linanthus androsaceus, 386.
Linanthus aureus, 388.
Linanthus breviculus, 386.
Linanthus dianthiflorus, 390.
Linanthus dichotomus, 388.
Linanthus liniflorus, 390.
Linanthus Parryae, 386.
Linanthus parviflorus, 388.
Linanthus parviflorus var. acicularis, 388.
Linaria, 474.
Linaria Canadensis, 474.

Linnaea borealis var. Americana, 514.
Linum, 270.
Linum Lewisii, 270.
Linum usitatissimum, 270.
Lion's-tooth, 578.
Lithophragma, 198.
Lithophragma heterophylla, 198.
Lithospermum, 424.
Lithospermum angustifolium, 426.
Lithospermum multiflorum, 426.
Lithospermum pilosum, 424.
Lizard-tail Family, 80.
Loasaceae, 300.
Loasa Family, 300.
Loco-weed, 256, 258, 260.
Lonicera, 512.
Lonicera Californica, 514.
Lonicera ciliosa, 512.
Lonicera hispidula, 514.
Lonicera involucrata, 512.
Lophanthus, 456.
Lotus, 242, 244.
Lousewort, 502.
Love-vine, 382.
Lungwort, 430.
Lupinus, 250.
Lupinus arboreus, 250.
Lupinus citrinus, 252.
Lupinus lacteus, 252.
Lupinus laxiflorus, 252.
Lupinus rivularis, 250.
Lupinus Stiversii, 252.
Lupine, Bi-colored, 253.
Lupine, False, 246.
Lupine, Milk-white, 252.
Lupine, Parti-colored, 252.
Lupine, River, 250.
Lupine, Tree.
Lycium, 464.
Lycium Cooperi, 464.

Machaeranthera incana, 556.
Madder Family, 506.
Madder, 506.
Madia, 538.
Madia dissitiflora, 538.
Madia elegans, 538.
Madia madioides, 538.
Madia, Common, 538.
Madia, Woodland, 538.
Mahala Mats, 282.
Maianthemum, 44.
Maianthemum bifolium, 44.
Malacothrix, 572.
Malacothrix Californica, 572.
Malacothrix Coulteri, 572.
Malacothrix Fendleri, 574.
Malacothrix glabrata, 572.
Malacothrix saxatilis, 572.
Mallow Family, 284.
Mallow, 286, 288.
Mallow, False, 290.
Mallow, Oregon, 286.
Mallow, Rose, 286.
Mallow, Salmon Globe, 291.
Mallow, Scarlet, 290.
Mallow, Spotted, 288.
Mallow, Tree, 290.
Malvaceae, 284.

Malvastrum, 288.
Malvastrum rotundifolium, 288.
Malvastrum Thurberi, 290.
Mamillaria, 310.
Manzanilla, 562.
Manzanita, 346.
Manzanita, Green, 346.
Mariana, 412.
Marigold, White Marsh, 146.
Marigold, Wild, 552.
Marigold, Yellow Marsh, 146.
Mariposa Tulip, 62, 64.
Mariposa Tulip, Orange, 64.
Mariposa Tulip, Yellow, 62.
Matricaria matricarioides, 562.
Matrimony, Desert, 464.
Matrimony Vine, 464.
Maurandia, 466.
Maurandia antirrhiniflora, 466.
Mayweed, 546.
Meadow Foam Family, 278.
Meadow Foam, 278.
Meadow Rue, 150.
Meadowsweet, Flat-top, 278.
Mentzelia, 300.
Mentzelia gracilenta, 302.
Mentzelia laevicaulis, 300.
Mentzelia Lindleyi, 302.
Mentzelia multiflora, 302.
Menyanthaceae, 380.
Menyanthes trifoliata, 380.
Menziesia, 350.
Menziesia ferruginea, 350.
Menziesia urcelolaria, 350.
Mertensia, 430.
Mertensia brevistyla, 430.
Mertensia Sibirica, 430.
Mesembryanthemum, 108.
Mesembryanthemum aequilaterale, 110.
Mesembryanthemum crystallinum, 108.
Micrampelis, 518.
Micrampelis fabacea, 518.
Micranthes, 202.
Micranthes Oregana, 202.
Micranthes rhomboidea, 202.
Micromeria, 436.
Micromeria Chamissonis, 436.
Micromeria Douglasii, 436.
Microseris, 576.
Microseris linearifolia, 576.
Milk Maids, 174.
Milkweed Family, 374.
Milkweed, Desert, 376.
Milkweed, Pale, 376.
Milkweed, Purple, 376.
Milkweed, Showy, 374.
Milkweed, Spider, 378.
Milkwort Family, 278.
Milkwort, California, 278.
Mimosaceae, 266.
Mimosa Family, 266.
Mimulus, 490, 492.
Mimulus brevipes, 492.
Mimulus cardinalis, 494.
Mimulus Fremontii, 494.
Mimulus Langsdorfii, 496.
Mimulus Lewisii, 492.
Mimulus moschatus, 496.

Mimulus primuloides, 494.
Mimulus Torreyi, 494.
Miner's Lettuce, 120.
Mint Family, 434.
Mint, Horse, 456.
Mint, Mustang, 436.
Mirabilis, 100, 102.
Myosotis, 422.
Mission Bells, 38.
Mitella, 204.
Mitella ovalis, 204.
Mitrewort, 204.
Moccasin, Indian, 78.
Mock-orange, 208.
Modesty, 204.
Monarda, 456.
Monarda citriodora, 456.
Monarda pectinata, 456.
Monardella, 436.
Monardella lanceolata, 436.
Moneses uniflora, 354.
Monkey-flower, 492.
Monkey-flower, Bush, 490.
Monkey-flower, Common-yellow, 496.
Monkey-flower, Desert, 494.
Monkey-flower, Little Pink, 494.
Monkey-flower, Little Yellow, 494.
Monkey-flower, Pink, 492.
Monkey-flower, Scarlet, 494.
Monkey-flower, Sticky, 490.
Monk's-head, 578.
Monkshood, 136.
Monotropaceae, 356.
Monotropa, 358.
Monotropa uniflora, 358.
Montia, 120.
Montia parviflora, 120.
Montia parvifolia, 122.
Montia perfoliata, 122.
Morning Bride, 548.
Morning-glory Family, 380.
Morning-glory, Field, 382.
Morning-glory, Yellow, 382.
Mosquito-bills, 364.
Moss Campion, 114.
Mountain Ash, 214.
Mountain Lilac, 282, 284.
Mountain Misery, 222.
Muilla, 26.
Muilla maritima, 26.
Mule-ears, 560.
Muscaria, 198.
Muscaria caespitosa, 198.
Musk-plant, 496.
Mustard Family, 174.
Mustard, 174.
Mustard, Black, 184.
Mustard, Tumbling, 98.
Myosotis, 422.

Nap-at-noon, 574.
Nemophila, 410.
Nemophila aurita, 414.
Nemophila insignis, 412.
Nemophila intermedia, 412.
Nemophila maculata, 412.
Nemophila, Climbing, 414.
Nemophila, Spotted, 412.

INDEX

Nemoseris Californica, 574.
Nemoseris Neo-Mexicana, 574.
Nettle, Common Hedge, 446.
Nettle, Hedge, 444.
Nicotiana, 464.
Nicotiana glauca, 464.
Nievitas, 428.
Nigger-babies, 70, 336.
Nightshade, 462.
Nightshade, Purple, 462.
Ninebark, 218.
Noonas, 56.
Nuphar, 156.
Nyctaginaceae, 100.
Nymphaceae, 156.
Nymphaea polysepala, 156.

Ocean Spray, 236.
Ocotillo, 294.
Oenothera, 324, 326, 328, 330.
Oenothera cheiranthifolia var. suffruticosa, 324.
Oleaceae, 366.
Olive Family, 366.
Onagraceae, 312.
Onagra, 330.
Onagra biennis, 330.
Onagra Hookeri, 330.
Onion, Pink Wild, 14.
Onion, Wild, 14.
Ookow, 16.
Opulaster, 218.
Opulaster malvaceus, 218.
Opuntia, 306, 310.
Opuntia acanthocarpa, 306.
Opuntia basilaris, 308.
Opuntia fulgida, 308.
Orchidaceae, 72.
Orchid Family, 72.
Orchis, Phantom, 72.
Orchis, Sierra Rein, 78.
Orchis, Stream, 74.
Oregon Grape, 154.
Oreocarya, 432.
Oreocarya multicaulis, 432.
Oreocarya setosissima, 432.
Ornithogalum, 200.
Orobanchaceae, 504.
Orobanche, 504.
Orogenia linearifolia, 332.
Orojo de Leabre 564.
Orpine Family, 192.
Orthocarpus, 496.
Orthocarpus attenuatus, 500.
Orthocarpus densiflorus, 500.
Orthocarpus erianthus, 498.
Orthocarpus erianthus var. roseus, 498.
Orthocarpus erianthus var. versicolor, 498.
Orthocarpus exsertus, 500.
Orthocarpus faucibarbatus, 498.
Orthocarpus luteus, 498.
Orthocarpus purpureo-albus, 500.
Orthocarpus purpurascens, 500.
Owl's-clover, 496, 500.
Owl's-clover, Yellow, 498.
Oxalidaceae, 272.
Oxalis, 272.
Oxalis corniculata, 272.

Oxalis Oregana, 272.
Oyster Plant, 574.
Oyster, Vegetable, 574.

Pachylophus, 326.
Pachylophus marginatus, 326.
Paeonia Brownii, 138.
Paint Brush, 472.
Paint Brush, Indian, 470.
Paint Brush, Scarlet, 472.
Painted Cup, 470.
Palo Verde, 264.
Pansy, Yellow, 300.
Papaveraceae, 160.
Papaver, 162.
Papaver heterophyllum, 164.
Papaver somniferum, 162.
Paper Flowers, 542.
Parnassia, 196.
Parnassia fimbriata, 196.
Parnassia Californica, 196.
Parosela, 246.
Parosela Californica, 248.
Parosela Emoryi, 248.
Parosela spinosa, 246.
Parsley Family, 332.
Parsley, 332.
Parsley, Whisk-broom, 334.
Parsnip, 332.
Parsnip, Indian, 336.
Pea Family, 242.
Pea, 242.
Pea, Chaparral, 248.
Pea, Golden, 246.
Pear, 214.
Pedicularis, 502.
Pedicularis centranthera, 504.
Pedicularis densiflora, 502.
Pedicularis Groenlandica, 504.
Pedicularis ornithorhynca, 502.
Pedicularis semibarbata, 504.
Pe-ik, 560.
Pelargonium, 274.
Pelican Flower, Yellow, 498.
Pennycress, 178.
Pennyroyal, Western, 436.
Penstemon, 478.
Penstemon acuminatus, 480.
Penstemon antirrhinoides, 482.
Penstemon breviflorus, 486.
Penstemon Bridgesii, 484.
Penstemon centranthifolius, 484.
Penstemon confertus, 482.
Penstemon confertus var. caeruleopurpureus, 482.
Penstemon cordifolius, 480.
Penstemon cyananthus, 480.
Penstemon Eatoni, 484.
Penstemon glandulosus, 478.
Penstemon heterophyllus, 484.
Penstemon laetus, 484.
Penstemon linarioides, 484.
Penstemon Newberryi, 480.
Penstemon Parryi, 482.
Penstemon Rattani var. minor, 478.
Penstemon Torreyi, 486.
Penstemon Wrightii, 484.
Penstemon, Blue, 480.
Penstemon, Cardinal, 482.

INDEX

Penstemon, Honeysuckle, 480.
Penstemon, Scarlet, 486.
Penstemon, Variable, 482.
Penstemon, Yawning, 486.
Pentachaeta aurea, 554.
Peony, Wild, 138.
Peppergrass, 174.
Pepper-root, 174.
Perezia nana, 536.
Perezia Wrightii, 536.
Persian Prince, 450.
Peucedanum Euryptera, 332.
Peucedanum simplex, 334.
Phacelia, 402, 404, 406, 408.
Phacelia alpina, 410.
Phacelia Arizonica, 410.
Phacelia crenulata, 410.
Phacelia distans, 404.
Phacelia Fremontii, 406.
Phacelia glechomaefolia, 402.
Phacelia grandiflora, 408.
Phacelia linearis, 406.
Phacelia longipes, 402.
Phacelia Parryi, 404.
Phacelia ramosissima, 406.
Phacelia sericea, 404.
Phacelia viscida, 408.
Phacelia viscida var. albiflora, 408.
Phacelia Whitlavia, 408.
Phacelia, *Alpine*, 410.
Phacelia, Arizona, 410.
Phacelia, Mountain, 405.
Philadelphus, 206.
Philadelphus Californicus, 208.
Philadelphus microphyllus, 208.
Phlox, 390.
Phlox Douglasii, 390.
Phlox longifolia, 392.
Phlox Stansburyi, 392.
Phlox Family, 384.
Phlox, Alpine, 390, 396.
Phyllodoce, 352.
Phyllodoce Breweri, 352.
Phyllodoce empetriformis, 352.
Phyllodoce glanduliflora, 352.
Physalis, 460.
Physalis crassifolia, 460.
Physalis Fendleri, 460.
Physocarpus, 218.
Pickeringia, 248.
Pigweed Family, 96.
Pimpernel, Scarlet, 294, 362.
Pinclover, 276.
Pineapple-weed, 562.
Pine-drops, 360.
Pine-sap, 358.
Pink Family, 112.
Pink, 112.
Pink, Cushion, 114.
Pink, Desert, 570.
Pink, Ground, 390.
Pink, Indian, 114, 116.
Pink, Windmill, 114.
Pink Lady-fingers, 258.
Pink Fairies, 322.
Pinkets, 276.
Pipe-stem, 148.
Pipsissewa, 356.
Plagiobothrys nothofulvus, 428.
Platystemon, 166.

Platystemon Californicus, 166.
Plectritis, 508.
Pleuricospora fimbriolata, 360.
Plum Family, 216.
Plum, 216.
Polecat Plant, 394.
Polemoniaceae, 384.
Polemonium, 384.
Polemonium carneum, 384.
Polemonium coeruleum, 384.
Polemonium occidentale, 384.
Polygalaceae, 278.
Polygala Californica, 278.
Polygonaceae, 86.
Polygonum, 96.
Polygonum bistortoides, 96.
Pomaceae, 214.
Poor-man's Weather-glass, 362.
Popcorn Beauty, 498.
Popcorn Flower, 428.
Popcorn Flower, Pink, 498.
Poppy Family, 160.
Poppy, Bush, 167.
Poppy, California, 164.
Poppy, Giant, 160.
Poppy, Matilija, 160.
Poppy, Thistle, 162.
Poppy, Tree, 166.
Poppy, Wind, 164.
Portulacaceae, 120.
Portulaca, 120.
Potato Family, 458.
Potato, 458.
Potentilla, 232, 234.
Potentilla emarginata, 234.
Potentilla pectinisecta, 234.
Prairie Pointers, 364.
Prickly Pear, 306, 308, 310.
Pride of California, 256.
Pride-of-the-mountain, 480.
Primulaceae, 362.
Primrose Family, 362.
Primrose, Beach, 324.
Prince's Plume, Golden, 182.
Prosartes, 54.
Prunus, 216.
Prunus ilicifolia, 216.
Prunella vulgaris, 444.
Psathyrotes annua, 530.
Psilostrophe Cooperi, 542.
*Psilostrophe tagetina var. sparsi-
flora*, 542.
Psoralea, 262.
Psoralea physodes, 262.
Pterospora Andromedea, 360.
Pteryxia Californica, 334.
Ptilonella scabra, 536.
Ptiloria, 570.
Ptiloria pauciflora, 570.
Ptiloria Wrightii, 570.
Puccoon, Hairy, 424.
Puccoon, Pretty, 426.
Purslane Family, 120.
Purslane-tree, 120.
Pusley, 120.
Pusley, Chinese, 432.
Pussy's Ears, Yellow, 60.
Pussy's Ears, White, 60.
Pussy-paws, 124.
Pussy-tai's, 224.

INDEX

Pyramid Bush, 228.
Pyrolaceae, 354.
Pyrola, 356.
Pyrola bracteata, 356.

Quaker Bonnets, 252.
Quamash, 48.
Quamoclidion, 100.
Quamoclidion multiflorum, 100.
Queen-cup, 50.
Quinine, 506.
Quinine Bush, 226.

Radish, 174.
Rafinesquia, 574.
Ragwort, 564.
Ramona, 438.
Ramona grandiflora, 438.
Ramona incana, 438.
Ramona nivea, 440.
Ramona polystachya, 440.
Ramona stachyoides, 442.
Ramona, Desert, 438.
Ranunculaceae, 126.
Ranunculus, 126.
Ranunculus Californicus, 126.
Raspberry, 236.
Raspberry, Creeping, 238.
Rattleweed, 256, 258.
Redbud, 264.
Red Feather, 470.
Red-pepper, 458.
Red-root, 282.
Reed-lily, 10.
Rhamnaceae, 282.
Rhododendron, 342, 344, 348.
Rhododendron Californicum, 344.
Ribes, 210, 212.
Ribes aureum, 214.
Ribes glutinosum, 212.
Ribes Hudsonianum, 212.
Ribes Nevadense, 212.
Rice Root, 38.
Riddellia, 542.
Rocket, 174.
Rock-rose Family, 304.
Rock-rose, 304.
Romanzoffia, 416.
Romanzoffia sitchensis, 416.
Romero, 454.
Romneya, 160.
Romneya Coulteri, 160.
Romneya trichocalyx, 160.
Rosaceae, 218.
Rosa, 220.
Rosa Californica, 220.
Rosa Fendleri, 220.
Rosa gymnocarpa, 222.
Rose Family, 218.
Rose Bay, California, 344.
Rose, California Wild, 220.
Rose, Cliff, 226.
Rose, Fendler's, 220.
Rose, Redwood, 222.
Rubiaceae, 506.
Rubus, 236.
Rubus parviflorus, 236, 238.
Rubus pedatus, 238.
Rubus spectabilis, 236.
Rubus vitifolius, 236.

Rudbeckia, 560.
Rudbeckia hirta, 560.
Rumex, 88.
Rumex venosus, 88.

Saccato Gordo, 428.
Sage, 436, 438.
Sage, Ball, 442.
Sage, Black, 442.
Sage, Hop, 98.
Sage, Humming-bird, 438.
Sage, Pitcher, 450.
Sage, Thistle, 450.
Sage, White, 440.
Sage, White Ball, 440.
Sage-brush, Common, 544.
Sagittaria, 2.
Sagittaria latifolia, 2.
Sahuaro, 310.
Sailors, Blue, 576.
Salal, 342.
Salazaria Mexicana, 448.
Salmon-berry, 236.
Salsify, 574.
Salvia, 438, 450.
Salvia apiana, 440.
Salvia columbariae, 452.
Salvia carduacea, 450.
Sandalwood Family, 82.
Sand Dock, 88.
Sanicle, Purple, 336.
Sanicula bipinnatifida, 336.
San Juan Tree, 464.
Sand Puffs, 104.
Sandwort, 112.
Sandwort, Fendler's, 112.
Santalaceae, 82.
Saponaria, 116.
Sarcodes sanguinea, 358.
Satin-bell, 58.
Saururaceae, 80.
Saxifragaceae, 196.
Saxifraga, 198, 202.
Saxifraga Bongardi, 204.
Saxifraga bronchialis, 198.
Saxifraga Nutkana, 204.
Saxifrage Family, 196.
Saxifrage, 202.
Saxifrage, Dotted, 198.
Saxifrage, Tall Swamp, 202.
Saxifrage, Tufted, 198.
Scarlet Bugler, 482, 484.
Schoenolirion, 10.
Scrophulariaceae, 466.
Scrophularia, 488.
Scrophularia Californica, 490.
*Scrophularia Californica var.
   floribunda*, 490.
Scutellaria, 446.
Scutellaria angustifolia, 446.
Scutellaria antirrhinoides, 446.
Scutellaria Californica, 446.
Scutellaria tuberosa, 448.
Sea Dahlia, 540.
Sea Fig, 110.
Sedum, 192.
Sedum Douglasii, 192.
Sedum Yosemitense, 192.
Sego Lily, 64.
Sego, Poison, 6.

593

INDEX

Self-heal, 444.
Senecio, 564.
Senecio cordatus, 566.
Senecio Douglasii, 564.
Senecio elegans, 568.
Senecio Lemmoni, 566.
Senecio multilobatus, 566.
Senecio perplexus var. dispar, 564.
Senecio Riddellii, 566.
Senecio, African, 568.
Senecio, Creek, 564.
Senna Family, 264.
Senna, Desert, 266.
Serapias, 74.
Serapias gigantea, 74.
Sericotheca, 236.
Sericotheca discolor, 236.
Service-berry, 216.
Shadbush, 214.
Shallon, 342.
Sheep-pod, 258.
Shepherd's Purse, 174.
Shield-leaf, 180.
Shinleaf, 356.
Shooting-star, 364.
Shooting-star, Large, 364.
Shooting-star, Small, 366.
Sidalcea, 286.
Sidalcea Californica, 286.
Sidalcea malvaeflora, 288.
Sidalcea Neo-Mexicana, 288.
Sidalcea Oregana, 286.
Silene, 112.
Silene acaulis, 114.
Silene Anglica, 114.
Silene Californica, 114.
Silene Gallica, 114.
Silene Hookeri, 114.
Silene laciniata, 116.
Silene laciniata var. Greggii, 116.
Silene Lyalli, 116.
Silver-puffs, 576.
Silver-weed, 232.
Single Beauty, 354.
Sisymbrium altissimum, 98.
Sisyrinchium, 70.
Sisyrinchium Arizonicum, 70.
Sisyrinchium bellum, 70.
Sisyrinchium Californicum, 70.
Sisyrinchium Elmeri, 70.
Skevish, 534.
Skullcap, 446.
Skunk-weed, 188.
Skyrocket, 392.
Smartweed, 86.
Smartweed, Alpine, 96.
Smoke Tree, 246.
Snake's Head, 572.
Snap-dragon, Sticky, 468.
Snap-dragon, Trailing, 470.
Snap-dragon Vine, 466.
Snap-dragon, White, 468.
Sneeze-weed, 538.
Snow-Balls, 92, 104.
Snowberry, 516.
Snow Brush, 282.
Snowdrop, 38.
Snow-plant, 358.
Soap-bush, 282.

Soap Plant, 12.
Solanaceae, 458.
Solanum, 462.
Solanum Douglasii, 462.
Solanum nigrum, 462.
Solanum umbelliferum, 462.
Solanum Xanti, 462.
Solidago, 562.
Solidago Californica, 564.
Solidago occidentalis, 564.
Solidago trinervata, 562.
Solomon's Seal, False, 52.
Solomon's Seal, Star-flowered, 52.
Sonchus, 576.
Sonchus oleraceus, 576.
Sorrel, 86.
Sorrel, Redwood, 272.
Sow Thistle, 576.
Spanish Bayonet, 40.
Spatter-dock, 156.
Spatularia, 204.
Spatularia Brunoniana, 204.
Speedwell, Alpine, 476.
Speedwell, Hairy, 476.
Spek-boom, 120.
Sphacele calycina, 450.
Sphaeralcea, 290.
Sphaeralcea pedata, 290.
Sphaerostigma, 324.
Sphaerostigma bistorta, 324.
Sphaerostigma tortuosa, 326.
Sphaerostigma Veitchianum, 324.
Sphaerostigma viridescens, 324.
Spikenard, Wild, 52.
Spinach, 98.
Spiraea, 228, 230, 236.
Spiraea aruncus, 226.
Spiraea betulaefolia, 228.
Spiraea corymbosa, 228.
Spiraea Douglasii, 230.
Spiraea pyramidata, 228.
Spraguea, 124.
Spraguea umbellata, 124.
Spring Beauty, 122.
Squaw Cabbage, 122.
Squaw Carpets, 282.
Squaw-grass, 44.
Squaw-weed, 564.
Squaw-weed, White, 566.
Squirrel Corn, 170.
Stachys, 444.
Stachys bullata, 446.
Stachys ciliata, 444.
Stachys coccinea, 444.
Stanleya, 182.
Stanleya pinnatifida, 182.
Star of Bethlehem, 200.
Star, Blazing, 300.
Star, Evening, 302.
Star-flower, 362.
Star Tulip, White, 60.
Star Tulip, Yellow, 60.
Star, Woodland, 198.
Steeple-bush, 230.
Steer's Head, 170.
Stellaria, 118.
Stellariopsis, 224.
Stellariopsis santolinoides, 224.
Stemodia, 474.

INDEX

Stemodia durantifolia, 474.
Stenanthella, 46.
Stenanthella occidentalis, 46.
Stephanomeria, 570.
Stephanomeria runcinata, 570.
Stickseed, 422.
Stitchwort, 118.
St. Johnswort Family, 292.
St. Johnswort, 292.
St. Johnswort, Creeping, 292.
Stock, 174.
Stonecrop, Douglas, 192.
Stonecrop, Yosemite, 192.
Storksbill, 276.
Strangle-weed, 382.
Strawberry, 240.
Strawberry, Sand, 240.
Strawberry, Wood, 240.
Strawberry Shrub Family, 158.
Strawberry Shrub, 158.
Strawberry-tomato, 460.
Streptanthus, 178, 180.
Streptanthus Arizonicus, 180.
Streptanthus tortuosus, 180.
Streptanthus, Arizona, 180.
Streptopus, 46.
Streptopus amplexifolius, 46.
Streptopus roseus, 46.
Stropholirion Californicum, 20.
Sulphur Flower, 94.
Sun-cups, 330.
Sunflower Family, 522.
Sunflower, 530, 550.
Sunflower, Common, 528.
Sunshine, 550.
Sweet-after-Death, 156.
Sweet Alyssum, 174.
Sweet Pea, Narrow - leaved, 254.
Sweet Pea, Utah, 254.
Sweet Shrub, 158.
Sweet William, Wild, 392.
Swollen-stalk, 90.
Symphoricarpos, 516.
Symphoricarpos longiflorus, 516.
Symphoricarpos oreophilus, 516.
Symphoricarpos racemosus, 516.
Syringa, 208.
Syringa, Small, 208.

Taraxia ovata, 330.
Taraxacum, 576.
Taraxacum Taraxacum, 576.
Tarweed, 222, 538.
Tea, Native California, 262.
Tea-tree, White, 284.
Tea-vine, 436.
Tetradymia spinosa, 562.
Thalesia uniflora, 504.
Thalictrum, 150.
Thalictrum Fendleri, 150.
Thalictrum Fendleri var. Wrightii, 150.
Thelypodium, 176.
Thelypodium torulosum, 176.
Themopsis, 246.
Themopsis Californica, 246.
Themopsis montana, 246.
Thimble-berry, 238.
Thistle, 522, 524.

Thistle, Arizona, 524.
Thistle, California, 524.
Thistle, Milk, 162.
Thistle, Sow, 576.
Thistle, Western, 524.
Thistle, Yellow-spined, 524.
Thlaspi, 178.
Thlaspi alpestre, 178.
Thlaspi glaucum, 178.
Thorn-Apple, 458.
Thurberia thespesioides, 286.
Thyme, 436.
Tickseed, 540.
Tidy-tips, White, 554.
Tidy-tips, Yellow, 554.
Tiny Tim, 556.
Toad-flax, 474.
Tobacco, 458, 464.
Tobacco, Tree, 464.
Tolguacha, 458.
Tolmiea, 200.
Tomato, 458.
Torosa, 164.
Townsendia exscapa, 530.
Tragopogon porrifolius, 574.
Trautvetteria, 142.
Trautvetteria grandis, 142.
Trefoil, 242.
Trichostema, 454.
Trichostema lanatum, 454.
Trichostema lanceolatum, 454.
Trientalis, 362.
Trientalis latifolia, 362.
Trifolium, 260.
Trifolium fucatum, 262.
Trifolium tridentatum, 262.
Trillium, 42.
Trillium ovatum, 42.
Triteleia, 24.
Triteleia grandiflora, 24.
Triteleia hyacinthina, 24.
Triteleia laxa, 18, 24.
Trixis, 540.
Trixis angustifolia var. latiuscula, 540.
Trollius laxus, 142.
Tule Potato, 2.
Tulip, Alabaster, 58.
Tulip, Butterfly, 62.
Tulip, Mariposa, 56, 62, 64.
Tulip, Orange Mariposa, 64.
Tulip, Yellow Mariposa, 62.
Tulip, Globe, 56.
Tulip, White Globe, 58.
Tulip, Yellow Globe, 56.
Tulip, Star, 56.
Tulip, White Star, 60.
Tulip, Yellow Star, 60.
Tumbleweed, 98.
Turkey Peas, 332.
Turkish Rugging, 86.
Turnip, 184.
Twinberry, Black, 512.
Twin-flower, 514.
Twisted Stalk, Pink, 46.
Twisted Stalk, White, 46.

Umbelliferae, 332.
Umbrella-wort, Narrow-leaved, 106.

INDEX

Vaccaria, 116.
Vaccaria vaccaria, 116.
Vaccinium, 348.
Vaccinium ovatum, 348.
Vagnera, 52.
Vagnera amplexicaulis, 52.
Vagnera sessilifolia, 52.
Valerianaceae, 508.
Valeriana, 510.
Valeriana Arizonica, 510.
Valeriana sylvatica, 510.
Valeriana sitchensis, 510.
Valerian Family, 508.
Valerian, Arizona, 510.
Valerian, Greek, 384.
Valerian, Wild, 510.
Valerianella, 508.
Valerianella macrosera, 508.
Vancouveria, 152.
Vancouveria chrysantha, 152.
Vancouveria hexandra, 152.
Vancouveria parviflora, 152.
Vanilla Leaf, 156.
Velaea arguta, 336.
Velvet-rosette, 530.
Venegasia carpesioides, 550.
Veratrum, 8.
Veratrum Californicum, 10.
Verbenaceae, 434.
Verbena, 434.
Verbena Arizonica, 434.
Verbena prostrata, 434.
Verbena Family, 434.
Verbena, Yellow Sand, 106.
Verbena, Pink Sand, 104.
Verbena, Wild, 434.
Veronica, 474.
Veronica Americana, 476.
Veronica Tournefortii, 476.
Veronica Wormskjoldii, 476.
Vervain, Common, 434.
Vervenia, 404.
Vetch, 250.
Vetch, Milk, 256.
Villela, 70.
Vinegar Weed, 454.
Violaceae, 296.
Viola, 296.
Viola adunca var. glabra, 298.
Viola adunca var. longipes, 300.
Viola Canadensis, 298.
Viola lobata, 296.
Viola ocellata, 296.
Viola pedunculata, 300.
Viola venosa, 298.
Violet Family, 296.
Violet, Blue, 300.
Violet, Canada, 298.
Violet, Dog-tooth, 28.
Violet, Pine, 296.
Violet, Pale Mountain, 298.

Violet, Yellow Mountain, 298.
Virgin's Bower, 148.

Wake-robin, 42.
Wallflower, Cream-colored, 178.
Wallflower, Western, 176.
Wapato, 2.
Water-cress, 174.
Waterleaf Family, 402, 422.
Waterleaf, 418.
Water Lily Family, 156.
Water-plantain Family, 2.
Whipplea modesta, 204.
Whispering Bells, 418.
Willow-herb, 316.
Willow-herb, Great, 314.
Willow-herb, Water, 314.
Wineflowers, 158.
Wintergreen Family, 354.
Wintergreen 340, 356.
Wintergreen, Western, 342.
Wolfsbane, 136.
Wood-balm, 450.
Woodland Star, 198.
Wood-sorrel Family, 272.
Wood-sorrel, Yellow, 272.
Wyethia, 560.
Wyethia amplexicaulis, 560.
Wyethia mollis, 560.
Wyethia, Woolly, 560.

Xerophyllum tenax, 44.
Xylorrhiza, 544.
Xylorrhiza tortifolia, 544.
Xylothermia montana, 248.

Yarrow, Golden, 546.
Yellows, 560.
Yerba Buena, 436.
Yerba Buena del Campo, 436.
Yerba Buena del Poso, 436.
Yerba Mansa, 80.
Yerba del Pasmo, 228.
Yerba Santa, 420.
Yerba Santa, Woolly, 420.
Youth-on-age, 200.
Yucca, 40.
Yucca Whipplei, 40.
Yucca, Tree, 40.

Zinnia, 552.
Zinnia, Desert, 552.
Zygadene, 6, 8.
Zygadene, Star, 8.
Zygadenus, 6.
Zygadenus elegans, 8.
Zygadenus Fremontii, 8.
Zygadenus paniculatus, 6.
Zygadenus venenosus, 8.
Zygophyllaceae, 268.